THE TRUTH ABOUT HISTORY

Reader's Digest

THE
ABOUT

TRUTH
HISTORY

How new evidence is transforming
the story of the past

Published by The Reader's Digest Association Limited
LONDON • NEW YORK • SYDNEY • MONTREAL

Contents

Origins of Man

Ancient Empires

Crowns and Conspiracies

Milestones of History

Death and Disaster

Fame and Reputation

Invention and Discovery

Fact and Fable

Exploring the

Anyone who picks up this book is entitled to ask: why do we need the truth about history? Isn't the accepted account of historical events broadly correct? We know the identity of the first president of the United States and the year the Berlin Wall fell. But these are just facts, and there is more to truth, and more to history, than facts.

It has been said that anyone who has ever heard two people describe the same traffic accident would lose all faith in history. The eminent British historian E.H. Carr once made the same point: 'No serious historian takes first-hand accounts at face-value.' In the end, all history consists of stories passed on from one person to another. Like any tale that goes through many tellings, historical accounts change along the way, skewed by bias and misinterpretation. Rumours can be promoted to truth, and facts can be demoted to supposition for lack of evidence.

More than that, only a tiny fraction of the events that happen in the world make it into the history books.

Someone has to decide what is worth recording, and these decisions are often made long after the event. So for example, the capture of the Bastille in 1789 and the storming of the Winter Palace in Petrograd in 1917 are seen as crucial and dramatic moments in the two greatest revolutions in history – at least as significant as the collapse of the Berlin Wall. But both events passed almost unnoticed at the time, as you can read on pages 116 and 140 of this book. 'The history we read is strictly speaking not factual at all,' said historian Geoffrey Barraclough, 'but a series of accepted judgments.'

Buried, but no longer invisible

In our age, those accepted judgments are constantly being challenged. Reams of new evidence have come to light as a result of a technological revolution in historical research. Archaeologists, the grimy-fingered workers at the coalface of history, have acquired a shiny box of tools in the past decade or two, and they are putting it to good use. Their new toys include all manner of equipment, from geo-stationary satellites carrying multispectral scanners to handheld ground-penetrating sensors. Once archaeologists worked blind. Now they have a good idea what they are going to find before they reach for their traditional spades and trowels. Sometimes they can see so clearly what is there beneath the soil that they can dispense altogether with the mucky business of digging holes.

Truth about History

Deskbound historians, meanwhile, have left the library and turned to the laboratory to get a clearer view of the past. Many of the most sensational new truths about history are the result of scientific enquiry. So for example the science of genetics, originally the exclusive sphere of medics and biotechnologists, has been enthusiastically applied to the problem of classifying ancient human remains (see page 296). Historians of early people once had nothing to go on but the age and location of unearthed skulls and bones; now DNA analysis of modern populations can reveal which are our oldest genes and so trace the movements of ancient humans, adding to the understanding of how our species spread across the world (see page 16 and page 272).

Tiny grains of truth

There are other examples. Carbon-dating, an incidental offshoot of nuclear physics, has become a key weapon in the historian's armoury. Electron microscopes can see ever further into the invisible minuteness of things, so now we can know where an artefact has been during its lifetime by the kinds of pollen that are stuck to it. This technique was used to prove that the Turin Shroud had once been present in the Holy Land. It also formed part of the investigation into the life and death of Ötzi the iceman (see page 177).

Some of the techniques of history have been borrowed wholesale from apparently unrelated lines of work such as police forensics. A lock of a dead emperor's hair was once nothing more than a macabre curio; now historians look on such things with the gimlet eye of the pathologist. In so doing they have answered an old historical question and solved a crime (see page 84). In the same way, an understanding of ballistics has made it possible to unravel what really happened at Custer's Last Stand (see page 224).

Making sense of the misunderstood

History has become a broader subject as a result of these changes. Whole new fields of study have opened up, generating yet more evidence that affects our understanding of the past. One of these new fields is historical epidemiology: looking at how disease and mortality affected our ancestors (see page 62 and page 166). Then there is historical ecology – the effect of land and climate on the course of events (see page 50 and page 38). These new ways of thinking have allowed us to spot historical undercurrents that were simply invisible to former generations.

All this activity adds up to a golden age for historical research. New truths about history are coming to light all the time, overturning the muddle and falsehood that infects many textbook accounts of the past. 'History has many cunning passages, contrived corridors and issues,' wrote the poet T.S. Eliot. *The Truth about History* goes deep into those dark passages and corridors, and brings some of the dusty issues out into the true, bright light of day.

ORIGINS
OF
MAN

OUR FIRST STEPS
Redrawing the 'Ascent of Man'

Almost 150 years after British naturalist Charles Darwin expounded the theory of evolution, there are still many misconceptions about how we came into being.

IN THE ZOO **Charles Darwin was lambasted in caricatures and accused of blasphemy by the Victorian clergy. But one of his supporters, Thomas Huxley, said that he would prefer to be descended from a 'miserable ape' than from a bishop who uses his brain 'for the mere purpose of introducing ridicule into a grave scientific discussion'.**

The first edition of *On the Origin of Species* makes no explicit claims about human evolution. The British naturalist Charles Darwin, who published the book in 1859, says only that, 'light will be thrown on the origin of man and his history'. The nervous young scientist preferred to leave readers to draw their own conclusions. And draw them they did.

On hearing of the theory, the wife of the Bishop of Worcester is said to have exclaimed: 'My dear, descended from the apes! Let us hope it is not true, but if it is, let us pray that it will not become generally known.' But, condemned from pulpits around the country and lampooned in newspaper cartoons and articles, the theory quickly gained notoriety. In the minds of the public, it was distilled to the simplistic statement: man is descended from the apes – a misconception which has dogged Darwin's theory to this day.

After all the scandal and controversy, Darwin must have felt that he ought to go further in later editions, because he altered the relevant passage to read: '*Much* light will be thrown on the origin of man...'

Contrary to what the Victorian public – and the public today – might have understood by the phrase 'descended from the apes', man did not descend from chimpanzees or gorillas. At some time in the past, we share with these apes a common ▶ **p.13**

Our early ancestors did not look like this...

The gradual progression from crouching to standing as shown in the series below, is almost certainly wrong. Our ancestors were able to walk upright a lot earlier than was thought when the first 'ascent of man' illustrations were published. In fact, like chimpanzees today, our ape ancestors could probably walk upright on two legs whenever it suited them.

There is no evidence of a creature that walked 'bent over', hovering between a two-legged and a four-legged stance like the second, third and fourth figures do.

Another error in many of the earliest diagrams was to include the Neanderthals as part of our lineage. They were not one of our ancestors, as we evolved directly from a *Homo erectus* type and so did they.

Standing for success

The action of 'knuckle walking' is the characteristic four-legged gait of chimpanzees and gorillas. Although chimpanzees live mainly on the ground they are adept at clambering in trees. As they balance along a branch, their feet and hands will curl around and under it, with the toe or thumb separated in order to grip. It appears that this specialised form of walking evolved in some ape species, while others experimented with bipedalism.

There are many advantages to standing up. Computer simulations have shown that bipedal apes, walking on two legs, travel far more efficiently than quadrupeds – four-legged walkers – at slow speeds. In other words they can travel farther while expending less energy.

The ability to cover more ground during the day may have provided the crucial adaptive edge for the isolated groups of apes from which we evolved. Walking on two legs frees both hands for carrying food, and it is seems likely that heavy competition for forest foods led to a need for foraged food to be brought from exposed open ground to the safety of the forest. This could explain why the adaptation came about, but research is continuing to find out which environments were preferred by the Australopithecines.

Another theory gaining support is concerned with how creatures dealt with the intense heat of the sun as they ventured from beneath the forest canopy to forage for food. In an upright position, the body absorbs far less of the sun's radiation than when walking on all fours, so walking upright may have enabled these creatures to stay longer in the sun.

12

...they looked like this

In the Tugen Hills of Kenya, fossils classified as *Orrorin tugenensis* have redrawn the picture of the 'ascent of man'. They are around 6 million years old, which is about the time that human ancestors diverged from the ape family tree.

The bones (right) show a mix of ape and hominid (early human) features. What is particularly noticeable is that the arm bones are extended and the shoulder joints are mobile enough for hanging and swinging in the trees, while the thigh bones – femurs – show the probable signs of early bipedalism. One shows a distinct groove which is identical to a groove carved on human femurs by a tendon that bends the hip joint. The rubbing of the tendon is caused by bipedal walking.

Tiny clues on the bones reveal the position and extent of the body's musculature. The muscles also suggest that the earliest hominids still had enough upper body strength to climb and swing through the trees. Their fingers could have supported their full weight while

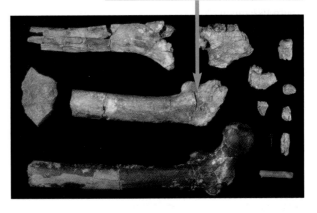

One tiny groove has had major implications for human origins.

hanging from a branch. On later hominid skeletons, the pelvis and leg bones are consistent with simple bipedalism, which means that the creatures would have had to shift their weight from side to side by swinging at the hip. Walking would still have been fully upright.

Around 9 million years ago
Early ape ancestors found insects and fruit in trees, but needed to cross open ground to reach new sources of food.

4-6 million years ago
The first two-legged gait was an ungainly rocking walk, as the pelvis and hips were not well adapted.

2-3 million years ago
Longer legs and a slightly angled thigh bone allowed early man to walk more smoothly.

ancestor – an ape-like primate. It may not seem like much of a difference, but it is crucial to our understanding of man's evolution and to our place in nature. When we look at gorillas and chimpanzees, we are not looking at our primitive past, we are looking at our modern cousins.

The misconception has long been reinforced by the iconic staged illustration, the 'ascent of man', shown in countless textbooks and encyclopedias. It seems to suggest a single evolutionary path from apes to man – a direct connection that simply does not exist. Most scientists would today redraw the illustration to show a huge diversity of species, only one of which is a true 'common ancestor' of humans and modern apes. From one tiny group, a process of adaptation (an adaptive path) led to us, the hominines. From another came the other modern apes.

Even with this in mind, it would be best to scrap the illustration altogether – because it gives rise to another huge misconception. The progression shown by the 'ascent' is reminiscent of a human baby first learning how to crawl and then how to walk. It shows a *Homo sapiens* or modern human, rising to his feet, nobly picking himself up from the crouched position of a grubbing, grunting ape ancestor. But recent finds, more exacting study of the fossil record and the new dimension brought by DNA analysis have been able to change this picture entirely and for ever. ▶ p.15

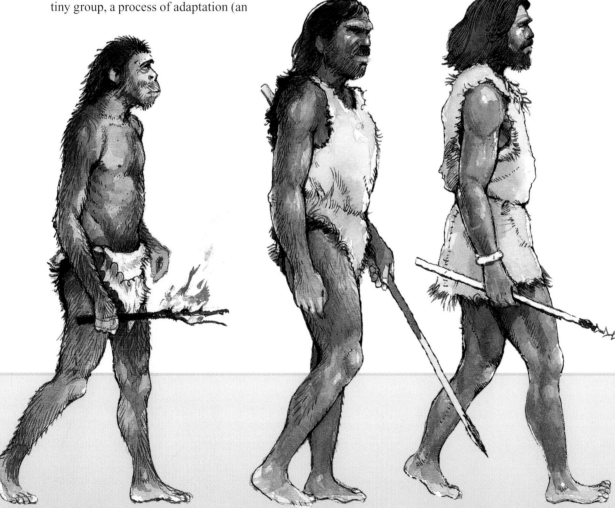

1.5-2 million years ago
The essentially modern skeleton had developed by around 1.8 million years ago.

300-400,000 years ago
The archaic *Homo* species confronted their prey and were more highly muscled than humans today.

20-50,000 years ago
With spears and bows, modern *Homo sapiens* hunted from a safer distance and needed agility more than brawn.

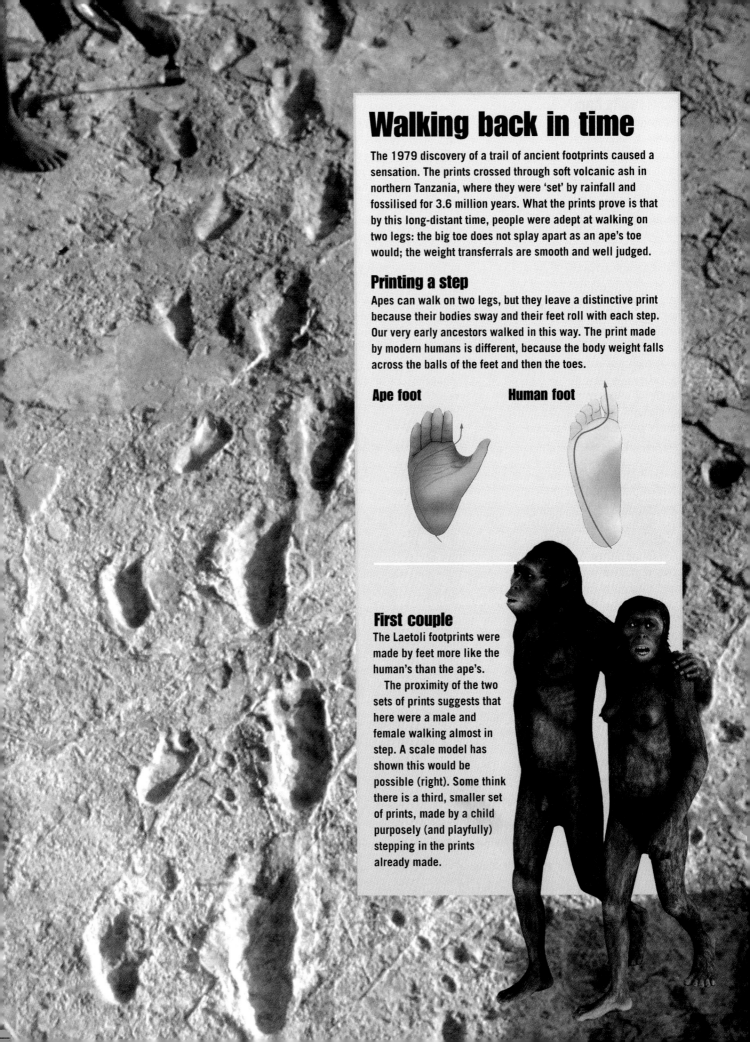

Walking back in time

The 1979 discovery of a trail of ancient footprints caused a sensation. The prints crossed through soft volcanic ash in northern Tanzania, where they were 'set' by rainfall and fossilised for 3.6 million years. What the prints prove is that by this long-distant time, people were adept at walking on two legs: the big toe does not splay apart as an ape's toe would; the weight transferrals are smooth and well judged.

Printing a step

Apes can walk on two legs, but they leave a distinctive print because their bodies sway and their feet roll with each step. Our very early ancestors walked in this way. The print made by modern humans is different, because the body weight falls across the balls of the feet and then the toes.

Ape foot   Human foot

First couple

The Laetoli footprints were made by feet more like the human's than the ape's.

The proximity of the two sets of prints suggests that here were a male and female walking almost in step. A scale model has shown this would be possible (right). Some think there is a third, smaller set of prints, made by a child purposely (and playfully) stepping in the prints already made.

What really happened

The common ancestors of modern apes and humans first appeared around 35 million years ago, when Earth really was the 'planet of the apes'. Dozens of species of primates – monkeys, apes and lemurs – lived in the forests of Africa and flourished for millions of years through the period known as the Miocene.

But some time between 10 and 5 million years ago, temperatures dropped and the forests began to give way to open savanna. The natural habitat for the ape-like creatures was diminishing and what was left of the jungle was populated by the rapidly reproducing ancestors of modern monkeys, who appear to have been quicker and more adaptable in the trees, out-competing the slower, heavier ape species.

Pushed out of the forest habitat, many of the early apes disappeared. The few that survived did so because they began to adapt to their new environment. The way they changed is shown in the fossil record. A skull recently recovered in Chad has shed light on the physiognomy of our prehistoric ancestors. 'Toumaï', as the specimen is nicknamed ('the hope of life' in the local desert language) has been dated to 7 million years old.

Even the most fragmentary of fossil finds can tell a palaeontologist a great deal about the way our ancestors lived and, most importantly, how they moved. The shape and position of the join between the skull and the spinal cord, for example, can establish a creature's posture. If the join is towards the back of the skull, it indicates that the creature spent time walking on all fours and needed to lift its head to see before it. If it is further forward, it indicates that the creature held its head on top of a vertical torso – and that it walked only on two feet.

Walking back in time

Toumaï was quickly identified as a biped, which means that our ancestors were already walking fully upright 7 million years ago, much earlier than was once suspected. But Toumaï fitted well with other discoveries. To develop the leg bones seen on some Australopithecines would certainly have taken a long time as they are quite unlike an ape's.

It seems that bipedalism did not work for every species that developed the ability. The landscape played a part in deciding how the pros and cons of using two legs weighed against each other.

The 'ascent of man' illustration is now wholly inconsistent with current scientific thinking: we did not crawl on all fours and then rise to our feet. Instead we found the adaptation that separated us from the line of the apes. Perhaps it was the single most important adaptation in the long story of human development – whatever the Bishop of Worcester's wife might say.

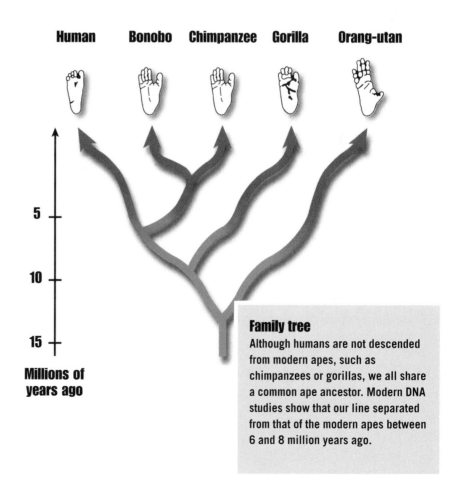

FACE OF A FOSSIL The fragmented skull of Toumaï, our 7-million-year-old ancestor, has an ape's flat face and high browline, and a brain no bigger than a chimpanzee's. But it walked upright on two feet, unlike the apes of today.

Human Bonobo Chimpanzee Gorilla Orang-utan

5

10

15

Millions of years ago

Family tree

Although humans are not descended from modern apes, such as chimpanzees or gorillas, we all share a common ape ancestor. Modern DNA studies show that our line separated from that of the modern apes between 6 and 8 million years ago.

WE WERE NOT ALONE
Other kinds of fully human people once lived alongside us

Homo sapiens – modern human beings – now dominate the Earth, but for some 100,000 years we shared the planet with another species that matched us in skill and strength: Homo erectus. Now scientists might be able to explain what happened to them.

KISSING COUSINS? Before the ascendancy of *Homo sapiens* (above, right), another human species – *Homo erectus* (above left) – was already living throughout Africa and Asia. Like us they hunted animals, lived in close-knit groups and cared for their own families.

About 2 million years ago, the world's first great nomads emerged in Africa. They were tall, muscular people, with smooth hairless skin, long legs and narrow hips. They had good stamina and were capable of a burst of speed. They had a taste for meat and a curiosity to discover what was over the next hill.

Their formidable physical attributes helped them to become established in many different terrains and swiftly they spread across the world, first to southern Europe and the Middle East, then throughout Asia.

The people were *Homo erectus* and, in a poor light and with a cap to conceal the heavy brow and receding forehead, they could have easily passed for modern man. But they were no such thing. They were not even going to become modern men. The *Homo erectus* people were quite distinct from our own ancestral population. As *Homo sapiens* gained in strength and grew in number, all the other ancient humans that filled the Earth were disappearing. Before long, they had died out completely.

Competing for survival

Scientists have only very recently been able to demonstrate through genetic studies what some palaeontologists have long believed: that our emergence has not consisted simply of one species evolving into another. We now know that human history is much crueller than this.

Homo sapiens evolved in one tiny part of Africa. The new species grew, spread and eventually replaced the ancient humans, almost certainly by competing for food, resources and territory, and eventually winning. This is the 'Out of Africa' or 'Replacement' theory and it fits so neatly with the discovery of *erectus* remains only 50,000 old that it has been accepted by most of the scientific community. Only a decade ago it was dismissed as a highly controversial idea.

So for the past few million years there have always been several species of human existing at once. Only now are we in the position of being the only ones.

The path that *Homo erectus* walked was a long and prosperous one. These early humans lived on Earth for at least 20 times as long as modern humans have even existed. In all that time, despite colonising much of the world, their technology evolved little. Stone Age they began and Stone Age they stayed for the best part of 2 million years.

We have evidence that some of the animal bones left by *Homo erectus* were 'cooked', but this could simply be meat that had dried out in the sun. It is impossible to be certain that they used fire to cook with. There is certainly no unambiguous evidence of deliberately constructed hearths.

In other words, unlike *Homo sapiens*, these people lived without putting down roots. They had no art, no culture, no religion, no burial practices. In short, they were not matching the advances made by *Homo sapiens* on the evolutionary journey. It may be that the absence of these adaptations was what sealed their fate.

The *Homo erectus* species remained fundamentally unchanged for more than a million years. Without any apparent pressure to adapt to challenges such as food shortages or changing land or climate conditions, they simply existed as they had always done.

Meanwhile, on the southern African plains, a new species did evolve. *Homo rhodesiensis* is the current prime candidate for our immediate ancestor; by 160,000 years ago he may have begun to evolve into *Homo sapiens*. The most obvious difference between these people and the older *erectus* people is the shape of the skull: *sapiens* had a more domed forehead, accommodating a brain at least 50 per cent bigger.

By 115,000 years ago, *Homo sapiens* had reached the Middle East. In time they replaced *Homo erectus*

> "Stone Age they began, and Stone Age they stayed, for the best part of 2 million years."

Meet the ancestors

The skull of *Homo erectus* (right) very close to that of modern man, but the brain is smaller. It had long been thought that the brain was not capable of adaptation. But the top part of a skull found in Java has shown that the brains *were* being used to address particular problems in an imaginative way. Dr Ralph Holloway of Columbia University, a specialist in neuroanatomy, studied an endocast – an interior cast of the skull – to evaluate the shape of the brain itself.

What he found was evidence of a distinct asymmetry between the brain's two hemispheres, showing that *Homo erectus* was addressing specific tasks with a degree of specialisation. In other words, these people would have been able to adapt to different environments and initiate useful skills.

The second notable feature was the size of the frontal lobes, the part of the brain used for language and understanding. Holloway concluded that *Homo erectus* had the potential to put thoughts into words.

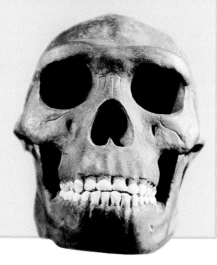

CUTTING EDGE TECHNOLOGY A million years ago *Homo erectus* would have used simple stone hand axes for chipping and flaking. All the evidence indicates that *erectus* never developed any tools more complex than this.

in every part of the world where they journeyed, including Africa, Asia, Southern Europe and even Australia, although no certain remains of *Homo erectus* have been discovered there.

Genetic track-finding

The scientific belief that all 6.5 billion modern humans must have originated from one small enclave is justified by the remarkable lack of genetic diversity found in humans today; in fact, there is more genetic variation in a single group of chimpanzees or a clan of gorillas than there is in the entire modern human population of the world.

For years, scientists have argued about what could have happened when the two species met. We know that the groups remained separate: no

mixed remains of the species have ever been found. But did they fight one another? Or did they interrelate and even interbreed?

While we can still only speculate about the first question, DNA evidence is now providing possible answers to the second.

One study has identified a variation of a beta-globin gene that arose more than 200,000 years ago in modern Asian populations. It is specific to that continent, so cannot be from a common ancestral group. Yet this was before any *Homo sapiens* arrived in the area, so one – albeit contentious – explanation is that the genetic material could have come from Asian *Homo erectus*.

Another study – of haplotypes, or DNA units – has found minute traces

Our distant family

There are around 20 and perhaps many more missing species that helped us – directly or indirectly – on the road to modernity since our ancestral line diverged from that of our cousins, the chimpanzees. All have died out.

Homo rudolfensis marks the transition from the archaic types of hominids to the new-style modern body around 2.5 million years ago. Until then, the Australopithecines, living in Africa's forests, were evolving in a different direction.

- ■ Earliest hominid skull yet found
- ■ Bones found; as yet no skull
- ■ *Ardipithecus* – early walking ape
- ☐ As yet not fully classified
- ■ *Australopithecus* – walking ape
- ■ Human species

The oldest skull

Breaking the 6 million year barrier was a milestone in the study of our ancestors. This is the oldest skull yet found that is not simply primate. It displays clearly non ape-like characteristics.

Sahelanthropus tchadensis

Ardipithecus ramidus kadabba

Orrorin tugenensis

Ardipithecus ramidus ramidus

Australopithecus anamensis

6 M

5 M

4 M

Where 'Lucy' fits in

Australopithecus afarensis was thought to be an ancestor of humans when the remains of a skeleton known as Lucy were found in the 1970s. Now we know that many of the Australopithecines that evolved from her species co-existed with *Homo erectus* and other *Homo* species. It could be that another species, *Kenyanthropus platyops*, is our ancestor, while Lucy's line of evolution led to *A. boisei* and *A. robustus*, who eventually died out.

of ancient DNA embedded in them. Geneticists are still considering the validity of the findings, but if they are accepted, they support the findings of the beta-globin study: that there was a certain amount of interbreeding between modern and ancient man.

The genetic trace of Asian or European *erectus* in our DNA is still hotly debated. What is not in doubt is that the tribes of *Homo erectus* were squeezed into ever-shrinking habitats and somehow driven to extinction. The fossil record in Asia illustrates how the species occupied smaller and smaller pockets and ever more obscure corners of the land masses they had made their home.

It is possible that conflict between the modern and archaic people was provoked by a global catastrophe (see page 163). In harsh conditions with little food, competition alone would be enough to drive the less successful species away to the more barren areas, where they could easily lose the battle to survive. It appears that tribe after tribe lost this battle.

We stand alone

For around 100,000 years, modern man existed alongside *Homo erectus,* occupying the same territory, living off the same land. When the older species dwindled and disappeared, then for the first time in human history only one species was left alive. It happened to be us, but we should remember that we are not the only possible outcome of human evolution. Until 30,000 years ago, that title was still up for grabs.

 As recently as 1997, Homo erectus was thought to have vanished from the Earth by the time Homo sapiens arrived. But the dating of buffalo teeth from sediment in Java set the age of erectus fossils to between 27,000 and 53,000 years, while the oldest sapiens remains yet found are from 160,000 years ago.

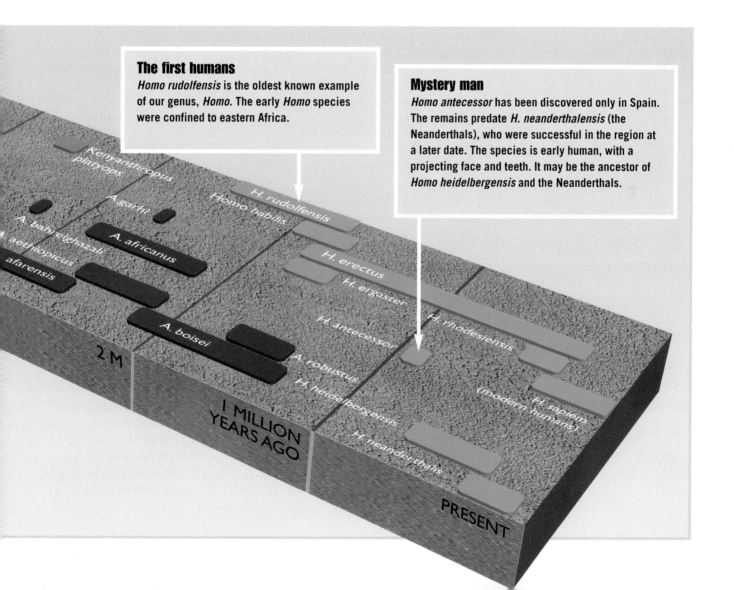

The first humans
Homo rudolfensis is the oldest known example of our genus, *Homo*. The early *Homo* species were confined to eastern Africa.

Mystery man
Homo antecessor has been discovered only in Spain. The remains predate *H. neanderthalensis* (the Neanderthals), who were successful in the region at a later date. The species is early human, with a projecting face and teeth. It may be the ancestor of *Homo heidelbergensis* and the Neanderthals.

DINNER FOR TWO
How meat and monogamy gave humankind the edge

Humans are one of the few species that indulge in long-term pair bonding. But why? A surprising link between families and the practice of eating animals has been suggested.

Our earliest ancestors lived in trees and the forest supplied all their food in the form of fruit, seeds and grubs. But at some point during the Miocene period, probably around 15 million years ago, the forests began to shrink and dry out. The apes who ventured out into the savanna found that the open ground provided far less of the food that formed their forest diet. It was dangerous: wild animals hunted the grazing herds of animals and the apes were slow movers in comparison to these grassland species.

The venture into the open, which occurred over many generations, could have been the death of our distant ancestors. In fact it was the making of them. It led to a discovery that guaranteed their survival as a species and gave a mighty boost to their evolution. The unexpected treasure that they found on the savanna was dead flesh: fatty, bloody, edible, and rich in nutrition beyond their wildest dreams.

Recent interpretations of skeletal evidence trace the evolution of the hominid body along with their diet. The large teeth of early hominids such as Australopithecines appear to be

BRINGING HOME THE BACON Like their prehistoric ancestors some 2.5 million years ago, modern tribespeople in Botswana range the African savanna in hunting packs.

well suited to grinding plants and leaves. The jaws and teeth of the later Australopithecines were even larger. But in the more human-like species, the front teeth become smaller and sharper. Many experts are convinced that the smaller teeth were an adaptive change, and so deduce that the diet of the line that led to humans was changing. They needed to cut and tear their food, not grind it.

The first meat-eating humans took what lions and other predators left behind. Later they became what anthropologists call 'power scavengers', driving animals away from a kill rather than waiting for them to abandon it.

Chop marks on fossilised antelope bones found in Ethiopia in 1997 testify that by 2.5 million years ago meat was being purposely butchered. Some bones have been hammered to take out the marrow.

Meat changed everything. The ribcage was much smaller by the time of *Homo ergaster* around 2 million years ago – perhaps evidence that stomachs had shrunk as people started to eat more meat, which is far easier to digest than tough plants or roots. Animal flesh is – pound for pound – far more nourishing than vegetable matter: a few mouthfuls can make a meal. It would have been more efficient to carry scavenged meat back to the family than fruit.

Brain power boost

More importantly, meat-eating allowed early humans, over the course of evolutionary time, to invest more energy in developing their brains, which grew larger with each emerging species. The bigger-brained men used their intelligence to find and collect more of the meat, thereby increasing their chances of being able to win attention from females with meat 'treats'. If they had more children their larger brains would pass on to future generations.

Alongside this, the early humans developed a strategy for making the most of the meat they found: they invented the family unit. Females who were pregnant or feeding infants could not trek to where the kill was, although they could still forage for food growing nearby. When the group left to find meat, the absent females needed some guarantee that they would receive some of what was brought back. The males for their part needed to know that their foraging would benefit their own offspring – their own genes – and not the children of others. In times of scarcity these needs may have become acute.

The neat answer was pair bonding. Individuals began to recognise partners and limit their sexual availability to just each other, making a self-supporting, mutually beneficial team of two. Family life, it seems, started with the sharing of a juicy, marrow-filled bone.

Meat menu

7 Hominids journey beyond the forest to scavenge for food.

4 Meat eating may be the reason for a slight increase in brain size.

2 Diet certainly includes meat: *Homo* skeleton has small abdomen and much larger brain cavity. Stone tools are used to scrape and crush bones and extract marrow.

1 Tools are designed purposely to cut and scrape meat. Co-operative hunting starts.

MILLIONS OF YEARS AGO

WHAT BONES TELL US

From a single bone, archaeologists can tell much about an ancient human's way of life. A complete joint reveals important details about how the human walked. Further analysis or X-rays can identify certain diseases, malnutrition and signs of stress.

A palaeoanthropologist's first examination of a bone will usually establish whether it belongs to a human or an animal, and where it belongs in the skeleton. Dating by eye is not possible, and unless its location (for instance in a Roman cemetery) gives its likely age, the bone may have to be radio-carbon dated.

TAKING IT WITH YOU Formal burials often include grave goods such food and weaponry. At a Neolithic grave found at Rössen in Germany, the skeleton had decorative metal bands around its arms and beads on each ankle.

The shape of the eye sockets can tell an expert whether the skull belongs to a male or a female.

Signs of sickness

Degeneration of the bones caused by diseases such as arthritis can be recognised by eye. That and ill-fitting shoes were responsible for the curved and partially fused foot bones on the skeleton of an elderly English woman from the 11th century AD (left).

Increased porosity – a bubbly texture to the bones – has a number of possible causes including anaemia and syphilis. DNA testing can be used to identify the disease as some vestiges of the pathogens may still be present in the body.

Researchers are collecting such bones to try to trace how syphilis spread around the world. Recent discoveries in Britain seem to suggest it was not brought to Europe by New World explorers as was commonly believed.

A broken bone can be examined for signs of healing to determine whether it broke during the owner's lifetime or after death. Broken bones from many ancient cultures may have been reset; splints were also used. More often the bone fused together wrongly, which would have left the patient with a permanent limp.

Bones before burials

The retrieval of prehistoric bones is a piecemeal operation. The famous 'skeleton' of the australopithecine 'Lucy', for instance, (right) is far from complete. Just 40 per cent of her bones have been found, including only five small fragments of the skull and a jawbone. The bones were scattered over a slope and many had been washed away by rain. But Lucy is still important for, fragmentary as it is, hers is the best set of bones of this great age that has been found.

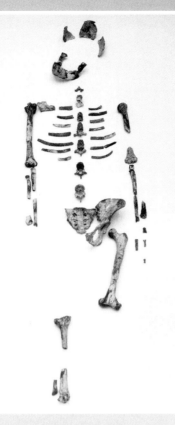

The scapula (shoulder blade) is more similar to a chimp's than to a human's. Lucy's arms could easily bear her weight while swinging from branches.

The angle of the femur (thigh bone) shows that Lucy's centre of gravity was right under her as she shifted balance from one foot to the other, giving her a modern gait.

The knee locks straight, unlike a chimp's, showing that Lucy's bones, not her leg muscles, bore the strain of standing upright.

The length of the femur (thigh bone) enables scientists to calculate the height of the person to whom it belonged, because the relationship between the lengths of leg (and arm) bones and overall height is more or less constant in all *Homo sapiens*. Multiplying the centimetre length of the femur by 2.6 and adding 65cm will give the height of a human of either sex.

X-rays of long bones such as the tibia (shin bone) may reveal 'Harris lines', which are caused by interrupted growth. The lines are often found in the bones of prehistoric populations as they started to experiment with farming and suffered food shortages. As their skills improved and they learned how to store food, the lines disappeared.

Nodules formed on the spine may indicate the constant use of a load-bearing strap for carrying wood or water.

Indentations in certain bones betray the habits of its owner. Notches at the ankle suggest a habitual squatting position was adopted.

PRIMITIVE PERCEPTIONS
Neanderthal man was neither savage nor brutish

We think of Neanderthals as little more than apes,or at best, ugly sub-humans. The latest evidence suggests that they were intelligent, compassionate and skilful.

ANIMAL CRUELTY The English author H.G. Wells described Neanderthals as 'grisly beasts' in his 1920 book *Outline of History.* Accompanying illustrations (below) confirmed this erroneous view.

On a hot day in August 1856, German workers blasting for lime uncovered the entrance to a small cave high up in the Neander Valley near Düsseldorf. Inside, they discovered the top of a strangely shaped skull and various other bones. The skull was incomplete. It was in fact just the skullcap, thick and round as a pie crust, and ending at the upper line of the eye sockets with an astonishingly prominent brow, like a deep, bony frown. At first, the bones were thought to belong to a cave bear, but someone thought they were strange enough to warrant a second look. So the quarrymen passed them on to a local schoolteacher, Johann Carl Fuhlrott, who was interested in archaeology. Fuhlrott realised that the bones belonged to 'a very ancient individual of the human race', but could say no more than that.

He took them to Herman Schaafhausen, a Professor of Anatomy at the University of Bonn. Schaafhausen agreed with Fuhlrott that the Neander Valley bones possessed human characteristics, but were markedly different from modern humans; that these were, in fact, the remains of an earlier and inferior race of men, now extinct.

The publication of his conclusions caused a storm among German scientists. Darwin was yet to publish his theory of evolution, but there was a debate raging in Europe concerning the origins of humanity. For many, even in scientific circles, the idea that species changed over time was blasphemous because it seemed to contradict the biblical account of creation. And the notion that mankind may be rooted in lower forms of life was an affront to human dignity as well as divine authority.

Character assassination
Schaafhausen's paper was met with all manner of counterclaims. It was said that the thick brow was a symptom of rickets or some other affliction, or that the bones belonged to an unfortunate lunatic. The most inventive theory came from Professor August Mayer, a colleague of Schaafhausen's at the university. After close examination of the bones he concluded that they belonged to a Russian Cossack who had died pursuing Napoleon's army across Europe. The bony brow, he proposed, was the result of constantly grimacing with the pain of his war wounds.

After the first discovery at the Neander Valley, other bones were found which clearly belonged to the same species. These finds proved beyond doubt that the first skull was ancient but they served only to exacerbate the confusion about who the Neanderthals were in relation to the human species.

Rogues' Gallery

How artists and curators smeared the Neanderthals

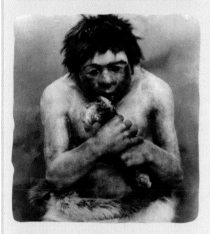

Museum oddity
Some representations of Neanderthal men show them as pathetically sub-human, consigned to extinction by their own witlessness.

Boule's law
An aggressive, ape-man image of a Neanderthal was approved by Marcellin Boule, author of *Fossil Men* (1912). 'What a contrast with the Cro-Magnons,' he wrote disparagingly.

Mark of the beast
One late-Victorian depiction of a Neanderthal has a chimpanzee's head, a man's body, and lives in a tree. The placing of Neanderthals in the animal kingdom undermined the Darwinian connection between man and other species of primate.

A particularly vexatious specimen was uncovered at La Chapelle-aux-Saints in France in 1908. It was thoroughly investigated by Marcellin Boule, professor of palaeontology at the Natural History Museum in Paris, who spent two years measuring, sketching and reconstructing the La Chapelle skeleton. He noted the long, low skull, heavy brow ridges, large jutting face and receding forehead. And he deduced from the bowed legs, bent knees, arched feet and C-shaped spine that this shuffling brute could not be related to modern humans.

But Boule had made a crucial error. The La Chapelle man was indeed a shambling, stooped individual – but only because he was riddled with arthritis. He had been in poor health for some years before his death at around 30 years of age – quite old for a Neanderthal. Boule's blunder was to infer from this that all Neanderthals shared the same traits.

Boule published a book, *Fossil Men*, which was widely translated. Boule's Neanderthal was pictured naked or in coarse furs, equipped with a club and placed in front of the stark caves that were assumed to be his home.

The brutish caveman version of Neanderthal man had been born. The anatomy was incorrect, the club and the bad attitude were imaginary, but the image stuck.

Modern analysis

That fearsome image of Neanderthal man has stayed with us, but the latest research has completely overturned the ape-man view. Anthropologists today can study the fossil remains of nearly 500 Neanderthals, a few dozen of which are almost complete skeletons. Mitochondrial DNA has been extracted from Neanderthal bones, and has provided a clearer understanding of their genetic relationship to us.

Computer tomographic scans allow us to look inside Neanderthal bones and see how they developed from childhood. An understanding of how movement affects bones has told us more about their lifestyle. In short, we can now

ELUSIVE FACE The skulls discovered at the start of the 20th century showed a strong, jutting jawline. From this, artists drew their own conclusions about the faces of Neanderthals. More recent computer-enhanced images based on the skulls offer a more sympathetic interpretation.

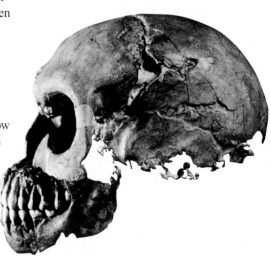

draw an accurate and vivid picture of Neanderthal life.

Neanderthals lived in the harsh climate of Northern Europe. Their anatomy reflects this: short limbs minimised skin surface area and conserved heat; large noses maximised the area through which cold, dry tundra air could be warmed and moisturised. Their brain growth, facial and dental development was faster than in the *Homo sapiens* who eventually forced them out.

Neanderthals were also far more muscular than *Homo sapiens*. Studies of their vertebrae suggest that they carried heavy loads – probably animal carcasses – over long distances. Healed fractures on their bones are common from a young age; it would be rare for a Neanderthal to reach his mid twenties without breaking something. Many died in adolescence, either in childbirth or as a result of injuries sustained in the hunt. Fractured bones among the females suggest that they took part in these dangerous activities alongside the males.

Neanderthal brains were on average larger than ours, even when offset against their bulky body size. The remains of a nine-year-old boy found in Teshik Tash in Uzbekistan show his brain capacity was 1500ml, which

is larger than the human adult average today. A study of a skull found in a cave on Mount Carmel in Israel suggests that Neanderthals could communicate verbally after a fashion, although probably did not possess the flexible tool of language as we know it. A reconstructed jaw cavity was tested and the conclusion was that three distinct vowel sounds could have been uttered through it.

The locations of Neanderthal kill sites show just how well they understood their local landscape. They used the lie of the land to corall bison, wild cattle or reindeer into valleys where they would be trapped. Woolly rhinos and mammoths were driven across country until they fell off ravines; a whittled wooden spear found in the rib cage of an elephant in Germany shows that they were prepared to confront their prey head on: Neanderthals did not lack courage. A flint knife preserved with mammoth remains suggests they may

FAMILY UNIT A diorama in the American Museum of Natural History makes reference to the supposed ability of Neanderthals to scrape and soften animal skins for their clothing. The wearing down of the front teeth in some Neanderthal skulls suggests how this activity might have been carried out.

The chilly world of the Neanderthals

The Neanderthals were Europeans. Most of their archaeological remains have been found in Western France, though sites have also been identified as far south as Iraq and as far east as Central Asia. The population flourished in the Ice Age, between 200,000 and 30,000 years ago, when their habitat would have been cold and inhospitable.

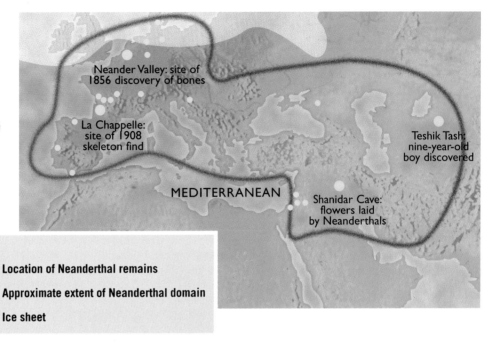

Neander Valley: site of 1856 discovery of bones

La Chappelle: site of 1908 skeleton find

Teshik Tash: nine-year-old boy discovered

MEDITERRANEAN

Shanidar Cave: flowers laid by Neanderthals

KEY

●　Location of Neanderthal remains

━━━　Approximate extent of Neanderthal domain

　Ice sheet

have used this weapon to penetrate the thick skin.

Neanderthals did not wear rough skins. Awls for punching holes in pelts have been discovered, showing that they fashioned clothes. They even made jewellery, piercing stones and teeth so that they could be hung on grass or strips of pelt.

The caves where the Neanderthals have left traces are often high in cliffs where they would have had an ideal vantage point from which to watch nearby game. We know they lit fires in the caves and sat around them, because the remains of a log found in a cave near Madrid in Spain show that it has been carefully placed as seating by the hearth.

Even more intriguing is the discovery of a prehistoric 'tent peg' driven into the ground at one site in France. Neanderthals were not necessarily 'cavemen'. Some preferred their own shelters to caves.

Care for the dead

The Neanderthals were also inventive: during the course of their sojourn in Europe they sought and found ways to make their short lives more bearable. They were sociable

people who lived in family groups. One Neanderthal skeleton belongs to an aged and disabled man who had obviously received constant care over many years.

But most strikingly of all, they had some degree of spiritual awareness. We cannot say that they prayed to a Neanderthal god, but we know that they took pains over the burial of their dead. A skeleton found in the Dordogne region of France was lying on its side in a sleeping position with an arm supporting its head. Remains found in Iraq were accompanied by deposits of pollen, suggesting that flowers had been strewn on the body as part of some unknowable ritual of mourning.

The Neanderthals were not benighted sub-humans; they were simply a different kind of human, an adaptation of the species that endured in Europe for 170,000 years. For the last 10,000 of those years our ancestors shared the world with them. We will have to endure for many more millennia before we can say that we were as successful as the hairy, stocky people of the Neander Valley.

OUT OF THE CAVE The latest thinking about Neanderthal man is reflected in modern facial reconstructions. Neanderthals are presented as being in possession of thoughtful intelligence – not so different from the *Homo sapiens* of the Ice Age.

COMING TO AMERICA
The first Americans may have been Japanese

We know that America was uninhabited, but when the first colonisers of the continent arrived and where they came from – Siberia, Europe, Australia or even Japan – are still mysteries waiting to be solved. Every new find fuels intense archaeological debate.

A flint spearhead discovered in 1933 at an archaeological dig near Clovis in New Mexico was hailed as the most ancient human artefact ever found in North or South America. The blade was sharpened on both sides, and it was clearly designed to kill. Indeed, it had killed. Beside the spearpoint was found the skeleton of a woolly mammoth, which was presumed to have died at the blade-owner's hand, and was estimated to be 11,500 years old. This dating identified the hunter who killed the mammoth as the oldest known American; his people the Adam and Eve of the New World.

After that first discovery, archaeologists began to dig up many more artefacts which seemed to date from the same period and to have been produced by the same people. It was noted that the spread of the 'Clovis people' (no-one knew what else to call them) coincided with the sudden extinction of all the colossal animals of North America – not just the mammoth, but the giant armadillo, the giant sloth and the great black bear. Whoever the Clovis people were, they were not afraid to take on big game, and their two-edged spears were devastatingly effective.

In search of the first-footers

The Clovis spearhead is the starting-point for all debates about the first Americans. There have been arguments about where the Clovis people came from, how they got there, and whether they really were the first people to set foot on American soil. The debate has been marked by a series of archaeological bombshells as new finds or interpretations appear to turn all previous theories on their heads.

These upheavals are possible because the timescale is extremely short. Most specialists in the prehistory of mankind are concerned with events that took place millions of years ago, so a margin of error of a few millennia is not significant. But the colonisation of America is recent. It happened only the day before yesterday in palaeological terms. This means that a shift of two or three thousand years has a big impact on the sequence of events. The extent of American archaeology, like the span of American history, is very brief.

After 1933, an accepted version of the story of the colonisation of America became established. The Clovis people, it was said, came

DOUBLE-EDGED The finely wrought spearheads found near Clovis in New Mexico prove that skilled big game hunters were in North America by 10,000 BC. The question is: did anyone get there sooner?

originally from Siberia at the end of the last Ice Age. At that time, sea levels were about 90m (300ft) lower than today and Siberia was linked to Alaska by a land bridge. The shrinking of the ice exposed a thin peninsula, a low, rich grassland full of game and edible plants, allowing people to make their way on foot to the continent beyond.

The Clovis Barrier

In the 1960s the earliest possible date for the arrival of people in the Americas was set at 10,000 BC. Before this time, the land bridge would have been buried by ice. This date became known as 'the Clovis Barrier': before it there was no-one in America; after it there were the Clovis people.

Certainly someone came to America from the eastern part of Asia around that time. The archaeological evidence is overwhelming. Finely worked spearpoints very similar to the American forms have been found in Siberia, near where the land bridge was before it flooded and the Arctic Ocean covered it at the end of the Ice Age. This part of Siberia was inhabited by a culture known as the Dyuktai: could they be the Clovis people?

If they were, there is no trace of them left today. Chromosomal studies conducted in the last few years point to a different part of eastern Eurasia as the origin of today's Native Americans. Their DNA shows a close link with the people of Mongolia. This genetic evidence is backed up by a surprising piece of physical evidence: something in the Mongolian smile. Some Native Americans have a distinctive 'shovel-shaped' tooth that is also found in present-day Mongolians. This cannot be a coincidence; it can only be the result of a distant family resemblance.

But while some archaeologists worked to find the people who wiped out the mammoth, others made it their business to demolish the Clovis Barrier altogether. This new generation of researchers claimed that there was plenty of evidence of human presence in the Americas long before the men with their two-edged spears arrived on the scene. The argument has become so heated that American palaeoanthropologists often define themselves as belonging either to the Clovis or to the 'pre-Clovis' camp.

Not that the pre-Clovis advocates agree with each other. All they have in common is the conviction that there were humans in the Americas before 10,000 BC. Their theories are bewilderingly contradictory.

Out of Europe

One theory holds that the Clovis people came not from eastern Eurasia, but from Western Europe in boats, across the Atlantic. Proponents argue that there are striking similarities between the Clovis spears and those made by the Solutrean people who, in the Stone Age, lived on the Iberian peninsula – modern Spain and Portugal. They also claim to have identified a link between the

FAST TRACK It was long believed that the first people in America must have come on foot from Siberia – over the Beringia land bridge and via a temperate gap between the ice sheets. But it is now thought that people in tiny boats had made their way down the Pacific coast of the continent long before that.

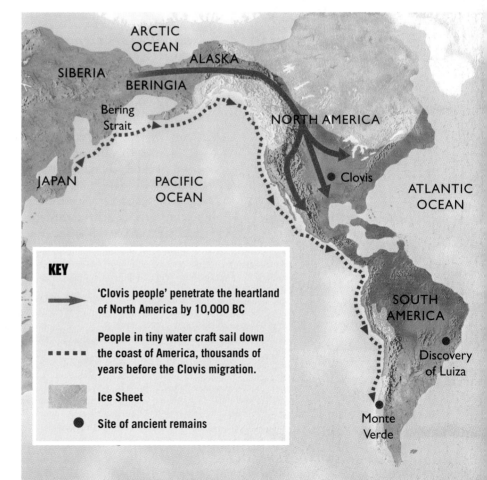

KEY

→ 'Clovis people' penetrate the heartland of North America by 10,000 BC

▪▪▪▪▪ People in tiny water craft sail down the coast of America, thousands of years before the Clovis migration.

▨ Ice Sheet

● Site of ancient remains

languages of the Cree Indians and of the Basque people of the Pyrenees. The journey across the turbulent Atlantic would have been possible during the Ice Age, they claim, because of the vast ice floes which dotted the sea like islands. People could have scrambled out of their boats on to the ice when the weather turned rough.

Most experts thought the Solutrean idea far-fetched. The idea was glibly summarised as 'Iberia not Siberia', and dismissed. But Spain is by no means the most distant location to be cited as the starting point for the peopling of America. Some scientists are convinced that the first Americans were Australian.

Siberian
Some ancient Siberians probably crossed into North America, but there is no genetic evidence of their descendants today.

Mongolian
The 'shovel-shaped' incisor tooth in modern Mongolians and also in some American Indians is proof of a genetic link.

Ainu
An ethnic minority in modern Japan, it is currently proposed that the Ainu may share ancestry with the Sioux, Blackfoot and Cherokee.

The southern route

In 1999, Richard Neave, a British forensic artist, was given a skull and asked to reconstruct its face. The skull belonged to a skeleton found in Brazil and nicknamed Luiza. At 12,000 years old (a date which itself broke through the Clovis Barrier) she was the most ancient skeleton yet found on the American landmass.

A shattering surprise came when Neave put flesh on Luiza's ancient bones: his reconstruction had features that were markedly negroid, similar to modern-day Africans, or Australian aborigines. Luiza's supposed face bore little resemblance to the historic peoples of Siberia or modern Native Americans. So it is possible that some of the early humans who migrated out of Africa to reach Australia 40,000 years ago found their way to South America.

There is a site at Monte Verde, in Chile, whose age could lend some weight to the Australia theory. It appears to be an ancient place of healing. The site has been confirmed to be at least 14,500 years old by corrected radio-carbon dating. Some studies show that there are signs of

human habitation below the remains at Monte Verde. This more ancient encampment, known as MV1, could be as old as 33,000 years.

As the dates mount, the foundations of the Clovis Barrier crumble away. Before the Clovis people crossed the Beringia land bridge, other people came to South America – perhaps from Australia or the South Pacific. Or, if they came from the north, then they must have travelled in boats many millennia earlier than was believed – before the land route could be taken. In canoes they could have hugged the coast, making frequent stops on the ice to hunt and rest.

By sea from Japan

Another convincing study published in 2001 put the focus back onto the northern route. Anthropologists at the University of Michigan compared modern and prehistoric skulls from around the world. Key measurements such as nasal bone height showed that the Jomon, the early indigenous population of the eastern part of the landmass that is now Japan, bore a close resemblance to some Native Americans who were established

Inuit
The Inuit are related to the Chukchi, who still live a nomadic life in Siberia.

Aleut
A genetic divergence from the Inuit around 9000 years ago shows that the Aleut branched out soon after crossing Beringia.

Blackfoot
Skull measurements have suggested that the Blackfoot, Sioux and Cherokee could have come from what is now Japan.

Cree
Apparent links between the language of the Cree and that spoken in the Basque region in France are regarded sceptically.

Apache
Apache and Navajo are ethnically distinct from other Native Americans. One researcher suggests that their language has Sino-Tibetan roots.

The peopling of America

Over the course of thousands of years, successive waves of people have made their way into North and South America. Some of the newcomers came on foot, others, almost certainly, by boat.

It is now possible to use a range of scientific methods – DNA profiling, linguistic studies, skull measurement – to trace the origins of these different peoples. These findings are being checked against the archaeological record to try to compile a timeframe and a map of the peopling of the Americas.

The tribal groups that we know today all hark back to different parts of north-eastern Asia, and they came in separate waves of immigration. If any people did come from Australia – or even Europe – they have vanished.

Yanomani
Genetic matches with the Inuit of the north show that the Yanomani must have originated in north-east Asia and moved south into Brazil.

deep in North America. Descendants of the Jomon, the Ainu, who are ethnically distinct from modern Japanese, still live on Hokkaido, the north island of Japan, which at the time was part of the north-east Asian mainland. Their American cousins are the tribes we know as the Sioux, the Blackfoot and the Cherokee.

Despite all the evidence – or rather because of the mass of conflicting evidence – the question of who the first Americans were remains open. Some scientists prefer to think of the colonisation of the Americas not as an event with a single starting point, but

as a series of waves. It may be that some of those waves of people left no trace in the archaeological record.

There is no simple answer to the question: who came first to America? But we can give an answer to the question: who are the truly native Americans? We can say that there is, in a sense, no such person. Everyone who has ever lived on the American continents – from Alaska to Tierra del Fuego, from the Stone Age to the present day – is an immigrant or the descendant of an immigrant.

That is something on which all the archaeologists agree.

PUTTING A DATE ON HISTORY

Scientific breakthroughs have made possible the precise measurement of the age of both artefacts and animal and human remains. Dating is no longer a matter of debate among archaeologists, but of demonstrable proof.

In traditional archaeology, soil and sediment are excavated layer by layer to reveal the chronology of a site. By matching artefacts to other finds from known periods of history, each layer is given a date. But one-off burials or objects found out of context always present problems. Now samples can be sent to the lab to be definitively dated. Where no comparisons are available, such as in prehistoric settings, radiometric dating, based on the rate of decay of radioactive isotopes, can reveal when sedimentation or mineralisation took place.

Feats of clay

Almost all natural minerals are 'thermoluminescent': over time they absorb electrons which are released in the form of light when the mineral is heated. The older an object is, the more light it produces. Scientists can measure the intensity of this light to work out how much time has passed since an object was last heated – when, for example, a clay pot was fired.

Long-ago natural events such as volcanic eruptions can be dated by thermoluminescence (TL), as can many flint tools made by Stone Age people – simply because they often heated the flint in fire to make it easier to work.

The oldest fired pottery so far discovered (left) dates from Japan's Early Jomon period, which began about 12,700 years ago. But sometimes the technique can reveal that an artefact is not ancient but surprisingly new – that it is, in fact, a clever fake. Many terracotta figures carved in the Zapotec style, initially thought to be 2500 years old, have been exposed as forgeries by TL dating.

Half life, whole story

Many chemical elements are radioactive. They break down at a set rate over a fixed period, expressed by the term 'half life', the time taken to lose half their radioactive component. Potassium-argon (K/Ar) dating is used for rocks and minerals.

Carbon-14 (radio-carbon) can date most organic remains such as wood, animal tissue, textiles and foodstuffs. All contain carbon-14, which starts to decay as soon as the living organism dies.

In 1999 the frozen remains of a man were found in a glacier in British Columbia, Canada. Beside his body was a pouch containing a hand tool (left). Radio-carbon dating showed that the objects were made between 1415 and 1445, 300 years before Europeans claimed to be the first to set foot on the north-west coast of the continent.

Every tree tells a story

As trees grow, their trunks thicken, laying down 'growth rings' each year. The width of each ring is determined by the climatic conditions of that year: wide in wet years, narrow in dry years. Now wooden artefacts can be dated by identifying the signature of a particular ring: a process known as dendrochronology.

The English Tudor warship, the *Mary Rose*, listed and sank in calm waters as she engaged with the French just outside Portsmouth Harbour. The ship's remains have been raised and many of her timbers have been dendrochronologically dated, revealing that the ship was refitted at least twice. A frame below one of the gun ports was made from a tree that one ring shows was alive in the year 1541, 30 years after her launch.

The discovery has led to the theory that the refit threw the *Mary Rose* out of balance. Her crew may have had no chance to make adjustments to their handling of the ship before the battle in 1545, with the result that water poured in through her newly carpented gun ports when they attempted a sharp turn to starboard.

Underground art

In 1994 a cache of ancient drawings was found by potholers at Chauvet, a network of caves northwest of Avignon in France. The vast chambers contained more than 400 black and ochre drawings. Because only tiny amounts of carbon from the charcoal used by the artists were available, a highly sensitive Accelerator Mass Spectrometer (right) was used to detect the carbon-14 atoms directly. The result astonished experts in Palaeolithic art: the drawings were around 30,000 to 32,000 years old.

Many experts found it incredible that art so accomplished could be so old, and while they were willing to accept the science, they refused to take the results at face value. It was possible, they proposed, that the artists could have used pieces of charcoal that were already several thousand years old; the burnt-out torches of earlier visitors to the caves would have made ideal drawing tools and probably littered the floor.

Then a 26,000-year-old torch mark was found in a calcite layer that was covering one of the drawings, and so post-dating it. Although the debate continues, this find silenced many of the sceptics.

HORNS APLENTY At Chauvet the walls have been scraped and prepared for cave paintings. Panthers, lions and bears are portrayed, but rhinos are particularly plentiful: most of them share small ears, dorsal bands and curved bellies, showing a consistent artistic style.

A controversial discovery on the island of Flores has raised the possibility that people were seafarers more than a million years ago. Flores appears never to have been linked to neighbouring islands, yet some archaeologists claim that stones found there bear the mark of *Homo erectus*, an early human species.

The ancient land of Sahul

Australia, New Guinea and Tasmania were once all linked by dry land in a continent, Sahul. Across the water lay Sunda, a landmass incorporating modern Indonesia, Java and other south-east Asian islands. The low sea levels of the Ice Ages allowed ancient man to walk on ground now covered by 150m (500ft) of water.

Sahul was much larger than Australia is now (right), but it was still an island and potential colonists had to cross the sea to get to it – either by taking a northerly route via Sulawesi, or southerly via Timor.

Migration routes of early humans

→ Land route

···· Sea route

● Site of ancient remains

SUMATRA

JAVA

NEW GUINEA

AUSTRALIA

TASMANIA

SUNDA

Sulawesi

Flores

Timor

Malakunanja

Jinmium

SAHUL

At the closest point, about 50km (30 miles) of water would have separated Sahul from the nearest island. Ocean currents would have carried buoyant objects towards the larger landmass.

The Earth's curvature meant that, despite its proximity, Sahul was probably not visible even from the highest point on Timor.

Allen's Cave

Willandra Lakes

Wareen

THE FIRST AUSTRALIANS
How prehistoric man found a continent he could not see

Ancient people living in Java could hardly see even the distant islands that led to the huge and uninhabited continent. So why did they take the plunge into the South Pacific, and how did they reach its shores?

The ancient landmass made up of Australia, New Guinea and Tasmania was not the distant and isolated corner of the world that is modern Australia. Just 50km (30 miles) separated it from Sunda, a conglomerate of south-east Asian islands. Though the inhabitants of Sunda could not see Sahul, smoke from forest fires and the smell of vegetation on the breeze would have alerted them to its presence.

Sahul was no further than other, known, neighbouring islands, and the people of that time were well used to ferrying themselves about. To them, the migration to the new continent was just one more push into the outer reaches of the territory available, part of a gradual migration by *Homo sapiens* out of Africa that lasted thousands of years.

Palm trunks and bamboo

There were materials for building rafts on the islands of Timor and Sulawesi. Palm trunks were buoyant, and bamboo, with its airtight segments, may have been used as an outrigger. The first explorers on Sahul would have been pleased with their new home: it was a land rich in large marsupials and other game. It is no coincidence that some of these species became extinct soon after the arrival of humans.

Radio-carbon dating of ancient stone tools found in Australia at sites such as Malakunanja and Allen's Cave, and Wareen in what is now Tasmania, has been difficult as the layers of dry sand are not stable enough to be sure how deep the tools were originally located. There is a consensus that these sites establish that there were humans on Sahul by 40,000 years ago, but any evidence of habitation before this date is highly disputed.

It was announced in 1998 that an adult male uncovered near Willandra Lakes in south-west Australia was 62,000 years old. But the radiometric techniques used to date 'Mungo Man' have since been questioned, and a recent re-evaluation suggests he lived some 20,000 years later.

The locations of the sites where remains have been found is consistent with a coastal-based migration around the continent, coupled with some tentative river exploration. The first Australians probably never reached the interior, but dating of the site at Jinmium suggests that by 22,000 years ago Aboriginal people had conquered this forbidding zone and made the desert core their home.

They were no longer a sea-going race and had no knowledge of raft-building. The folklore that survives among modern-day Aborigines reveals no vestigial memory of the sea, asserting rather that people were created with and as part of the land.

False! The proclaimed age of 62,000 years for Mungo Man's remains was finally proved false in 2003, when it was found that sand containing uranium that gave the age had not been taken from the close vicinity of his skeleton.

FAR HORIZONS Not all the islands of the South Pacific were inhabitable. But, just as today, those that offered fresh water, easily caught shellfish, safety from wild animals and comfortable shade and shelter could be minor paradises for humans.

ANCIENT
EMPIRES

A COSTLY SACRIFICE
Easter Island's stone monoliths were the ruination of those who built them

The natives who greeted Dutch explorers on Easter Sunday, 1722, had no apparent connection to their island's mighty statues. Now, detailed geological analysis and new archaeological findings have solved the mysteries of the island, its statues and the tragic story of its people.

MONUMENTAL FOLLY Hundreds of sentinel statues once stared across Easter Island's landscape. Most faced inland as though watching over the island's inhabitants, but if this was their purpose it failed. The island became a wasteland and the statues fell; many slid into the sea. A few of the remaining ones have been re-erected.

Easter Island is a tiny scrap of land far out in the Pacific Ocean between Tahiti and Chile. It is the world's most remote inhabited place: the closest human habitations are on Pitcairn Island, 1900km (1300 miles) away, where the mutineers from HMS *Bounty* were marooned in 1790.

The coastline of Easter Island is studded with hundreds of huge beetle-browed statues, *moai* in the island's Rapa Nui language. Each one is carved from a single block of volcanic stone; some are nearly 10m (33ft) high. All the figures have distinct features: a prominent nose, stretched earlobes, downturned mouth and long chin atop a stunted torso with arms held tightly at the sides and hands resting on the midriff.

Many of the *moai* have been sited with astronomical precision – in one group of seven, for example, all face the point where the sun sets during the equinox. More than a hundred lie abandoned and unfinished in the island's quarry, half hewn or apparently awaiting transportation.

For more than 250 years, historians and archaeologists were at a loss to understand how a primitive island race with few resources, totally cut off from the outside world, could fashion these great monoliths, shift them over miles of rough terrain and then erect them. Among the many theories and wild speculation, a number of experts suggested that the island had once been home to a vanished civilisation or lost culture, perhaps an advanced society of American Indians, who were wiped out by a cataclysmic

Gatekeepers of paradise

Easter Island or Rapa Nui flourished in the 12th century when trees covered the hillsides, settlements abounded and the population wanted for nothing. Hundreds of statues, maybe double the number that survives today, ringed the island's coastline.

Vegetation was lush; parrots and monkeys lived in the subtropical forest.

La Perouse Bay

The extensive ruins of settlements imply that a far greater population than first encountered was living on Rapa Nui by the 9th century AD.

Tahai Bay

2

The laval rock from which the statues were carved was only available from volcanic craters, which became huge quarry sites.

1 Rano Lau crater lake

2 Rano Raraku volcanic lake

1

SOUTH PACIFIC OCEAN

SEAFARING NATION **The islanders once fished for dolphins from canoes hollowed out of a single palm tree trunk. But when the Dutch arrived, they saw canoes built of second-hand planks, stitched together.**

event before they were able to finish their work.

Now, with the help of detailed scientific analysis of core samples taken from the island's soil, the mystery has unravelled. The truth of what happened on Easter Island has sobering implications, which reach far beyond its shores.

Startling discovery

On Easter Sunday, 1722, three Dutch ships under the command of Captain Jacob Roggeveen sighted an island in the South Pacific, unmarked on any charts. As the fleet anchored offshore, a few of the inhabitants paddled out to the ships in crude canoes.

Roggeveen was unimpressed. The canoes, he reported, were 'bad and frail... put together with manifold small planks and light inner timbers'. They leaked so badly that all the occupants were obliged to spend as much time bailing as paddling. As for the island itself, he noted sourly, 'its wasted appearance could give no other impression than of a singular poverty and barrenness'.

Despite the apparent friendliness of the brightly painted natives, the Dutchmen rowed ashore armed and ready for trouble. They took up a battle formation, watched by a crowd who had never encountered people from outside their own island, let alone Europeans with firearms.

Tragedy soon marred the visit. Someone fired a shot, claiming later he'd seen some of the islanders pick up stones and make threatening gestures. The panicky sailors instantly opened up with a fusillade which left 'ten or twelve' islanders dead and a similar number wounded. The islanders fled in terror, eventually returning to the beach with fruit, vegetables and poultry to appease the

Dutch. Roggeveen recorded in his journal that the island was an almost treeless wasteland with no shrub taller than 3m (10ft). Only the extraordinary statues erected on huge stone platforms along the coastline gave him reason to think that the place he named 'Easter Island' was of any further interest:

> *These stone images at first caused us to be struck with astonishment because we could not comprehend how it was possible that these people, who are devoid of any thick timber for making machines, as well as strong ropes, nevertheless had been able to erect such images.*

Lost generations

When the English explorer Captain James Cook arrived 50 years later in March 1774, he found the population ill-nourished and reduced to around 700 people. He concluded that the island had perhaps been devastated by a volcanic eruption, since many of the stone statues had toppled from their platforms. Cook was convinced that the statues had been carved and erected by much earlier generations:

> *They must have been the work of immense time, and sufficiently show the ingenuity and perseverance of the islanders in the age in which they were built; for the present inhabitants have almost certainly had no hand in them, as they do not even repair the foundations of those which are going to decay.*

Scientific investigations have only recently provided some answers to the riddle of Easter Island's statues. The analysis of pollen grains found in the sediment that has built up at the bottom of swamps on the island revealed that the island was once covered with thick forests, ferns and flowering shrubs, and was abundantly rich in wildlife.

Scientists examined sections of sediment and found the lowest strata packed with pollen from a tree closely related to the Chilean wine palm, which grows up to 25m (82ft)

CLASH OF CIVILISATIONS **There are Easter Island statues in collections in Paris and London, but it was no easy matter to take them. The islanders had names for each statue and were not willing to relinquish any of them. Crowds were held back at gunpoint in 1875, when the French took a moai from the island.**

Who were the Easter islanders?

People first settled on Easter Island in around AD 400. It is widely accepted that they paddled huge canoes from eastern Polynesia: the Rapa Nui language is related to that spoken by Polynesian people on Hawaii and the Marquesas Islands, and ancient fish hooks and stone adzes discovered on the island are similar to those used on the Marquesas.

Early Western explorers described the islanders as being naked, but by the 19th century they wove their own cloth. Families treasured old heirlooms rather than sustain ancient crafts. Men sometimes wore headdresses made from the feathers of birds long vanished from the island (near right). Women still wove straw hats (far right). Both sexes pierced their ears and wore bone or wooden ornaments; this left earlobes that dangled almost to their shoulders.

GOOD MEASURE The French explorer le Comte de La Pérouse landed on Easter Island in 1786, bringing a diarist, three naturalists, an astronomer and a physicist. After extensive surveys he speculated that the island might have once been forested.

high and 1.8m (6ft) in diameter. Its tall, straight, branchless trunks would have made ideal rollers for shifting weights of around 80 tonnes. Also found was pollen from the hauhau tree, which is used elsewhere in Polynesia for making ropes.

Proof that the early inhabitants of Easter Island had plenty to eat came from DNA analysis of food remains on cooking pots. The islanders ate bananas, sweet potatoes, sugar cane and taro root.

Yet the island's botanical history shows how the idyllic lifestyle slowly disappeared. Core samples of sediment show that, by AD 800, the destruction of the forest environment was underway. Pollen from trees and ferns in the deepest strata represented the island during the unspoilt times; in the more recent strata these gave way to charcoal from wood fires. Humans were using up the trees at an ever-increasing rate.

The loss of the trees had huge repercussions for the islanders' way of life; particularly for their diet. Analysis of bones left on refuse piles showed that, at one time, dolphin meat was a staple part of the diet on the island. In order to pursue and kill the dolphins swimming far out in the deep sea they hollowed seaworthy canoes out of the thick palm trees.

But with the trees becoming rare the islanders were unable to build the canoes that were needed for ocean fishing. In 1786, the diarist with a French expedition led by the explorer le Comte de La Pérouse recorded that

the islanders ate only shellfish snatched from shallow water and from rock pools.

Tragedy of the moai

Statue building started around the 10th century, probably to honour Polynesian gods or deified ancestors. Local legend has it that they were erected by *mana*, a magical force, and that the statues were able to walk about at night, offering protection for members of the clan that had created them. Rival groups may therefore have tried to upstage each other by building bigger and more elaborate statues on even larger platforms.

Virtually no statues were carved after AD 1500: the despoiled island had run out of the trees needed to move and erect them. Palm tree pollen disappears from the core samples around this time and dolphin bones vanish from the archaeological record. The destruction also affected the wildlife: all the native land birds and half the seabirds were wiped out.

With food in increasingly short supply, a population that had numbered around 7000 went into decline. From 1805, South American slave raiders carried off unwary natives and infected many of those left behind with smallpox. The number dropped to a few hundred.

The Easter Islanders erected the moai to ensure spiritual protection for their homeland. That their actions led to its ultimate and irreversible destruction is an irony, but also a terrible testament to human folly.

> " Palm tree pollen disappears from the core samples and dolphin bones vanish from the record… all the native land birds and half the seabirds were wiped out. "

MARK OF THE SCORPION
A tiny sign scratched on a rock may solve the mystery of Egypt's origins

How did the widely separated kingdoms of Upper and Lower Egypt unite to form a mighty empire? Now experts think they have the answer.

Despite all we know about Ancient Egypt, there are still many questions surrounding its origins. A particular mystery is how the two separate kingdoms of Upper and Lower Egypt came into being and joined together to form a single nation. Now the image of a scorpion scratched on a rock – perhaps by a soldier fleeing in haste from an ancient battlefield – has provided a vital clue. The symbol itself, and the story it tells, seem to point to a ruler we now know as the 'Scorpion King'.

By 5000 BC the early Egyptians were living in small settlements, on land that is now a desert but was then a savanna. The land was dotted with waterholes and many seasonal rivers fed into the great River Nile. Rock carvings dating from these long-ago times attest to the presence of hippos and crocodiles. Boats ferried people and goods through what are now dry gorges.

Each of these many village states had its own animal or plant deity: excavations have unearthed cult objects and pottery showing the special totems for each village. These simple cult figures may well have evolved to become Egypt's complex pantheon of animal-headed gods.

Forced into conflict by the shrinking Nile

By the middle of the 4th millennium BC, there is evidence of at least 42 such village states. Conflicts over territory had forced them to band together into alliances: about 20 made up Lower Egypt, around the Nile delta, and 22 formed Upper Egypt in the original settled region.

But the people people of Upper Egypt faced an impending crisis so severe that it may have provoked the wars that led to Egypt's unification. Geological surveys show that the rivers were starting to dry up and the land could no longer support its inhabitants. The dried tracks of these rivers can still be seen etched into the landscape east of the Nile. The people there urgently needed to move north towards the floodplains of the great river itself, where the settlements of Lower Egypt were concentrated around the floodplains of the Nile delta.

Writing thousands of years later in the 4th century BC, the Egyptian historian Manetho told of a conqueror

SYMBOL OF UNITY **For thousands of years Egypt had two crowns: the white skittle-shaped crown of Upper Egypt and the red ladle-like crown of Lower Egypt. The crowns could be worn individually or stacked together to present the pharaoh as 'Ruler of the Two Lands', one of the regal titles. But which ruler first unified the two warring peoples?**

LOWER EGYPT

Heliopolis and Giza are both now suburbs of the sprawling city of Cairo.

● Heliopolis

Giza ●

Memphis ●

Seasonal rivers or 'wadis' (shown with a white edge on the map) fed into the upper Nile during the rainy season. As climatic changes caused the wadis to dry up, the people of Upper Egypt began to move to the fertile plains of the Nile delta

Wadi

Nile

who arose in the dry desert, defeated the king of Lower Egypt's floodplains and called himself ruler of all Egypt. Upon his victory, he united the red and white crowns of Upper and Lower Egypt and established his capital at Mennefer (now Memphis). He gave rise to a great dynasty and his name, said Manetho, was Menes. Manetho also tells us that Menes was killed by a crocodile after reigning for 62 years.

The rise of the empire

Until 1898, this was all that was known of Egypt's origins. Then the Narmer palette was unearthed at Nekhen, the ancient capital of Upper Egypt, about 600km (375 miles) south of Cairo. This was a skilfully carved tablet made from a hard mineral called schist, which showed a powerful king subduing his enemies – even inspecting the slaughtered dead as they lay in rows. The king was wearing each of the two crowns of Egypt on either side of the tablet.

At the top of the tablet, pictographic writing described the king as Narmer: 'n'r' (fish) coupled with 'mr' (chisel). 'Chisel fish' actually means 'Catfish'. The presence of the two crowns suggested to many archaeologists that Narmer was the king who had unified Upper and Lower Egypt.

Nekhen was a powerful republic, the centre of the cult of Horus the falcon, and the finds there contained references to kings known by such names as 'Crocodile' and 'Scorpion' as well as 'Catfish'. Their icons often appeared alongside the Horus falcon symbol of Nekhen. Other clues seemed to suggest that the kings of Nekhen were buried at Abydos, which became a site for frantic excavation. Many tombs of the first and second dynasties were found, as well as those of even earlier rulers.

A giant mace head was also found at Nekhen at around this time. It is far too large to have been used in combat and was almost certainly ceremonial. It, too, is covered with scenes of a pharaoh's victories and the subjugation of his enemies, though it shows only the crown of Upper Egypt. But the king, identified by a scorpion symbol, may now have more than a mace head to his name. We may have found out who he really is.

The victory of Narmer

The Narmer palette dates from around 3100 BC: it is 60cm (2ft) long and would have hung on a column in the Temple of Horus at Nekhen. Two pegs on a column in the temple still fit the holes in the top. Now thought to be more dynastic propaganda than historical document, the palette was probably commissioned by a later king to glorify Narmer's victories. It is the oldest known artefact to show a king wearing both of Egypt's crowns, suggesting that Narmer was seen as the unifier of the country by his successors, who allowed the palette to be displayed.

FRONT

BACK

The king wears the red crown of Lower Egypt. His name 'N'r mr' (Narmer) is shown just in front of his face.

Wearing the crown of Upper Egypt and wielding a mace, Narmer subdues an enemy of rank from Lower Egypt.

Horus, sign of the king, in the victorious position.

Decapitated enemies are piled up to show the numbers killed.

Narmer, represented by a bull, crushes his enemies.

Downtrodden and defeated army.

The papyrus may symbolise Ta Mehu, the delta region of Lower Egypt, now conquered by Narmer.

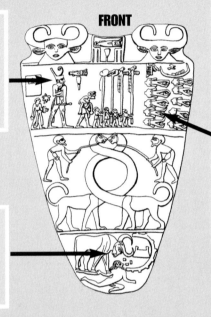

UPPER EGYPT

Wadi

Gebel Tjauti

Naqada   Karnak

Abydos

Nekhen

NUBIA

N

The rise of Scorpion

The Scorpion mace head was the first known artefact thought to show a king named 'Scorpion'. The scorpion symbol appears clearly beneath a rosette that signifies kingship (inset). Only recently has this reading been borne out by other references to a King Scorpion.

The mace head shows Scorpion wearing the white crown. Could he have risen from powerful regional leader to the first king of all Upper Egypt?

The new interpretation of the symbols on the mace head suggest that he could. He wears the bull's tail – a symbol of power. Along the top, birds hanging by their necks represent at least seven vanquished cities. In his hand he holds a hoe, often appearing in later reliefs as a ceremonial tool used to flood the fields or cut the first furrow for a temple or city. Now scholars are speculating that he built up the force that eventually conquered Lower Egypt.

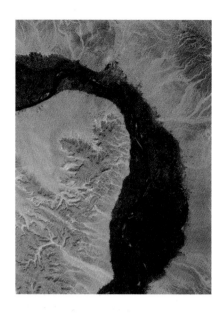

RUNNING ON EMPTY In Upper Egypt, the Nile is flanked by the tracks of dry river courses – wadis – which can most easily be seen in aerial photographs (above). The banks are rocky and there is little farmland. Closer to the delta, there are fertile floodplains on either bank.

The oldest message

In the hills a hundred or so miles from Nekhen, at a desert pass called Gebel Tjauti, rough outlines have been found etched into a rock face. These are very different from the carefully fashioned clay mace heads or the Narmer palette: the figures and symbols here are artlessly etched with flint into the hard limestone, and appear to refer to a battle.

By matching the images to reliably dated artworks in tombs, the Scorpion tableau has been dated to 3200 BC or slightly earlier. The pictures seem to have been used to tell a story, not merely as decoration, making the tableau the world's oldest historical document. Its discoverers, John and Deborah Darnell, believe it tells of a real event and other scholars agree that the etchings do relate a narrative.

The tableau shows a vanquished ruler, and the Darnells believe they have identified him by the bull's horns on his staff. Other symbols have convinced them that the conquered army was from Naqada, a large settlement on the west bank of the Nile, where the god Set was worshipped. The battle was about the consolidation of power in Upper Egypt, and the carving is proclaiming King Scorpion's victory.

Such a battle would have been a significant one, and the location of the carving, the Darnells believe, is also of great importance. They propose that it was carved at the site of the battle and probably soon after the moment of victory. The immediacy of the scratching suggests that it has been done in the heat of the moment, not as a considered artwork.

The first red crown

Naqada may be important for another reason. A pottery fragment found there, far older than the mace heads or the rock carving, appears to depict a primitive red crown. Red was the colour associated with Set. One theory is that the crown was taken by King Scorpion, and later became associated with rule over Lower Egypt, perhaps by Narmer.

The Scorpion tableau's interpretation is supported in part by the findings of Dr Gunter Dreyer, director of the German Archaeological Institute in Egypt. In the early 1990s, Dreyer opened up a vast mud brick tomb at Abydos in which he found an ivory sceptre, and pottery fragments depicting the scorpion, from which he surmised that here was the tomb of a King Scorpion. Hundreds of minute, carved bone and ivory tags proved to be accounts for goods delivered to the king in the form of tithes.

The 'Scorpion tomb' was of great interest to the Darnells. When they compared the iconography of the carving with the slightly more refined symbols in the tomb, they concluded that the two were closely related. They speculated that the owner of the tomb was one and the same as the victor at the battle of Gebel Tjauti.

Dreyer has yet to be convinced, but many Egyptologists find the idea of the battle at Gebel Tjauti highly credible. It would mean that unification was achieved not by a single confrontation, but by a series of clashes throughout the reigns of Scorpion and Narmer. Initially King Scorpion subdued neighbouring cities and settlements in Upper Egypt; subsequently Narmer battled against the southerly people of the Nile delta.

The pharaonic dynasties start with the semi-legendary King Menes at the head of Dynasty 1. But the new finds at Abydos and Gebel Tjauti suggest that Egyptian history should start before Menes, with the kings who fought for dominance as Egypt's landscape began to assume the form we see today. Now a new dynasty has been accepted as valid by many Egyptologists. To it belong kings such as Scorpion, who laid the foundations of the most glorious of the ancient civilisations. Its name: Dynasty 0.

MOUNTAIN PASS Gebel Tjauti is the crossing point of several caravan trails that date from the period of the Scorpion carving and much earlier. It is a strategic location and a likely site for a battle.

Rock carving claims victory

The carving is rough, and covers just 50cm (20in) of rock. It was not carved by skilled artisans, but probably by victorious fighters. Some experts now see the images as 'proto-hieroglyphs', which have a literal translation just like words. Some of the symbols on the carving signify meanings just as on the mace head and Narmer palette. For instance, the falcon is used above the scorpion to show the meaning 'king'.

According to these experts, the 'Scorpion Tableau' relates how King Scorpion emerged victorious from battle, with his opponent captured and humiliated.

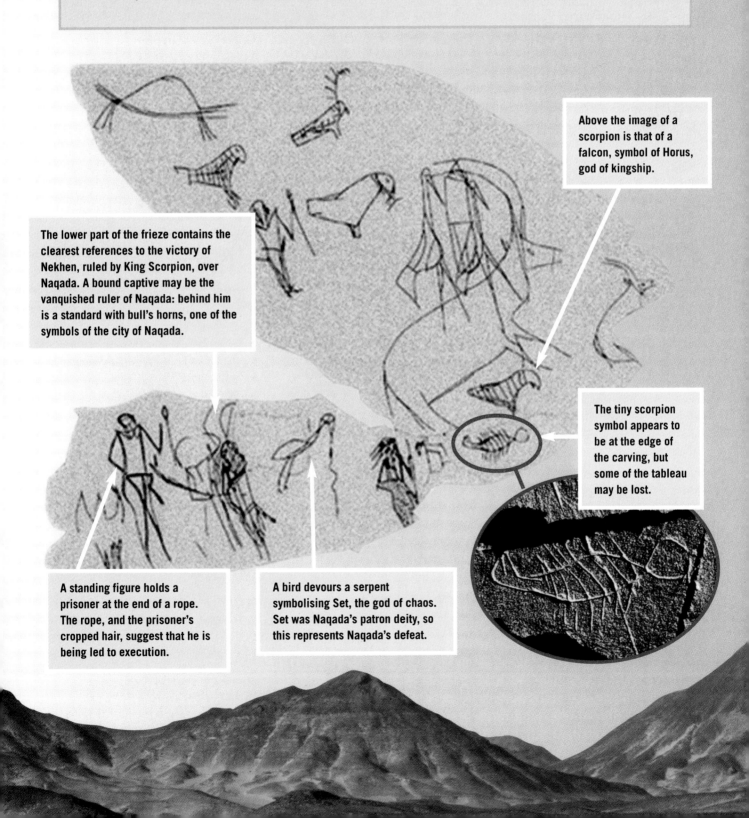

Above the image of a scorpion is that of a falcon, symbol of Horus, god of kingship.

The lower part of the frieze contains the clearest references to the victory of Nekhen, ruled by King Scorpion, over Naqada. A bound captive may be the vanquished ruler of Naqada: behind him is a standard with bull's horns, one of the symbols of the city of Naqada.

The tiny scorpion symbol appears to be at the edge of the carving, but some of the tableau may be lost.

A standing figure holds a prisoner at the end of a rope. The rope, and the prisoner's cropped hair, suggest that he is being led to execution.

A bird devours a serpent symbolising Set, the god of chaos. Set was Naqada's patron deity, so this represents Naqada's defeat.

HISTORY BY REMOTE

Images from space and 3D maps drawn by radio waves are now commonplace in archaeology. The ability to examine an undug site remotely with scanners and sensors has been hailed as the greatest breakthrough since the shovel.

Aerial photography has long been used to locate and map archaeological sites. Such images only capture and enhance what the human eye can see, but more advanced cameras can register wavelengths beyond the visible spectrum, revealing structures undetectable in a photograph. Images formed by the scattering of sonar or radar waves show variance in the land's texture, while radiometric sensors measure the wavelengths of radiation, giving the chemical composition of the land. Ground-penetrating sensors go below the surface, sending sound or radio waves down into the soil to find what lies buried within it.

Atlantis of the sands

A photograph of southern Oman taken from a Landsat satellite by a multi-spectral scanner eventually led two archaeologists to the fabled lost city of Ubar. Once termed by Lawrence of Arabia the 'Atlantis of the Sands', Ubar is mentioned in both the Koran and *Arabian Nights*. It was a bustling trading centre 5000 years ago, and was believed by some scholars to have been where the wise men bought frankincense for the infant Jesus.

The Landsat image commissioned by the archaeologists showed no trace of a fortress, but they hypothesised that the faint scratches of tracks that they could see might be old enough to lead to the city.

Field studies confirmed that the tracks were ancient. A more detailed photograph taken from the space shuttle *Endeavour* showed them to converge at a little-visited place called Ash Shisr. Here, excavations finally revealed the fabled fortress and other ruins of Ubar (inset, above).

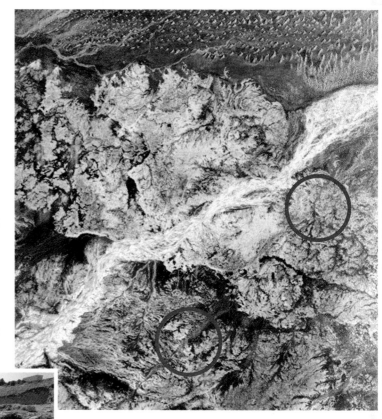

READING THE IMAGE Radar waves transmitted from space bounce back from flat surfaces on the ground and 'scatter' on textured terrain. The resulting image represents the scatter thrown up from the radar waves. Dunes show up as purple; rock as green. White areas are dry stream beds, which reflect the most scatter. The pink lines (circled) are ancient tracks that have been trampled flat over time.

What lies beneath?

Many different types of sensors can be used to scan a site at ground level. Magnetometers measure disturbances in the Earth's magnetic field caused by water that has collected in ditches or trenches, or by metallic remains. They identify land where people have lived by registering the effects of campfires and soil compaction. Ground Penetrating Radar (GPR) devices are used to detect objects underground. Archaeologists first insert probes to test the electrical resistance of the sand or soil on a site. Then they use a GPR device to send electromagnetic waves into the ground. Whenever the waves meet an object with different electromagnetic properties to those measured in the host dirt, they are bounced back to the surface where they are detected by the GPR device.

A sensor survey carried out in 2002 helped archaeologists locate a 2500-year-old Egyptian town. Its remains are buried below 6m (20ft) of sand a few kilometres from the step pyramid of Djoser at Saqqara in Egypt. The results suggest the presence of large temple-like structures and smaller buildings on either side of a ramped causeway. The town probably housed up to 4000 people – perhaps at one time the craftsmen and masons who built the pyramid itself.

BOX OF TRICKS The geophysics team at Saqqara used light, mobile GPR devices to survey the Egyptian desert.

Seen from above

● In 2001, satellite images of recently drained territory in southern Iraq showed the ring of a meteor crater 3km (2 miles) in diameter. Mineral analysis fixed the date of the impact at about 2300 BC. The disaster would explain the disappearance of early cultures such as the Akkad, and perhaps that of 'lost' tribes of Israel.

● Radiometric sensors on satellites can identify the radiation emitted by different minerals and vegetation on the ground. This technique was used to locate ancient quarries in Montana hacked out 10,000 years ago by early Americans.

Out of bounds

Images from a NASA satellite taken in 1996 showed that the ancient Khmer capital city around Angkor Wat was highly developed, with 1000 km² (500 sq miles) of roads and canals. Although the temple – built in the 12th century – is a popular tourist destination today, much of the domain around it is inaccessible, covered with vegetation and dangerously studded with Khmer Rouge landmines. As archaeologists examined the extent of the city for the first time, theories about poor planning, overcrowding and pollution were put forward to explain the sudden collapse of the Khmer empire in the 15th century.

More recently, NASA produced an interferometric image (right), which combines two angles of view to show varying elevations. At the corner of the temple boundary wall, a 'Kapilapura' mound sprang into view, now known to be a religious building dating from the 10th century.

Other previously undetected earthworks may help scholars to understand how the Angkoreans used dams, ditches and reservoirs to control the rise and fall of water from the Tonle Sap lake, which doubles in size during the monsoon.

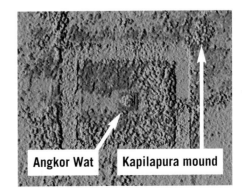

Angkor Wat   Kapilapura mound

HOW GREECE SLID DOWNHILL
Olive trees symbolised wealth and victory, but brought tragedy

Olive oil was a liquid fortune that made ancient Greece secure and prosperous. But the olive tree's root system undermined a fragile ecology and turned the land rocky and barren.

SCANT LEGACY The sparse Greek countryside of today bears little resemblance to that of 2000 years ago. Soil slips and exposed patches reveal the instability of the topsoil, but evidence of soil deposits shows that trees, grass and fields once covered the now-bare hills.

Human affairs are judged in human terms: the actions of leaders and the ebb and flow of marching armies. Ecology is not seen as a critical factor affecting ancient history, perhaps because we assume that these are recent problems, caused by the huge and expanding population of today. But even in prehistoric times, human habitation

could put a strain on the land. Once people started to practise widespread cultivation, their efforts sometimes led to devastation. In the case of the Greeks, intensive farming may have led to the erosion of the empire from right under their feet.

Well oiled economy
For the Greek city states, olives were the ideal cash crop: the trees were reliable, long-lasting and very

productive. Once the oil had been pressed, it was easily stored in pots, usually giant clay vessels called amphorae. The oil kept for weeks, travelled well and there was a market for it in countries all around the Mediterranean.

Agricultural levies comprised most of the country's tax base, so olive oil helped to finance the building of cities and the fighting of wars.

The olive was also of immense symbolic importance. It was believed to be a gift from the goddess Athena and the Greeks revered a particular olive tree growing on the Acropolis in Athens because it was held to have been planted by her. It was associated with joy, purity, victory and honour: ancient Olympians were rewarded for their athletic prowess with wreaths of olive leaves. No one realised that Athena's gift contained a highly destructive drawback.

Analysis of soil particles from deposits now lining stream beds in Greece is able to give some idea of the extent of rich soil that once covered high ground. The sheer amount of displaced soil suggests that much of the ancient countryside was once lush and green. Large areas were covered by forest, but the trees were gradually cleared and replaced with cereal crops. Although the soil on higher ground was often difficult to maintain, the farmers managed to do so by using a series of banked terraces and mixed planting.

Taproots versus topsoil

With the rise of olive farming, mixed crops were abandoned and the land began to lose irreplaceable soil. Most trees have a branching network of roots that helps to hold shifting soil in place, but each olive tree has only a single taproot that burrows right down to the limestone shelf beneath the soil. This root enables the olive tree to survive in dry conditions without much watering; in fact the less it is watered, the deeper the taproot will grow.

With the land cleared for olive trees, the topsoil became unstable. On flat ground it stayed put, but on sloping ground, the precious soil was soon swept away, and with it the ability to grow vegetables or to pasture domestic animals. Instead of cramming in olive trees, farmers should have planted them at least 20m (66ft) apart, allowing other kinds of trees with surface root systems to grow in between and anchor the soil in place.

The Greeks soon became aware of the scale of the problem: the dramatist Sophocles delivered a grave warning about intensive farming methods in his play *Antigone*:

And she, the greatest of the gods, Earth,
Ageless she is and unwearied,
[Man] wears her away as the ploughs go up and down from year to year,
And his mules turn up the soil.

The Roman writer Pliny, writing 500 years later in the 1st century AD, was also aware of the importance of properly ditching and terracing olive groves. These precautions would

> The olive was associated with joy, purity, victory and honour...

BUMPER CROP Compared with most ancient agriculture, olive harvesting was not labour intensive. As the decoration on this Greek vase from 520 BC shows, all workers had to do was beat the trees with sticks and gather the fallen fruit. The olives were then pressed to make olive oil.

TRADING VESSELS Oil was stored in tall, thick clay amphorae, like this one from the 7th century BC. Such flasks are common archaelogical finds around the Mediterranean.

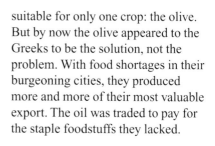

ensure that soil did not wash away and could be properly irrigated. As Pliny presented the practices as traditional ones, it is reasonable to assume that most farmers in ancient Greece, given the time and the means, would have used ditching and terracing.

But for terraces to be successful at holding unstable soil, they required constant upkeep. Farm maintenance was often disrupted by war. Greek republics such as Sparta and Athens were frequently feuding, and it was hard to keep farms in good repair with marauding armies tramping over the fields. A farmer's absence at war could be just as destructive. Just a few weeks of missed repairs to stone terracing could allow patches of soil to slip. Often, grazing goats would be allowed onto the fields, kicking away the terracing stones and creating tracks down which topsoil would be washed when it rained.

While farmers would at least attempt to tend their own land, tenant farmers had less incentive. Many olive groves were investments for rich landlords who could afford to wait the 30 years it took for the trees to mature. After becoming established, olive trees managed well on poor, unwatered soil, so the tenants simply left the plantations untended. Such neglect rendered parts of the land

suitable for only one crop: the olive. But by now the olive appeared to the Greeks to be the solution, not the problem. With food shortages in their burgeoning cities, they produced more and more of their most valuable export. The oil was traded to pay for the staple foodstuffs they lacked.

War and famine

There is no record that the olive crop itself ever failed the Greeks. What failed them was international trade. The Peloponnesian war between Athens and Sparta (431-425 BC) was the turning point. Greece was utterly dependent on corn imports from abroad, which were paid for by the profits of olive oil. When a strategic naval passage called the Hellespont was seized by the Spartan ruler Lysander in 405 BC, Athens was effectively blockaded, and shipments of corn and other foodstuffs arriving by sea were easily commandeered by the Athenians' Spartan enemy.

Once, farms might have been able to make up the deficits. But with only depleted arable land available to grow vegetables and crops, a series of famines ensued and the empire was fatally weakened.

Deforestation and neglect caused the erosion of Greece's once fertile soil, but the olive tree hastened the tragedy – by distracting farmers from the need to conserve the environment.

MARKET FORCES Olives were so crucial to the Greek economy that an early stock exchange was based on their export value. The product is still of commercial importance today.

Decline of Greece's Arcadian landscape

The measurement of soil deposits in stream beds can account for the lost lush fields of ancient times. Huge levels of deposits appear that can be dated to around the late 3rd century BC, exactly matching the rise in cash cropping and the likelihood of neglect. It is even possible to match deposits to the dates of wars in the locality. Farmers deserting their farms or failing to keep the soil terraced would return to find their fields unworkable. Once lost, eroded soil cannot be replaced.

KEY

Land with poor soil

Soil ideal for farming, but prone to erosion if not properly terraced

Rich soil washed off the hillsides builds up in stream beds

Ermióni

Kranidhion

Island of Dhokós

Porto Khéli

MIRTOAN SEA

Peninsula, eastern Greece, c.400 BC
At the height of Greek civilisation, workable land was plentiful, as this detail of one region shows. The green areas represent rich agricultural soil.

Olive trees have no surface-level roots, and so do not hold the topsoil (lighter).

The deep taproot draws water to sustain the tree through dry months.

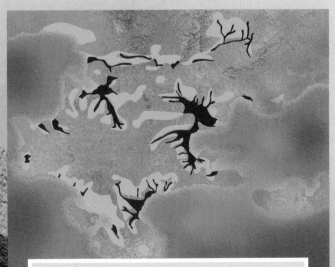

Five centuries later
By AD 100, when the Roman Empire had eclipsed the Greeks, cultivable areas in the same region had shrunk to a quarter of their previous size. Here, the dark shading indicates where soil deposits washed from the hills has accumulated in stream beds.

STRANGERS IN THE FORBIDDEN LAND
The Europeans who travelled 3000 miles to make their home in China

China has long been seen as a closed society, for centuries impenetrable to outsiders, and aloof from the cultures that existed beyond its walled borders. But new discoveries show that Europeans visited China as far back as the Bronze Age, and even made their homes there.

FACE OF AN ENIGMA The body of the 3000-year-old 'Cherchen Man' has been preserved by the climatic conditions in the Taklimakan desert. His facial features are neither Chinese nor Mongolian, and he lies thousands of miles away from his apparent homeland.

Surrounded by mountains, deserts, oceans and the Steppes, China has a natural physical isolation. As a result the people became isolated, too: separate, unvisited and ethnically distinct. In the eyes of its leaders and their people, China was the centre of civilisation, culturally and intellectually undiluted. Most Western scholars have accepted that China had no contact with the

West before around 140 BC. Certainly, over the centuries, there had been scant cultural interchange. When Marco Polo returned from Cathay to Venice in 1295, it was with tales of a distant land exotic beyond European imagining. Then, in the early 1970s, a discovery was made which would stand conventional wisdom on its head.

Loosely covered by the salt sand of the Taklimakan desert were the miraculously well-preserved and

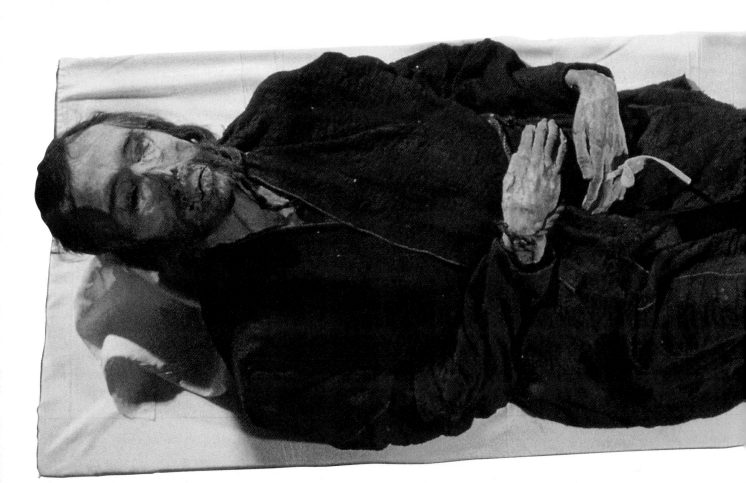

colourfully clothed bodies of men, women and children, some of whom, carbon dating would show, had lived as long ago as 2000 BC. The first discoveries were at Cherchen, a remote town 1600 miles to the west of Beijing. The townsfolk knew of the bodies; soon, as archaeologists investigated, it became evident that there were hundreds of people preserved in the desert over a wide area. They appeared to represent groups from a culture that spanned at least 1000 years.

Braids and beards

Some of the dried-out bodies were blond, others redheaded. Some were extremely tall: a blond male – 'Cherchen Man' – found in 1978 and dating from 1000 BC, had stood 2m (6ft 6in) tall. A woman in a red dress was a rangy 1.8m (6ft). But most intriguing were their facial features: recognisably Caucasian in origin, they had none of the typical characteristics of either Chinese or

Mongols. The mummies had great swathes of braided light hair, large eye sockets, aquiline noses and jutting European jawlines. Winter temperatures as low as -50°C (-58°F) prevented the bodies from decomposing; in summer the searing heat and desert salt dried them out. They were 'mummified' by the elements.

The bodies were an astonishing find, but they also had political significance for the modern Chinese state. They challenged the idea that Chinese civilisation had evolved in isolation and undermined the claim that Xinjiang, the province where the mummies had been found, had always been a part of China.

The records of the Han dynasty describe people first moving into the region in around 120 BC, striving to open up trade routes with the West. The very name Xinjiang means 'new territory'. The existence of the mummies shows that someone else

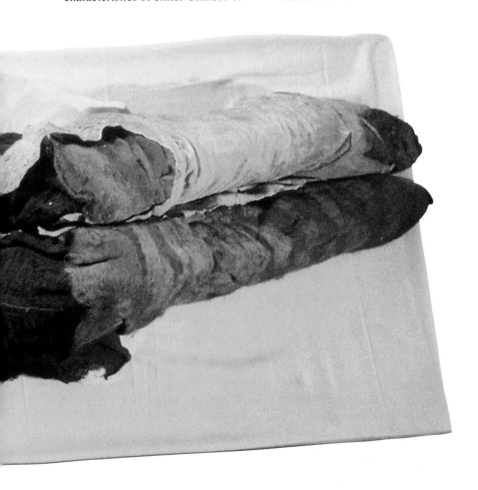

FARMER'S WIFE The 'Beauty of Loulan' is, at 4000 years old, one of the most ancient of the mummies. Her fur moccasins, wool hood and the winnowing tray lying by her shoulder show that she lived in a settled, agricultural community.

was there long before their arrival. The majority population of the province, the Turkic Uighurs, have never considered themselves Chinese and could use the discovery to strengthen appeals for independence.

Behind the curtain

The Chinese authorities made sure that the mummies were quietly put into storage – buried once again. There they might have remained, had it not been for an initiative by the museum of Urumchi, provincial capital of Xinjiang. Some of the mummies were put on display, albeit in a discreetly curtained-off area.

In 1987 an intrigued visitor pulled the curtain aside: he was Victor Mair, professor of Chinese studies at the University of Pennsylvania. Mair had been to the museum before, and assumed that he had already viewed the best exhibits. What he saw that day hit him with the force of a revelation. As he recalled, 'I came across a new exhibit so beautiful, so breathtaking, so defying of the imagination, I thought at first it had to be a hoax.'

Although he was dazzled by the discovery, Mair was sensitive to its implications. He made cautious approaches to the authorities, and secured permission for himself and a small group of fellow experts to investigate some of the bodies in more detail. They started by carrying out a precise dating procedure. The oldest of the mummies were Bronze Age people, who had settled in Loulan around 2000 BC. At least 100 mummies had been found at Loulan, where they were buried not just with tools and utensils such as clay pots, wool and spindles, but with flat bread and skewered meat to sustain them in the hereafter.

If the Loulan settlers were the first to journey

east into this inhospitable desert, they were not the last. The settlers at neighbouring Cherchen must have arrived in a second wave of colonisation. The bodies found there dated from around 3000 years ago, and belonged to a more advanced culture. While the Loulan mummies wear sack-like wraps and loose leggings in neutral, earthy colours, the Cherchen people are dressed in high fashion. Their shirts, skirts, coats and trousers incorporate bold designs in high-contrast colours: spirals and zigzags in red, blue, ochre and brown.

For one of the team, the textiles expert and professor of archaeology Dr Elizabeth Wayland Barber, these were the most exciting discoveries of her career. For 13 years she had travelled across Europe, and beyond to Iran, poring over the threads, shreds and tatters of degraded cloth. Nothing had prepared her for this. The fabrics, preserved in the desert salt, had hardly rotted at all. They might have been no more than a century old.

'The first thing that struck me was that it was all sheep's wool,' said Barber. 'I had expected most of it to be plant fibre. Sheep are not indigenous to that part of the world, so the early travellers must have brought them with them.' As well as livestock, the settlers carried their own seeds to grow crops. Wheat found in the Cherchen graves was found to be a non-local variety.

The possessions buried with the mummies contradict the ancient Chinese view that nomads were primitive; there is evidence that they were skilled jewellers, bakers, leather-workers, potters and weavers. They were also mobile – the later arrivals used the wheel and rode on horseback long before the Chinese.

Celtic cousins

It was the mummies from the third site, Hami, that were to offer the most fascinating lead. Some of their clothes were woven in diagonal twill, with wide and narrow stripes. ▶ **p.58**

TEXTILE MESSAGES At Hami, the form of the weave used in the mummies' clothes alerted an expert in ancient fabrics, Dr Elizabeth Wayland Barber, to a possible origin for the settlers. The telltale signs are the diagonal weave (twill) and the decorative blue stripe (plaid).

Where did the strangers come from?

The oldest remains of woven woollen fabrics have been found at grave sites north of the Caucasus, between the Black Sea and the Caspian Sea. From this region, people are thought to have migrated both east to China and west into the Alps, taking their sheep and their weaving techniques with them.

The Taklimakan desert is 4500km (3100 miles) from the Caucasus, so their migration would have been gradual. Remains found 500km (300 miles) to the north of the desert show that nomads lived there from around 4500 BC, but no link between them and the mummies of the Taklimakan desert has been proven.

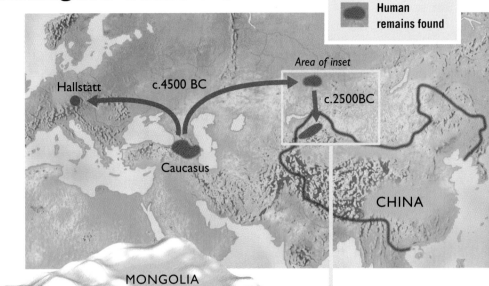

KEY

Human remains found

Hallstatt

c.4500 BC

Area of inset

c.2500BC

Caucasus

CHINA

MONGOLIA

Urumchi

Hami

Loulan

KAZAKHSTAN

Qizil   TAKLIMAKAN DESERT

GOBI DESERT

Cherchen

TIBETAN AUTONOMOUS ZONE

Waking the dead

Mummies have been found around Hami, Loulan and Cherchen. Each site presents a particular reason for interest: Cherchen has the most recent and best-kept garments and textiles; Loulan, with drier ground, has better-preserved bodies, although they are much older. But it is at Hami that a 'tartan' weave has been found (inset) that one expert has matched to cloth from Hallstatt in Europe.

Faces on the wall

Paintings at the Caves of the Thousand Buddhas in Qizil show that in the 5th century AD there were people with Western features such as red hair, bushy beards and prominent noses living in China alongside Oriental people.

They reminded Barber of a cloth woven by the Celts. She had seen it at a Bronze Age Celtic site at Hallstatt near Salzburg in Austria.

These two communities, more than 8000km (5000 miles) apart, were both able to produce the same type of plaid twill, or tartan, and they were doing it at about the same time. Barber thought the technique was so distinctive that it indicated a common ancestry for the two cultures. She suggested a region north of the Caucasus, now part of Russia. From this region, she deduced, some groups of migrants moved west, and others journeyed east.

Other evidence supports the story told by the bodies. Around the 2nd century BC, the Chinese mentioned sightings in the Xinjiang province of people who, they said, had red hair, bluish-green eyes and long noses, and looked like monkeys. A little further south there are depictions of such blue-eyed men among the wall paintings in the Caves of the Thousand Buddhas, in Qizil, near the city of Kucha. The paintings are the work of Buddhists who lived centuries after the era of the mummies, but the curly hair and thick beards on the men show them to bear more resemblance to the mummies than to any Chinese or Mongolian.

Buddhist texts describe these distinctive people as the Tokharians. They even had their own language, no longer spoken, but still studied. Analysis of words used in the old religious documents suggests that the Tokharians did not originate in China or anywhere nearby. The language appears to have its roots in the Indo-European tongues of Europe and the Near East. The Tokharian words 'Pacer' and 'Macer', for instance, probably share the same root as 'Father' and 'Mother'.

Blue eyes and red hair

Living proof of influx from the West can be witnessed by any traveller on the 4000-mile Silk Road from Italy and Greece to China, passing through the city of Kashgar to Xinjiang. Blue eyes and red hair are common among the Uighurs, who also have their own religion, language, history and traditions of art, dance and music.

Many modern Uighurs believe that the Tokharians are the link between themselves and the mummies. They can trace their ties to the region back no farther than to around AD 800, and suggest that, as this is close to the time when the Tokharians disappear from Chinese historical records, they may be one and the same.

The original settlers would by now have been absorbed into other communities, interbreeding with Mongols and Han Chinese. Their cultural heritage was lost, but their genetic legacy lived on.

The Chinese authorities permitted Victor Mair to take skin and bone samples from two of the mummies. Genetics expert Paolo Francalacci showed that the tissue contained a genetic combination shared by many Europeans but few East Asians.

The finding was significant enough for China's President Jiang Zemin to make a statement. His view is that if the bodies do turn out to be of European origin, there is 'nothing wrong with that'.

Meanwhile the mummies are starting to crumble in Urumchi's underfunded museum; its humidity may destroy the tissues that the desert preserved. Whether or not they are Chinese, the Cherchen, Loulan and Hami mummies do not deserve to be forgotten again by history.

PLAIN PLAID **The fabric found at Loulan is a plain weave in neutral colours. It was used to make simple wraps, which were belted and topped with furs in cold weather. Square pieces of woollen felt were worn as headscarves.**

An outpost of the Roman foreign legion

③ **36 BC** Texts suggest Romans were fighting for the Hun warlord Jzh-Jzh in modern Uzbekistan.

④ **AD 5** Liqian in Gansu Province first appears in a census. It is a Chinese name for the Greco-Roman world.

① **53 BC** Ten thousand Roman legionaries captured by Parthians at the disastrous battle of Carrhae, in modern-day Turkey.

② **50 BC** Prisoners are taken to guard the border of the Parthian Empire.

UZBEKISTAN
TURKEY
Beijing
Liqian
Carrhae IRAN
CHINA

Recent DNA tests on 200 villagers in a far corner of Gansu Province in China found that 40 of them had European aspects to their genes. Some even display European characteristics, with curly hair and light-coloured eyes. Two discoveries at the modern town of Zhelazhai have provided a startling explanation: that these people are descendants of an ancient village populated by lost Roman legionaries.

Official permission to inspect the site has been refused, so the artefacts have not yet been authenticated, but they are tantalising. A Roman-style pot could be proof of a link, and a helmet with the inscription *zhao* – 'one of the surrendered' – could provide an astonishing vindication of a theory advanced more than half a century ago.

In the 1930s, Homer Hasenphlug Dubs, a professor of Chinese at Oxford University, put forward the idea that a city in China had been home to a group of Roman legionaries. The mention of a particular defensive formation in the *Book of the Late Han Dynasty* piqued his curiosity, as he believed it was a distinctly Roman tactic. He traced an epic series of battles from Rome to China, uncovering piecemeal evidence of Roman participation all along the way.

In 53 BC, 42,000 troops set out under the command of Crassus to fight the Persian Parthians. They were defeated at the battle of Carrhae, and 10,000 men were taken prisoner. According to the Roman historian Pliny, some of the prisoners were taken to guard the eastern border of the Parthian land, now Syria. What interested Dubs was a battle that took place in 36 BC between the Chinese (the

Hans) and the Central Asian 'Huns'. The citadel of the warlike Hun emperor, Jzh-Jzh, was guarded by a 'double palisade of wood' – a defence that only the Romans used. Furthermore, a group of the emperor's soldiers fought in a complex formation with their shields linked. The record described the defensive formation as 'fish scale', although students of Roman military techniques would recognise it as the *testudo* or tortoise, a hallmark of the Roman army.

Resettled prisoners

Dubs proposed that some legionaries had cut their losses and offered their services to Jzh-Jzh as mercenaries. The Han records supply the story's final chapter: it states that 145 prisoners were taken back to China and placed in an outpost on the northern frontier.

Dubs was determined to find this outpost. He studied China's place names in censuses and found that in AD 5 there was a northern village called Liqian, an ancient Chinese term for the Greco-Roman world. Two other cities on the rolls had foreign names that derived from the place of origin of immigrants who lived there, leading Dubs to hypothesise that the inhabitants of Liqian could have come from the Mediterranean. Even more suggestive is the fact that, in AD 9, the Emperor Wang Mang decreed that all city names should 'tell what is true'. Liqian was renamed Jieh-lu, which can be translated as 'prisoners raised up'.

TAKING COVER Roman soldiers overlapped their shields in defence. Could this be what Chinese records describe as the 'fish scale' formation?

THAT EUREKA MOMENT
How the lost work of Archimedes was rediscovered by modern science

When a 13th-century monk scratched out 94 pages of notes to make a prayer book, he destroyed some of mathematics' most ground-breaking work. But today's techniques can bring back Archimedes' lost 'Eureka texts'.

CROSSING THE LINES Just visible behind the densely written Greek script of this 13th-century prayer book are other lines of text, running at right angles. The original ink was scraped off so the parchment could be reused, but this was the work of Archimedes.

Archimedes possessed a most remarkable mathematical mind. His lost treatise, *The Method of Mechanical Theorems*, was known only from references made to it by other scholars until it was found in the 20th century, under layers of overwritten text and paint, in what appeared to be a forgotten and little used Greek Orthodox church service book, lying in a library in Constantinople.

In *The Method*, the Greek thinker of the 3rd century BC formulated mathematical concepts that were 2000 years ahead of their time, such as adding up an infinite sequence of numbers to make a finite sum.

Elsewhere in the prayer book that hid Archimedes' text, diagrams show that he used differential and integral calculus to come to precise conclusions about areas, volumes and rates of change.

Now Archimedes' lost work has been rescued by a technique called multispectral imaging, which can separate the faint underlying stains left by tannins in faded ink from text that has been written over the top. It is a process that would have pleased Archimedes, as much a practical

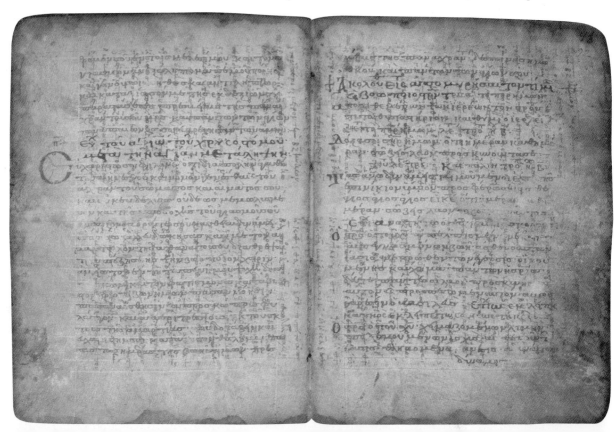

scientist as he was a mathematician. The method enables researchers to detect differing wavelengths of light reflected when examining a piece of parchment to reproduce a clear image from the mere ghost of something that has long been erased.

Archimedes wrote in two columns on scrolls of parchment, which were then copied and recopied. The text erased by the unwitting monk was a 10th-century transcription, but this badly damaged copy is the closest we will get to the original versions of some of Archimedes' greatest works. Because the transcription is in the style used by Archimedes, scholars can be confident that it is faithful to the original.

Paper recycling

That the monk treated the work so lightly reflects changing values over the course of history. Parchment was in short supply in the 13th century and recycling of library manuscripts to make palimpsests (from the Greek word meaning 'rescraped') was common practice.

The monk dunked Archimedes' text in natural bleach then scraped off the ink to make a fresh surface. He then doubled the pages for his prayer book by cutting each of the original pages in two and rebinding them.

The 20th century saw more devious machinations. A Danish classicist, Johan Ludvig Heiberg, recognised Archimedes' faintly decipherable text when he saw the book in a library in 1906, but before he could convince the world of its importance it had been sold to a collector of religious works. Illuminated pictures from a later period were glued over some pages and the book was torn and stained to increase its value as a religious relic.

In the end, it was technological advances in imaging, and not the efforts of a greedy forger, that did most to increase the value of this ancient parchment. In 1998, the rediscovered work of one of the greatest minds the world has ever known was sold for $2 million.

Lines of enquiry

From faint reddish staining in a forgotten prayer book, modern imaging cameras and computer software can provide a crystal-clear view of an ancient Greek mathematical legacy.

1

The horizontal lines of reddish text that will be enhanced by the spectral imaging can just be seen behind the pointing hand drawn by the monk to demarcate sections of the prayer book. The circular diagram below the bright red capital letter is also part of Archimedes' treatise, but can hardly be made out.

2

When ultraviolet light is shone on the parchment, the lost text responds to the different wavelength and becomes darker and clearer. By altering the lighting and the filters over the camera lens, the text can be enhanced. Sensors identify the wavelengths reflected from the ink that Archimedes used.

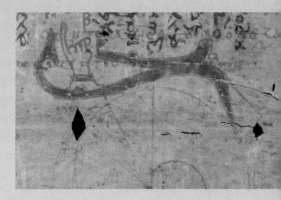

3

A computer is programmed to recognise the particular 'spectral signature' of the wavelengths emitted by the Archimedes text, and to suppress any other signals. The resulting black and white image reveals the lost text much more clearly. Two lines of strong white script are now evident at the top of the picture.

4

At the final stage, also on computer, the lost text is digitally coloured green so that it can be sent for transcription and translation by scholars. The diagram appears to show how Archimedes used the principles of integral calculus to find the area under a curve: he added together the areas of triangles below it.

ROMAN SICKNESS
How the humble mosquito helped to bring down an empire

Countless thousands of words have been written about the reasons for the fall of Rome. But a decisive medical factor has only now been acknowledged.

DANCE OF DEATH The Roman word for funeral meant 'parade'. The annointed corpse was carried on a bier to the family vault in the catacombs or to burial in a graveyard. Now the DNA in the bones of dead Romans is shedding light on why some of them died.

By the beginning of the 5th century AD the Roman Empire was on its knees. Its borders were under constant attack from raiding barbarians: Huns, Goths, Visigoths, Ostrogoths and Saxons. Religious dissent had created an irreparable rift between the two halves of the empire, creating bitter enmity between its eastern Greek Orthodox territories and the Latin west. There was also corruption in the government and the army, and civil wars that left the empire poorly defended against supposedly inferior enemy forces.

But 'fall' is too dramatic a word to describe the lingering process of the empire's decay, and many complex factors played their part. When the last western emperor was deposed in AD 476, it was the culmination of a long, slow decline.

And the Asian and Germanic hordes were not the only enemies that Rome faced, nor perhaps the most threatening. An invader of a quite different kind played a crucial role in bringing down the empire – the *anopheles* mosquito – and its effect on the Romans meant that when the German barbarians finally attacked, they may have met an enemy no longer able to fight.

Invisible army

The Romans certainly knew about malaria, but had no effective way to combat it. One writer had even identified its cause. In 40 BC, the soldier and agriculturist Lucius Junius Columella wrote:

And neither should there be any marsh-land near the buildings, and no military highway adjoining, for the former throws off a baneful stench in hot weather and breeds insects armed with annoying stings, which attack us in dense swarms... from which are often contracted mysterious diseases whose causes are even beyond the understanding of physicians.

But the notion that mosquitoes were responsible for infecting malarial victims did not become common knowledge. On his way to Rome in AD 467, the aristocratic letter-writer Sidonius Apollinaris reported falling victim to a disease which struck when 'the wind Atabulus from Calabria or else the pestilential region of Etruria entered my body'.

The Romans were certainly aware that some parts of the country were more dangerous than others, and during warm and wet months wealthy Romans often withdrew to country villas in the hills. But the notion that the pestilence itself was airborne was a misconception that persisted well into the 18th century: malaria

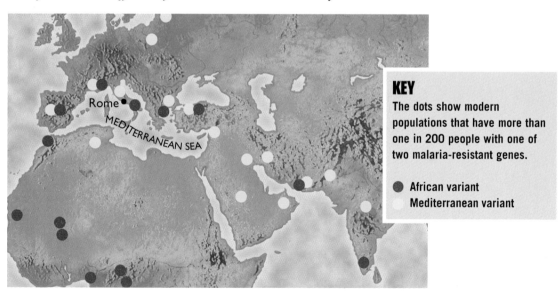

Rome

MEDITERRANEAN SEA

KEY
The dots show modern populations that have more than one in 200 people with one of two malaria-resistant genes.

● African variant
○ Mediterranean variant

Advance of the mosquito

Researchers have identified certain genes that confer resistance to malaria, and measured their presence in African and European populations. Testing shows that a gene that started in Africa (red) is now well established in European populations, indicating that a strain of malaria from Africa – *Plasmodium falciparum* – must have crossed the Mediterranean. The European gene variant (yellow) only offers protection against milder forms of the disease. The mix of African and Mediterranean gene variants found in southern Europe fits with the possibility that a virulent African malaria attacked the Mediterranean in ancient times, weakening the Roman population but gradually giving rise to the resistant gene.

actually means 'bad air'. In reality, low-lying land can be dangerous because of the pools of warm, stagnant water where the malaria-carrying mosquitoes lay their eggs. By moving to higher ground, people could protect themselves from being bitten, and hence from infection.

Though the Romans were aware of malaria, no commentator observed any increase in deaths during the last two centuries of the republic. Contemporary Roman writers and physicians relate how most adults who fell ill with malaria could be nursed through high fever; only weak and vulnerable patients would actually die. Exposure made victims – such as Julius Caesar – resistant to further attacks. The population even developed some genetic resistance which Italians still carry today.

But in 1907 a British professor, W.H.S. Jones, proposed the amazing notion that malaria was responsible for bringing down the Roman Empire. His argument was based on army records showing that Italians in the lower, hotter regions of Italy were no longer contributing young soldiers to Rome's legions; they were recruited mainly from mountainous territory. By the middle of the 5th

BLOOD LINES Without a tiny insect to transmit it, the deadly *Plasmodium falciparum* microbe (inset) would not be dangerous. The female anopheles mosquito carries the parasite in its salivary glands and infects the blood of healthy people when it bites them.

century AD most of the Roman army was German.

Professor Jones reckoned that the number of malaria deaths increased from the 2nd century AD onwards, and that a depleted and weakened population could not spare healthy men to fight. He suggested that the disease was introduced to Italy by the soldiers of the Carthaginian emperor Hannibal during the Second Punic War. But few experts believed that malaria could reach epidemic proportions, nor that it could wipe out entire populations in the way that the plague virus did.

Deadly microbe

New evidence now suggests that Professor Jones may have been right after all. The sudden arrival in Europe of a strain of malaria against which the Romans had no immunity would have had the debilitating effects he describes. *Plasmodium falciparum* – still the world's deadliest infection, killing around 3 million people every year – could be the culprit. The

microbe is usually associated with tropical climates and is most widespread in Africa.

Dr Sarah Tishkoff, a researcher from the University of Maryland in America, has found genetic evidence that *Plasmodium falciparum* entered Europe from Africa comparatively recently. Dr Tishkoff places the incursion before AD 400, but no earlier than 4400 BC. Her suspicion

EARTH WORK **The remains of 47 infants were found in a cemetery at a Roman villa in Lugnano. Analysis of the burial earth suggested that the bodies had been interred within one month around AD 450. The community had apparently been devastated by an epidemic.**

is that the increasing trade between Rome and North Africa could have led to mosquitoes being transported across the Mediterranean on board merchant ships.

There is archaeological evidence too. The recent uncovering of a late Roman cemetery at a villa at Lugnano, 70 miles north of Rome, provides tantalising evidence of a catastrophic outbreak of malaria there, dated to AD 450. In a grave site alongside the villa were found the skeletons of 47 infants – most of them premature stillbirths or newborns. The archaeologists decided the bodies had been buried within days or weeks of each other, indicating a major epidemic of a killer disease.

Exposed community

The villa was set near the marshes along the Tiber, a typically malarial zone. Honeysuckle seeds found in the grave told the archaeologists that it may have been dug in summer, the only season when malaria strikes.

Analysis of even the best preserved bones was difficult, but one was found to contain the DNA of the *Plasmodium falciparum* microbe. The large number of foetuses present also pointed to *Plasmodium falciparum*: miscarriage is one symptom of this type of malaria when pregnant women are infected. It had taken 21st-century scientific procedures to prove that an Edwardian academic's hunch could be right.

A new form of malaria would have taken the rural communities most prone to malaria by surprise. Instead of throwing off the fever and chills as they had come to expect, adult sufferers could die within hours of the onset of symptoms. Others

would be sufficiently weakened to succumb to diseases such as influenza or tuberculosis. The infection can also appear to be gastric, with symptoms very like typhoid. The way the fatalities would have been disguised could explain why there are no clear accounts of a new disease in texts from the time.

The bones in the Lugnano cemetery back up the scientific evidence of *Plasmodium falciparum* in Italy during the time of the empire's decline. And if the insects had penetrated as far as Rome, other epidemics must have already occurred farther south.

Through heavily farmed lakeland terrain the mosquitoes were infiltrating deep into Italy. To a population that was economically, politically and agriculturally crippled, the disease could well have delivered a decisive blow.

CHILD VICTIM **At first, the burials were in ones and twos. But at the highest level, up to seven infants were found in a single tomb – indicative of an epidemic that had worsened rapidly. The burials were hastily arranged: one child was laid to rest on a terracotta roof tile.**

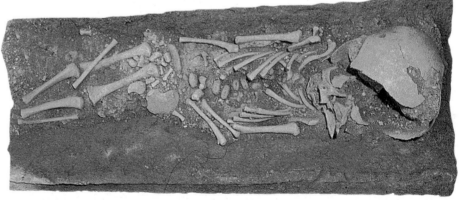

WANDERING STONES

Stonehenge has been altered many times – even in our own age

We assume that Stonehenge is as constant as it is ancient, that it has stood as we now see it for thousands of years. But the monument has often been changed – the stones have collapsed, been realigned, restored and repeatedly vandalised.

One expects Stonehenge to stand in bleak and silent isolation, a fixed point in the shifting annals of history. But really it has never been left in any kind of peace, by turn augmented, reshaped, wrecked and rebuilt. In the 20th century there were three major restorations. Fallen stones were re-erected, leaning stones were straightened, and many were set permanently in concrete. Some of the massive horizontal lintels on top of the standing stones were put there by a 60-ton crane, not by the efforts of a Bronze Age builder.

Forgotten photographs of the restoration work recently rediscovered by the Stonehenge historian Christopher Chippindale challenge our view of the monument: is it an ancient edifice, or is it more truthful to call it a modern reconstruction? After all, most of the 162 stones have been moved – many of them in the last hundred years. The Stonehenge that we see today is not as it appeared to any generation before the 1960s.

Nobody can say how Stonehenge ought to look, because there has never been a definitive version. None of the ancient people who contributed to it had a finished building in mind – as is the case with, say, the pyramids. Stonehenge has always been evolving.

It began as a circular earthwork, then around 4000 years ago bluestones were brought from Wales and erected in a U-shape. Later these were removed and the circle of trilithons – upright stones supporting a horizontal – was constructed on the site. Over the centuries, the bluestones were brought back inside the main circle and reconfigured in various arrangements: rounds, ovals and horseshoes.

About 3000 years ago, Stonehenge was wrecked – possibly by the action of the weather, but more likely by human hand. One of the stones toppled in that first and most serious act of vandalism – known to modern

BLOCK AND TACKLE More of the stones were moved in the 20th century than in the previous 3000 years. The restoration in 1901 directed by Professor William Gowland (centre) was the first to use modern heavy-lifting gear to raise the stones, and concrete to fix them in place.

hengologists as Stone 55 – snapped in half like a twig and still lies where it fell. Thirty-one of the great rectangular sarsen stones and 29 of the smaller bluestones have been plundered – either in antiquity or in more recent times.

Toad repellent

The 17th-century historian John Aubrey, who studied Stonehenge for much of his life, heard an account of stones being carted off to make a bridge. He was also told that villagers liked to take pieces of the stones and grind them to a powder, which they put in their wells to keep away toads.

Much damage has been done to the stones that remain. In January 1797 one of the central trilithons crashed down after being destabilised by a rapid thaw; in 1900, an ominous hour or two before the dawn of the 20th century, another of the trilithons came down in a gale.

The worst disfigurement of the monument in recent centuries has been caused not by locals or the weather, but by tourists. Dr William Stukeley, one of the many learned men to become fascinated by Stonehenge, complained in 1740 that visitors were breaking off pieces with hammers. This new custom continued in the Victorian era. One visitor wrote that on a sunny day 'a constant chipping of stone broke the solitude of the place'. Not all the hammerers were souvenir hunters; some were graffiti artists. One sarsen stone has

ARTIST'S EVIDENCE John Constable painted Stonehenge in 1835. His meticulous study shows that in the 19th century the monument was far more dilapidated than today (inset).

MAKER'S MARK The trilithon that fell in 1797 was winched upright in 1958 and the lintel was replaced. The restoration revealed beautifully crafted tenons on the two upright stones which fitted exactly into the two mortices gouged out of the underside of the lintel.

been engraved with neat capital letters, which spell out 'H. Bridger, 1866, Chichester'. Chippindale remarks wryly that writing this inscription must have taken up most of Mr Bridger's day out.

The vandalism did not cease in the 20th century. An army camp built on Salisbury Plain during the First World War obliterated the eastern end of the 'cursus', an ancient 2-mile ditch that runs north of the monument. There is even a rumour that Stonehenge was slated for demolition in the First World War, because it was a hazard to

the newfangled aircraft of the Royal Flying Corps.

The greatest changes to the aspect of Stonehenge have been wrought not by those who defaced it, but by those who made it their life's work to restore it. In 1898 Sir Edmund Antrobus inherited Stonehenge from his uncle, on whose land it stood. The new owner at first hinted that he might sell the whole edifice and ship it to America, but then instead appointed Professor William Gowland to halt the deterioration of his property. Under Gowland's

Avebury Stone Circles: very old but very new

Fifteen miles north of Stonehenge, on the opposite side of Salisbury Plain, lie the Avebury Stone Circles. They are a magnificent sight, an eerie ensemble of ditches and earthworks a mile round. The circles are dotted with dozens of standing stones, like megalithic exclamation marks.

The Avebury stones look for all the world is if they have been there forever, but the site as it now appears was created by one man: a millionaire by the name of Alexander Keiller, who made his fortune in marmalade.

Keiller bought the entire village of Avebury in 1934 with the intention of reconstructing the circles in what, in his opinion, was their original state. At that time only four stones were standing and fully in view. The rest had been buried, destroyed or taken for building materials in the 17th and 18th centuries. The medieval village occupied the heart of the main circle, which was in a deeply delapidated state.

Keiller's first goal was to remove all human habitation from inside the circle, and he pursued this ruthlessly. He demolished buildings and relocated their tenants, removed fences and pig enclosures, and dynamited obtrusive trees. Most contentiously, he dug up all the buried stones and re-erected them where he believed they once stood (left).

Avebury is now protected from further interference. It is a genuinely ancient place – at least as old as Stonehenge – and it is full of mystery. But the rough-hewn megaliths and clearly defined earthworks that visitors see today have been in their current positions for less than a lifetime.

direction one stone was straightened, others were shored up with timbers, and much useful archeological work was done on the site. Gowland also began the practice of anchoring the stones in cement.

Cemented into place

A second round of restoration was undertaken after the First World War. Lintels that had not been moved in four millennia were lifted from the most unstable uprights, which were brought back to the vertical using jacks and steel supports. More concrete was poured beneath their feet; then, as photographers and newsreel cameramen captured the moment, the lintels were popped back on like lids on a jar.

The trilithons that had fallen in 1797 and 1900 had to wait until 1958 to be pulled back up to the vertical. A

huge crane designed to lift aircraft was employed to raise the stones. At the end of this final round of work only seven of the sarsens were actually standing in their original chalk sockets: most of Stonehenge now was embedded in metre-thick cement. But to the naked eye, and from a distance, the stones looked pretty much as they had done in the 16th century. At least they did until 1963, when Stone 23 fell down, having previously received a whack from Stone 22 while it was being moved with a winch.

The righting of Stone 23 in 1964 was the most recent major task of restoration. For a brief half-century, Stonehenge has stood undisturbed apart from the clamour of traffic on the nearby main road, which sometimes rattles the brooding monoliths in their concrete boots.

 True! In 1919, a bottle of port was found in a hole beneath the 'Slaughter Stone', left there by the 18th-century antiquarian William Cunnington. Unfortunately the cork had rotted and the wine was undrinkable.

DEATH OR GLORY
Gladiators were professional showmen, not hapless victims

They occupied the lowest social rank – on a par with slaves – but not all gladiators were badly treated, shackled and forced to fight for their lives. Many of them were the pop stars and sports celebrities of the day, complete with their own pet names and fan clubs.

HEAT OF BATTLE A mosaic found in a villa near Zliten in Libya (above) shows that a gladiatorial contest was not a free fight. The men in the white tunics are referees; one to the right considers an appeal from a fighter whose upraised finger denotes his surrender. On the left, a referee stops a gladiator attacking when his opponent is down.

Countless screen epics have fashioned our image of Roman gladiatorial contests as terrifying fights to the death, in which unwilling gladiators were thrown into the arena and forced to kill – or be killed – for public entertainment. The drama begins with the ringing gladiatorial cry: 'We who are about to die salute you!'

These contests were in fact not orgies of blood and inevitable death, but carefully orchestrated duels fought under the watchful eye of a referee – much like an armed version of modern-day boxing matches. Particularly adept thrusts, feints or parries would draw enthusiastic cheers from the crowd. And, although the poignant salute seems to suggest otherwise, many gladiators lived to fight another day.

Certainly when they fought, gladiators risked their lives. But the element of danger was an important part of the sport – it heightened the entertainment. According to Professor Fritz Krinzinger of the Austrian Archaeological Institute, gladiators were in this sense like modern racing drivers, 'the Schumachers of the ancient world'. They were in danger every time they performed, and they were ready to risk their lives for sport.

Judging from the admiring graffiti scratched on the walls of Pompeii, the gladiators' mixture of brawn and bravery drew particular support from female spectators. Inscriptions

FREE FIGHTER A gladiator who earned his freedom was presented with a token engraved with his name (left). His sponsor then had to be paid off.

testified to the fact that 'Celadus, the Thracian, makes all the girls sigh'. The suggestive names of some gladiators – 'Eros', 'Narcissus' – imply that organisers were keen to emphasise their sex appeal. In the 2nd century AD the satirist Juvenal lampooned a noblewoman who abandoned her husband and ran off with a gladiator:

There were sundry deformities in his face: a scar caused by the helmet, a huge wen on his nose. But what women love is the sword.

Not everyone thought the erotic appeal of the gladiators was funny. The Emperor Augustus judged it so potent that women were only allowed to watch the fighters from the back seats of the arena.

Protected species

The first images of gladiatorial combat date from the 4th century BC, and the shows increased in popularity over the succeeding centuries. By the start of the 1st century AD, there were as many as 186 amphitheatres in operation at any time across the Roman Empire.

New evidence uncovered from a gladiator burial site at Ephesus in Turkey has revealed much about those who fought in the arena there from AD 200 to 300. The bones show various wounds. Three holes in a skull were made by a trident that had been thrust into a man's head; another loser was killed by a blow to the throat. But the remains also reveal the quality of the medical

treatment that was given to gladiators. One of the bones – a fractured forearm – had healed almost invisibly, indicating that recovery had been assisted with physiotherapy.

Records confirm that some gladiators had their own private doctors and masseurs: at Ephesus these specialists could have learnt their skills from the famed Greek physician Galen, who lived close by at Pergamum.

Too precious to die

Fight organisers tried hard to protect their gladiators inside the arena as much as outside. Fully trained gladiators were an investment. To let a good gladiator die was to lose a valuable asset, and so the organisers kept a close eye on every fight and ensured that referees knew which gladiators were to be spared. Inscriptions about fight results prove that veteran fighters could be defeated yet still leave the arena alive.

Contrary to popular myth, neither the crowd nor the presiding dignitary necessarily dictated who lived or died at the end of a gladiatorial bout. This was because the financial interests of the *lanistae*, entrepreneurs who bought or recruited gladiators to rent out for events, were paramount.

Lanistae ran gladiatorial schools where the trainees were subject to strict discipline and a harsh, physical regime aimed at building fitness and strength. They even ate carbohydrate-rich meals of pulses and barley porridge to build up their weight.

WEAPON OF CHOICE Gladiators took their name from the *gladius* – the short sword of the Roman Army. One *gladius* found at the gladiators' barracks in Pompeii is only 30cm (12in) in length, shorter than a soldier's, very likely to ensure that fights in the arena had to take place at close quarters.

RULES OF THE GAME In his 1872 painting *Pollice Verso* the artist Jean-Léon Gérome depicted a bloodthirsty audience baying for execution. In reality the victorious gladiator would not appeal to the crowd, but would await the referee's decision. Nor would a slain fighter be left lying in the arena. He would be borne off on a stretcher.

Meticulous records were kept of each fighter's performance, as his value depended on his success in the arena.

A lanista had a vested interest in the outcome of a fight involving one of his gladiators, and could instruct the referees to spare certain fighters or even call a draw to prevent too many injuries being inflicted.

A referee could control the fight – and its outcome – and still try to satisfy the demands of the crowd. There were no rounds in a gladiatorial contest, but if the fight went on for a long time the referee could call for an interval. As no time limit was imposed, the duel ended only when the referee said so. Surrender was signalled either by throwing down shield and sword or by raising a

hand with the forefinger extended. If a contestant had fought bravely and capitulated only when he could fight no more, the crowd would wave the hems of their togas and cloaks and call '*missio*' (mercy). However, if they were dissatisfied with his performance, they would roar out '*iugula*!' (Cut his throat!).

The politician or nobleman who had put on the show may have had the final decision at moments of such drama, but even he would have weighed financial considerations as well as wishing to appease the bloodlust of the crowd. He had to recompense the lanista for every gladiator killed in the arena. One historian who has analysed the outcomes of 100 contests fought

Adoring fans

Graffiti from the walls of Pompeii attested to the romantic allure of certain gladiators. This inscription refers to 'Crescens, the net fighter, healer of the girls at night'.

during the 1st century AD found that only 19 of the 200 gladiators involved actually died in the arena.

Rich prizes

Sponsors, too, hated to see anyone of value needlessly wasted. The writer Suetonius recorded how, during a gladiatorial show organised by Julius Caesar for his daughter Julia, he 'gave orders that whenever famous gladiators fought without winning the favour of the people, they should be rescued by force and kept for him'. Suetonius also noted how the Emperor Nero, for all his bloodthirsty reputation, ordered that no one be killed during a show at Campus Martius. In other words, it appears that gladiators – the best and most popular at any rate – were a protected species.

For those fighters who did emerge victorious, the rewards could be great. After the contest, the victor would ascend a flight of steps to the officials' box, where he received the palm branch and a bag of money, which he kept even if he was a slave. For an outstanding performance he could receive a laurel wreath.

These would have been highly prized by the combatants, for most gladiators came from lowly positions: they were slaves, criminals or captured soldiers. Some gladiators, *auctorati*, were volunteers. These fighters could buy themselves out of service, although they were not allowed to hold public office.

For all the danger and harsh conditions, being a gladiator could be a very glamorous occupation: celebrity, wealth and freedom were the rewards for the stars who made a fight into a drama worth watching.

 False! The crowd demanded the death of a gladiator by turning their thumbs upward, not by 'thumbs down' as is often shown. Some historians think that sign was made after a formal execution.

Let the games commence

In the film *Gladiator* (2000), particular care was taken to present authentic fight sequences. Although group fights, as shown in the film, were not commonplace, the clear vested interests of the arena officials and the gladiators' keepers ring true. Arena assistants – *harenarii* – are also shown. These men carried long sticks to discipline the fighters, or prod them if they were deemed to be insufficiently aggressive.

There are records of whips, torches and red-hot irons being used to 'persuade' contestants to fight, but most historians believe that such reluctant combatants were probably criminals condemned to death.

Playing to the gallery

The games usually followed a certain order of events. The day began with a display of animal acts, such as a staged animal hunt. The public execution of convicted criminals by various means, ranging from crucifixion to being eaten by lions, took place later on during the lunch break. This grisly spectacle, much enjoyed by Roman audiences, preceded an athletic or dance display, or sometimes a comedy interlude.

In the afternoon, the gladiators, wearing lavishly decorated armour, made their first appearance to the accompaniment of drum rolls and fanfares. Full details of all the fighters taking part – notably their previous wins and any awards they had received – were published in the programme. The gladiators warmed up and showed off their skills by fighting with blunted or wooden weapons. It is easy to imagine that this part of the presentation was the gladiators' chance to play to the crowd and impress their supporters. Pre-choreographed moves, much like in today's wrestling shows, would draw gasps and applause.

Then the real contests began. Most games comprised a series of duels fought to agreed rules, officiated by a referee with the power to interrupt the fight and order the combatants back to their starting positions. A usual day would see perhaps 12 to 15 paired fights.

CROWNS
AND
CONSPIRACIES

LIBELS THAT KILLED A QUEEN

Pamphlets, not cakes, were the ruin of Marie Antoinette

History judges the last queen of France harshly, as though her own selfish and stupid actions sealed her fate. But the evidence shows that a vile and unstoppable campaign of slander turned the mob against her.

The decade leading up to the French Revolution saw an unending supply of cheaply and anonymously produced scandal sheets peddled on the street corners of Paris. They could be bought by anyone with a few centimes to spare. Courtiers, politicians and publicity seekers were singled out in turn for vilification that was vulgar in the extreme. But one woman was ceaselessly attacked in print. By the time of the Revolution, Marie Antoinette drew popular derision and hatred on such a scale that the mob was baying for her blood long before her trial. One scandal sheet of 1781 tells of the 26-year-old queen's orgies with aristocrats of all sexes, ranks and ages, and has the young queen confessing:

Barbaric queen, unfaithful wife,
woman without morals,
sullied with crime and debauchery –
these are the titles that identify me.

But Marie Antoinette was not always hated by the Parisian mob. She was born into the Austrian royal family in 1755. It was at the age of 14, barely able to read and write even in German, her native language, that she was plucked from among her sisters for marriage to crown prince Louis of France, himself aged only 15. Her politically ambitious mother, the Austrian Empress Maria-Theresa, had already arranged for three of her elder sisters to marry into European royal families.

The transformation of the Austrian princess Maria Antonia into the French Marie Antoinette was turned into a highly symbolic ceremony. At a house specially built on the French border, the young girl descended from her carriage and undressed, leaving all her belongings with her old attendants. She crossed the threshold naked into a room on French soil where she was

REGAL PORTRAIT In 1767 12-year-old Marie Antoinette – then the Austrian archduchess Maria Antonia – sat for her portrait. Two years later, she was engaged to Louis of France.

reclothed and even renamed in the French style. Her carefree Viennese childhood over, she was faced with immediate marriage to Louis. Within five years she was Queen of France.

A vivacious, beautiful and innocent girl, Marie Antoinette captivated France – she was a Lady Diana of her time. The populace loved their fairytale bride. But at court in Versailles, south-west of Paris, it was a different story. To the sophisticated French aristocrats she appeared hardly better bred than a commoner. Many had soon joined in the new sport of making snide comments behind the princess's back.

Marie Antoinette's behaviour soon made her plenty of enemies. She disliked conforming to the finer points of French etiquette, so formed a circle of friends with whom she engaged in dancing and gambling. One of Louis' dowager aunts coined the nickname *l'Autrichienne* – literally meaning 'the Austrian woman', but containing a pun on *chienne* – 'bitch'. One contemporary, Madame de Staël, commented that the queen was condemned from the start by her marriage into such a corrupt nest of vipers.

Cruel slander

Rumours spread about the queen – at first in whispers and then in a host of pamphlets, called 'libelles'. These libelles were the crueller ancestors of our tabloids and are the root of the English term 'libel', a written slander.

The scandal sheets were always published anonymously. Some

FINAL JOURNEY **The French artist Jacques Louis David made a quick pencil sketch of Marie Antoinette as she was carried in an open cart, or tumbril, to the guillotine. Her execution took place on a scaffold in the Place de la Révolution on October 16, 1793.**

Cult of simplicity

As the queen of France, Marie Antoinette often had her portrait painted – at least 20 were painted by her friend, Elisabeth Vigée-Lebrun, one of the most brilliant artists of the time. Unlike other more formal images, this one from 1783 captures the 28-year-old Marie Antoinette in the simple, 'unaffected' style Vigée-Lebrun preferred. Many, however, felt that the informality of such portraits was unbecoming and cheapened the queen's status.

historians even believe that at least one of the libelles against the queen was financed by her brothers-in-law, the Comte d'Artois and the Comte de Provence, as part of a campaign against her.

The queen's good name was compromised by early misfortune. For a long while she and Louis were unable to have children, because Louis apparently suffered from phimosis (erectile dysfunction). He was examined by a few discreet doctors, but his naïve child bride could not understand his condition.

The fact that Marie Antoinette was not getting pregnant should have been sufficient proof of her fidelity; but the snobbish and prurient logic of the court interpreted it as the opposite. As she was clearly spending little time in bed with the king, the whispers ran, she must be engaging in sexual exploits elsewhere.

An operation finally corrected the king's problem and the couple had four children, but the damage had been done in the seven years of childless marriage.

Nor did Marie Antoinette's concern for the poor save her name, although

PRINTED POISON The libelles drew a grossly distorted picture of Marie Antoinette. She was described as a monster with insatiable passions. Some had pornographic illustrations.

it was certainly genuine. At the beginning of her reign, she cancelled a tax known as the 'Queen's Belt' with the remark, 'Belts are no longer worn'. This was not to be the quip that survived for posterity. A year later, during the 'Flour War' of 1775 – violent rioting triggered by a rise in bread prices – she wrote to her mother that '…seeing the people who treat us so well in spite of their own misfortune, we are more obliged than ever to work hard for their happiness.' Her obligations extended to charity work and personal visits to institutions serving the needy, where her artless manners and lack of schooling helped

Diamonds in the night

In 1784, Marie Antoinette's reputation suffered a serious blow with the scandal of the Diamond Necklace Affair. In truth, this was a confidence trick that exploited the princess's status. A trickster calling herself Contesse de La Motte convinced the wealthy Prince de Rohan that she was a confidante of the queen, and he agreed to purchase a diamond necklace (right) that Marie Antoinette supposedly wanted. Royal gratitude, even physical favours, seemed forthcoming when he was rewarded by a meeting in a darkened courtyard of the palace with 'Her Majesty' – really a prostitute in a gown similar to one of the queen's. When the jeweller came for payment, the plot unravelled in public.

La Motte and the prince were arrested but, in a slight to the queen, Rohan was acquitted. Despite the fact that Marie Antoinette knew nothing about the plot, the insulting notion that she could trade sexual favours for diamonds was considered to have been credible enough for the prince to have acted in good faith.

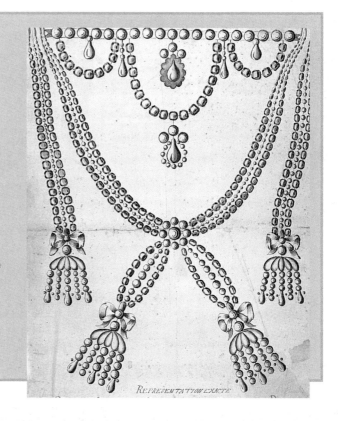

REPRESENTATION EXACTE

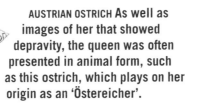

AUSTRIAN OSTRICH As well as images of her that showed depravity, the queen was often presented in animal form, such as this ostrich, which plays on her origin as an 'Östereicher'.

establish her early rapport with the common people.

For all her compassion, Marie Antoinette loved the frivolity that came with her status. She was often to be seen in the galleries and theatres of Paris. But as her popularity waned, she found herself being booed on her evenings at the theatre and she visited Paris less and less. To escape loneliness and unhappiness at court, she would disappear to her small, private chateau, Le Petit Trianon, in the grounds of Versailles, where she would hold tea parties and sumptuous balls. A quarter of a mile away, she had a rustic hamlet of farmhouses and a dairy built, where she could dress as a peasant woman, complete with mob cap, crook and

silver-plated milk pails. Her lambs were shampooed to a dazzling white; each one lovingly decorated with a satin ribbon.

These girlish bouts of dressing-up could be interpreted as a naïve attempt to express fellow feeling for the French people, but they attracted derisive gossip at court. Now the libelles doubled their doses of poison. The astronomical sums the queen spent on her farmhouse folly and on costume balls were published as proof of her intention to bankrupt France and divert misappropriated funds to the Austrian royal coffers.

In fact, much of the hostility towards the queen was rooted in her Austrian nationality. She made no secret of her loyalty to her native country, promoting pro-Austrian ministers to positions of power and maintaining regular contact with her family back in Vienna.

This, after all, was her *raison d'etre* as queen: her marriage itself had been the diplomatic expression of the Franco-Austrian alliance. But anti-Austrian feelings were endemic in France, and the alliance was deeply

'Let them eat cake'

It is one of the great myths of the Revolution that Marie Antoinette, hearing people were suffering a shortage of bread, replied – cynically or naïvely – 'Let them eat cake.' But the saying was already in circulation at the French court long before she came to the throne. It is known that the phrase did not originate with the queen (caricatured in 1775 for her extravagance, right).

In his *Confessions*, the French political writer Jean-Jacques Rousseau recalled an incident in which this phrase had been uttered by 'a great princess' when told the peasants had no bread. But this book was written in 1767, three years before Marie Antoinette came to France. When it was finally published during the final years of her reign, the phrase became linked with the wrong queen.

unpopular. The queen's enemies accused her of wanting to turn the king into a puppet of Austria, and their words found a ready audience. In a libelle entitled *The Austrian on the Booze*, Louis XVI passes out after drinking too much champagne while Marie Antoinette engages in an orgy with her courtiers.

Printing presses churned on with *The Royal Bordello, The Hen-Hooker of Austria* and *The Austrian Harpy.* The anonymous stories became a potent means of political agitation against the queen. She could have taken the publishers of the libelles to court, but that would have drawn more attention to the slanders. Marie Antoinette chose to maintain a dignified silence.

Madame Deficit

Marie Antoinette took refuge in her role as a mother and, realising the extent of the financial crisis in France, pared down her extravagant lifestyle. She tried to convey a simpler image, and commissioned portraits of herself as a devoted mother wearing plain, uncorseted clothes.

But this attempt to redefine her image failed. The queen continued to shower her favourites with special offices, privileges and money. Her brother-in-law, the Comte de Provence, mocked her for it, dubbing her 'Madame Deficit'. The implication was that the queen's spending was responsible for the national debt.

When the Revolution came in 1789, the royal family was brought to Paris as prisoners of the people. They made appeals to various foreign powers to save the monarchy and, when Austria and Prussia declared war on France in 1792, were accused of passing secrets to the enemy – a charge of treason.

Marie Antoinette was at first imprisoned with her husband and children, but towards the end was in solitary confinement. Her treatment in prison was harsh and demeaning. At one point, the severed head of her friend Madame de Lamballe was paraded on a pike past her window.

LAID LOW Prison conditions turned the glamorous Marie Antoinette into the careworn 'Widow Capet'. She was now an ordinary citizen of the new French republic, the name Capet a reference to an earlier dynasty of unpopular French rulers.

The victorious revolutionaries were also giving thought to her children. When Marie Antoinette came to trial in 1793, she was accused not only of plotting with the Austrians, but also of incestuous relations with her sickly ten-year-old son. Such a crime would have been no more than routine for the insatiable harlot of the libelles, but the crowd outside knew when a dirty joke had gone too far. The queen struck exactly the right note in her response. 'I appeal to all the mothers in this room,' she said. 'Is such a crime possible?' Her restrained bearing aroused a clamour of support, and the news of her dignity under interrogation nearly set off rioting in the chaotic streets outside.

Sensing the mood of the mob, the people's court dropped the incest charge. The hated queen had won a measure of sympathy from the common people of France. But it was too little and too late. She was found guilty of treason and condemned to the guillotine.

On the day of Marie Antionette's execution – October 16, 1793 – the hawkers of the libelles were out in force once again. They were selling copies to the crowd of *Les adieux de la Reine à ses mignons et mignonnes*: the queen's farewell to all her lovers and mistresses.

False! His name is forever associated with the apparatus of the Terror, but Joseph Guillotin (1738-1814) – the inventor of the killing machine – was not a supporter of executions. His hope was that the guillotine's swift decapitation would lessen the victim's suffering and discourage spectators.

SHAKESPEARE'S HISTORY

William Shakespeare was a playwright, not a historian, but many of his works feature real people and real events. So popular are the bard's plays that – true or not – some of them have become the most widely-known version of events.

Character assassination

As Henry VII's defeated rival for the throne, Richard III received short shrift from the Tudor chroniclers. Drawing heavily on an earlier play (now lost) and Sir Thomas More's *History of King Richard the Third*, Shakespeare portrays Richard as evil, twisted and full of hate. Not only that but also as a hunchback (which was untrue), the murderer of the two innocent young princes in the Tower (uncertain) and a coward on the battlefield (untrue). Shakespeare's work is great drama but bad history.

HAMMING IT UP The real Richard III (above) was not the deformed hunchback described by Shakespeare and portrayed by Antony Sher (right).

❝ Cheated of feature by dissembling nature, Deform'd, unfinish'd, sent before my time... – Richard III ❞

Under the influence

Shakespeare dramatised the reigns of six English monarchs, the last of whom, Henry VIII, died only 17 years before the playwright was born. Many of his plots came from a book entitled *Chronicles of England, Scotlande and Irelande* (1577) by Raphael Holinshed, a historian who sought to emphasise the virtues of the Tudors by highlighting – and occasionally inventing – the shortcomings of previous rulers.

The play's the thing

The tragedy *Hamlet* is based on a 13th-century book in Latin by Saxo, a Danish historian who made no attempt to discriminate between myth and fact. It is unclear whether the Prince of Denmark ever existed, let alone lived the life described in the story. To Shakespeare, it was just a good plot. He expanded the basic tale of medieval revenge and added some inventions of his own – Rosencrantz and Guildenstern (left) could not have been students at Wittenberg, because the university there was not founded until the 16th century.

Playing with the facts

- *The Winter's Tale* features scenes set in 'Bohemia – a desert country near the sea'. The real Bohemia (part of the modern Czech Republic) is landlocked.

- In *Henry V*, the English king receives a gift of tennis balls from the French Dauphin – mocking the king's youth and inexperience in battle. Shakespeare invented this episode.

- A stage direction in *Julius Caesar* reads, 'A clock strikes'. The play is set in 44 BC, more than a thousand years before such timepieces were invented.

The witch guide

The plot of *Macbeth* was embellished to please James I, the patron of Shakespeare's theatre company. James had written a book called *Daemonologie*, and Shakespeare's witches echo some of the passages from it.

James liked to think that he was descended from a Scottish nobleman called Banquo, but this was a fabrication. Banquo had been invented to validate the family line of the Stuarts, the royal house of which James was a member. The Stuarts were actually descended from a Norman named Walter FitzAlan, a humble steward to David I of Scotland. Shakespeare treats Banquo as a real character from history, murdered by Macbeth because the witches prophesy that his descendants (including James) will come to sit on the throne of Scotland.

DEATH OF AN EMPEROR
Mementos held the key to Napoleon's gruesome death

The French Emperor Napoleon dominated European history for a decade. But, during his final days in exile on the island of St Helena, he was to prove vulnerable to the murderous intent of one of those around him. Now we know how and by whom he was assassinated.

MURDER VICTIM During his years of exile on the island of St Helena, Napoleon had no idea that there was an assassin in his entourage.

Napoleon Bonaparte died at eleven minutes to six on the evening of May 5, 1821, at Longwood House on the south Atlantic island of St Helena. After a post-mortem examination the following day, his doctors announced that he had died from 'a condition leading to cancer'. He had not been in good health, and in recent months his decline had been unremitting. Doctors and servants recorded more than 30 symptoms which came and went at different times, and occurred in various combinations. The symptoms included uncontrollable weight gain, loss of body hair, swollen feet, nausea, diarrhoea, constipation, headache, dizziness, irregular pulse, pain in the liver and stomach, loose teeth, bleeding gums, weakness in the legs, deafness, impaired vision and excessive thirst.

Ten weeks before Napoleon died, his Italian doctor Francesco Antommarchi had noted with concern: 'The Emperor, who was feeling fairly well on Feb 21, has a sudden relapse. Dry cough. Vomiting. Sensation of heat in intestines. Generally disturbed. Discomfort. Burning feeling that is almost unbearable, accompanied by burning thirst.' By the next day the situation was even worse: 'The cough has become more violent, and the painful nausea did not stop until seven in the morning.'

In desperation the doctors tried to induce their patient to purge with emetics and laxatives. After a particularly strong dose of calomel laxative on the evening of May 3, he suffered complete muscular paralysis and fell into unconsciousness. According to a member of his entourage, General Gratien Bertrand: 'He could not even swallow.' The emperor remained in a coma and died two days later. He was buried on St Helena, but nearly 20 years later his body was exhumed and removed to a tomb in the Hôtel des Invalides, Paris.

At the time of Napoleon's death, and for more than 130 years afterwards, no one questioned the doctors' last diagnosis: the history books recorded that he had died of stomach cancer.

And there the matter would have rested, had it not been for his habit of giving locks of hair as mementos for visitors and servants. Many of these have survived as family heirlooms. The possible significance of this was not realised until 1955, when a Swedish scientist, Sten Forshufvud, read the recently published journals of Napoleon's valet,

Napoleon exhumed

On October 15 1840, 19 years after his burial, Napoleon's coffin was opened in front of officials and former attendants. It was then sent from St Helena to France for a state funeral. The coffin lid was lifted for two minutes and the crowd reportedly gasped on seeing the condition of the body.

Although it had not been embalmed, Napoleon's corpse was still life-like. It had been interred in four coffins – two of wood, one of lead and one of tin. But there was an explanation for its preserved appearance: the arsenic that killed Napleon would also have slowed the process of his body's decay.

Louis Marchand. In Marchand's meticulously detailed account of the last months of the emperor's life, Forshufvud saw a puzzle. If Napoleon had died of stomach cancer, as historians insisted, then why had Marchand not noticed any symptom of that disease? And why, when cancer typically emaciates its victims, had Napoleon died fat?

The more he read, the more Forshufvud came to realise that the catalogue of mysteries – the large number of apparently unrelated symptoms, the short-term recoveries and relapses, the obesity, the swollen liver noted at the autopsy – all indicated a very different diagnosis from the one recorded by the doctors.

It was a diagnosis which, if it were true, would rewrite history – a diagnosis so dramatic and so politically charged that Forshufvud knew it could never be accepted unless he had proof.

Methodically, over a period of 20 years, Forshufvud traced surviving locks of Napoleon's hair in France, Switzerland, England, Russia and Austria, and persuaded each owner to provide a sample.

In total, 140 samples were sent for analysis, initially by Dr Hamilton Smith at the department of forensic medicine at Glasgow University, and subsequently by the Atomic Energy Research Establishment at Harwell, England. The results were exactly as Forshufvud had predicted. All the samples were from the same person, and that person had swallowed a great deal of arsenic.

Attempts were made to suggest that the poisoning had been accidental: there might have been arsenic in Napoleon's hair oil, for example, or he might have inhaled arsenic fumes from the green dye in his wallpaper. But a hair sample taken after his death puts the issue beyond doubt.

Forensic record

The value of the forensic tests was that they do not simply give a single overall reading, but grade the hair in sections. If the date a sample was taken is known, then a scientist can work back along the entire length of the hair and calculate almost to the day when arsenic entered the body. If the concentrations vary significantly, contamination by a background source such as wallpaper or hair oil can be ruled out. Constant exposure would result in constant levels of absorption and this would have been unlikely to affect one man alone.

Marchand had carefully put in an envelope a lock of hair shaved from Napoleon just after his death. The 3in long lock – kept in its envelope by the valet's descendants – was an incontrovertible record of the last six months of his life. The variations in arsenic levels were not just significant – they were startling. At a time when the average concentration of arsenic in the

Key to the lock

After Napoleon's death in 1821 his head was shaved and his valet Louis Marchand took a lock home with him in an envelope to France. The 3in long hair represents the last six months of the emperor's life.

The amount of arsenic a person has ingested at a particular time can be determined in parts per million (ppm) by testing the hair at intervals from root to tip.

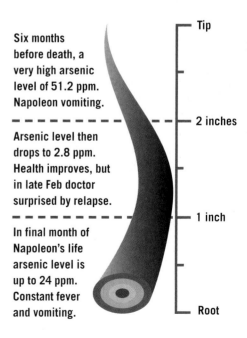

Tip

Six months before death, a very high arsenic level of 51.2 ppm. Napoleon vomiting.

– – – – 2 inches

Arsenic level then drops to 2.8 ppm. Health improves, but in late Feb doctor surprised by relapse.

– – – – 1 inch

In final month of Napoleon's life arsenic level is up to 24 ppm. Constant fever and vomiting.

Root

population was approximately 0.08 parts per million, Napoleon's readings veered between 2.8 and 51.2. Napoleon at times had more than 600 times the amount of arsenic in his hair than one might expect.

Working now with Ben Weider, president of the Montreal-based International Napoleonic Society, Forshufvud made a time chart of the symptoms recorded by Marchand and the doctors, then compared this with the daily analysis of Napoleon's hair. They matched precisely. Whenever the arsenic increased, so did the symptoms. Earlier samples told the same story: the more arsenic in Napoleon's body, the sicker he was. The slow poisoning had been going on at intervals throughout his exile.

But what finally killed Napoleon was not the arsenic itself but the medicines prescribed to treat its symptoms. In the month before he died, he was given lemonade spiked with 'tartar emetic' to make him vomit. To a modern chemist, tartar emetic is better known as antimony potassium tartrate. It is highly toxic and corrodes the stomach lining. It also inhibits the very vomiting reflex

it is intended to stimulate. It is not an emetic at all; on the contrary it robs the stomach of its natural ability to expel poisons.

At about the same time, Napoleon was given an orange-flavoured drink called orgeat, along with calomel laxative. Between them, these would deliver the coup de grâce. An ingredient of orgeat is oil of bitter almonds – a source of prussic acid. Calomel contains mercury chloride. In the stomach this combines with the acid in the orgeat to form mercury cyanide. If not expelled by vomiting, it further damages the stomach wall and eventually causes muscular paralysis – precisely the effects noted in Napoleon's last hours.

Death by degrees
Slow poisoning by arsenic was, from the poisoner's point of viewpoint, exactly the right way to go about killing the emperor. The murderer would not have wanted to kill him outright. An obvious case of murder would have inflamed republican passions in France, and the Bourbon royal family – only recently restored to the throne in 1816 – could not risk

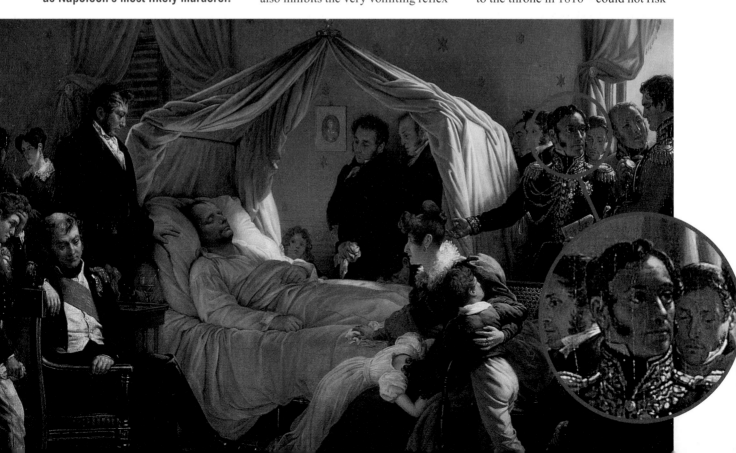

DEATHBED SCENE **Several years after Napoleon's death the artist Carl von Steuben visualised the scene at his deathbed. The deceased emperor is shown surrounded by a host of mourners, including the courtier Count Charles-Tristan de Montholon (encircled), who has been identified as Napoleon's most likely murderer.**

another revolution. It would have been safer to poison him by degrees, making his gradual deterioration look like chronic disease.

Plotting poisoner

The evidence amassed by Forshufvud was enough to convince 20th-century crime agencies. In 1995, the US Department of Justice declared that the results of hair analysis were 'consistent with arsenic poisoning', and, in a letter written to Ben Weider in 1997, Scotland Yard agreed.

Then, in June 2001, Weider swept away most of the remaining objections. For years, French historians had refused to accept the evidence of forensic tests conducted outside France. Now Weider was able to reveal that samples of Napoleon's hair had been examined by Dr Pascal Kintz in the department of toxicology at the University of Louis Pasteur in Strasbourg. Kintz's conclusion allowed no room for doubt: 'There was major exposure, and I stress major, to arsenic.'

But who was the murderer? The only two people who were with Napoleon throughout his exile, and had access to his food and drink, were his valet Marchand and a courtier, Count Charles-Tristan de Montholon.

The unquestionable loyalty of Marchand and his lack of motive make him an unlikely suspect. Montholon, on the other hand, had both motive and opportunity. He had a grudge – Napoleon had once dismissed him from a diplomatic position for making an unsuitable marriage. It also seems clear that his wife became Napoleon's mistress on St Helena. Montholon was a known royalist, with links to both Louis XVIII and his brother the Duke d'Artois, later to become Charles X. D'Artois had tried to kill Napoleon before, in a bomb attack in 1800.

D'Artois had also saved Montholon from punishment after he had embezzled army funds. It could be that this favour was now being repaid, and that Montholon volunteered for exile at the insistence of the royalist faction in France. On St Helena he endured the pain of exile and the humiliation of being cuckolded in order to fulfil a greater purpose: to kill Napoleon.

So how was the crime committed? Montholon would have had access to Napoleon's private supply of wine. Arsenic lacks odour and taste, so Napoleon would have noticed nothing. Although circumstantial, the evidence against Montholon is compelling. In October 2002, his descendant, François de Cande-Montholon, wrote to Weider from his home in Noyant-la-Gravoyère, accepting his ancestor's guilt.

Napoleon had once remarked that 'It is only a step from the sublime to the ridiculous'. His murder, if not actually ridiculous, was certainly a pathetic end to a life filled with sublime glories and epoch-making achievements. A decade earlier, Napoleon bestrode continents and decided the fate of nations; he died at the hand of an embittered servant, unwittingly abetted by a gaggle of baffled physicians. From the sublime to the ridiculous – not so much a step as a hair's breadth.

LOYAL VALET Louis Marchand was Napoleon's faithful servant. It was Marchand's detailed account of his master's eating and drinking habits on St Helena – only published in the 1950s – that helped to identify the means of murder.

DEATH MASK This bronze cast shows the Emperor's face after he had succumbed to poison and the ministrations of his doctors.

THE LOST COLONY OF ROANOKE
Uncovering a conspiracy that killed the first English settlers in America

In 1587 a colony of 123 English men, women and children was founded on Roanoke Island in Virginia. Three years later their settlement had disappeared without trace. Now one historian believes that they were the victims of an English court conspiracy, led by one of the most powerful men of the time.

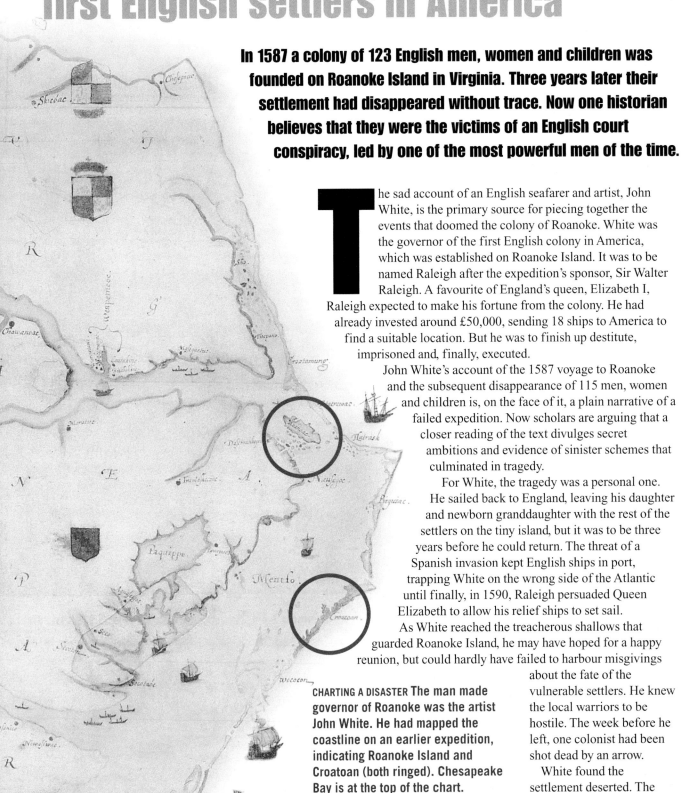

The sad account of an English seafarer and artist, John White, is the primary source for piecing together the events that doomed the colony of Roanoke. White was the governor of the first English colony in America, which was established on Roanoke Island. It was to be named Raleigh after the expedition's sponsor, Sir Walter Raleigh. A favourite of England's queen, Elizabeth I, Raleigh expected to make his fortune from the colony. He had already invested around £50,000, sending 18 ships to America to find a suitable location. But he was to finish up destitute, imprisoned and, finally, executed.

John White's account of the 1587 voyage to Roanoke and the subsequent disappearance of 115 men, women and children is, on the face of it, a plain narrative of a failed expedition. Now scholars are arguing that a closer reading of the text divulges secret ambitions and evidence of sinister schemes that culminated in tragedy.

For White, the tragedy was a personal one. He sailed back to England, leaving his daughter and newborn granddaughter with the rest of the settlers on the tiny island, but it was to be three years before he could return. The threat of a Spanish invasion kept English ships in port, trapping White on the wrong side of the Atlantic until finally, in 1590, Raleigh persuaded Queen Elizabeth to allow his relief ships to set sail.

As White reached the treacherous shallows that guarded Roanoke Island, he may have hoped for a happy reunion, but could hardly have failed to harbour misgivings about the fate of the vulnerable settlers. He knew the local warriors to be hostile. The week before he left, one colonist had been shot dead by an arrow.

White found the settlement deserted. The

CHARTING A DISASTER The man made governor of Roanoke was the artist John White. He had mapped the coastline on an earlier expedition, indicating Roanoke Island and Croatoan (both ringed). Chesapeake Bay is at the top of the chart.

single clue to the settlers' fate was a lone word carved into a wooden stake: 'CROATOAN'.

Enduring mystery

Roanoke was meant to be the first permanent English colony in America – 33 years before the Pilgrim Fathers set foot in the New World. Yet the colonists disappeared, and were never seen by Europeans again. Now historians argue that they may have been pawns sacrificed as part of an English conspiracy that permeated the highest echelons of power.

Throughout the 16th century the thought of conquering North America captivated English traders and adventurers. They were lured by the prospect of mineral riches and the lucrative returns from 'privateering' – state-sanctioned piracy that in 1580 accounted for 20 per cent of English imports. An American settlement also had the potential, should an inland passage to the Pacific be found, of becoming the great mercantile gateway to the Orient.

Raleigh had won from the queen the patent to 8.5 million acres of American land. But he was undecided about which land to choose. One explorer, Captain Arthur Barlowe, had written of Roanoke that it was 'plentiful, sweet and fruitful... and bringeth forth all things in abundance, without toile or labour'. But Raleigh's first attempt to set a colony on Roanoke had failed, with the settlers giving up after just ten months. They fell out with the local Secotan tribe, and burned one of their villages after a quarrel over a stolen silver cup. In retaliation, the Native Americans withdrew food supplies, forcing the settlers to hunt for crabs.

Raleigh and his backers decided to move the settlement some 50 miles north, to the sheltered deep-water ports of Chesapeake Bay, away from hostile neighbours. A small garrison remained on Roanoke to guard the old site, but the island was deemed to be too risky for civilians unless the Secotan were brought under control. John White, the prospective governor,

was charged by Raleigh to recruit 150 colonists, each of whom would receive 500 acres of farmland. Time was pressing if the colonists were to reach Chesapeake for the planting season. Under strength, with only 115 recruits, the ships set sail at the end of April 1587.

White's account of the voyage shows that they were immediately beset by puzzling difficulties. It is

clear that in White's opinion these all stemmed from one man: his Portuguese pilot, Simon Fernandez.

Fernandez was a former pirate. His navigational skills and knowledge of the eastern seaboard of America were undoubted – there was even a stretch of coastline named after him. His judgment was less assured. White wrote in his diary how Fernandez 'lewdly' – that is, deliberately – abandoned the flyboat that carried stores for the settlement as it foundered in the water off Portugal. In the Caribbean, White recorded, the crew failed to take on necessary supplies of water and salt because of Fernandez's obstruction.

The expedition made slow progress. In mid July the ships were brought to a complete halt for several days off the coast of Carolina as – despite his familiarity with the area – Fernandez attempted to get his bearings. White wrote that 'such was

LOCAL INHABITANTS Near the original Roanoke settlement was the village of Pomeiooc, populated by Secotan Indians. At first, relations were good and there was trading between the two groups, but the peaceful accord was short-lived.

DEADLY ENEMIES There was a great rivalry between Sir Walter Raleigh (right) and Sir Francis Walsingham (left) at the court of Elizabeth I. Walsingham was notorious for his underhand methods. A writer of the time reckoned that, 'he could overthrow any matter by undertaking it and moving it so as it must fall.'

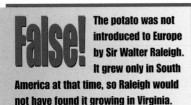

False! The potato was not introduced to Europe by Sir Walter Raleigh. It grew only in South America at that time, so Raleigh would not have found it growing in Virginia.

[Fernandez's] carelessness and ignorance' that he nearly ran the boat aground on the Cape of Fear. These delays had desperate consequences for the settlers. They had reached land too late to plant their grain, while the failure to stock up on food meant that supplies were running low.

Worse was to come. Raleigh had instructed White to go ashore at Roanoke for a conference 'concerning the state of the country' with the small garrison of men left there from the 1585 trip. But as White and 40 of his men were being rowed ashore, one of Fernandez's deputies shouted that they would not be let back on board. The ship would only stay at Roanoke long enough for all the settlers to be ferried ashore.

White was dumbfounded. His pilot had overruled the orders of Sir Walter Raleigh himself. Fernandez refused to take the colonists any further; he said he was too pressed for time. They were to be marooned with insufficient supplies, in unseasonal conditions and in hostile territory.

Alone, and with their only source of advice, support and protection the garrison at Roanoke, the settlers' next discovery was a chilling one. All that remained of the 15 soldiers were bleached skeletons. The Secotan had exacted a terrible revenge for their destroyed village.

The colony's salvation appeared only with the late arrival of their

flyboat, carrying surplus provisions. The settlers decided to send White back to England on the ship to seek assistance for their predicament.

Fernandez's ship's log, meanwhile, shows that he idled on the American coastline for 36 days – easily enough time to take the colonists to Chesapeake Bay. Why did Fernandez, an investor in the expedition, choose to abandon the colonists? The answer lay across the Atlantic Ocean, at the court of Queen Elizabeth I.

Court intrigue

Among all the noblemen jostling for position and favour at court, Sir Walter Raleigh stood out. He was only a courtier, but possessed the wardrobe and demeanour of a prince, and was a particular favourite of the queen – 'the darling of the English Cleopatra', as one Flemish visitor to the court put it. On foreign policy his buccaneering style often held sway with her, overruling her more cautious advisers, such as the secretary of state Sir Francis Walsingham. Raleigh was well rewarded for his loyalty to Elizabeth. Following the execution of Anthony Babington (who had plotted to assassinate the queen), Raleigh was given Babington's sizable estates.

Raleigh's power and influence ensured that he was a target for others with ambition. Few men had the power to organise Raleigh's downfall, but one certainly did. Sir Francis Walsingham had both motive and means. He was facing financial ruin, and, as the mastermind behind the exposure of the Babington conspiracy, had expected to be rewarded with the estates that were given to Raleigh. Walsingham knew that the Roanoke settlement was Raleigh's long-held dream – and his weakest spot. Its failure would lead to his ruination.

An American historian, Lee Miller, has argued that the loss of the colonists stems from Walsingham's plot to bankrupt Raleigh, and take the land titles for himself. Miller found evidence of a vital connection between Walsingham and Fernandez. The Portuguese pirate should have gone to the gallows, but Walsingham signed papers that released him. Could Fernandez have repaid this debt by sabotaging the Roanoke colony in order to ruin Raleigh?

John White's diary certainly suggests dark purposes at work. He wrote how he told the colonists that 'some enemies to him... would not spare to slander him, saying he went to Virginia but politikely... to lead so many into a countrey and there to leave them behind'. He could have been referring to rival entrepreneurs aiming to discredit Raleigh and set up their own colonies.

Miller has also found that, on two occasions, ships Raleigh tried to send to the aid of the colonists were barred from departure on the direct orders of Walsingham. When John White was eventually authorised to return to Roanoke in 1590, it was one month after Walsingham's death.

The missing clue

John White never found his family or the other settlers. On his first attempt he was attacked by pirates. His second rescue ship, the *Hopewell,* was damaged by storms and only just made it back to England. White wrote in 1604 that he was 'committing the relief of my discomfortable company the planters in Virginia, to the merciful help of the Almighty.' He is thought to have died in Ireland at around this time.

By this time there had been five rescue missions, all of which were unsuccessful. Raleigh was running out of money. He may never have learnt of the vital 'Croatoan' message carved by the settlers and found by John White. If not, the rescuers would have searched in vain at Chesapeake Bay or on Roanoke, instead of on Croatoan, which is an island 50 miles to the south.

Raleigh's legal right to the title to the land was in jeopardy: it depended on having settled a permanent colony within seven years. As the former favourite descended into ruin and disgrace, Walsingham's old allies – Robert Devereux, Earl of Essex and Robert Cecil – eyed up his assets. Following the death of Elizabeth I, the new king, James I, was soon convinced of Raleigh's disloyalty. He was tried for treason and imprisoned in the Tower of London in 1606. Soon after, his land title was won by Robert Cecil, along with the two men responsible for the charges against him: the Attorney General Sir Edward Coke and Chief Justice Popham.

Epilogue to the mystery

It was reported in 1608 that the chief of the Powhatan tribe had told settlers in Jamestown, Virginia, that the Roanoke survivors had been slaughtered. Historians now suspect this was a trumped-up charge against the Powhatan to justify violent incursions into their territory.

Then in 1701 the English surveyor John Lawson wrote of an unusual group of light-skinned American Indians he met on the dunes of Croatoan Island. As far as he could comprehend it, 'several of their ancestors were white people and could talk in a book as we do'. Could the settlers have survived to be the first European colonists in America, after all? That mystery is one that may never be solved.

LASTING MYSTERY **The Roanoke settlers may have been massacred by American Indians, or they may have integrated into one of the tribes that John White painted a decade before their disappearance.**

VICTORS' HISTORY

Few countries admit to conquering another nation: they often claim to have 'liberated' it. History is written by the victors: brave leaders can become evil tyrants in the telling, while places, people and events can be wiped from maps and historical records at a single stroke.

Idealism is essential to warfare. Victory is its own vindication: the winners feel that their success proves that they were right, and that the enemy was wrong. Yet in reality war is almost always morally ambiguous, every argument has two sides and history's verdict on individuals changes as often as the times in which the account was written. If history has a lesson it is this: do not take it at face value.

The lesser of two evils?

In the early 16th century Spain was making inroads into South America. Hernán Cortés began the conquest of Mexico and Francisco Pizarro captured Peru. For many years both men were hailed as liberators, but most accounts of their exploits were written by European clerics who welcomed the spread of Catholicism.

Later, as South Americans found their own voice, Cortés began to be depicted as an evil conqueror, Pizarro as a thug who duped and murdered the courteous Inca emperor Atahualpa. Yet neither viewpoint was impartial, and the truth must lie somewhere in between. The Inca empire was a militaristic theocracy, not unlike that of the Spaniards who overthrew it. In Mexico, the Aztecs regarded mass human sacrifice as an article of faith and the other indigenous Indian tribes there were so persecuted that they welcomed Cortés as their liberator from tyranny.

CONQUEST OR LIBERATION? When the Spanish conquistador Hernán Cortés landed in Mexico in 1519, he was welcomed by the Aztecs, who thought he was a reincarnation of one of their gods, Quetzalcoatlxuahatl, and that he had come to save them.

Given a bad press

Could this be the worst king of England? William Rufus (right) robbed churches and indulged in devil worship. But this account of him comes from churchmen writing during the reign of his brother Henry I, who succeeded him in 1100.

In the 20th century, historians began to re-evaluate Rufus and a new picture emerged of a fair-minded monarch. He promoted many court favourites into bishoprics, depriving the Church of revenue and influence, which could explain why its chroniclers hit back with accusations of ungodliness. The circumstances of his death were also re-examined. He had been killed while hunting, supposedly by an arrow that glanced off a tree, but to redirect an arrow this way is impossible. Many now think Rufus was assassinated. The obvious suspect was Henry, who was present at the hunt and swiftly seized control of the treasury.

The pen that blunted the sword

The 1st-century Jewish historian Joseph ben Mattathias wrote an account of the assault on Jerusalem led by the Roman emperor Vespasian (below). Mattathias presented the Jews as hapless victims – not of efficient Roman soldiers pressing home a military advantage, but of freak weather conditions.

There arose such a Divine storm against [the Jews] as was instrumental to their destruction; this carried the Roman darts upon them, and made those which they threw return back, and drove them obliquely away from them; nor could the Jews indeed stand upon their precipices, by reason of the violence of the wind, having nothing that was stable to stand upon, nor could they see those that were ascending up to them; so the Romans got up and surrounded them.

The historian had reason to present the Romans in a positive light. As a young soldier captured in Galilee, Mattathias fell under sentence of death, but persuaded Vespasian, then a mere general, to spare his life by foretelling that he would one day become emperor. When the prophecy came true, Vespasian rewarded his captive with Roman citizenship: Mattathias moved to Rome and was renamed Flavius Josephus. His intention in writing the history of the war was to encourage his fellow Jews to accept their conquest and live peacefully under Roman rule.

MILITARY MIGHT Vespasian was a fair and just emperor, but his army's campaigns were brutal affairs. During the siege that Josephus described, thousands of Jews were slain and the temple was torched.

History is all quotations

● *History to the defeated may say Alas but cannot help or pardon.*
W.H. Auden

● *Who controls the past controls the future. Who controls the present controls the past.*
George Orwell

● *Tell a lie enough times and it becomes the truth.*
Josef Goebbels

● *The one duty we owe to history is to rewrite it.*
Oscar Wilde

● *'What is truth?' said jesting Pilate, and would not stay for an answer.*
Francis Bacon

● *History is a pack of lies about events that never happened told by people who weren't there.*
George Santayana

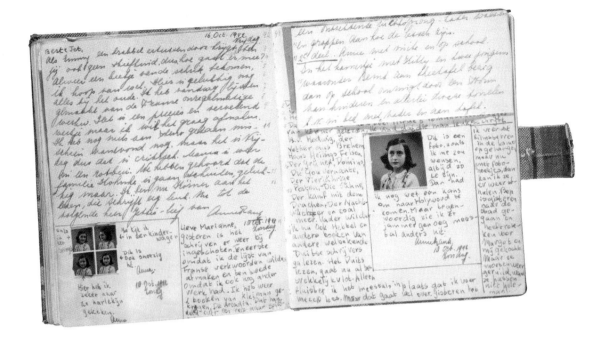

ANNE FRANK'S BETRAYER
The real identity of the man responsible for her capture

The facts of Anne Frank's life, hiding from the Gestapo in a secret annexe, are set out in her own vivid account. We also know that she died in Bergen-Belsen concentration camp. But the identity of the person who betrayed her hiding place has only recently come to light.

BIRTHDAY GIFT Anne Frank received a diary for her 13th birthday on June 12 1942. She used it in the secret annexe as a personal journal and scrapbook for photos and comments (above) throughout her time in hiding.

Early on the morning of August 4, 1944, Gestapo headquarters in Nazi-occupied Amsterdam received an anonymous telephone call. The caller said that Jewish people were hiding in a secret annexe of a house bordering the canal at 263 Prinsengracht. Within hours, Gestapo officials and Dutch Nazis had raided the house. There, behind a bookcase, was the entrance to the rooms where the Frank family had been hiding for 25 months.

The occupants of the annexe – the Franks, Fritz Pfeffer and Hermann, Auguste and Peter van Pel – were taken first to a prison on the Weteringschans. Within weeks they were deported to the concentration camp at Auschwitz. The timing was cruel: they caught the last train ever to leave the Netherlands carrying Jews to the death camp.

Otto and Edith Frank's 15-year-old daughter, Anne, had kept a meticulous diary of the two years she and her family spent in hiding. Anne did not survive the war, but her personal account of life in Nazi Europe became an enduring record of the horrors of the Holocaust.

After the publication of *The Diary of a Young Girl* in 1947, speculation grew as to who had been responsible for the Franks' betrayal. The first agents to look into the raid at 263 Prinsengracht were the Dutch police. They began their investigation in January 1948. The prime suspect at that time was Wilhelm van Maaren, the man who managed the warehouse below the Franks' hiding place. He had sometimes queried the purpose of the annexe with his co-workers.

During police interviews about his role in the case van Maaren denied betraying the Franks, and was granted a conditional discharge.

Another suspect questioned was Lena Hartog. She was a cleaner in the warehouse and wife of van Maaren's assistant. Hartog had reportedly confided to another woman that she thought that Jews were being hidden in the building, and was worried she would be arrested if she did not say something. Her testimony was evasive, yet the police did not question her again. The investigation was closed after four months, with no conclusions drawn.

The Nazi hunter

The trail then grew cold until the 1960s, when the Nazi hunter Simon Wiesenthal conducted his own investigation into the Franks' betrayal. In 1963 he tracked down the official who had overseen the Franks' arrest. His name was Karl Josef Silberbauer, and he was living in Vienna. When questioned, the former Gestapo man admitted that the speed with which the tip-off was followed up suggested that the caller was a trusted Nazi informant, but he claimed not to have

Concealed in the secret annexe

1 Peter van Pel
Anne and Peter became very close during their long captivity. She described Peter's room as 'very narrow, very dark and damp', but said that he had turned it into a 'real room'.

2 Hermann and Auguste van Pel
The van Pels' room doubled as a communal living room. Every evening the occupants of the annexe sat down together to eat there.

3 Otto, Edith and Margot Frank
The three Franks moved into the same room after the arrival of Fritz Pfeffer in November 1942.

4 Anne Frank and Fritz Pfeffer
Anne and Fritz lived together in a room dominated by Anne's collection of Hollywood movie posters. She wrote that the walls were 'one gigantic picture'.

5 The movable bookcase
The bookcase concealed the doorway leading to five tiny rooms that, for two years, were home to eight people.

6 Private office and kitchen
The office was reached via the front door and a door in the hallway that only opened from the inside.

7 The warehouse
When the building was sold in 1944, the new owner employed Wilhelm van Maaren as head warehouseman. The Franks believed that he was their betrayer. Lena Hartog, wife of van Maaren's assistant and also the warehouse cleaner, admitted she had known of the presence of Jews in the annexe.

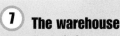

BETRAYER'S FACE Tonny Ahlers (ringed) – the man who boasted of having handed the Frank family over to the Nazis – was photographed at the funeral of a Dutch Nazi in February 1941. Ahlers stands next to Anton Mussert, who had founded the Dutch Nazi Party in 1931.

spoken to him. He also refuted both the claims of the police, and the Dutch publication *Revue*, that the betrayer was van Maaren.

Wiesenthal gave up on his investigation. But wild speculation continued through the decades. A 1998 biography of Anne asserted that the guilty party was certainly Lena Hartog. But with Hartog proclaiming her innocence until her death, the assertion remained unproven. Van Maaren, too, died still denying any responsibility. The mystery was set to stay unsolved.

Then in 2002 a researcher's persistence brought about a surprising acknowledgment of guilt – not from the man himself, but from his family.

According to this researcher, the man who betrayed Anne Frank was someone known to her father, Otto. His name was Tonny (Anton) Ahlers. Tonny Ahlers strode into Frank's life in April 1941. He entered Frank's office brandishing a letter that had been sent to the NSB, the Dutch Nazi Party, claiming that Frank was an anti-Nazi. Ahlers agreed to keep the letter secret: money changed hands, although Frank would always refute the suggestion that he had been a victim of blackmail.

Ahlers was a violent, unstable anti-Semite, who had ingratiated himself with the German occupiers of Holland. He is known to have denounced Jews and members of the Dutch Resistance. Before the war, Ahlers had been arrested for incidents involving anti-Semitic violence; he was also a member of the NSB.

On July 5, 1942, the Franks' eldest daughter Margot was ordered to report for deportation to Germany. The next day the family went into hiding, having prepared the annexe behind Otto Frank's office for just such an eventuality. Anne had celebrated her 13th birthday only a few weeks earlier.

At the time the Franks vanished into their upstairs hiding place, Ahlers' business was thriving. He was well regarded by the Germans and was looking forward to a comfortable life after Germany won the war. But by the summer of 1944 everything had changed. His business was in trouble, he was deeply in debt and his Nazi friends were turning against him. He badly needed money and to re-establish his credentials with the Gestapo, who had previously served as much-needed protection from Ahlers' many enemies.

The betrayal

Germany was offering 40 florins in payment for every Jew betrayed. There were four other Jews hiding with the Frank family at 263 Prinsengracht – making the secret annexe worth a total of 320 florins. It was a lot of money for a man in desperate financial straits. Ahlers claimed after the war that he had known all along where the Franks were hiding. If so, he kept the secret as a kind of insurance policy. On August 4 he phoned the Gestapo, and cashed in.

Ahlers' betrayal led to the deaths of three of the Frank family. Edith died in Auschwitz in January 1945. Her teenage daughters, Margot and Anne, succumbed to typhus at Bergen-Belsen some time in March 1945, a few weeks before the camp was liberated. Otto survived his imprisonment in Auschwitz, and after the war returned to Amsterdam.

Otto Frank's behaviour after the war was puzzling. When Ahlers was arrested as a collaborator in June 1945, he wrote letters on his behalf pleading for his release. He argued with Wiesenthal, and defended both Karl Silberbauer – whom he claimed had shown him courtesy and respect during his arrest – and Willem van Maaren.

Wiesenthal remained convinced that Otto Frank knew who his betrayer was, and was suspicious of the inconsistent accounts he gave of his relationship with Ahlers.

Then in 2002 a British researcher, Carol Ann Lee, published a book in which she named Ahlers as the informant. Her conclusions were immediately confirmed by members of Ahlers' family. Tonny's younger brother Casper claimed that Tonny had said he was proud of turning in the Frank family, and had told him so after the war. He did it for money and for whatever he had been able to steal from the annexe. Casper claimed to own a candlestick that his brother had stolen from the Franks.

Casper's testimony was supported by Tonny's son, Anton, who admitted that his father was obsessed by Otto Frank and talked about him incessantly. Anton also believed that Ahlers knew about certain business dealings between Otto Frank's pectin company and the German Army during the war. He said that Frank's company had made a small profit by trading with the Nazis, and Ahlers used this information to blackmail Otto Frank. According to Anton, a regular payment from an unexplained source landed in Tonny Ahlers' bank account every month.

To many this idea was fanciful. In 2003 a report by the Netherlands Institute of Documentation criticised the blackmail theory, pointing out that it was based indirectly on the unreliable testimony of the boastful Ahlers himself. It gave no contrary evidence, but concluded that Ahlers could have misled his family, making them believe falsely that he had betrayed the location of Frank family. Their conclusion: that the identity of the informant was still a mystery.

It may be that Otto Frank did know more than he let on about his betrayer. But whatever his motive for keeping quiet, he was more concerned with protecting his daughter's work than raking over the past. Her book became an international best-seller, partly because of the vibrancy of her writing, but also because as one person's story it expresses all the millions of separate human tragedies of the Nazi genocide. Her words are as powerful now as they were then. On November 19, 1942, she wrote:

The Germans ring at every door to enquire if there are any Jews living in the house… In the evenings, when it's dark, I see rows of good, innocent people accompanied by crying children, walking on and on, bullied and knocked about until they almost drop. No one is spared – old people, babies, expectant mothers, the sick – each and all join in the march of death.

DEATH TRAIN In 1945, after liberation by the Russians, the concentration camp known as Auschwitz II (Birkenau) lies desolate, with snow covering the belongings of people brought by train for labour or extermination. The Franks arrived here in September 1944 on the last train from Westerbork transit camp in the Netherlands.

THE WITCHES OF SALEM
What really lay behind the deadly accusations of witchcraft

The Salem witch trials tore a 17th-century village apart and led to the execution of 19 of those convicted. The 'bewitching' of the villagers has been attributed to hysteria or hallucinogenic bread. Only now has geographical analysis uncovered the uncomfortable truth.

AS GOD IS MY WITNESS **Depositions such as those by Elizabeth Hubbard (above) attested to the evil powers of the witches, in this case three girls who 'pressed, squeezed and choked' their victim. Hubbard was an orphan and was, at 17, the oldest girl to be afflicted. She testified against 29 people during the trials, but was also herself the subject of rumours of witchcraft.**

On August 19, 1692, a cart rolled out of Salem Village, Massachusetts. It was carrying five prisoners to a hill east of the settlement, where they were to be put to death. One of the five had been a leading figure in the community. His name was George Burroughs, ex-minister and condemned witch.

As Burroughs was being led to the noose he made a declaration of his innocence. The historian Robert Calef wrote in his *More Wonders of the Invisible World* (1700) that this speech was 'uttered with such composure and such fervency of spirit as was very affecting and drew tears from many'. The minister's eloquence and his flawless recitation of the Lord's Prayer were in vain. The presiding magistrate, Cotton Mather, stepped forward and argued that 'the devil has often been transformed into an angel of light', and the minister was hanged.

The Salem witch hunts began with a harmless game of fortune-telling. Betty Parris – daughter of the vicar of Salem Village, Samuel Parris – was playing with some of her friends. The girls dropped egg whites into a pan of water and tried to read the shapes that formed. The Parrises' West Indian servant Tituba had introduced the girls to the game to while away the cold winter nights. One child thought she saw a coffin and this frightened her and the others: they began shouting and shaking.

The Reverend Parris sought the help of the village physician William Griggs, who observed the girls having what appeared to be fits and shouting obscenities. Lacking a medical explanation for the girls' erratic behaviour, Griggs suspected the 'evil hand' of witchcraft.

A month passed; the condition of the girls did not improve. Indeed, the strange 'distempers' spread to other young women in the village. Under intense questioning the afflicted girls claimed that they had been bewitched. They pointed the finger at three local women: Sarah Osborne, Sarah Good and the servant Tituba.

Spectral evidence

The three suspects were not well placed to rebuff the accusations. Osborne had a record of poor church attendance and was not well liked, Good was a beggar and Tituba was a foreigner, on the lowest rung of the social ladder. On February 29, warrants were issued for their arrest. Yet their imprisonment did not end the witch hunt. In an atmosphere of growing hysteria, the girls' strange behaviour continued. Some screamed of seeing visions, others stood up in church to mock the sermons. At the same time the afflicted made more and more accusations of witchcraft. By May 1692, the sheer number of these forced Sir William Phips, governor of Massachusetts, to set up a special Court of Oyer (hearing) and Terminer (deciding) to try the witchcraft cases.

The court sessions were chaotic and deeply sinister. The afflicted girls would writhe and scream at a glance from the accused. Prosecution testimonies relied upon 'spectral evidence', in which the accused's spectre had supposedly appeared in front of the afflicted girls and hurt them. Local innkeeper Nathaniel Ingersoll testified during the trial of one Sarah Wilds that 'if she did clinch her hands or hold her head aside the afflicted persons... were... tortured'.

The devil himself made regular appearances in the transcripts of testimony: a ship-owner, Philip English, was seen by Susannah Sheldon with 'a black man with a high crowned hat on his head and a book in his hands'.

The trial of Rebecca Nurse caused the most chaos. Nurse, a 71-year-old mother of eight well respected in the community, was accused by members of the Putnam family of 'haveing donne Much hurt and Injury to the Body' of eight-year-old Anne Putnam and her mother, also named Anne. Nurse was acquitted by the court, only for the afflicted girls to recommence their screams of pain. Asked to reconsider their verdict, the judges found the elderly lady guilty.

Hallucinations and fever

The trials continued for four months. In the course of the witch hunt, more than 20 people were executed or died in jail. The village never recovered from the trauma.

Over the years, many explanations have been put forward for the paroxysm of violence that overtook this small, God-fearing community. Some have argued that the visions were symptoms of mass hysteria caused by Freudian repression; others, that a fungus called ergot growing on the local wheat was making the villagers hallucinate. Another theory suggested that the village had suffered from an epidemic of viral sleeping sickness, *encephalitis lethargica,* a highly

CURSED BLEMISH One way of proving that the accused was a witch was finding the 'Devil's mark' upon their body, as portrayed in the 1853 painting by Tompkins H. Matteson, *Examination of a Witch* (above).

IF LOOKS COULD KILL One testimony, from a witness called Abigail Williams, revealed the depth of hysteria in the belief that she had, more than once, been 'almost killed' by the sight of an apparition.

The Testimony of Abigail williams witnesseth & saith that sundry times she hath seen & been almost killed by the Apparition of John willard of Salem village Husbandman at & before the 18 May. 1692

abigall williams did deliuer this testimony to us the Jurriors [...] Inquist this 3. of June: 1692: and did afarme to the truth of it

Josiah H. Benton Fd.
Mar. 13, 1939
B

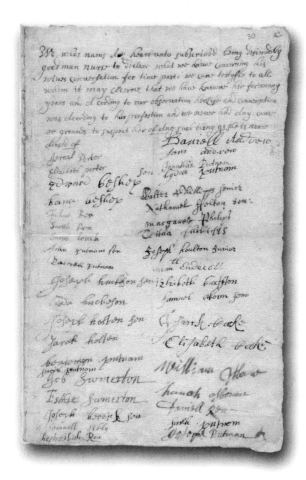

SIGN OF REASON The prosecution of Rebecca Nurse caused an outcry. A petition signed by 41 villagers stated '...we have known her for many years... and never had any grounds to suspect her of what she is accused of'. It was in vain: Nurse was hanged on July 19, 1692.

...tious, potentially ... disease, usually ...ed by high fever. ... recent investigation ...ts to a less exotic ...anation, and it was ...d map that provided ...irst clue.

... 1867 Charles W. ...am made a map of ...m as it stood in ..., pinpointing the ...es of all the major ...cipants of the trials. ...e map shows that ...ally all the ...sations were ...led against those in ...ast half of the ...ge by those living in ...est. Of the 14 ...le found guilty of ...hcraft, 12 were from ...astern half, while ...f the 32 accusers ...located in the west. ...eover, 24 of the 29 ...tics' or defenders of those on trial could also be found in the east. If the devil really had come to Salem, then he was being choosy about which homes he visited.

The curious division of the village into eastern 'witches' and their western accusers led two historians to examine Salem's past more closely.

East versus west

In 1626 a harbour had been built nearby in the larger settlement of Salem Town, attracting merchants and making the town a thriving market centre, distinct from the older rural area of Salem Village.

The sudden economic expansion of the town caused a rift in the neighbouring village. The eastern half of the village grew prosperous: it was only a short distance from the town along the Ipswich Road and had flat meadowland to farm on. Many who lived there branched out into new professions: shoemaking, innkeeping and pottery. By contrast, those in the western half of the village were scattered over poor farmland,

where life was less profitable. Families such as the Ingersolls and the Putnams may have been heavily involved in village politics, but economically and socially they were second-class citizens. From the 1660s onwards they argued that Salem Village should break away from Salem Town and become self-governing.

The eastern half of the village – fearing such a move would end their new-found prosperity – fought against the prospect of a separate community. Villager Jeremiah Watts described the atmosphere in 1682:

Brother is against brother and neighbours against neighbours, all quarreling and smiting one another.

These arguments about village politics had a religious basis. Like many of the immigrants who had settled in Massachusetts after the 1630s, the 'westerners' were Puritans, who followed a strict and austere religious code that shunned luxury. By contrast, the businessmen of Salem Town were perceived by the Puritans as devoting their lives to the pursuit of sinful profit. In an effort to distance themselves from the entrepreneurs, the Puritans pressed the Salem Town administration for their own meeting-house. Their request was granted in 1672, but the question of who should be appointed as minister only caused further friction in the village.

In 1689, after a series of short-lived incumbents, the Reverend Samuel Parris took over, and under his leadership the meeting-house became dominated by the Puritans. The Putnam family made up more than half of the congregation, while those in the eastern half of the village boycotted the meetings and fought to have Parris removed.

The battle-lines – social, economic and religious – had been drawn, and remained in place throughout the trials, defining the pattern of accusation and defence.

In the later stages of the witch hunt, it was as though anyone who lived in

Hill against valley

Using Charles W. Upham's map of Salem Village from 1692, two American academics –
Paul Boyer and Stephen Nissenbaum – located the addresses of supposed witches and
the key witnesses at the witch trials. There was a marked west-east split between the
two groups. The villagers living in the hills to the west, who frequented the Puritan
meeting-house in the centre of the village, made accusations against the inhabitants of
the more affluent east, who had campaigned to have the minister replaced. Accused and
accuser could be identified almost solely on the basis of geography.

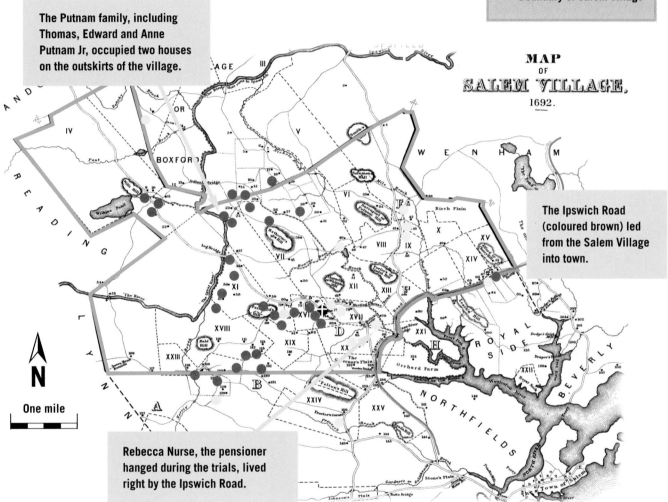

KEY

● house of an accuser
○ house of an accused
✝ Puritan meeting-house
━ Boundary of Salem Village

The Putnam family, including
Thomas, Edward and Anne
Putnam Jr, occupied two houses
on the outskirts of the village.

MAP
OF
SALEM VILLAGE,
1692.

The Ipswich Road
(coloured brown) led
from the Salem Village
into town.

Rebecca Nurse, the pensioner
hanged during the trials, lived
right by the Ipswich Road.

One mile

The development of the harbour (above,
on the map) brought prosperity to
Salem Town. Inland, Salem Village
remained isolated and poor, as shown
by an 18th-century woodcut (below).

The deposition of Ann Putnam who testifieth and saith that I have ben most greviously afflected by George Jacobs Sen but most dreadfully tormented by him on 11 may of may 1692 dureing the time of his examination also on the day of his examination I saw George Jacobs or his Appearanc most greviously torment mary walcott and Eliz: Hubbard and I beleve in my hart that George Jacobs is a dreadful wizzard and that he hath very often afflect me and the afore mentioned persons by his acts of witchcraft.

ann putnam owned this har testimony before the Juriars of Inquest: one har oath this 4 day of agust: 1692

Jurat in Curia

the eastern half of the village could find themselves branded as witches; some who went on trial found themselves accused by 'afflicted' from the west who could not even identify them in court.

Particularly harrowing was the evidence of children, who in the absence of any physical proof could make such accusations as:

Sarah Good most violently pulled down my head behind a chest and tied my hands with a wheel band and almost choked me to death.

The children's hysteria is more understandable in the light of the hostile relationships between the households in the village. The object of a child's allegations was likely to be a person known to and disliked by their parents.

Neighbourhood feuds

Some of the 'witches' had been involved in long-running feuds with their accusers. Sarah Wilds' husband John was on a committee that settled land disputes. In fixing a boundary between Salem and neighbouring Topsfield, he had made enemies by siding in favour of the latter.

The executed minister George Burroughs did not even live in Salem in 1692; he had left in 1683 after falling out with the Putnam brothers over money. In 1681 Burroughs had

borrowed from Captain John Putnam to pay for his wife's funeral. To recover the debt, Putnam had issued a warrant for his arrest. Although the matter was settled out of court, bad blood remained.

Nine years later, George Burroughs was brought back to Salem from Maine, New Jersey, to face formal charges of witchcraft. During his trial Anne Putnam Jr testified that: 'I was tortored by him being Racked and all most choaked by him, and he tempted me to write in his book.'

Eight-year-old Anne faithfully followed her family's prejudices. She made 21 formal accusations during the trials, the most by any individual. But eight other members of her family also testified, including her mother and father, and 46 of the 141 formal accusations of witchcraft emanated from them. Young Anne could hardly have been unaware of her family's long-running feud with Burroughs, or the dispute between the Putnams and the Wilds.

Years later she repented her part in the trials, blaming 'a great delusion of Satan' for her actions. It appears that Satan may well have known the 'afflicted' better than he did those who stood trial. For all the hysteria and rhetoric, the Salem witch trials signified little more than a vindictive social grudge match.

DEADLY ACCUSATIONS Anne Putnam tesified during the trial of George Jacobs that she believed him to be a 'dreadful wizzard'. Jacobs was hanged at the age of 72 – one of the first men executed for witchcraft in Salem. His granddaughter Margaret was among those who testified against him in court.

NOT LONG TO REIGN OVER US
How accident and violence has decided the fate of the English throne

When kings and queens die, their children aren't always the ones to inherit the throne. From medieval times to the present day, the English line of succession has taken unexpected and desperate turns.

As a child she could not have imagined that she would be queen. Her claim to the throne was slender until the shock fall of her uncle, the king. Her father had become monarch, only to die at an early age, and her uncle's abdication meant that the royal line would now pass to her children, who – under other circumstances – would have been minor members of the royal clan. This is what the future held for the new queen. Her name was Elizabeth; she was 26 years old; and the year was 1952.

The monarchy is, for many British citizens, a rock of tradition and stability. For them the story of the English throne is a stately procession of kings and queens from one generation to the next. In fact, even in the 20th century an unsuitable king such as Edward VIII could be forced off the throne. And the stakes were much higher in earlier centuries, when monarchs held great power, and ruled as well as reigned. Then it was all the more important – and all the more tempting – to get rid of inadequate kings. In consequence crucial moments of English history have seen violent and bloody struggles for the crown.

Such conflicts were normal in Anglo-Saxon times. When Alfred the Great succeeded his brother on the throne in the 9th century, he did so by disinheriting his brother's son. In 1066, when Edward the Confessor died childless, it took three great battles – Fulford Gate, Stamford Bridge and Hastings – to settle the disputed succession in favour of Edward's distant Norman relative, William I.

Even in more recent times, foreign rulers have played a major role in deciding the succession. In the 17th century the Dutch prince William of Orange was persuaded by the English parliament to lead a revolt against their own monarch, who happened to be William's father-in-law, James II. James was forced to abdicate and flee to France. Even Queen Victoria was of foreign descent: the daughter of Princess Victoria of Leiningen, she spoke English with a German accent throughout her life.

Fight for the throne

But one family's line of succession was more tumultuous than any other. They fought wars, used wheedling diplomacy and sheer skulduggery to edge closer to the throne. Cousins and brothers whose claim to be king was insufficient channelled their energies into making – and breaking – alliances. Mothers and sisters hatched extraordinary schemes to undermine the claims of other branches of the family, often leading to declarations of bastardy that debarred rivals from taking the throne. Most of all, though, the family members killed each other until so few were left that the ▶ p.106

ROYAL COMMAND **According to Norman chroniclers, Edward the Confessor promised England's throne to a Norman, William. On the Bayeux Tapestry, Edward is shown sending his emissary Harold to France to meet William and swear allegiance. But in 1066, William had to fight Harold to win the 'promised' crown.**

A FAMILY AFFAIR

The Plantagenet succession was complicated by the warring factions of the Houses of York and Lancaster. The gold arrows trace the zigzagging path of the crown as it was passed on, usurped, and snatched from dead men's hands.

The House of York

EDWARD III

Edward = Joan, daughter of
Prince of Wales   Earl of Kent

Lionel, = Elizabeth de
Duke of   Burgh
Clarence

Philippa = Edward,
Earl of March

RICHARD II
- b. 1367, d. 1400, ruled 1377-99
- Only ten when he became king
- While fighting in Ireland rebel Henry Bolingboke seized the crown
- Murdered months after his abdication

Roger, = Eleanor
Earl of March   Holland

Richard, = Anne
Earl of Cambridge   Mortimer

Richard, = Cecily
Duke of York   Neville

BASTARDS

In 1483 Richard of Gloucester declared his brother's son, the boy-king Edward V, illegitimate. According to Richard, Edward's parents were not married; he claimed Edward IV was previously another woman's husband. For good measure he spread the rumour that Edward IV was also a bastard, the son of his mother's affair with an archer. Ironically the man who defeated Richard in 1485 was the descendant of the Beauforts, illegitimately born children of John of Gaunt and Katherine Swynford, who were subsequently legitimised by Act of Parliament.

EDWARD IV
- b. 1442, d. 1483, ruled 1461-70, 1471-83
- Deposed in 1470 by Henry VI and Earl of Warwick – returned a year later
- Had Henry VI imprisoned then murdered
- Died suddenly aged 40

= Elizabeth, daughter of
Sir Richard Woodville

RICHARD III

- b. 1452, d. 1485, ruled 1483-5
- Yorkist king widely thought to have murdered the teenage Edward V
- Killed by Lancastrian forces at the battle of Bosworth

= Anne, daughter
of Richard,
Earl of Warwick

EDWARD V
- b. 1470, d. 1483, ruled 1483
- Only 12 when he became king
- Declared a bastard by uncle and Protector Richard of Gloucester
- Disappeared in Tower of London

Richard,
Duke of York

BETROTHALS

Marriages were an essential means of getting closer to the throne for noble families. The Earl of Warwick – known as the 'Kingmaker' – treated his daughters Anne and Isobel as bargaining chips. After failing to marry off Anne to Edward IV, he had her wed Edward, Prince of Wales. Isobel was married to Edward IV's brother. Anne's husband was killed in battle against Richard III; Richard married Anne a year later.

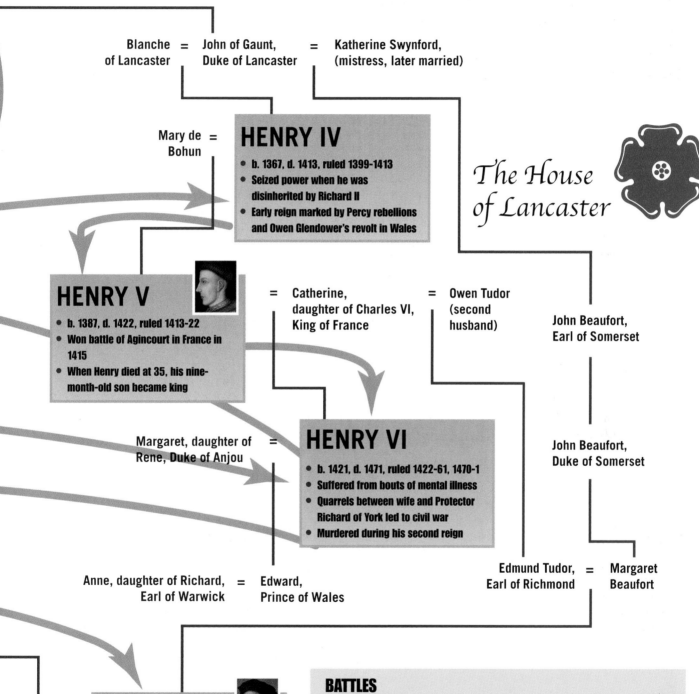

= Philippa, daughter of Count
of Hainault and Holland

Blanche = John of Gaunt, = Katherine Swynford,
of Lancaster   Duke of Lancaster   (mistress, later married)

Mary de = **HENRY IV**
Bohun
- b. 1367, d. 1413, ruled 1399-1413
- Seized power when he was
  disinherited by Richard II
- Early reign marked by Percy rebellions
  and Owen Glendower's revolt in Wales

*The House
of Lancaster*

HENRY V
- b. 1387, d. 1422, ruled 1413-22
- Won battle of Agincourt in France in
  1415
- When Henry died at 35, his nine-
  month-old son became king

= Catherine,
daughter of Charles VI,
King of France

= Owen Tudor
(second
husband)

John Beaufort,
Earl of Somerset

Margaret, daughter of = **HENRY VI**
Rene, Duke of Anjou
- b. 1421, d. 1471, ruled 1422-61, 1470-1
- Suffered from bouts of mental illness
- Quarrels between wife and Protector
  Richard of York led to civil war
- Murdered during his second reign

John Beaufort,
Duke of Somerset

Anne, daughter of Richard, = Edward,
Earl of Warwick   Prince of Wales

Edmund Tudor, = Margaret
Earl of Richmond   Beaufort

Elizabeth = **HENRY VII**
of York
- b. 1457, d. 1509, ruled 1485-1509
- Married Elizabeth of York, uniting the
  houses of York and Lancaster
- First king of the new Tudor dynasty.
  Father of Henry VIII

BATTLES

Armed conflict was a traditional way to sort out succession disputes.
Most decisive were those battles in which the king or one of his heirs
was killed. The most recent king to fall in battle was Richard III: on
August 22, 1485, his mutilated body was carried from the battlefield of
Bosworth on the back of a horse. The previous king to die defending his
throne was Harold II at Hastings in 1066.

crown had little choice about upon whose head it came to rest. That family was the Plantagenet dynasty; the conflict, the Wars of the Roses.

The Plantagenets were a line of kings that dated back to Henry II, who had succeeded the Norman invaders in 1154. The Plantagenets ruled to the end of the 15th century, yet their successors – the Tudors – were the descendants of a Welshman whose highest position at court is thought to have been Keeper of the Queen's Wardrobe. How could an established royal dynasty have been usurped in such a manner?

Feuding families

In many ways the Plantagenets were the authors of their own downfall. The succession was muddied in 1399, when Henry Bolingbroke overthrew his cousin, Richard II. Soon after parliament recognised Bolingbroke as Henry IV, Richard was found murdered, and Henry's branch of the dynasty, the Lancastrians, took over.

Henry IV's son, Henry V, became one of England's favourite warrior-kings, but when he died at the age of 35, he left on the throne a nine-month-old baby whom he had never seen. As the boy grew up surrounded by powerful nobles, the house of Lancaster became embroiled in a succession conflict with the rival house of York.

During the course of this struggle two kings and three heirs to the throne were killed. Between 1455 and 1487, 13 battles between Lancastrians and Yorkists – later represented by red and white roses – took a heavy toll on the aristocracy, eliminating a number of potential claimants to the throne.

The situation was not helped by the fact that Henry VI was plagued by bouts of hereditary mental illness. Faced with the rival claim of Richard, Duke of York, the king's wife, Margaret of Anjou, took control. In 1453 the country slid into civil war as Anjou's and York's forces clashed. Richard was killed at Wakefield in 1460, but his 18-year-old son Edward defeated the Lancastrians and was

crowned Edward IV in 1461. Henry was captured and put into the Tower of London, but in 1470 found himself back on the throne again, mainly due to Edward's previously staunch ally, the nobleman Warwick 'the Kingmaker', changing sides.

Henry's second reign was brief – he was murdered within a year, allowing Edward to become king again. When Edward died suddenly at the age of 40, his 13-year-old son, now Edward V, was presented with a 'protector' to ensure his safety. This was his uncle Richard, Duke of Gloucester. Gloucester promptly declared the king and his brother bastards. The two boys were locked in the Tower of London, supposedly for their own safety. In 1483 they disappeared; Richard became king.

The brutal suddenness of Richard III's coup split the Yorkist party, and opened the way for a contender who until this moment had lived in obscurity in Brittany: Henry Tudor. His shaky royal claim was based on the fact that his mother, Margaret Beaufort, was a great granddaughter of Edward III's son, John of Gaunt. His grandfather was Owen Tudor, the Welsh keeper of the wardrobe who had shocked society by marrying Henry V's widow. In 1485, at the head of a French army and with crucial help from his mother's third husband, Thomas Stanley, Henry Tudor defeated and killed Richard at the battle of Bosworth.

Henry was now king. To cement his position he married Elizabeth of York, uniting the warring houses. The Tudor dynasty had begun. The last Plantagenet was Edward, Earl of Warwick. He spent most of his life in prison; Henry VII arrested him following Bosworth. Edward died in a manner befitting of his lineage – he was beheaded in 1499, for allegedly conspiring in an attempted coup.

The Tudors would be remembered as a popular and archetypally English line of monarchs. But they flourished only after the bitter taste left by the Plantagenets had gone, and the bloody dust of battle had settled.

True! The Plantagenet dynasty is named after the 'planta genesta', or broom, the flower that counts of Anjou took as their emblem.

HOW DID TUTANKHAMUN DIE?

The sinister fate of Egypt's boy-king

Ever since the door of his opulent burial chamber was first prised open, the life of Tutankhamun has been the subject of wonder and speculation. Now historians believe he may have been murdered, and are attempting to find a 3000-year-old killer.

A single rough-cut stone step uncovered from the sand in Egypt's Valley of the Kings heralded one of the greatest archaeological finds ever made. It was the top step of a staircase that led down to the tomb of the boy-king Tutankhamun. British archaeologist Howard Carter's sensational find of November 1922 made headlines around the world.

It took a decade to examine and catalogue all the treasures found in the tomb, yet much remained unexplained. 'The mystery of his life still eludes us,' Carter wrote. 'The shadows move but the dark is never quite dispersed.'

Eighty years on, historians believe that they are now able to shed some light on how that mysterious life came to be snuffed out when Tutankhamun was just 19. His body may be shrouded in plastic and unavailable for further study, and the existing hard evidence is little more than an autopsy report from 1922 and a handful of 40-year-old X-rays – but the clues are all there, and they pose an intriguing question: was Tutankhamun murdered?

Historians have spent years combing through Egyptian texts, hoping for insights into the identity of Tutankhamun. It is now believed that he was the son of Akhenaten, the tenth king of the 18th Dynasty.

Akhenaten plunged Egypt into turmoil during his 17-year reign. He abolished the priesthood, closed the temples and banned the worship of all gods save one: Aten, a deity with

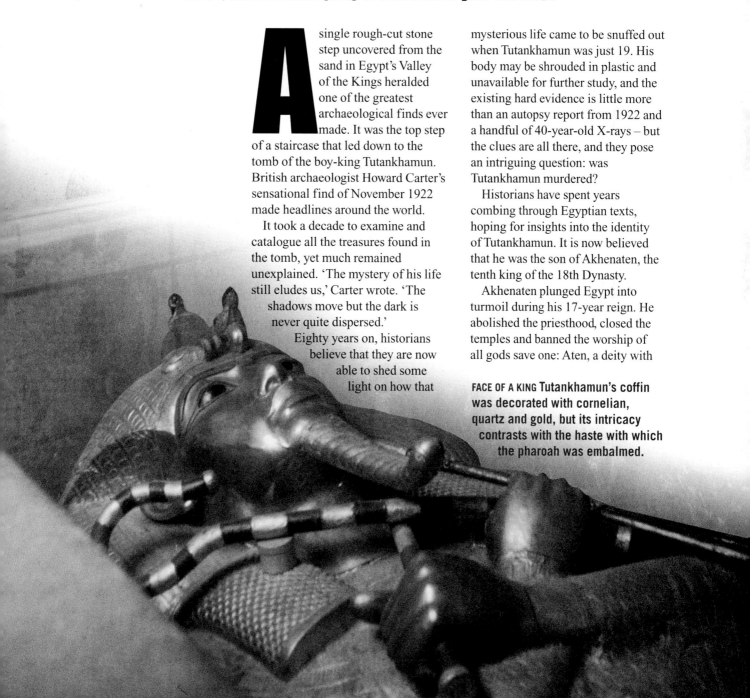

FACE OF A KING Tutankhamun's coffin was decorated with cornelian, quartz and gold, but its intricacy contrasts with the haste with which the pharoah was embalmed.

FRIENDS OR ENEMIES? **Tutankhamun was surrounded by influential advisers throughout his adolescence. The grand vizier Ay (left) and General Horemheb (right) are both suspects in his murder.**

no earthly form who was represented by the sun's rays.

Akhenaten built an opulent new capital city at a place now called Tell el Armana for his court and family, virtually bankrupting the country in the process. It was here, surrounded by palace intrigue, and political turmoil, that Tutankhamun grew up.

After Akhenaten's death, nine-year-old Tutankhamun's life utterly changed: almost all records of his father's reign were destroyed in an attempt to erase Akhenaten's name from history. The tomb of Akhenaten himself has never been found.

Change and conflict

Young Tutankhamun must have accepted the advice of those who had rejected his father's policies. He reinstated the traditional religion, restoring the status of the priests and reopening the temples. On a huge stone at Thebes, now known as the Restoration Stela, was carved this proclamation:

He [Tutankhamun] restored everything that was ruined, to be his monument forever and ever. He

SUN WORSHIPPER **Amenhotep IV was the tenth or eleventh pharaoh of the 18th Dynasty. He renamed himself 'Aken-Aten' (he who is of service to Aten) in honour of the sun, the manifestation of the one great deity at the centre of the cult religion he imposed on Egypt.**

has vanquished chaos from the whole land and has restored Ma'at to her place. He has made lying a crime, the whole land being made as it was at the time of creation.

Tutankhamun returned his court to the old capital of Memphis. He married his older half sister, Ankhesenamun, and probably anticipated a long and prosperous reign. In fact, his rule was to last less than a decade.

The mystery surrounding the sudden demise of the young pharaoh only deepened with the initial examination of his body. Tutankhamun was interred in a nest of three coffins – the innermost one made of beaten gold and bearing a death mask. Carter and his assistant, Dr Douglas Derry, a professor of anatomy from Cairo University, had enormous difficulty opening the coffins; and when they had finally prised open the lid of the last of the three, they discovered that a resin-like substance had glued the mummy into its coffin.

Derry used a chisel to extricate the mummy and then conducted a post-mortem, during which the body was decapitated and the torso sliced in half lengthways. Little of any significance was discovered. The skin was hard and caked in gluey resin; Derry failed to notice that the breastbone and part of the ribcage had been removed prior to mummification, and was unable to ascertain the cause of death.

Tutankhamun's tomb itself had indicated that the pharaoh's death had been a sudden one: it was far more humble than would normally be expected for someone of royal status. The tomb was probably being prepared for some senior official, and commandeered at short notice in order to complete the burial ritual and embalming process for the pharaoh within the customary 70 days.

The case for murder

The first theories proposing murder were put forward in 1968, when the mummy was re-examined using

X-ray equipment. The man who interpreted these first X-rays was British anatomist Professor Ronald Harrison. He noticed a small, loose piece of bone in the left side of the skull cavity. 'The X-rays suggest that the piece of bone is fused with the overlying skull,' he wrote. 'This could mean that Tutankhamun died from a brain haemorrhage caused by a blow to his skull from a blunt instrument.'

This was not conclusive evidence of murder. During the initial post-mortem, Derry's chisel could have flaked off a piece of cervical vertebra and driven it high up into the skull. Alternatively, since Tutankhamun's

mummification was a poor job compared with other work done during the 18th Dynasty period, hasty embalming could have been to blame for dislodging the bone.

But in 1996, an American Egyptologist, Bob Brier, passed transparencies of the X-rays to Dr Gerald Irwin, a trauma specialist at Long Island University. Dr Irwin noted a 'dark shadow' on the transparency. He suggested that this was a blood clot, possibly caused by a blow to the head. Was this more convincing proof that the pharaoh had been murdered? It was hard to be sure. The position of the shadow put

Anatomy of a murder inquiry

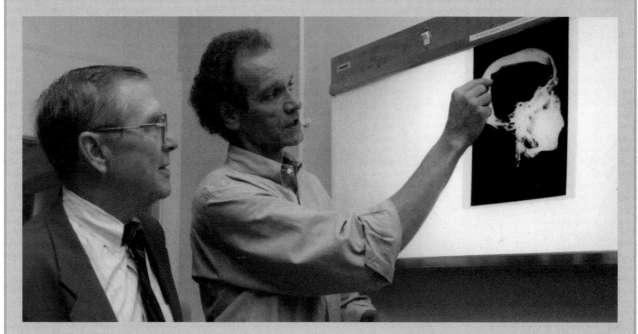

Egyptologist Bob Brier of Long Island University (above right) is the latest scholar to claim to have solved one of the world's oldest murder mysteries. Brier announced at a news conference in January 1997 that Tutankhamun's murderer was none other than the prime minister and closest confidant, Ay (pronounced 'I').

Bloody feud
Brier's proof stemmed from medical evidence that Tutankhamun had been killed by a blow to the back of his head, perhaps while he was sleeping. Brier and his

associate Dr Gerald Irwin, medical director of the Radiologic Technology Department at Long Island University, believe that the X-ray also shows fluid leakages, suggesting Tutankhamun lingered in pain for months before finally dying from his injury.

Brier nominates Ay on the basis of motive and opportunity. It is known that Ay succeeded Tutankhamun and married his widow, Ankhesenamun. In the absence of any royal heir or relative, this was not a usurpation of the throne. But Brier's contention is that Ay gave Queen Ankhesenamun no choice.

the injury at the underside of the back of Tutankhamun's head, an unlikely spot for an assassin to attack, as it is well protected by neck musculature.

Who could have wanted the pharaoh dead? His wife Ankhesenamun would have had the easiest access to him, but she is an unlikely aggressor. All the ancient murals portray the pharaoh and his wife as a close and tender couple. Two mummified foetuses in Tutankhamun's tomb indicate that the couple were trying to have children.

One man who stood to benefit from Tutankhamun's death was the elderly Ay, chief adviser to the former king and still the highest-ranking courtier in the land. Although he was not a close blood relation, Ay followed Tutankhamun onto the throne of Egypt and married his widow. Bob Brier suggested that as Ay would have controlled access to the king he could have arranged an assassination.

When the young king came of age and began making decisions in his own right, Ay's influence must have waned. He must have realised that his time was running out: if Ankhesenamun produced a son and heir, Ay's hopes of succession would be dashed.

Another suspect was General Horemheb, commander-in-chief of the Imperial Egyptian army and one of the king's closest advisers. Horemheb, an ambitious man of low birth, was the only courtier not to place an engraved memento in the dead king's tomb, which was a mark

UNCOVERING THE PAST Before the body of Tutankhamun could be autopsied, the archaeologist Harold Carter had to brush away the remnants of a shroud kept in the second of the three coffins in which the young pharaoh had been interred.

of great disrespect. Just four years after Tutankhamun's death, Horemheb himself took the throne and ordered artisans to travel the land erasing any engraved references to Tutankhamun, replacing the young pharaoh's name with his own. A compelling theory is that Ay and Horemheb could have plotted together to kill the king.

Conflicting evidence

With the evidence as it stands, historians cannot say for certain that Tutankhamun was murdered. Other theories about his death have their supporters. Derry's original X-ray of the body of Tutankhamun has also been interpreted as showing the spinal malformation usually known as scoliosis, and the inclusion of 130 walking sticks in his tomb tends to support this theory. If Tutankhamun was sickly, his early demise is easily explained. He would have had a short life expectancy, and could have easily succumbed to plague or infection.

On the other hand, there are artworks depicting a healthy looking Tutankhamun out hunting in a horse-drawn chariot, the reins wrapped around his waist to free his hands to aim a spear. While this conflicts with the theory that Tutankhamun was deformed, it has given some credence to a new one. The king could have had an accident during one of his chariot rides, thus necessitating the removal of his crushed ribs and sternum during his embalming. This would explain the poor state of Tutankhamun's remains.

It could also explain the presence of so much resin in the coffin. If death had occurred at a hunting ground far from the palace, copious quantities would have been needed to mask the stench of the corpse, which would have begun to decompose within 24 hours. Is it possible that the boy-king slipped from his

chariot to be dragged to his death under its wheels?

Although an accident sounds plausible, it does nothing to explain the sense of fear that Tutankhamun's death created at court. The letters sent by the young king's widow Ankhesenamun are full of apprehension and voice the premonition that one character in particular – a servant – was a source of threat. Could this be further evidence to support Brier's theory that the former minister Ay, who was soon to become pharaoh partly through his marriage to Ankhesenamun, was guilty of regicide?

We glimpse the queen's fragile state of mind in her letter to the king of the Hittites – Egypt's neighbours and bitter enemies – in which she begged for a Hittite prince to come to Egypt to marry her. Miraculously preserved on a clay tablet, her desperate words echo down the millennia.

'Never shall I pick out a servant of mine and make him my husband,' she wrote. 'I am very afraid.'

CONFLICTING IMAGES **A decorated wooden chest found in Tutankhamun's tomb shows him leaning on a walking stick. Some scholars think this shows the young pharaoh had some disability. Other depictions such as that on an engraved gold fan holder show the pharaoh as an athletic sportsman, hunter and charioteer. But which was the real Tutankhamun?**

SUBMERGED SECRETS

Water covers three-quarters of the Earth's surface, leaving the terrain beneath largely unexplored. Yet slowly but surely even this frontier is being pushed back by technology that enables us to look more closely at the secrets of the ocean floors.

Shipwrecks are fertile finds for the historian: a single dramatic moment in time, preserved beneath the waves, can yield fascinating insights into trade and seafaring techniques. Rising water levels and coastal earthquakes have also flooded ports and settlements, making the seabed a rich hunting ground for marine archaeologists.

Underwater detection

Surveying instruments such as magnetometers can be used from ships or in the water by divers (left) to find anomalies in the composition of the seabed. These pinpoint possible remains that can be investigated by scuba divers or in submersibles.

In very deep water, sonar can pick up distinctive 'scatter' in the echoed soundwaves. A Byzantine trading ship was discovered at a depth of 324m (1100ft) in the Black Sea using the technique. At this depth, the sea is oxygen-depleted, so when the wreck was investigated it was found to be remarkably well preserved for its age.

Fathoming the pharaohs

Alexandria's ancient royal port and Cleopatra's palace were destroyed by an earthquake in AD 365 and subsided beneath the waters of the Mediterranean. Polluted water with a visibility of less than 5m (16ft) made it impossible to map Alexandria's east harbour using video, but variation in the magnetic fields gave possible sites. From electronic scans, marine archaeologist Franck Goddio built up a topographical map of the silt and what lay beneath. From it, divers were able to find the possible remains of the palace and thousands of treasures including a statue of the great priest of Isis (right).

PRESERVED IN BRINE
Artefacts that would be in fragments in a land site can survive intact on the seabed. Encrustations protect glass and pottery, such as these thousand-year-old clay jars in Limani Bay, Turkey. Even organic materials such as wood and leather can avoid decomposition if they are lodged in silt.

Deeper and deeper

Many scientists have carried out underwater exploration, but the name of Robert Ballard has become synonymous with marine archaeology. In 1977 he pioneered the use of remote-operated vehicles or ROVs: unmanned submarines equipped with a video camera, surveying equipment, and a robotic arm for retrieval of finds (right).

A tethered ROV can be steered remotely using a joystick, allowing scientists to explore deep and dangerous wrecks beyond the scope of a diver. Images from its 'eyes' are transmitted directly along a fibre-optic cable to the surface vessel, allowing the ROV to be operated as though its controller were sitting right in it.

The discovery by ROV sonar scanning of sunken trading vessels at depths of up to 750m (2500ft) in the Mediterranean has disproved the notion that ancient sailors 'hugged the shoreline' and shows they could navigate across open sea. An ROV sent down to the site retrieved about 150 amphorae containing wine, olive oil and fish sauce.

Digital technology allows ROVs to be small enough to penetrate tiny spaces, such as the cramped hold of a silted up fishing boat or the portholes of ships. These 'flying eyes' are hardly any bigger than the CCTV camera they carry. They can be precisely manoeuvred and have a slow propeller setting so that the sand is not whisked up from the sea bed, obscuring the view.

Wreck reckoning

The wreck of the *Titanic* was located by a team led by Robert Ballard in 1985, 73 years after it had sunk. The great ship lay partly buried in mud under 3.8km (2 miles) of water off the coast of Newfoundland. The wreck is far too deep for scuba divers, who can venture no deeper than 60m (200ft), but with the help of ROVs (remote-operated vehicles) Ballard was able to document the wreck. He used sonar

scans and video cameras to build up a complete picture of the *Titanic*'s condition (below, left) and his findings demolished many long-held theories about the circumstances of the disaster.

Since 1912 it had been widely thought that the iceberg ripped a huge gash, perhaps as long as 90m (300ft), in the side of the ship. But Ballard found there was little damage to the hull – no more than six thin openings covering around 1.1m² (12 sq ft) along the starboard side.

The ship went down not because of the size of the holes, but because of their location – directly over six watertight holds that were critical to its buoyancy.

For deep investigations such as this, manned submersibles built to withstand extreme pressures can be commandeered by archaeologists. They cost up to £18 million and can only be used on heavily sponsored projects.

MILESTONES
OF
HISTORY

STORMING OF THE BASTILLE
The uprising of the Parisian mob was about gunpowder, not people power

The fall of the Bastille on July 14, 1789, is celebrated as the start of the French Revolution. Yet the citizens who died in the uprising were not revolutionary martyrs, but victims of poor crowd control, swept along in a hunt for some missing barrels of gunpowder.

T ension and unrest filled Paris during the summer of 1789. The people were enraged at the rising price of food, and political meetings attracted huge and rowdy audiences. The king and queen rarely emerged from Versailles, their huge palace beyond the outskirts of Paris. A large consignment of troops had been deployed by the king inside the city. Although the soldiers had no specific orders, the people found their presence threatening. The message was clear: the king feared civil disturbance.

One politician who had tried to address the common concerns of inflation and national debt was Jacques Necker, the popular minister of finance in the government of Louis XVI. The sudden announcement that Necker had been dismissed by the king brought angry crowds out onto the streets. On the afternoon of July 12, a mob milling in the gardens of the Tuileries palace, in central Paris, was set upon by a German cavalry unit ordered to clear the area. Rumours quickly circulated that some kind of military action against the people was imminent, and by the evening of that day thousands of Parisians were desperately trying to arm themselves.

Confusion and turmoil spread rapidly. Foreign troops had been placed at Paris's 54 *barrières*, the gatehouses that led into the city, and by midnight at least 40 of these were ablaze. Later that day, a delegation of Electors of Paris, self-appointed representatives of the citizens, was despatched to the armoury at Les Invalides to demand arms for the newly formed 'civic militia'. The delegation was turned away.

By the morning of July 14, a huge crowd had gathered on the parade ground at Les Invalides. Undeterred by the presence of 5000 troops, the mob swarmed into the armoury and began indiscriminately handing out more than 30,000 muskets. Only a small amount of gunpowder was stored in the armoury, but the mob soon learned that 250 barrels of powder had been moved to the Bastille, an old fortress-prison across the river Seine in the quarter known as the Faubourg St Antoine.

No word from the king

About 1000 people rapidly gathered in front of the outer courtyard of the Bastille, demanding the powder. During the morning the governor, Bernard-René de Launay, received delegations from the citizens' army, but refused to hand over any munitions without authorisation from the king. The angry crowd soon lost patience. A group managed to cut the ropes holding the counterweights of the first drawbridge; the bridge came down and the crowd poured through and filled the outer courtyard. Inside the Bastille, Governor de Launay feared for the safety of his guards and ordered them to fire their muskets, hoping to disperse the

DRUMBEAT OF REVOLT Citizens wore a revolutionary 'uniform': the red cockade hat – symbol of liberty – and rosettes or sashes emblazoned with the red, white and blue of republican France.

Monument to tyranny

Perceptions of the Bastille's physical proportions grew to match the symbolic importance attached to its fall. Paintings such as Hubert Robert's *Demolition of the Bastille* of 1789 (below) shows a structure that dwarfs ant-size humans, yet in reality the highest point of the fortress was little more than 21m (70ft). A contemporary lithograph (right) depicts a Bastille that is closer to the correct dimensions. It also conveys confusion and dismay, rather than suggesting that the crowd was heroically storming the Bastille. The episode was a messy and unnecessary riot, not the key opening skirmish of a popular revolution.

GRISLY TROPHY Bernard de Launay, govenor of the Bastille, was killed in the storming of the prison. His head was stuck on a pike (below) and paraded through the streets. Earlier in the day, the wax heads of politicians – lent out by Madame Tussaud – had been displayed in the streets, but this was the real thing.

crowd. He may not have realised that the people in the outer courtyard were unable to leave, pressed in by crowds collecting outside.

To these people – who assumed that the lowering of the first drawbridge had been ordered from within – it appeared that they had been welcomed into the Bastille's compound only to be fired upon.

Until this point the crowd had fired shots only from their own personal firearms. These numbered a few; most of the crowd were unable to fire their weapons as they had no powder. No one succeeded in hitting any of the Bastille's defenders. Angered by what they perceived as an attack, the crowd readily parted to allow through two cannon, brought up by a group of renegade French soldiers sympathetic to the republican cause.

On hearing of the approaching cannon, de Launay wrote a note, threatening to blow up the fortress and the surrounding area unless those inside were given safe passage, but the crowd was in no mood to negotiate, shouting 'Lower the bridges' and 'No capitulation'.

As preparations were made to fire the heavy cannon at the second drawbridge, it suddenly rattled down,

having been opened from within by the guards.

After a moment's hesitation, the crowd rushed in, disarmed the terrified defenders and set about ransacking the fortress.

Mob revenge

During the 'storming' of the Bastille, 83 members of the citizens' army had died – shot by soldiers on the parapets – whereas only three of the guards had been killed. The mob took their revenge on the hapless de Launay, who was paraded through the streets towards the people's headquarters at Hôtel de Ville, the seat of local government in the city.

He arrived badly beaten and covered in spittle. As the crowd debated how he should be killed – one suggestion was that he should be tied to a horse's tail and dragged through the cobbled streets – de Launay suddenly shouted 'Let me die' and lashed out with his foot.

Instantly the crowd fell on the governor, slashing at him with swords, bayonets and knives. He was rolled into the gutter and finished off with a volley of pistol shots. De Launay's head was then cut off, stuck on a pike, and paraded through the

The Bastille's inmates

Prints produced after the revolution depicted naked prisoners, shackled and left to rot in the dungeons of the Bastille. But conditions in the prison were in fact far from inhumane. Most cells were furnished with basic amenities, and many inmates brought in their own possessions. Alcohol and tobacco were permitted, and – for those who could pay – meals could be lavish.

Nor were the prisoners the political martyrs that some of the revolutionary literature presented them to be. Of the seven men released, four were petty forgers – Jean de la Corrége, Jean Bèchade, Bernard Laroche and Jean-Antoine Pujade. They were rearrested later the same day. Also freed was the Count of Solages, who had been charged with incest. The other two were madmen. One had been imprisoned for 30 years, while the other, an Irishman known as Major Whyte, was carried aloft by the cheering crowd, though he had no idea where he was at all.

streets to the cheers and laughter of the crowd. As the governor was being murdered, Louis XVI, in Versailles, ordered the troops to withdraw from the city.

These were the events of July 14, 1789. They consisted of a misunderstanding, some impulsive and violent behaviour and a good deal of futile bloodshed. In France, this day is celebrated as 'Bastille Day'. It symbolises the victory of liberty, equality and fraternity over oppression, the arbitrary power of royalty and the yoke of tyranny.

In the popular version of events, embellished by 19th-century romantic historians, the fortress prison is the hub of the despotic *ancien régime*, a place where prisoners of the monarch were incarcerated and tortured. The fall of the Bastille took on a great historical and heroic dimension as the first example, in modern times, of a people in a European country expressing their right to self-determination.

Contemporary paintings tend to propagate this view of events, showing the Bastille as an immense monolithic structure. Revolutionary propaganda made much of the Bastille's fearsome reputation.

The foundations for this mythologised version of events were being laid within three days of the Bastille's fall. The first issue of the *Revolutions de Paris* contained a fanciful account of children and women embroiled in bitter fighting, and the cells finally being thrown open to 'set free innocent victims and venerable old men who were amazed to behold the light of day'.

The same newspaper was responsible for bolstering the story in the days following the bloodshed:
The fighting grew steadily more intense; the citizens had become

BLOCK BY BLOCK Two days after the Bastille was stormed, the people began to tear it down. By the end of the year it had been flattened and a statue of the goddess Nature was built in its place.

hardened to the fire; from all directions they clambered onto the roofs or broke into the rooms; as soon as an enemy appeared among the turrets on the tower, he was fixed in the sights of a hundred guns and mown down in an instant... People bravely faced death and every danger... even the children, after the discharge of fire from the fortress, ran hither and thither picking up the bullets and shot... Serene and blessed liberty... has at last been introduced into this abode of horrors, this frightful refuge of monstrous despotism and its crimes.

The vivid descriptions of wizened prisoners blinking in the first daylight they had seen for decades were certainly embellished. The keys to the prison had, in fact, been carried off in triumph before anyone bothered to release the prisoners. It transpired that there were only seven inmates, memorably described as 'two fools, four forgers and a debaucher'. None were guilty of offences against the 'monstrous despot'. Far from being a bastion of oppression, the Bastille had ceased to be a political prison some years earlier.

The storming of the Bastille would be glorified over and over again as an epic uprising of the people in which the giant edifice was overrun. In truth, a new era of popular power was ushered in by a handful of people striding unopposed across an unguarded drawbridge. This crossing of the threshold, however, was to herald a future darkened by the shadow of another, greater, terror: the guillotine.

THE MASS STEAL **For many in the crowd, the storming of the Bastille was an opportunity for looting rather than the dawn of a republican age. A political drawing making this point shows an ignored yellow crate – the sought-for gunpowder lies forgotten. In later street processions (below) celebrating Bastille Day patriots bore aloft a replica of the prison.**

AN ACT OF WAR

The torpedo that was fired at the Lusitania found her Achilles' heel

The sinking of the Lusitania in 1915 transformed America's stance on the First World War. But no one could explain how a single torpedo had sunk so large a ship in 18 minutes. Now, technical analysis and underwater study of the wreck have revealed what happened.

On the afternoon of May 7, 1915, the British merchant ship RMS *Lusitania*, the world's biggest and fastest passenger liner, was 16km (10 miles) off the south coast of Ireland, en route to Liverpool. A bitter war was waging in Europe: one unlike any the world had ever seen. Britain and Germany had both declared arbitrary 'war zones' in which any merchant ships belonging

to the enemy were liable to be attacked without warning. But passengers on the ship relaxed in the lounges and saloons as they neared the end of their transatlantic crossing. No one on board believed that the huge ship would be targeted by a German submarine.

The first indication that the *Lusitania* was in danger came as passengers in the café on the veranda deck looked out to sea. They noticed a stream of bubbles forging through the

PERILOUS JOURNEY As passengers embarked, many must have read the warnings issued by the German embassy. One such warning appeared in a newspaper beside an advertisement for the Cunard Line. Nobody asked for a refund on their ticket and no government statement was made.

OCEAN STEAMSHIPS.

CUNARD

EUROPE VIA LIVERPOOL

LUSITANIA

Fastest and Largest Steamer
now in Atlantic Service Sails
SATURDAY, MAY 1, 10 A.M.
Transylvania, Fri., May 7, 5 P.M.
Orduna, - - Tues.,May 18, 10 A.M.
Tuscania, - - Fri., May 21, 5 P.M.
LUSITANIA, Sat., May 29, 10 A.M.
Transylvania, Fri., June 4, 5 P.M.

Gibraltar—Genoa—Naples—Piraeus
S.S. Carpathia, Thur., May 13, Noon

ROUND THE WORLD TOURS
Through bookings to all principal Ports
of the World.
Company's Office. 21-24 State St., N. Y.

NOTICE!

TRAVELLERS intending to embark on the Atlantic voyage are reminded that a state of war exists between Germany and her allies and Great Britain and her allies; that the zone of war includes the waters adjacent to the British Isles; that, in accordance with formal notice given by the Imperial German Government, vessels flying the flag of Great Britain, or of any of her allies, are liable to destruction in those waters and that travellers sailing in the war-zone on ships of Great Britain or her allies do so at their own risk.

IMPERIAL GERMAN EMBASSY

WASHINGTON, D. C., APRIL 22, 1915.

LIFEBOAT RESCUE The chaos of the ship's evacuation is captured in illustrations from British newspapers published immediately after the event. The speed of the sinking and the lack of crew training contributed to the deaths of almost two-thirds of those on board.

water and heading directly for the ship. Seconds later there was an enormous explosion. The blast sent up a plume of water, higher than the *Lusitania*'s bridge, and showered the decks with debris. One lifeboat was blown off its davits and into the sea.

Final countdown

Within a few minutes the great ship had started to list to starboard. Water began to pour in at the rate of 800 tonnes a minute as passengers and crew trapped below decks struggled to escape. On the decks there was panic: lifeboats on the port side swung inwards and could not be launched; lifeboats on the starboard side swung out beyond reach.

Able Seaman Leslie Moreton later described how he had lowered a lifeboat full of people into the water, only for the water alongside the still-

speeding ship to carry it directly under another lifeboat. The second boat dropped from a height right on top of the first, crushing everyone. Around him was utter panic.

The turmoil of passengers and lifebelts, many people losing their hold on the deck and slipping down and over the side, and a gradual crescendo of noise building up as hundreds and hundreds of people began to realise that, not only was she going down very fast, but in all probability too fast for them all to get away...

As the ship went down there was, according to most survivors, a second explosion. The RMS *Lusitania*, pride of the Cunard fleet, slid below the water just 18 minutes after being hit. Survivors reported a 'long lingering moan' rising to a 'mighty crescendo of screams' as she sank.

A woman named Margaret Gwyer was sucked into one of the funnels as the ship disappeared, only to shoot out, covered in oil and soot. She survived, but of the 1257 passengers on board, 785 died; among them 128 children and infants, their bodies bobbing around the liferafts 'like lily pads on a pond'. Of the 702-strong crew, 413 were lost.

By the time the *Lusitania* had disappeared under the waves, Kapitänleutnant Walter Schwieger, commander of the German submarine U-20, which fired the fatal torpedo, had set a course for home – and for a place in the annals of infamy.

One hundred and twenty eight Americans were among those killed, and news of the disaster led to rioting in New York City. Most of the passengers were Irish and, although just a third of the bodies were recovered, the number of dead required mass graves to be dug at Queenstown, in County Cork, southern Ireland.

The right to ram

The U-boat captain could not have anticipated the severe loss of life – ships of the *Lusitania*'s size would be expected to take hours or even days to sink. When hit, she was almost within hailing distance of the Irish coast and, although the sea was wretchedly cold, there were 48 lifeboats on board.

The Hague Conventions of 1899 and 1907 had introduced new codes of practice for neutral countries in the event of war. But these rules had been drawn up before the advent of organised submarine warfare. Neutral ships such as cargo vessels and passenger liners were meant to be immune from attack.

The captain of an attacking vessel was required by law to give due warning and allow the crew to disembark. But for a U-boat to come to the surface and hail or warn a ship before attacking would put the submarine's own crew at risk. As a non-neutral vessel, it would immediately be vulnerable to being rammed. And since the convention allowed merchant vessels to be armed, surfacing could also make a submarine vulnerable to cannon. Observing the laws of neutrality was a luxury submarine commanders could not afford.

The Kaiser's government was internationally condemned for ignoring neutrality. But the British government was downplaying a potentially disastrous revelation: that its Admiralty had issued instructions that any merchant ship confronted by a U-boat should ram it or open fire from mobile guns.

The Germans were well aware of these orders after finding copies of them on captured ships. Any action by Kapitänleutnant Schwieger was

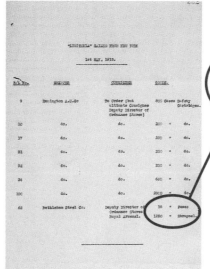

taken in the knowledge that his submarine would never survive being rammed by a leviathan such as the *Lusitania*. But in less threatening circumstances, Schwieger was a lot less ruthless. Earlier that day he had encountered a much smaller schooner and had allowed an evacuation before sinking the vessel.

The *Lusitania* soon became the focus of a worldwide argument about the rules of permissible warfare on 'merchant' ships. The Germans tried to justify their action by calling attention to the *Lusitania*'s cargo of military supplies – 4200 cases of rifle bullets, 1250 cases of shrapnel shells and 18 cases of percussion fuses. But technically this cargo was 'non-explosive' (it would not explode in the event of a torpedo attack), and

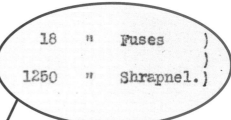

WATER LOGGED The *Lusitania*'s manifest listed percussive fuses, shrapnel and cartridges. Claims that this cargo exploded and blew up the ship were not supported by tests. One of the fuses (below) was recovered from the wreck and shown to be safe. It could not have detonated during the attack.

Tasteless token

This medallion celebrating the sinking of the *Lusitania* was struck by a Munich metalworker called Karl Goetz. Passengers are shown queuing up at the Cunard office to buy tickets from Death. On the reverse side, the sinking ship is pictured laden with guns, aircraft and weaponry, while the banner above reads 'no contraband goods'.

The medal did nothing to help the German government's efforts to defend their military policy: they moved swiftly to prevent the medallions from being distributed. But some did get into circulation and ended up in the hands of British propagandists, who wasted no time in commissioning Gordon Selfridge, owner of the London store, to make 250,000 copies for worldwide distribution.

was judged legal to be carried by neutral vessels. The Germans began to allege that other, illegally carried, munitions had been on board.

Stash of explosives

One claim was that the *Lusitania* had been secretly – and illegally – loaded with highly volatile guncotton hidden in crates of butter and cheese, and it was this that caused the mysterious second explosion that hastened her end. If true, it would have meant that the British government and the Cunard Line had colluded to put passengers' lives at risk.

The exploration of the wreck by sophisticated underwater cameras in 1993 put paid to this hypothesis. The ship's magazine is virtually intact and the tearing of the hull, as revealed by 3D imaging, is inconsistent with the effects of an armaments explosion.

The exploration of the wreck also helped to solve the mystery of why such a stoutly built ship sank so quickly from a single hit. The torpedo happened to find the liner's weakest point, just behind the main bulkhead (one of several barriers between the compartments in the ship's hold). The breach in the hull allowed water to flood into two long coalbunkers at the heart of the ship. As the weight of the water built up, the other internal bulkheads buckled, opening more compartments and compromising the structure of the entire ship. Amazing as it seemed at the time, one torpedo was enough.

The loss of life was exacerbated by the complacency of the *Lusitania*'s

On impact

The torpedo punches a hole about 3m x 6m (10ft x 20ft) in the ship's steel hull, just below the waterline on the starboard side. The impact loosens rivets and sends out a pressure wave that causes major structural damage on the two lowest decks. The ship yaws to starboard, and more rivets and steel plating tear free. Seconds after impact, 1000m^2 (10,000ft^2) of the starboard hull is letting in water. Electrical power is lost and the engines cannot be reversed to slow from 18 knots. The ship takes in seawater at a rate of 800 tonnes a minute.

Why she sank so quickly

When news of the *Lusitania* came through, few could accept that a single torpedo could sink such a large ship in just 18 minutes. Alternative explanations ranged from a second unreported torpedo strike to an explosion of illegal armaments aboard the liner. But one researcher decided to calculate just how much damage the torpedo could have caused. Her findings propose a sequence of events that tallies closely with the known details of the sinking.

7 minutes after impact

As the ship lists further to starboard it takes on even more water through scores of open portholes on that side. The loss of power means that hydraulically operated safety doors cannot be closed. Crucially, these could have isolated the coal bunkers that run the length of the ship below the water line. As they are breached, water fills the entire lower decks very rapidly.

15 minutes after impact

As the ship continues to fill with water the bulkheads buckle and twist under the strain with an explosive rumble, eventually tearing apart. The sheer weight of water in the starboard bow now causes the stern of the ship to lift up and rotate, the hole in her side opens even further. The ship continues to list, the bow dips under the water and the ship slides to the ocean floor.

captain, William Turner. Some lifeboats had been bolted down to ensure they did not slide across the deck. Safety drills had been ignored, Turner explained later, for fear of alarming the passengers. Many put their lifebelts on upside-down, which forced their heads under the water.

Turner had believed that in the event of an attack his ship would stay afloat long enough for orderly evacuation, so he did not enforce orders to keep all the portholes shut.

Worse, it seems that Turner had disregarded an Admiralty telegraph sent on May 6 warning him that there were U-boats in the area. His apparent insouciance prompted one Admiralty official to suggest that he had been 'got at by the Germans'. Conspiracy theorists still claim that Turner purposely allowed the ship to be sunk, acting on secret orders from the Admiralty. The reason for the deliberate sacrifice, they suggest, was to draw the United States into the war.

The absence of an armed escort for the *Lusitania* has been another cause for suspicion about British motives, but the simple explanation for this was that ships with an armed escort were legal targets for attack under the existing 'cruiser rules'.

Last orders

The last message telegraphed to the *Lusitania* was acknowledged at 11:52 on May 7. It stated simply: 'Submarines active in southern part of Irish Channel. Last heard of 20 miles south of Coninberg Lightship.' Turner's orders were to set an evasive zigzag course should he encounter U-boat activity. In the event, he slowed the engines and tried to delay his arrival into Liverpool so that he would not be left vulnerable outside a major port on the outgoing tide. Captain Turner was not a naval officer, but a merchant seaman with no experience of wartime engagement. He did not zigzag, saying later in court that he had interpreted this instruction to mean the ship was to be turned if it came under attack.

The *Lusitania* was duly following a straight course when, on board U20, Kapitänleutnant Schwieger looked through his periscope, caught sight of her distinctive four funnels, and gave the order to fire.

CAUSE FOR THE LOST The sinking of the *Lusitania* prompted a surge in army enlistment in Ireland. Many were persuaded by powerfully illustrated recruitment posters, which appeared throughout the country.

Neutrality no longer an option

The sinking of the Lusitania did not bring America into the war, despite the widespread horror it evoked. The decisive factor in US involvement was a decoded telegram and a subtle piece of British diplomacy.

The United States declared war on Germany in April 1917. The immediate cause was neither outrage at attacks on US citizens, nor a desire to come to the aid of Britain. What brought America into the European conflict was, bizarrely, the need to protect its own southern states from invasion by Mexico. In March 1917, the American media published a telegram. It was a coded message sent from the German foreign minister, Arthur Zimmermann, to the German ambassador in Washington, Count Johann von Bernstoff. It caused public uproar. Zimmermann had signalled the initiation of 'unrestricted submarine warfare' in the Atlantic, the very policy cancelled by the German Kaiser after the *Lusitania* sinking.

Shocking offer

More chilling for Americans reading the telegram was the implication that Germany was proposing to ally itself with Mexico and Japan. In the event of a German victory, Mexico was promised the disputed territories of Texas, Arizona and New Mexico. It seemed obvious that Germany hoped to stir up trouble on America's doorstep, in order to preclude any US involvement in the European war.

How had this top-secret communique fallen into American hands? Zimmermann had been unaware that, on the first day of the war, the British had tapped into the Germans' underwater transatlantic cables. Every message subsequently sent was intercepted by the British and studied in Room 40 of the Admiralty office. When the Zimmermann telegram was sent on January 17, 1917, its great

CODED CABLE The Zimmermann telegram was intercepted by British intelligence. Their decoding notes include the names 'Texas', 'New Mexico' and 'Arizona', indicating Germany's warlike intentions.

length aroused immediate suspicion and two cryptographers, William Montgomery and Nigel de Grey, set about trying to decode it. The initial decryption of the words 'Mexico' and 'US and Japan' indicated the potential importance of the document, but it took several more weeks of painstaking effort until the entire message could be read.

The British were now faced with a dilemma. Announcing the telegram's contents would alert the Germans that their lines of communication were vulnerable.

To avoid this, the coded version of the message and a copy of the German code book was handed to the Americans, who duly cracked it on their own soil. When the American President Woodrow Wilson announced that he had received the telegram, he made no mention at all of any British involvement.

Even so, the authenticity of the message was immediately called into question, but extraordinarily, Zimmermann confirmed that he had sent it: 'I cannot deny it… It is true.' The president was left with no choice. The threat had been placed too close to home for him to ignore. On April 2, 1917, Wilson told Congress that 'Neutrality is no longer feasible or desirable where the peace of the world is involved', and – in a veiled reference to the Zimmermann telegram – 'We are accepting this challenge of hostile purpose'.

Four days later, the United States declared war on Germany.

LOOKING UP THE DATES

Many events in early history are well documented, but lack a precise date. Modern astronomy has helped to pinpoint some events in time even though there may be no contemporary record of when they took place.

What goes around

Halley's comet has long been feared as a portent of doom. Its appearance in 1066 caused panic throughout Europe, and earned it a place in the Bayeux Tapestry (circled, right). In 1456, the comet was blamed for earthquakes, plagues, a mysterious red rain and the births of two-headed farm animals in Switzerland.

In 1705 the English astronomer Edmond Halley proved that the comet which now bears his name was orbiting the Earth and that it would reappear in the sky approximately every 75 years. Working backwards, this gave rise to the theory that the passage in the Book of Joshua which describes the Sun standing still in the sky – the so-called 'long day' – may be a reference to a sighting of the comet. This would mean that the Israelites were occupying the land of Canaan in 1404 BC.

Finding Jesus' birth in the stars

Astronomy has helped to estimate the date of birth of Jesus Christ. According to St Matthew's Gospel, Jesus was born during the reign of Herod the Great. The Jewish historian Josephus, who died in AD 100, did not record the year of Herod's death, but he noted that the king died near Passover shortly after an eclipse of the Moon. Modern astronomers have dated this eclipse to March 12 or 13, 4 BC. Passover that year fell on April 14. If the Bible is accurate, this is the latest Jesus can have been born. With that in mind, astronomers looked for evidence of the star that guided the Wise Men to the stable in Bethlehem. They believe that it was probably not a star at all but a conjunction of Jupiter and Saturn which produced an unusually bright light in the sky. Astronomers now know that this celestial event took place in late March or early April, 7 BC.

Days to remember

Dates have not always been written by day, month and year. Ancient chronicles tell of events taking place in a certain year of a monarch's reign, making it impossible for later readers to know exactly when they happened. But solar eclipses – events so spectacular that they are mentioned in contemporary accounts whenever they occur – can now be predicted and backdated historically by calculating the orbits of the Earth and the Moon.

Using these calculations, historians can now put dates to ancient events. For example, in the Book of Amos, God says: 'On that day I will make the Sun go down at noon, and darken the Earth in broad daylight'. This is a reference to a total eclipse, which has been dated to June 15, 763 BC.

In the Middle East, a five-year war between the Lydians and the Medes came to a sudden halt when 'day was turned into night'. This dramatic and frightening event was a total eclipse that is now known to have happened on May 28, 585 BC.

ON THE RECORD The eerie effects of a solar eclipse – when the Moon blocks out the Sun – struck fear into ancient people, who recorded the events with awe.

Stardating

Egyptians believed that their pharaohs became stars in the northern sky when they died, so to help them find their way they built the pyramids to face true north. The Great Pyramid of Cheops is aligned to within a tenth of a degree.

Research suggests that they located true north by watching two stars – Mizar and Kochab – which both traced a circle around the same axis of rotation as the Earth. When the stars were vertically aligned, a plumb line through them would cut the horizon at true north.

This is not always the case. Our planet wobbles on its axis, and the stars change position relative to the Earth. Polaris is the star now aligned with true north, but astronomers have calculated that true north did line up with Mizar and Kochab in 2467 BC. Thereafter the stars appeared to shift slightly to the west. Pyramids built after the Great Pyramid of Cheops are all very slightly misaligned by a fraction of a degree to the west; those built before it point slightly to the east. By measuring the angle of deviation, the Great Pyramid's construction can be dated to 2478 BC.

Kochab

Little Bear

N Celestial North Pole in 2467 BC

Mizar

Great Bear

RENAISSANCE MAN
A forgotten artist changed the way that people look at paintings

The Italian city of Florence is famous as the birthplace of the Renaissance. Yet the rediscovery of a little-known master who lived in Rome and predated the great Florentine artists suggests otherwise. Pietro Cavallini may be the true father of modern European art.

The city of Florence, set among the hills of Chianti, north-west Italy, is home to fewer than half a million people – and to a treasure-trove of Europe's greatest works of art. Here, in the Uffizi Gallery, you can see the paintings of Leonardo and Botticelli; in the Bargello, the sculptures of Michelangelo and Donatello; in the Accademia, Michelangelo's David. Once described as a 'little treasure-city' by the American author Henry James, Florence is home to 50 galleries and museums and is crammed with public buildings, churches and palaces.

For centuries art historians have assumed that Florence was the epicentre of the Renaissance – the revival of art and learning in Europe in the 14th to 16th centuries. Intellectually, the Renaissance marked the transition from a medieval to a modern Europe. In art, it saw paintings develop from the flat, stylised Byzantine works popular during the Middle Ages to more naturalistic paintings with genuine feeling and realistic perspective. The

BY WHOSE BRUSH? As the Renaissance began, subjects such as angels and apostles took on a more earthy solidity and beauty. Half these images are details from works by Pietro Cavallini; the others are by the more celebrated Giotto di Bondone. To find out who painted each picture, turn the page.

Renaissance was an artistic revolution – but it now appears that its origins have been misattributed.

Giorgio Vasari's 1550 *Lives of the Most Eminent Painters* was the first internationally influential work of art history and criticism. The book credited Florentine artists with ushering in the Renaissance, most notably Giotto di Bondone (1266-1337), a farmer's son turned painter and sculptor. Its argument has passed into history as fact.

Florentine supporter

Vasari was by no means an impartial observer. Although born in Assisi, he was a fiercely partisan resident of Florence, where he enjoyed the patronage of the Medicis, an immensely wealthy family of nobles and generous benefactors of the Florentine arts. Vasari's *Lives* was dedicated to Francesco's father, Cosimo de'Medici, and its emphasis on Florentine artists such as Giotto and Donatello makes it a work more of civic propaganda than history.

This is not to downplay Giotto's influence. Great works such as the fresco cycle in the Arena Chapel at Padua testify to his genius. His work featured ground-breaking use of light and perspective that made figures look real and substantial. He was perhaps the first Florentine artist to apply this technique, but he was certainly not the first in Italy.

Pietro dei Cerroni, nicknamed Cavallini, is a little-known figure in the history of art. There are only the

ARTISTIC LICENCE While Raphael and Michelangelo (both Florentines) deserve their accolades in Giorgio Vasari's *Lives of the Most Eminent Painters*, the downplaying of Pietro Cavallini may have put the birth of the Renaissance in the wrong city.

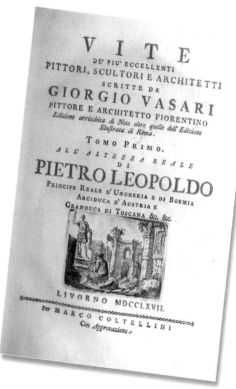

Cavallini 1293: angel's head from *The Last Judgment* in the church of Santa Cecilia in Trastevere, Rome.

Cavallini, 1293: head of St James from *The Last Judgment*.

Cavallini, 1292: crowd detail from *Scenes from the Life of St Agnes* in the church of Santa Maria Donnaregina, Naples.

Giotto, 1306: angel from *The Last Judgment* in the Scrovegni Chapel, Padua.

Giotto, 1305: head of a disciple from *Christ Washing the Disciples' Feet*, Scrovegni Chapel.

Giotto, 1320: crowd detail from *The Miracle of Drusiana* at the Peruzzi Chapel, Florence.

merest scraps of information about his life. He was born around 1240-50 in the city of Rome. His son Giovanni wrote a single sentence about his father, claiming that he lived to be over 100 and never wore a hat against the cold.

Yet during his lifetime this obscure, mysterious figure was acknowledged to be one of the finest painters of his day. The Florentine Lorenzo Ghiberti described him as 'a master... the most learned of all the masters and one who did much work'. When Giotto was a child, Cavallini was at the height of his fame, and most scholars agree that his work influenced Giotto, who is known to have visited Rome. So how did this crucial figure disappear from the history of art?

The problem was that Cavallini's reputation allowed him to work on the most famous churches of his time. These were the churches that suffered the most wear and tear and were often repainted with new decoration. With every brushstroke, the original work of Cavallini was further obscured.

Only 100 years after his death, the destruction of Cavallini's work was recognised as a problem. Giorgio

Vasari wrote that Cavallini had 'painted over the door of the sacristy of Aracoeli some scenes which are now destroyed by time'.

But new light was shed on the subject in the year 2000, when the art historian Tommaso Strinati discovered a hidden fresco in the church of Santa Maria in Aracoeli, on the Capitoline Hill in Rome, the very church referred to by Vasari. The fresco depicted a stern Madonna with a plump, precocious infant Jesus, against a chapel background. Almost certainly by Cavallini, the *Madonna col Bambino* is dated to 1290 and displays the naturalistic style and use of perspective that – according to Vasari – was not developed until the 14th century. It was finished in the year that Giotto completed his apprenticeship with the artist Christo del Cimabue; the same year that he is said to have visited Rome. Could he

TURNING POINT **The seraph, from Cavallini's *The Last Judgment,* shows a roundness to the portrayal of the human figure, turning it from a mere representation into a living, breathing entity.**

A new perspective on Renaissance innovation

The 16th-century art historian Giorgio Vasari cited Christo del Cimabue as the teacher of and chief influence on Giotto. Cimabue was a Florentine artist, and had continuing contact with Giotto, but there is little resemblance between their painting styles. By contrast there is a marked similarity between Giotto's work and that of the Roman artist Pietro Cavallini.

Impossible buildings

Cimabue had no apparent ability to show buildings in correct perspective. His ceiling fresco in the church of St Francis in Assisi shows a storeyed building with skewed roofs and arches that defy the laws of perspective (left). By comparison Giotto's ability was extraordinary. Only 13 years after Cimabue's painting was complete, Giotto was producing realistic representations of three-dimensional buildings that included roofs and balustrades correctly rendered (right). Could he have learnt this from Cimabue?

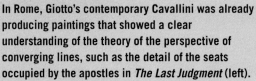

Light and shade

In Rome, Giotto's contemporary Cavallini was already producing paintings that showed a clear understanding of the theory of the perspective of converging lines, such as the detail of the seats occupied by the apostles in *The Last Judgment* (left).

Cavallini has long been credited by art experts for using light and shadow on forms to depict volume. He conveys the solid shapes of the human body with a skill more advanced than his contemporaries.

Real people

The Florentine school took up the challenge, and rapidly developed the use of perspective in art. Giotto himself was the first to foreshorten the figures in the foreground to suggest their proximity. In his painting of the Garden of Gethsemane, Giotto shows the sleeping apostles in this compressed form (below). Soon after, Giotto's pupil Taddeo Gaddi became the first to paint the shadows cast by figures, confirming their reality in a landscape or interior.

With the advent of the new style, the old Gothic manner of showing figures frontally and without depth was immediately rendered obsolete.

have climbed the 124 steps to the church of Santa Maria? Was he inspired by what he saw inside?

The fresco of the Madonna was not Cavallini's only work in the Santa Maria. A fragment of fresco uncovered in the early 1970s consisted of a column painted as a *trompe l'oeil*, a device that used perspective to deceive the viewer into thinking it was a three-dimensional object. The column was decorated with inlaid mosaics in a style known as Cosmati – after the family of craftsmen who invented it. This decoration was Cavallini's trademark: it also appeared in his 1293 work *The Last Judgment*, in the church of Santa Cecila in the Roman district of Trastevere.

Cavallini would not have been working alone. The late 13th century saw the advent of the 'worksite': a collective of artists all painting in the same style under the unifying direction of a master painter. Strinati believes that the Santa Maria church is proof that Cavallini was in charge of a Roman worksite that heralded the start of the Renaissance.

Key fresco cycle

The achievements of the Cavallini worksite may be greater than are already imagined. One prime example of the artistic techniques developed by both Cavallini and Giotto can be seen in the church of San Francesco at Assisi, midway between Florence and Rome. This is the fresco cycle of the *Life of St Francis*, widely considered to be the first great Renaissance fresco, and confidently attributed to Giotto by Vasari.

However, the restorer Bruno Zanardi, who cleaned the frescoes between 1978 and 1982, has argued that it was actually the creation of one or more Roman master, probably Cavallini and his school. 'In the 13th century,' reasoned Zanardi, 'Rome was the most important city in the world. It just makes sense that the Renaissance began there.' The discovery of the Santa Maria frescoes

backed up Zanardi's hunch. Art historians can now be sure that Cavallini possessed the technical skill and knowledge of perspective to create the Assisi frescoes.

The Assisi works also bear several of his trademarks. There are the little cherubs holding festoons (strings of leaves, flowers or ribbons suspended between two points) and a red tower with pillared balustrade. There are also the *trompe l'oeil* Cosmati columns identical to those painted by Cavallini. It is clear that, even if Cavallini was not responsible for the painting of the Assisi frescoes, then he was certainly a major influence on whoever was.

The more that is learned about Cavallini and the Roman school of painting, the more Vasari's assertion that Florence was the sole inspiration for the Renaissance looks misleading. The debate is complicated by the fact that not all Renaissance artists working in Florence were born or bred there. In fact, while the debate still rages among patriots of Rome and Florence, the truth may be that the Renaissance was born when Giotto di Bondone first saw the face of an angel, painted by the hand of Pietro Cavallini.

AWAKENING THE SENSES *The Dream of the Palace* from the frescoes in the Upper Church of San Francesco in Assisi is attributed to Giotto. It shows his figurative style and penetrative observation in the hand poised to rouse the saint, but some scholars now believe it may have been painted by Cavallini.

MAGNA CARTA
A charter of noble self-interest

It is often said that the right to trial by jury goes back to Magna Carta, but in fact this clause only meant that people should be tried in courts composed of their social equals. Trial by jury in criminal cases did not exist in 1215.

Magna Carta is seen as the first step towards democracy, but it won little if any benefit for England's landless serfs and villeins. Close analysis shows that it was a smokescreen to hide the motives of the self-serving nobility.

From all over the world visitors come to the British Library to inspect a piece of parchment covered with line after line of Latin written in faded brown ink. Why so much interest in a nondescript document written in a dead language? Because this is Magna Carta – the most famous document in English history and one revered in Africa, America, Asia and Australasia as much as in Britain. People who prize liberty and democracy think of Magna Carta as the foundation-stone of the values they cherish, and they look upon the English barons who in 1215 forced King John to agree to the terms of the 'great charter' as our first champions of freedom.

UNHAPPY REIGN **King John's rule was marked by foreign military defeats and domestic unpopularity. After being driven out of Normandy by Philip of France in 1204 he acquired the nickname 'Softsword'.**

The free and the unfree

But this is to succumb to the myth of Magna Carta. The barons were not fighting for democracy. True, they made King John grant Magna Carta 'to all the free men of our realm and their heirs for ever' (Clause 1). But the term 'free men' meant something quite specific. English society during the reign of King John was divided into two classes: the free and the unfree. The unfree, who were known as serfs or villeins, made up about half of the total population. They were peasant farmers at the beck and call of their landlords, the lords of the manors of England.

The barons were the richest of the manorial lords and they had no intention of dismantling the fundamental social divide on which their own power rested. So although villeins are mentioned in Magna Carta, it was not for them. There is nothing in it about the rights of man, only the rights of 'free men'.

In 1215 England was dominated by a few dozen baronial families, each of whom had dozens of manors. The king's job was to prevent this small elite from fighting among themselves, and to retain their loyalty.

The rebels' reward

John, by the grace of God King of England, Lord of Ireland, Duke of Normandy and Aquitaine… grants the Magna Carta. But to whom? The charter lists the following: his archbishops, bishops, abbots, earls, barons, justiciaries, foresters, sheriffs, stewards, servants, bailiffs and loyal subjects. Careful interpretation of each clause of the Magna Carta shows that every single one of the 63 directly benefits the aristocratic or landed classes – except for two that pertain to the Church and one stating that all fish weirs are to be removed.

If the heir of one of our tenants has been in wardship, when he comes of age he shall have his inheritance without having to pay a relief.

While an heir was under age, the king 'looked after' his estates – and pocketed the revenues. So making an heir pay inheritance tax seemed unjust. When Magna Carta was reissued after John's death, this was given more precision. An heir, it said, came of age at 21.

No free man can be made to pay a heavy fine for a trivial offence, and even for a serious offence the fine imposed must not deprive him of his livelihood. …In the same way a fine imposed on a villein must not deprive him of the means to carry on farming.

This is the only clause in which villeins are mentioned. It would not have been in the interests of manorial lords to have villeins who were unable to work efficiently for them.

We will restore lands, castles, liberties and rights to anyone from whom we have unjustly taken them….If any disagreement arises about this, let it be settled by the judgement of the 25 barons.

This clause demonstrates that by 'liberties and rights' the barons meant privileges and property rights. By insisting that disputes should be decided by the 25, the rebels reveal just how central this was to the quarrel with King John.

The barons shall choose 25 of their number who with all their might shall ensure that the peace and liberties granted by our charter are properly observed and maintained…Anyone in the land who wishes may take an oath to obey the 25.

Because the rebels did not trust John to keep his word, they had this clause written into the 1215 charter. Its effect was to destroy the sovereignty of the crown. The clause was dropped from all subsequent reissues.

Pope Innocent III had a difficult relationship with John. After a disagreement over the appointment of the Archbishop of Canterbury in 1209, John was excommunicated. But the pope aided John in 1215 by declaring Magna Carta void.

John was the son of Henry II and Eleanor of Aquitaine. He came to the throne in 1199 as the ruler of the most powerful state in Europe. But by 1204 he had lost Normandy, Anjou and a large part of the Aquitaine to Philip II of France, his great rival. After 1204 John stayed mostly in England. Here too he failed dismally, and Magna Carta is the record of his failure.

The Great Charter contains 63 clauses dealing with all manner of grievances against the king's government. Some of these clauses are famous, for example: 'To no one will we sell, to no one deny or delay justice'. But this is clause 40. It is the early clauses that tell us what the rebels cared about most. Fourteen of the first 15 deal with taxation and with the property rights of wealthy landowners and their widows. These early clauses were the squeals of rich men who had been squeezed hard by King John, and were often deeply in debt to him. Traditionally the king had the right in time of war to demand help in the form of money and service, especially military service, from these landowners – they were, after all, his tenants.

But John had gone way beyond tradition. Landowners had to pay a kind of inheritance tax known as a 'relief'. Magna Carta fixed the rate of relief for a barony at £100, whereas John had been imposing reliefs of hundreds, even thousands, of pounds. He imposed taxes, especially the war-tax known as 'scutage', more frequently and at much higher rates than his predecessors.

Revolt of the barons

John's exchequer had been bringing in vast amounts of money. During the rule of Henry II and Richard the Lionheart – John's father and older brother – revenue had averaged £20,000-£25,000 a year. For the years 1210 to 1212 John's Exchequer averaged about £64,000, which is a phenomenal rise in the amount of money the king was taking from his subjects.

It wasn't only the barons who suffered. John was accused of violent extortion against a wealthy Jew of Bristol, who had suffered the daily removal of a tooth until he agreed to pay more than £6000. But it was the barons who had the power to do something about the situation, and some of them had other grievances.

No matter how much money John raised, he still could not win his wars. In 1214, in a bid to recover his dominions in France, he spent nearly all the money he had accumulated, but his troops – in his absence – were defeated by Philip in a great battle at Bouvines in north-east France. Despite his poor record as a war leader, John continued to press for payment of a heavy scutage. There was a widespread refusal to pay, and discontent was turning into a co-ordinated rebellion.

But the rebels had their problems too. Why should other people join them, risking life and limb, if the leading rebels were fighting only for their own private interests? They needed a cause. Opponents of an incumbent king usually claim to be

The common clauses

Only two clauses were of direct benefit to the lowest strata of society – the landless labourers. The first stated that no man, including villeins, could be punished by being deprived of the means of his livelihood, and that such fines or punishments had to be imposed by the oath of honest men of the neighbourhood. The second required that 'all subjects of the realm' enjoyed the 'customs and liberties' that Magna Carta had outlined. Although this clause attempted to guarantee that everyone felt the benefits of the treaty there was no stated means by which it could be enforced.

fighting for someone else's legitimate rights, usually another member of the royal family. But in 1215 there was no prince whose discontent could serve as a focus for revolt. John's own sons were much too young to play this role. So John's enemies invented a new kind of focus for rebellion, a programme of reform.

For all the freemen

They could not afford to be identified with a programme which suited only themselves. They drew up a charter of liberties which contained something for 'all the freemen of the realm', that is to say for people of substance in country and in town, whose support they were bidding for. If they could not fight for the rights of a prince they would fight instead for the rights of what they called 'the community of the land' (Clause 62).

This programme soon won a decisive victory. The city of London opened its gates to a rebel force in May 1215, and John realised he would have to play for time and pretend to make major concessions. On June 15 he agreed terms at Runnymede and set his seal on the final draft of the charter.

Magna Carta was meant to be a peace treaty between king and barons, but it failed. Within three months civil war had broken out again. The pope declared the charter void, and threatened to excommunicate anyone who observed it. This did not stop John's enemies. They appealed for outside help and were joined by the rulers of Scotland and Wales.

Reverting to the old style of revolt, the rebels now named another claimant as the rightful king: Louis, heir to the throne of France.

The Magna Carta looked doomed, but what revived it was John's own death in October 1216. His heir, Henry III, was only nine years old. Some of the nobles rallied behind this young prince and issued a revised Magna Carta. The opposing rebels soon gave up the fight, and in 1217 Louis returned to France.

The barons revised Magna Carta yet again, and once more in 1225. All these reissues kept Magna Carta alive, and people came to think of it as a touchstone of good government.

The charter of 1225 remained on the Statute Book for more than 600 years – even today three of its clauses are still part of the law of the land. Although Magna Carta actually did nothing for the common man, and said very little about democratic rights, it came to be seen as a powerful symbol of the struggle against tyranny.

The English poet Rudyard Kipling summed up the popular image of Magna Carta in his poem, 'What Say the Reeds of Runnymede?'

At Runnymede, at Runnymede,
Your rights were won at Runnymede
No freeman shall be fined or bound
Or dispossessed of freehold ground
Except by lawful judgment found.

It is a fine poetic vision of the birth of British democracy, but as a piece of history it is utterly false.

UNDER PRESSURE **Faced with widespread baronial revolt, King John had little option but to agree to Magna Carta. Popular engravings of later centuries showed him reluctantly put pen to paper at Runnymede, a meadow on the banks of the River Thames.**

FARCE AT THE WINTER PALACE
The true story of how the Russian Revolution took place

The Great October Socialist Revolution, which brought the Bolsheviks to power in Russia, would pass into history as a popular uprising that won a bloody yet heroic victory. In fact it was a chaotic coup d'état – and it went almost unnoticed even while it was happening.

FEEBLE DEFENCE There was scant military resistance to the Bolshevik Revolution. In Petrograd, Imperial Horse Guards quickly vacated their barracks, leaving the streets clear for the Red Guards.

October 24, 1917, was a quiet night in Petrograd. Actors on the theatre stage finished their performances and received their measure of applause. Waiters bustled from table to table. Audiences and diners went home, as usual, by tram. In one district of the city the only event reported by the police was the arrest of two drunken soldiers. Factory workers slept soundly after a long day and rose early for the next.

If Soviet legend is to be believed, they missed an event of monumental importance. Tens of thousands of soldiers and workers – countless numbers of them dying for the cause – stormed the Winter Palace and won a fierce battle against heavily armed government troops. It was a victory inspired by Vladimir Lenin, the leader of the Bolsheviks, and driven by the will of the proletariat. It was the workers' finest hour.

The truth is rather different. Where history insists on a popular triumph unmatched in the 20th century, the facts record only a farcically mismanaged military coup that succeeded despite the almost comical incompetence of its leaders.

The subsequent revision of the event as a glorious uprising against a bourgeois government was written into Soviet history as pure fact. School textbooks described heroic deeds that never took place. Through the sheer force of its conviction the account was largely accepted in the West and rarely questioned. Not until the collapse of communism in Russia did the real story emerge.

The October events came at the end of a tumultuous year for Russia. In March, violent bread riots in Petrograd and a string of defeats for the Russian troops fighting in the First World War had led to the abdication of Tsar Nicholas II. The 300-year-old Romanov dynasty was replaced by a new Provisional Government, whose leader since July had been the liberal revolutionary Alexander Kerensky. The government's reluctance to disengage from the war had caused widespread unrest and defections from the army. Russia's political parties bickered among themselves. The Bolshevik party alone lobbied for an end to the war. But meanwhile they recruited their own army of Red Guards and planned – optimistically – to seize power when the revolutionary moment was right.

Great October

The date they set was October 24, and they intended to finish the job by midday. But the revolt simply failed to materialise, and Kerensky's ministers were still meeting in the afternoon at the Winter Palace – no longer the royal residence but now the seat of government. Lenin falsely told a crowded meeting of the Petrograd Soviet that the Provisional Government had already fallen. In fact it would not surrender for another 11 hours, as the Bolsheviks' battle plan disintegrated into chaos. First, some of their essential fighting

men – sailors from the Baltic fleet – failed to arrive in time. And then their heavy guns wouldn't fire.

The plan had been to bombard the Winter Palace with artillery from the Peter and Paul fortress on the far bank of the Neva River, which the rebels had occupied. But the Bolshevik commander of the fortress, G.I. Blagonravov, soon found he had to think again. 'The guns standing formidably on the parapets,' he would write later, 'were not fit to be fired and were emplaced solely for better appearances.' The only one that worked was a muzzle-loaded cannon that was fired to signal the hour. In place of the rusted museum pieces,

RED HERRING This heroic image of the storming of the Winter Palace reflects the Soviet view of the revolution. But everything about it, from the size of the army to the warlike assault of a well-defended building, is fanciful and unhistoric.

STANDING FIRM The leader of the Provisional Government, Alexander Kerensky, stayed at his desk for much of the Russian Revolution, while Bolshevik forces outside struggled to find working artillery.

Blagonravov's men hauled out a battery of three-inch guns which they found standing in a courtyard. At the same time Blagonravov himself went off in search of gunners to fire them.

It had been agreed that a red lantern would be hoisted on a flagpole to signal the battery's readiness for action. The cruiser *Aurora*, moored in the Neva, would then fire its guns into the air to encourage the government to surrender. If this didn't work, the fortress gunners would fire directly upon the Winter Palace. Finally, if there were still no surrender, the *Aurora*'s guns would join the bombardment.

Blagonravov's day of misery, however, showed no sign of improvement. 'A small unforeseen circumstance disrupted our plan,' he wrote. 'There was no lantern for the signal.' After a long search a light was

REPLAYING HISTORY Fake pictures of the Revolution circulated worldwide after 1920. They had been taken at the outdoor production *Storming of the Winter Palace*, which involved 8000 actors and 500 musicians.

eventually found, but it was not red and they repeatedly failed to find any way of raising it on the flagpole. Life in the city meanwhile continued with almost mocking normality. 'The trolleybuses with their sharp bells and racket stretched in a row across the Trinity Bridge, and cars and the figures of pedestrians shone there,' Blagonravov recalled. 'Nothing hinted at the October battle.' Things were soon to get even worse:

The second lieutenant came to meet us and reported that they could not fire the guns since they were out of order – they had rusted through, and there was not a drop of oil in the recoil mechanisms, and at the first shot they could blow up.

Delay and frustration

On the way to inspect the battery for himself, Blagonravov fell into puddles and became lost in the fortress's maze of passageways. When he did eventually reach the guns it was only to recognise the truth of what he had been told. 'Firing the guns was undoubtedly associated with tremendous risk. What to do?

Could we find a comrade who knew how to fire the guns and would sacrifice his life for the revolution?'

As it happened, none of this mattered much. Kerensky had already left the Winter Palace to try to recruit military reinforcements, and those remaining had little idea of how to defend the building and little stomach for a fight. If the delays in attack were frustrating for the Bolsheviks – Lenin was said to be pacing like a lion in a cage, screaming at his commanders – they were terrifying for the defenders.

By early evening the forces within the Winter Palace, which hitherto had been packed with troops like a barracks, were reduced to just 300 men. Fear played its part, but so did hunger – there was little food left in the palace and many of the men headed for the city's restaurants. The remainder kept up a sporadic exchange of small arms fire with the Bolsheviks outside.

The reality was that at any time the Bolsheviks could have walked without serious challenge through the palace's flimsy defences and forced the Provisional Government to surrender. Instead they clung to the wreckage of their assault plan and so delayed the moment of victory until the early hours of the next morning.

At 6.30pm they sent the government an ultimatum – surrender or face bombardment from the Peter and Paul fortress and the *Aurora*. Though unaware that the fortress's guns were inoperable, or that the *Aurora* had no live ammunition, the ministers continued to hold out, fortified by the hope that Kerensky would reappear at any moment with a column of loyal troops. At 9pm the *Aurora* let off a salvo of blanks. At 11pm the fortress, having at last recruited enough gunners willing to risk their lives, fired between 30 and 35 rounds of live ammunition.

But the gunners' bravery was not matched by their accuracy. Only two shells struck glancing hits on the palace, resulting in a chipped cornice and a broken window. It was of no account. By this time the only defenders remaining inside were a company of women – the grandiosely named Death Battalion – and a few teenage cadets.

Inside the palace

The gunfire from within the palace soon stopped altogether. The sailors and Red Guards climbed in through open windows and walked through the unlocked gates, followed by a mob of looters. The last few ignominious moments of the Provisional Government were vividly described by the minister of justice, P.N. Maliantovich:

One could hear sharp, excited sounds of a mass of voices, a few isolated shots, the stamping of feet, some pounding, movements, the commingled, mounting, integrated chaos of sounds and the ever-mounting fear... Defence was useless; victims would be sacrificed in vain.

An officer rushed in, snapped to attention and saluted: did the ministers want the cadets to fight to the last man? Maliantovich recorded the horrified response of the cabinet: 'No need for this! It would be useless! No bloodshed! Surrender!'

And that was that. At 2.10am they were all arrested and taken to prison. There had been no heroic storm of workers; just a bungled military coup and the acquiescent arrest of unarmed politicians. The total number of deaths was five, mostly caused by random bullets. Revolutions need heroes, however, and the new Bolshevik government made sure it got them.

In 1920 a huge theatrical spectacle, *The Storming of the Winter Palace*, was enacted in front of the Winter Palace itself before an audience of 100,000. Grainy photographs of the 'assault' were later passed off as pictures of the revolution itself. The illusion was compounded in 1927 when the Soviet filmmaker Sergei Eisenstein made his silent classic *October*, which was filled with pseudo-historical images of workers battling for victory.

> By this time the only defenders of the Winter Palace were a company of women and a few teenage cadets.

AMBIGUOUS IMAGES

Ever since photographs first appeared in newspapers, images have been used as powerful tools for reporting news about current affairs. In the early days it was widely assumed that the camera never lied, but a closer examination of the evidence reveals a different kind of truth.

We now know that seeing is not – or at least should not be – believing. Photographs and films can be doctored or deliberately misrepresented for propaganda purposes. People and objects can be added to or removed from film and no one need ever know the difference unless they have seen the original image. Photographs should be regarded with the same degree of scepticism as any other form of evidence.

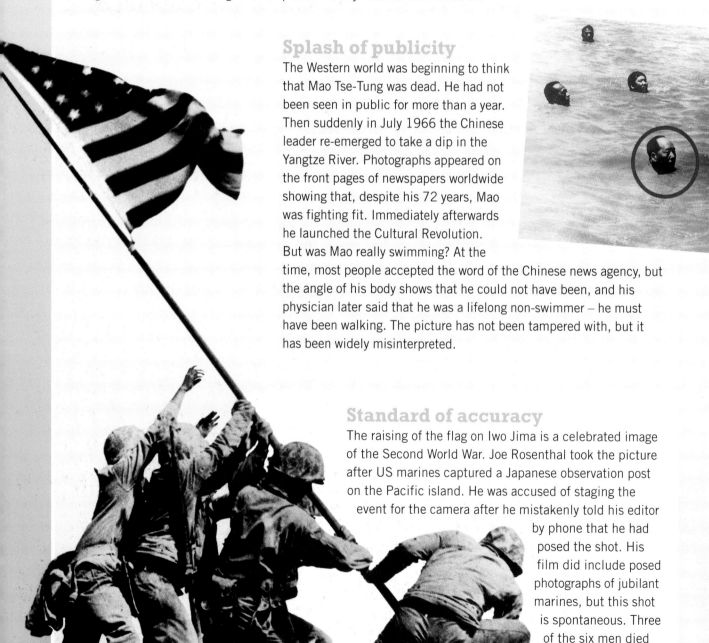

Splash of publicity

The Western world was beginning to think that Mao Tse-Tung was dead. He had not been seen in public for more than a year. Then suddenly in July 1966 the Chinese leader re-emerged to take a dip in the Yangtze River. Photographs appeared on the front pages of newspapers worldwide showing that, despite his 72 years, Mao was fighting fit. Immediately afterwards he launched the Cultural Revolution. But was Mao really swimming? At the time, most people accepted the word of the Chinese news agency, but the angle of his body shows that he could not have been, and his physician later said that he was a lifelong non-swimmer – he must have been walking. The picture has not been tampered with, but it has been widely misinterpreted.

Standard of accuracy

The raising of the flag on Iwo Jima is a celebrated image of the Second World War. Joe Rosenthal took the picture after US marines captured a Japanese observation post on the Pacific island. He was accused of staging the event for the camera after he mistakenly told his editor by phone that he had posed the shot. His film did include posed photographs of jubilant marines, but this shot is spontaneous. Three of the six men died fighting on the island.

Spot the difference

A photographer recorded Soviet leader Vladimir Lenin addressing troops in Sverdlov Square, Moscow, in 1920 during the Russian Civil War. On the podium to his left is Leon Trotsky, another founding father of the Russian Revolution, then commissar of war.

After the death of Lenin in 1924, Joseph Stalin became leader of the Soviet Union and Trotsky fell from favour. The photograph was reissued but in a revised version, from which Trotsky and the man on his left are absent. Photographic archives made public since the fall of the Soviet Union in 1991 have revealed that thousands of other enemies of the state were airbrushed out of history in this way.

Little local colour

In 2000 two American universities admitted that photographs of their students had been doctored to ensure that the intake looked multi-racial.

The cover of the University of Wisconsin at Madison's admissions brochure featured the face of an ethnic minority student who had not appeared in the original photograph. The University of Idaho removed from its website a picture of eight students – six white, one Asian and one black – after it was revealed that the faces of the last two had been pasted over those of white students.

These adjustments were exposed only when people who were really in the pictures realised what had been done – the work was otherwise undetectable. In the digital age, can we trust any published image to represent the truth?

UNHOLY CRUSADERS
Mass murder in the name of God

We still think of the Crusades as a broadly noble undertaking. The Crusaders, we believe, were idealists who fought for their faith. But their actions were stained by ignorance, bigotry and indiscriminate cruelty on a terrifying scale.

NO SANCTUARY The siege of Jerusalem, shown as a heroic battle in a 15th-century manuscript, came to a bloody end. Even many of the frightened citizens who fled to holy refuges were slaughtered by the rampaging Crusaders.

The soldiers of Christ entered Jerusalem on July 15, 1099, after a siege of more than a month. The Muslim governor's surrender was accepted, and he was allowed to march out of the city with his troops.

Then the slaughter began. Killing was without regard to age, sex or religion. The Crusaders did not even spare Oriental Christians, because they could not distinguish them in language or appearance from Muslims. On July 16 the soldiers broke into the huge mosque of Al Aqsa, which had already surrendered to another Crusader – Tancred, the Christian prince of Antioch – and was flying his banner. All the Muslims sheltering inside were put to the sword. Jews taking refuge in the main synagogue were burnt alive as it was razed to the ground. Survivors of the massacre were employed to dispose of the heaps of corpses that filled the squares and streets of the Holy City, but six months later Jerusalem still stank of death.

This was the bloody culmination of the First Crusade. The attackers admitted to killing 10,000 people, while one Muslim chronicler claimed that 70,000 died in the sanctified part of the city that included the Al Aqsa mosque. Modern historians estimate that the Crusader army killed around 40,000 unarmed civilians, or 80 per cent of the city's population.

Sign of the cross

If the First Crusade were to happen today, we would view it as an act of genocide. But the fact that we are separated from the slaughter of July 1099 by the passage of 1000 years means that many of us do not look back on the Crusades as the barbarous acts they were. The word Crusade now usually has positive overtones that bear no relation to historical events.

Not that anyone in Christendom condemned the First Crusade at the time. The Crusaders saw the sack of Jerusalem as a glorious victory, a testament to their faith and perseverance. 'Now that our men had possession of the walls and towers, wonderful sights were to be seen,' wrote the chronicler Raymond d'Aguilers. He continued:

> *Some of our men cut off the heads of their enemies; others shot them with arrows, so that they fell from the towers; others tortured them longer by casting them into the flames. Piles of heads, hands and feet were to be seen in the streets of the city. In the Temple and Porch of Solomon, men rode in blood up to their knees and bridle reins. Indeed, it was a just and splendid judgment of God that this place should be filled with the blood of unbelievers, since it had suffered so long from their blasphemies.*

D'Aguilers and his fellows had no doubt that they were doing God's will – as expressed three years earlier by Christ's representative on Earth, the pope. On November 27, 1095, Urban II had spoken in colourful and often violent language of the oppression of the Christian churches in the east.

But the pope's call to arms was motivated by politics as much as religion. Jerusalem had been in Muslim hands for more than 450 years, and Oriental Christians had rarely been persecuted. The pope was responding to a request for help from the Christian Byzantine Emperor Alexius I, whose lands in Anatolia were under threat from the Muslim Seljuk Turks. So, with promises of rich earthly rewards as well as heavenly ones, Urban urged his listeners to free the Holy City from Muslim rule:

> *With earnest prayer I, or rather the Lord, exhort you as heralds of Christ to urge men of all ranks, knights as well as foot soldiers, rich and poor, to hasten to exterminate this vile race from our lands…*

To those who would go in a spirit of true devotion he promised that joining the expedition would count as a penance for all their sins. To many of his listeners this was tantamount to a promise that when they died they would go straight to heaven.

So successfully did he stir his audience that there and then many

SEAL OF APPROVAL **William of Tyre's** *Latin History of the Crusades* **(illustration, below) of the 12th century became the main source for later Western accounts. The** *History* **did not fully describe the sheer desperation of the assaults on Antioch and Jerusalem. At Antioch, about half the Crusader army starved to death in the cold winter.**

'took the cross' – pieces of cloth cut into the shape of a cross were fastened to their shoulders as signs that they had sworn to go on crusade. Many thousands more joined as the pope and bishops sent out preachers among the people.

Waves of invaders

Some Crusaders must have been driven by the thought of plunder as much as by promises of glory and a passport to heaven. To those who were suffering famine after a run of bad harvests in parts of France and Belgium, the very word Jerusalem would have offered the allure of plenty: the heavenly city with its gates of sapphire.

It is not possible to say exactly how many set out on the long march east – a journey of three years. But to the Byzantine princess, Anna Comnena, who saw them pass through Constantinople, it seemed as though they outnumbered the grains of sand on the shore or the stars of heaven.

Pope Urban had decided that the Crusade should start in August 1096, but thousands of the poor would not wait so long. An unruly multitude, including women and children, set off on a 'People's Crusade' of their own. They were encouraged along their way by Peter the Hermit, an

electrifyingly eloquent preacher, who claimed that he had a letter from heaven in which God told him that Christians would, if they only dared to try, drive the heathen from the Holy Places. After reaching Constantinople and crossing the Bosporus, Peter and his poorly armed followers entered Turkish territory, where they were soon wiped out.

Other rag-tag groups followed in Peter's wake from England, France and Flanders. They had nothing in the way of supplies or backing and resorted to plundering the Rhineland towns they passed through such as Cologne and Mainz. The Jews who lived here provided the obvious target as they were not fellow Christians. With the encouragement of politically motivated regional leaders such as the notorious Count Emico of Mainz, looting soon turned to massacre. The atrocities committed in the Rhineland were the first in the long history of pogroms in Europe.

These murderous bands were soon followed by organised contingents led by noblemen such as the ambitious brothers Godfrey and Baldwin of Bouillon and the pious Robert of Flanders. The most prominent was Raymond of Toulouse – a 55-year-old veteran who had fought against the Muslims in Spain. Such men had experience of planning campaigns and were able to raise the money to supply properly equipped forces.

The first rendezvous was at Constantinople. From the moment they crossed the Black Sea in the spring of 1097 the Crusader knights faced huge obstacles. There were long marches through difficult terrain in enemy-held territory; the heat of the summer; shortages of water and food; Turkish towns and strongholds such as Nicaea (modern Iznik) which had to be besieged; Muslim armies to overcome in battle.

HOLY RHETORIC The 15th-century painter Jean Fouquet depicted Pope Urban II preaching the First Crusade at Clermont in 1095. Below him sits Philip I of France, although he was not present. It was not until the Third Crusade that European monarchs embraced the idea of crusading.

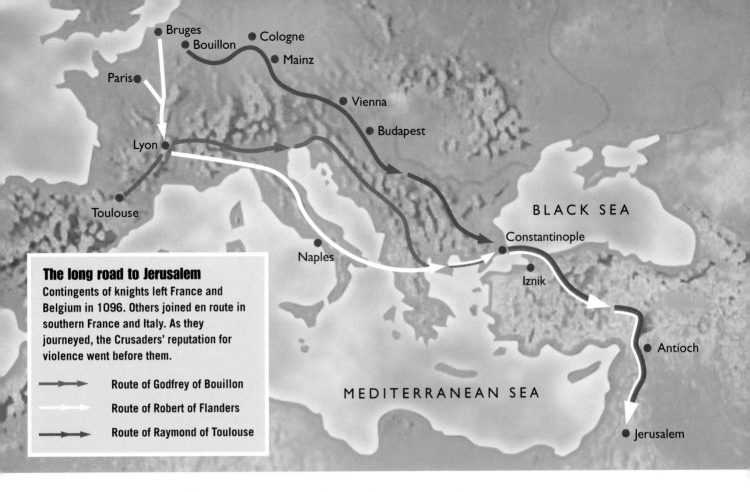

The long road to Jerusalem

Contingents of knights left France and Belgium in 1096. Others joined en route in southern France and Italy. As they journeyed, the Crusaders' reputation for violence went before them.

→ Route of Godfrey of Bouillon

→ Route of Robert of Flanders

→ Route of Raymond of Toulouse

But by October 1097, after a long, hard slog through Anatolia, the Crusaders reached Antioch. This great fortress-city held them up until June 1098. Many Crusaders starved to death outside the city walls. Some kept alive by turning cannibal. Many more deserted. And no sooner had they taken Antioch than they were themselves besieged by a much larger Muslim army.

Strength of the faith

In the midst of this crisis, one among a number who experienced visions of Christ and the saints was Peter Bartholomew. He said that St Andrew had shown him where the Holy Lance – used to pierce Christ's side on the cross – lay buried. When a lance was duly unearthed, the soldiers, inspired, sallied forth to break the siege.

Then came Jerusalem, and what has come to be seen as one of the saddest episodes in history. Once again heat, hunger and the knowledge that a large Muslim army was on its way from Egypt reduced the Crusaders to desperate straits. They spent a month hauling timber 70km (40 miles) to build siege towers. As many as

35,000 had died along the way, so that no more than 15,000 were camped outside the huge walls. It seemed that only God could help them now.

A priest claimed that he had seen a vision telling that they could not enter the Holy City until they had humbled themselves before God. On July 8, to the astonishment of the besieged, the army turned itself into a barefoot procession of pilgrims, solemnly winding around the walls behind chanting priests. The horrifying bloodbath that followed seven days later was born out of this religious fanaticism and the intoxicating relief of a victory at the journey's end, after three years of unrelenting self-imposed pressure on mind and body.

The men who hacked and stabbed their way through Jerusalem must surely have held it to be a miracle that they had come this far. They believed passionately, faithfully, in the literal truth of their battle cry: 'Dieu li volt!' – 'God wills it!'

No wonder the Scottish historian David Hume called the Crusades 'the most signal and durable monument to human folly that has yet appeared in any age or realm'.

UNLOCKING THE ENIGMA
The secret weapon that won the Second World War

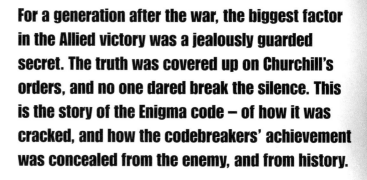

> **The German ships were being sent to the bottom like hulks at target practice.**

For a generation after the war, the biggest factor in the Allied victory was a jealously guarded secret. The truth was covered up on Churchill's orders, and no one dared break the silence. This is the story of the Enigma code – of how it was cracked, and how the codebreakers' achievement was concealed from the enemy, and from history.

Crews of German supply ships crossing the Mediterranean during 1941 and 1942 watched and listened with the heightened senses of hunted animals. Upon them rested the success of Erwin Rommel's swashbuckling tank campaign in the African desert. If the ships kept the supply lines open, then Germany's Panzers would succeed in their campaign to grind the British Eighth Army into the dust. If they did not, then even the dashing Rommel – starved of fuel and military hardware – would face defeat. The seamen's responsibility was immense.

Submarine hunt

But their nervousness, too, was well-founded. The British, no less than the Germans, were keenly aware of the ships' importance and were determined to hunt them down. The skies were thick with Allied aircraft, the seas infested with their submarines. Six of every ten Axis ships putting out from North Africa or the northern shore of the Mediterranean were being sunk. The Germans and Italians calculated that they faced a fleet of no fewer than 400 hunter submarines, guided from the air by a huge force of reconnaissance aircraft based on the island of Malta.

The facts, however, were very different. The huge air force contained just three aeroplanes. The entire 2.5 million km^2 (1 million square miles) of the Mediterranean were patrolled by only 25 submarines. And yet the ships with their precious supplies were being sent to the bottom like hulks at target practice. For British commanders the only question was how many ships they had time to sink each day, and in which order they should be torpedoed. How was it being done?

CRYPTIC KEYBOARD The Enigma machine looked like a bulky portable typewriter, but it could generate more than ten trillion combinations. No wonder the Germans thought their code was unbreakable.

KEY ERRORS Operators in the field and on U-boats unwittingly made it easy for Bletchley. They often began messages with formulaic phrases such as 'Heil Hitler'. For the codebreakers at Bletchley, knowing these ten letters could be the key to cracking an encrypted message.

The answer, one of the most closely guarded secrets of the war, would remain unknown for another 30 years. It had little to do with the command centres in Malta, Cairo or Algiers. Still less did it depend on luck, or even on military strategy. Indeed, the men responsible for it were so far removed from military discipline, so unwarlike in their dress and neglect of command structures that they were an offence to army sensibilities.

Many of them were derided as war-shy cowards or shirkers. And yet, if they did not directly win the war, they

certainly shortened it. Their hunting ground was not the sea, or the sky, but several unprepossessing huts in the grounds of Bletchley Park – code name Station X – a country house in Buckinghamshire. Their weapons were not bombs or torpedoes but instinct, imagination and logic.

Led by the dishevelled mathematical genius Alan Turing, these were the 'men of the professor type' (as they were described by Commander Alastair Denniston, director of the top secret Government Code and Cipher School) who cracked the ciphers that were used by the Germans in their Enigma encryption machines.

Through a system of rotors and cross-wirings, Enigma produced 17,576 substitution alphabets and automatically changed the code each time a letter-key was pressed. The Germans regarded the system as

> **Churchill called the workers at Bletchley Park 'the geese who laid the golden eggs and never cackled'.**

Campaigns won by stealth

The decryption of Enigma codes at Bletchley Park was critical for Allied success in two major theatres of war – the Mediterranean and the North Atlantic. In both places, supply ships were the targets.

In the North Atlantic, it was England's supply convoys that were the prey, and Germany's much feared *Unterseebooten*, or U-boats, were the predators. With huge merchant shipping losses, and national survival at stake, the British had to turn the tables on the U-boats, but without alerting the Germans that their navy's Enigma ciphers (code-named 'Ultra') had been broken.

The policy was not to destroy the submarines – too obvious a response – but to evade them and bomb their supply vessels. As a result, the U-boats intercepted fewer and fewer convoys. In May 1943, the British went on the offensive, destroying about a third of the U-boat fleet. Bletchley's trail was covered by a contrived story that the Allies had developed a new radar that worked underwater. By summer, the Germans gave up the fight, having only sunk a handful of convoy vessels.

Keeping decryption secret

In the Mediterranean, the roles were reversed and the ships were German. They were taking fuel and military hardware from Italy (then an Axis power) to troops fighting in North Africa. Three planes flying out of Malta – in the early 1940s, an island still holding out against the Nazis – were getting their target directions from Bletchley Park's cryptanalysts, who were intercepting German signals.

To preserve Bletchley's secret – and to encourage the misapprehension that British successes were due to a large number of reconaissance planes – no German vessel could be sunk until it had been observed by an aircraft. An easy-to-intercept signal was then sent by the air crew to confirm their sighting before an attack was made.

More than a thousand Allied convoy ships were sunk before the U-boat menace was finally crushed in 1943.

CANADA

Nova Scotia

Halifax

Operational U-boats numbered around 200, and they worked in groups of up to 40, known as 'wolf packs'.

---

impenetrable, so it was essential to the Allies that the enemy should never suspect their signals were being read by the Buckinghamshire 'professors'.

The tale of the Bletchley Park boffins has captured imaginations more than almost any other episode of the Second World War. But the shroud of secrecy around them was maintained long after VE Day. Amazingly, it was not until 1975 that those who fought and survived the war on the Allied side learned of the intelligence breakthrough that had saved many of their lives.

Yet while the staff of Bletchley Park deserved every word of the plaudits they received, there were others whose crucial contribution has not received the same attention.

First breakthrough

The foundations for Bletchley had actually been laid in Eastern Europe during the 1930s, when three brilliant young mathematicians from the University of Poznań were recruited to work for the Polish General Staff's code department. Marian Rejewski, Jerry Rózycki and Henryk Zylgaski spent the rest of the decade analysing encoded German messages.

Poland's precarious geographical position, between a resurgent Nazi

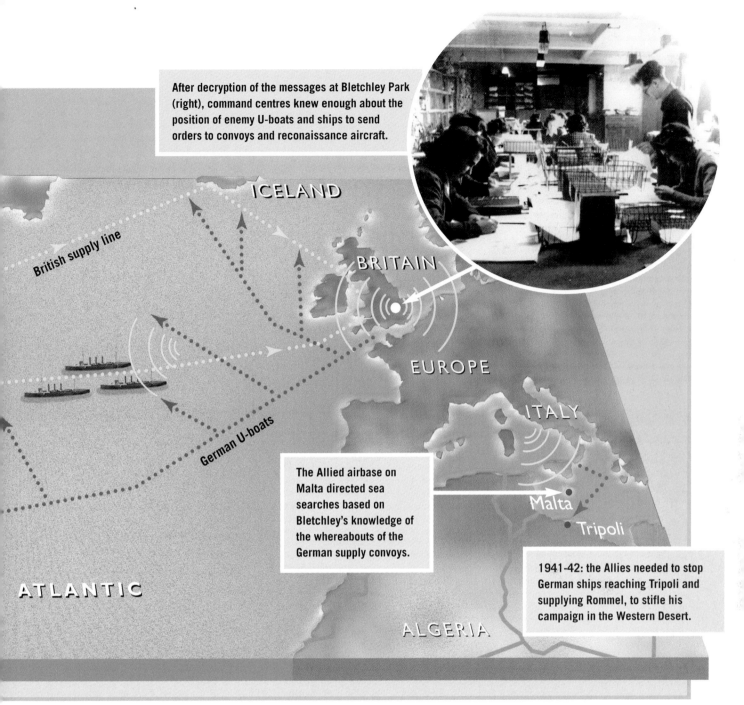

After decryption of the messages at Bletchley Park (right), command centres knew enough about the position of enemy U-boats and ships to send orders to convoys and reconaissance aircraft.

ICELAND

BRITAIN

EUROPE

British supply line

German U-boats

ITALY

Malta

Tripoli

The Allied airbase on Malta directed sea searches based on Bletchley's knowledge of the whereabouts of the German supply convoys.

1941-42: the Allies needed to stop German ships reaching Tripoli and supplying Rommel, to stifle his campaign in the Western Desert.

ATLANTIC

ALGERIA

Germany and a bellicose Stalinist Russia, had led them to place great emphasis on intelligence resources. They had received an unexpected boost in 1929, when a German package was wrongly directed to Poland. Alerted by a suspicious customs official, the Polish authorities opened it and found a working commercial Enigma machine. It was studied in minute detail, before being carefully re-wrapped and sent on to the correct destination. This postal sleight-of-hand allowed the Poles to build fully working replicas without the Germans having any idea that a

machine had fallen into their hands.

The difficulty was that the German Army used a different set of internal wirings on the rotors of their machines from the commerical versions. Through a combination of inspired guesswork and mathematical theory, Marian Rejewski was able to work out the wirings, so he and his two colleagues were now set the task of decrypting the messages.

The Germans' practice of starting messages with the settings they were using – to allow the intended recipient to decode them – gave the code-breakers opportunities to spot patterns in the different codes and

ALAN TURING
1912-1954

crack them. In this fashion the Poles enjoyed five years of intelligence supremacy, but by the end of the decade the Germans had increased the sophistication of the process. There were extra connections in the plugboard and more rotor wheels. Even worse, the settings were now being changed every single day. This daily setting change proved too great a demand on the Polish resources: they had to admit that Enigma had become unbreakable.

Under skies darkened by the threat of all-out war, the Poles handed over working models of the machine to the British and French in Warsaw in July 1939. These products of a decade's work provided Bletchley with a platform from which to begin their own assault on Enigma.

The baton passed

By late 1942, and after the capture of an Enigma codebook from a floundering U-boat in the eastern Mediterranean, Britain was able to read all the German messages. Another problem then arose. How could the British use this information without alerting their enemy to the vulnerability of their codes?

Undoubtedly, the greatest asset of the Allied intelligence charged with protecting the secret of the Enigma codebreakers was the Germans' own confidence in the security of their system. Even with English destroyers hunting down U-boats with unerring consistency, they simply did not believe that the Allies could break their ciphers.

As the number of decrypts from Bletchley rose to 90,000 a month, the Enigma decoders affected almost every aspect of the war. They helped British forces to minimise their losses in the withdrawal from Crete, and also represented immense value to the American and Russian allies. The Russians, however, unlike the Americans, were officially allowed only selected titbits of information passed through diplomatic channels and disguised to appear as the results of routine espionage.

Allied naval successes in the Mediterranean and Atlantic crucially accelerated the shifting balance of power after the Americans entered the war in December 1941, and almost certainly brought forward the Normandy landings.

Nobody can know precisely how many months or years the war would have continued without the intervention of Poland's code-crackers and Bletchley's professors – estimates vary between two and three years. But this would have been at crippling cost and catastrophic loss of life.

And then there is the very real possibility that, with an extended war, the triumph of America's science boffins – the atom bomb – might have been dropped on Berlin.

How Enigma worked

The code books

German code books gave 'set-up' strings of letters that were typed in at the start of each day. This meant that the Enigma would be coding in a different way each day. Without captured code books, Bletchley would not have had a chance to decrypt the messages.

The light board

Once a key was pressed, after a short delay a letter would light up on the second keyboard above the typewriter keys. This letter was noted down until the whole message was encrypted and ready for the signal operator to send.

The buttons

Enigma machines worked both ways: the operator receiving the message would key in the coded message and, letter by letter, the light board would show the original.

The rotors and plug board

Each rotor was wired internally and turned independently. Every time a button was pressed, the rotors moved round, recoding every letter differently. The wiring of the plug board gave an extra layer of encryption, and was reset differently each day, according to code books.

Rotors: wired to encrypt messages

Keyboard: typed messages are encrypted, letter by letter

Light board: to display encrypted messages

Plug board: circuitry to create an extra layer of encryption

How the codes were cracked

There were different Enigma codes in use by the German navy, army and submarines: each had their own code books. British 'Y stations', listening posts, intercepted and transcribed the signals, dating and labelling them. Bletchley dealt with thousands of signals every day, at first taking weeks to decrypt them but later, with code books and bombes, needing only hours.

Serial number, date and time of interception.

SC29/04/43 0140 7305 A783
RCU 0110/29/04/43 UDIF FWCM EGFS LFKZ QU

The initial three letters were not in code, but referred to the set-up of the rotors for that particular message. Each message was therefore encrypted differently.

Next came numerals that referred to the time and date of the message, followed by the message itself. The opening words often gave code breakers important clues or 'cribs' as they could be weather reports or greetings. Within the message were grid positions in written numbers and status reports.

DEATH
AND
DISASTER

MILLER'S CROSSING
The explanation for Glenn Miller's disappearance lay in the archives

Bandleader Glenn Miller was listed as missing when his plane failed to arrive in Paris. Severe weather was blamed, but one man said otherwise. He had seen the plane, he said, and he knew what had happened to it. Now the facts that prove him right have been unearthed.

FLYING LOW Major Glenn Miller was one of three men crossing the English Channel in a tiny aircraft. Overhead they would have heard the drone of more than a hundred Lancaster bombers returning from a mission over Germany.

Shortly after midday on Sunday, December 15, 1944, in the last months of the Second World War, a single-engine nine-seater aircraft took off from Twinwood in southern England, bound for Paris. On board were two American air force officers and Major Glenn Miller, the celebrated bandleader. The weather was clearing, but within a few minutes the plane disappeared into the clouds. It was never seen again.

Miller was on his way to newly liberated Paris to organise a Christmas concert for the troops. News of his disappearance spread rapidly, causing widespread dismay. The Glenn Miller Army Air Force Band was immensely popular, and the loss of its leader was a blow both to the troops in Europe and to the American public. Almost immediately wild rumours sprang up concerning his fate. Some suggested that he had been captured by the Nazis and tortured to death; others that his death had been covered up because it had occurred in a Parisian brothel.

With no distress signal, no word from the pilot on the radio, and no wreckage found, the bandleader's fate remained unknown for more than 50 years. But a 1984 South African television programme on Miller's death brought so many enquiries from his fans that the Air Historical Branch of the British Ministry of Defence decided to conduct an investigation.

The ministry called in Roy Nesbit, an aviation historian who had himself flown during the Second World War. Nesbit had the perfect credentials for such detective work. And buried within the logbooks and route maps kept at the Public Record Office in London, he found the reason for Miller's disappearance.

The Glenn Miller sound

From the moment he was given his first trombone at the age of 11, Glenn Miller adored playing music. He often quoted Duke Ellington's aphorism: 'It don't mean a thing if it ain't got that swing.'

By the age of 34, Miller had formed his own band and showcased his idea of having a clarinet lead the saxophone section. This distinctive and revolutionary 'Glenn Miller sound' quickly propelled him into the big time. With hits like 'Tuxedo Junction', 'In The Mood' and 'Pennsylvania 6-5000', the Glenn Miller Orchestra wowed audiences across America. In 1941, the orchestra's recording of 'Chattanooga Choo Choo' became the first million-selling gold disc in history.

But then came the war. After the Japanese attack on Pearl Harbor, Miller abandoned his career, disbanded his orchestra and joined the US Army. But his talent was immediately enlisted in the cause of troop morale: it was decided that he should organise the modernisation of the army band. The Glenn Miller Army Air Force Band was an instant success, giving more than 800 performances in one year, including 500 broadcasts to troops in Europe and Africa.

In June, 1944, a few days after D-Day, the band was shipped to England and quartered at the Sloane Court Hotel in Chelsea. As London was under nightly attack from doodlebugs, Miller decided to move the band to the comparative safety of Bedfordshire. The day after they moved, the Sloane Court was destroyed by a German bomb. But Miller's luck was not to last and his disappearance in December 1944 confounded attempts at explanation.

The first hint of what might have really happened came after the release of a successful biopic, *The Glenn Miller Story*, in 1956. After

SWING INTO ACTION Glenn Miller was a gifted trombonist, but as a band leader he introduced highly original arrangements, bringing precise syncopation and catchy harmony to the New Orleans jazz sound.

watching the film, a man called Fred Shaw came forward with the sensational claim that Miller's plane had been accidentally bombed by the Royal Air Force. On December 15, 1944, Shaw had been a navigator on a Lancaster bomber, one of a large formation returning from an aborted raid on Germany. Ordered to jettison their bombs over the Channel before landing, Shaw said he had seen a light aircraft, a Noorduyn Norseman, underneath them and that it had crashed into the sea. He remembered saying to the rear gunner: 'There's a kite gone in.' Only after seeing the movie did he fit together the dates and times and realise that it was probably Miller's plane.

Dangerous territory

Shaw was at first dismissed as a publicity seeker. There seemed to be significant holes in his story. How was it that he had happened to recognise a Canadian-built Norseman, one of only a handful operating in Britain? How was it that the Norseman had strayed into the dangerous territory of the 'jettison zone', where returning Allied aircraft with bombs still aboard always released their loads? Most damning of all was that the times did not add up – the records indicated that the Lancasters began dumping their bombs at 1.40pm, whereas Miller's Norseman did not take off from Twinwood until 1.55pm.

But not everyone disbelieved Shaw's theory. Nesbit was swayed by the testimony of his companions in the Lancaster, who attested to his honesty although they could not confirm his story. The only crew members who, according to Shaw, had also seen the plane dive into the sea – bomb aimer Ivor Pritchard and gunner Harry Fellows – were both dead. But with the number of discrepancies in the story, how could it be true?

One matter of doubt was easily cleared up. Nesbit established that Shaw would have been able to recognise Miller's plane because he

All flights grounded by fog

At Twinwood airbase in Bedfordshire, poor weather and low visibility prevented any aircraft taking off on the morning of Sunday, December 15, 1944. Major Miller could have delayed by a day – his orders from General Eisenhower were to leave 'on or about December 16' – but the plane left for Paris at 13.55pm. Its time of departure was thought for many years to disprove the bombing theory until it transpired that the Lancasters were operating on Greenwich Mean Time, which was one hour different.

Twinwood airbase

London

'There's a kite gone in'

Miller's tiny plane was about half the size of a Lancaster. Its flat, rounded wings gave it a distinctive outline when viewed from above. The plane was a Noorduyn Norseman, a light aircraft that was in constant use in Canada where bomber navigator Fred Shaw was trained. He recognised the high-wing monoplane and saw it crash.

The Lancasters: homeward bound

With their mission to Siegen in Germany aborted, 139 RAF Lancasters were heading back to base in Norfolk. For safety reasons, they were not allowed to land with ordnance (bomb loads) on board, so returned via the jettison zone to drop them into the English Channel.

FRANCE

Beachy
Head

Safe air corridor

Jettison zone

ENGLISH CHANNEL

Danger spot

The jettison zone was a circular area 16km (10 miles) in diameter, located some 45km (30 miles) south of Beachy Head. It was not marked on official maps. Friendly shipping and Allied planes which traversed the Channel were briefed on the zone's position and avoided it. Air traffic was supposed to cross the Channel using the Supreme Headquarters Allied Expeditionary Forces (SHAEF) safe air corridor, a defined shuttle route that passed the jettison zone 10 miles to the east.

N

Date	Aircraft Type & Number	Crew	Duty	Time Up	Time Down	Details of Sortie or Flight	References
15th Dec.	Lancaster I "K" NF.973	F/O.V.H. Gregory, P/O.I.J. Pritchard, P/O.T.H. Shaw, Sgt.Thurman, D., Sgt.O'Hanlon, R.A., Sgt.Arnold, E.T., Sgt.Fellows, H.	Capt. Nav. A/B. F/E. W/Op. M/U. R/G.	11.37	14.20	Target: SEIGEN. Bomb load 1 x 4,000 HC.MINOL.2., 14 x 500lb. clusters 4lb. incend. Aircraft recalled.	
"	Lancaster I "L" HK.598	Signal. NZ.13228, F/S.Dodds, R. NZ.27836 NZ, P/O.S.R.McLaughlin, NZ.12405 NZ, Sgt.Cressey, ., F/O.Gibson, J. NZ.26152 NZ, Sgt.McCutcheon, W., Sgt.Jefferies, H.	Nav. A/B. W/Op. M/U. R/G.	11.29	12.55	Target: SEIGEN. Bomb load 1 x 4,000 HC.MINOL.2., 14 x 500 clusters 4 lb. incend.	
"	Lancaster I "M" HK.699	P/O.L.F.Robinson, NZ.210092 NZ, F/S.J. Cockerill, R190564, CAN, Sgt.Cullen, J., Sgt.Stubbs, L., Sgt.Birch, F., Sgt.Wheeler, J., Sgt.Coombs, C.	Capt. A/B. F/E. W/Op. M/U. R/G.	11.30	14.05	Target: SEIGEN. Bomb load 1 x 4,000HC.MINOL.2., 14 x 500lb. clusters 4lb. incend. Aircraft recalled.	
"	Lancaster I "N" PD.284	F/Lt.R.D.Davidson, F/S.Sharpe, R., Sgt.Crane, R., Sgt.Lay, D.J., Sgt.Owen, E.A., Sgt.Green, D.H., F/S.Prosser, L.	Capt. Nav. A/B. F/E. W/Op. M/U. R/G.	11.32	13.57	Target: SEIGEN. Bomb load 1 x 4,000HC.MINOL.2., 14 x 500lb. clusters 4 incend. Aircraft re...	

Date	Aircraft Type & Number	Crew
th Dec.	Lancaster I "K" NF.973	F/O.V.H. Gregory, P/O.I.J. Pritchard, P/O.T.H. Shaw, Sgt.Thurman, D., Sgt.O'Hanlon, R.A., Sgt.Arnold, E.T., Sgt.Fellows, H.
	Lancaster I	F/O.R.V. S...

had been trained in Manitoba, Canada, where the Norseman was commonly used by novice navigators.

But to check the feasibility of Shaw's and Miller's planes meeting over the Channel, Nesbit had to plot their flights. He was aided by the Air Historical Branch, who allowed him to photocopy the official file on Miller. Access to other files enabled Nesbit to pinpoint the location of the 'jettison zone', which was never marked on public maps. For the first time it could be placed alongside the flight path of the Norseman – they were about 10 miles apart.

Only a tiny misjudgment in navigation, a degree or so on the dial, could have taken Miller's plane into the jettison zone. The American Air Force records on the pilot, John Morgan, suggested this was a strong possibility. They showed that he had only recently qualified and, according to a fellow pilot Nesbit interviewed, he had little experience of flying with instruments in poor weather. He would have had to rely on a simple magnetic compass for the flight across the Channel and could easily have strayed off course.

Nesbit could now argue that the planes' paths had crossed, but still the time differential remained. Back in the Public Record Office, he scoured through the logs. Suddenly it became clear: the RAF was operating on Greenwich Mean Time. They always

did, to ensure the fixed position of the sun, moon, planets and stars. The American airbase at Methwold, Norfolk – where Fred Shaw's squadron flew from – was operating on local time. This meant a one-hour time difference because a special wartime Statutory Rule and Order (Defence) gave Britons an added hour of daylight during winter. Miller had in fact set off 45 minutes before the Lancasters reached the bomb zone – not 15 minutes afterwards. Fred Shaw's adamance and Roy Nesbit's persistence had been vindicated.

Thus it was that the little Norseman with Major Glenn Miller aboard was well into its trip across the Channel when the returning RAF Lancasters were ordered to begin dumping their bombs. Roy Nesbit is convinced that the Norseman, with an inexperienced pilot at the controls, and the world-famous musician in the back, headed directly under the lumbering giants as they began cranking open their bomb doors.

ON THE RECORD **The logbook kept at the American airbase in Norfolk, England, recorded the sortie made by the Lancaster in which Fred Shaw was the navigator. The landing time of 14.20 shows that the Lancasters would have been over the Channel at the same time as Glenn Miller's aircraft. The note 'aircraft recalled' shows that the planes returned without bombing and had to drop their loads in the jettison zone.**

Miller's last tunes

Two weeks before his death, Miller recorded at the Abbey Road Studios in London. Regular collaborators such as Sergeant Ray McKinley and the 'GI Sinatra', Sergeant Johnny Desmond, joined him to record what would become his last album. The tracklist comprised a mix of popular favourites played by the Army Air Force Band; unlike his pre-war band, it had a giant string section.

Miller had used rousing tunes throughout the war in his so-called 'Secret Broadcasts'. These broadcasts, specially commissioned by the US Office of War Information, were transmitted to Allied troops in enemy territory and were considered part of the war effort. Their ability to boost the soldiers' spirits was appreciated by the commanders of the US forces. As General Jimmy Doolittle put it: 'Next to letters from home, the Glenn Miller Army Air Force Band was the greatest morale builder we had in the European Theatre of Operations.'

ENDANGERED SPECIES
A natural disaster took humankind to the brink of extinction

Everyone assumes that from the earliest times humanity has enjoyed steady and inexorable population increase, but 70 millennia ago Homo sapiens very nearly died out.

About 3000 generations ago – a mere blink of an eye in the evolutionary timescale – the human population of Earth dwindled to the point where everyone on the planet could have fitted inside a small football stadium. Mounting DNA evidence indicates that the human population was reduced to perhaps fewer than 10,000. One study even suggests that the number of women dropped to just 500 individuals. For centuries, each new generation of *Homo sapiens* could easily have been the last.

The evidence for this population crisis (or 'bottleneck') lies within each and every one of us – in the DNA that we all carry. There is very little variation in the modern human gene pool, a fact that researchers recently sought to explain by tracing our genetic heritage back through time. The amount of variation that they measured pointed to a period when there can only have been a tiny number of procreating females in the species. Other DNA studies supported the finding and began to offer more certainty on its timing: the crisis had occurred around 70,000 years ago. After hundreds of thousands of years of evolution, the human species came close to falling at the final hurdle.

Global catastrophe
Although geneticists were able to pinpoint the scale and timing of the population crisis, they could not offer any explanation for it. In fact the reason for the collapse of our species might be right under our feet. Deposits of ash and debris have provided evidence for one of the most severe natural disasters in the history of life on Earth. It has been dated by palaeoclimatologists and geoscientists to exactly 71,000 years ago.

BARREN LANDSCAPE Geoscientists have found evidence of a very sudden shift in the world's climate, which happened recently in geophysical terms. It threw the Earth into a harsh volcanic winter: as many as three-quarters of the plants in the northern hemisphere perished and most existing humans died of hunger.

RUSSIA

ASIA

CHINA

The size of the eruption
Toba spewed 2800km³ of volcanic material into the atmosphere, making it the most violent eruption of the last two million years. Mount St Helens, the largest eruption in living memory, produced just 1km³ in 1980.

SAUDI
ARABIA

BORNEO

MALAYSIA

INDIA

Toba

SOUTH
CHINA
SEA

INDIAN
OCEAN

Raining ash
The cloud of ash ejected from the volcano billowed out westwards across the Indian Ocean as far as the Middle East. Deposits of ash 6m (20ft) thick have been found during archaeological digs in India.

SUMATRA

Dissection of a disaster

Toba was a catastrophe precisely because of the suddenness of the event. A more gradual climate change would have allowed people to adapt to the reduction in plant and animal life, but there was no warning of the destruction to come.

● Scientists calculate that Toba's plume would have been at least 30km (19 miles) high, double the height needed to bring about an alteration in global climate. The effects would have been felt across the world within days.

● Worse was to come: ratios of oxygen isotopes in cores – cross-sectional samples of the Earth's surface – reveal that summer temperatures dropped by as much as 12°C (22°F) in the wake of the eruption.

● As glaciers formed, the sea level dropped, baring a raw landscape where exposed soils could be whipped away by the wind. Calcium from the dispersed soil is found in glaciers in Greenland, showing that dust storms probably raged for days on end, killing plants and so depriving animals and humans of food.

Scars on the earth
The giant blast hole left by the Toba eruption is now the largest crater-lake in the world, with an average depth of 450m (1485ft). It is 100km (60 miles) long, with a coastline measuring nearly 300km (200 miles).

The cause of this disaster was the eruption of the Toba volcano on the Indonesian island of Sumatra. The largest volcanic explosion of the previous two million years, and one of the biggest of the past 450 million years, its effects were felt right across the Earth. The crater it left behind measured 100km (60 miles) across.

The big chill

The scale and impact of the explosion are recorded not just in the size of the crater but in the deposits of ash, sulphur and calcium found in rock and ice samples taken from locations as distant as Greenland, 11,000km (7000 miles) away.

The eruption itself appears to have lasted for about two weeks. It was followed by six years of 'volcanic winter', in which thick clouds of ash blocked out the sun. Then came at least a further thousand years of global cooling. Some early humans may have perished at once in the eruption, but the population crisis identified by the geneticists was almost certainly the result of the aftermath, when temperatures across the globe fell by up to 12°C (22°F).

The environment in which the human population lived became cooler and drier, sending many ecosystems spiralling into decline. Seeds would have failed to lodge and germinate; inadequate sunlight would have left plants weak and tasteless. Animals would have died in their thousands, leaving rotting carcasses of inedible meat strewn over the land.

Starving and desperate, the people would have found it hard to have children, let alone raise them. Wasted by severe famine, the children would have been the first to die, followed by the women. It was a crushing blow to our chances of survival.

Populations that had already dispersed from tropical and subtropical regions would probably have been wiped out by the cold. At higher latitudes the Neanderthals, while biologically adapted to harsh environments, seem to have shrunk in number and left northern Europe.

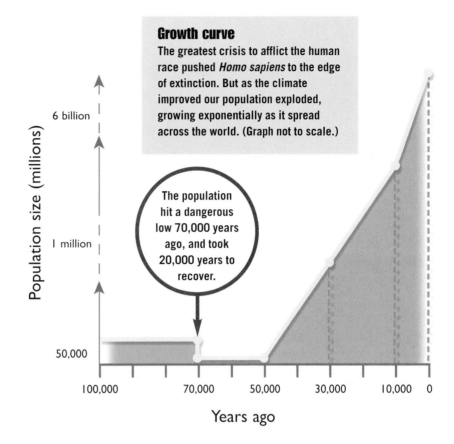

Growth curve
The greatest crisis to afflict the human race pushed *Homo sapiens* to the edge of extinction. But as the climate improved our population exploded, growing exponentially as it spread across the world. (Graph not to scale.)

The population hit a dangerous low 70,000 years ago, and took 20,000 years to recover.

Although population figures are not known for the period before the Toba disaster, it is certain that after the eruption our species fell dangerously close to extinction.

We could have been wiped out centuries before we started cave-painting or hunting woolly mammoths, leaving no greater mark on the world than the Neanderthals, or other extinct species that were once part of the family of the apes.

Weathering the storm
Homo sapiens survived because there were three tropical areas of high rainfall in the world, where the land was able to support larger numbers of people. All were in Africa, where there is archaeological evidence for human expansion after the crisis. Tools and carvings, dating from 70,000 years ago, indicate that developments in human behaviour occurred in Africa long before anywhere else.

We owe our very existence to those few populations that – through luck or ingenuity – managed to survive the geological disaster that killed the rest of our species.

TIME CAPSULE **Samples of ice taken from bore holes in the world's glaciers hold sulphur and ash deposits and telltale microbes, such as pollen. These can help to pinpoint the time of the Toba eruption and record how long its effects were felt across the world.**

ALL THE PRESIDENT'S PILLS
Abraham Lincoln's medicine drove him into fits of rage

Blue mass pills were a standard remedy in the 19th century, but their high mercury content could render the patient moody and prone to erratic behaviour. These mood swings were known to Lincoln's colleagues, but they had no idea that the pills were to blame.

MELANCHOLY MAN The early years of the great leader's life were marred by bereavement and extreme poverty. Even after he married and gained employment as a lawyer, he would be wracked by self-doubt.

There were two Abraham Lincolns. One was the 'Great Emancipator', a formidable statesman, compassionate, idealistic, patient, thoughtful, wise. The other, in the years before his inauguration in 1861, was melancholic, irascible, prone to mood swings, towering rages, fits of maniacal laughter and bizarre behaviour. Almost certainly Lincoln suffered from clinical depression, and he became accustomed to living with it. These bouts of mental illness were brought on by a series of tragic events in his early life. He himself wrote when president: 'I have been driven many times to my knees by the overwhelming conviction that I had nowhere else to go.' But his other option – a trip to the pharmacologist's – may have driven him much closer to the edge.

To counter his feelings of despair Lincoln took pills for hypochondriasis – the 18th-century name for paranoia and melancholia, often ascribed to bowel malfunction. Now that the toxic content of these pills can be scientifically assessed, a new and convincing explanation for Lincoln's peculiar outbursts is forthcoming.

Mercury and rose petals

John Todd Stuart, Lincoln's law partner of those early years and the cousin of Lincoln's wife, Mary, claimed that it was he who suggested Lincoln try pills called 'blue mass' for his melancholia. The drug was a mix of mercury, liquorice root, rosewater, honey and dried rose petals.

Stuart claimed after Lincoln's death that he was an 'unfortunate and miserable man'… 'the most striking picture of dejection I had ever seen'. The lawyer stated that Lincoln definitely started taking the pills 'before he went to Washington and for five months while he was president'. Another of Lincoln's friends also confirms that the president took blue mass as a medicinal remedy. Mercury is an extremely potent neurotoxin and each pill contained 65mg of mercury – thousands of times the current maximum allowable daily intake today. Most of this mercury, in its metallic state, would not have been absorbed by the body, but a recent study has shown that an ordinary pestle and mortar – widely used for grinding pill mixtures – would have crushed some of the mercury into particles small enough to be absorbed.

Dr Robert G. Feldman, a professor of pharmacology and neurology at Boston University, was one of the authors of the 2001 study that tested the pills' toxicity. He asserted that: 'Mercury poisoning certainly could explain Lincoln's known neurological symptoms: insomnia, tremor and rage attacks'.

Terrifying wrath

According to Henry Clay Whitney, one of Lincoln's companions on the trial circuit when he practised law, in anger he was 'lurid with majestic and terrifying wrath'. At a congressional debate in 1858, he was so out of control that he seized a former aide and shook him until his teeth rattled. Yet he went on to become the 16th US President, to steer the nation through the Civil War and, despite its great human cost, to become renowned as America's greatest and most humane leader.

Abraham Lincoln was born into a pioneer family in 1809, and, with his elder sister, Sarah, grew up in poverty. A brother, Thomas, died in infancy when Lincoln was three. Then his mother, Nancy, and his aunt and uncle died when he was nine, and Sarah died in childbirth when Lincoln was 18. In 1835, his first sweetheart died.

Even Lincoln's marriage started unhappily: Mary Todd broke off the engagement on New Year's Day 1841, propelling Lincoln into what his friends feared was a near suicidal state. This extract from a letter of that year gives some idea of the extent of the depression that had descended:

I am now the most miserable man living. If what I feel were equally distributed to the whole human family, there would not be one cheerful face on the earth. Whether I shall ever be better I can not tell; I awfully forebode I shall not. To remain as I am is impossible; I must die or be better, it appears to me.

On this occasion, as on others before it, Lincoln refers specifically to his state as hypochondriasis. He wrote in another letter: 'I have, within the last few days, been making a most

False! It is well known that Lincoln wrote a sympathetic letter to Mrs Bixby, a mother of five sons all killed in the Civil War. But War Department statistics show that only two were in fact killed. One son deserted, one was discharged and one became a Confederate soldier.

A repeat prescription

Researchers tested the toxicity of the mercury in blue mass pills by making a batch of their own tablets, following a 19th-century recipe. They pounded the ingredients with a pestle and mortar, then rolled and cut the pills to size. The pestle crushed the mercury into particles that were found to be small enough to pass into the bloodstream.

In a further experiment, the pills were combined with hydrochloric acid to replicate the stomach's digestive juices and then strained through a membrane resembling the intestinal wall. The amount of solid mercury that would have been absorbed from two pills was found to be 190 micrograms. A great deal more could have been breathed in as mercury vapour when the pills were crushed.

Blue mass was prescribed as a purgative and a fever suppressant. It was a convenient remedy for a host of ailments, but it affected the nervous system by attaching to molecules in the cells, and the side effects of ingesting such a large quantity included irritability, hostility, memory loss and insomnia.

KINDRED SPIRITS **Hat makers often suffered from the same syndrome as Lincoln. Constant exposure to a mercury compound used to treat felt hats gave them violent mood swings, inspiring the Mad Hatter in Lewis Carroll's** *Alice in Wonderland*.

discreditable exhibition of myself in the way of hypochondriaism.' Lincoln's early political career, meanwhile, was beset by failures, such as the defeat for nomination for Congress in 1843 and then again for Vice President in 1856.

Norbert Hirschhorn, who led the team that undertook the research into Lincoln's pills, points out that no one can be certain of exactly how many pills the man took, or how often. But all of those who knew Lincoln were aware of his reliance on physicians, and there is no doubt that the favoured prescription for hypochondriasis was blue mass. No such prescriptions for Lincoln survive, if any were ever written down, although an order for 'pills' – six boxes of them – does survive. What we do know is that Lincoln made the decision to stop taking the pills early in his presidency. John Todd Stuart records that he said they made him 'cross'. But his troubles were far from over, and he may have

craved relief more than ever before. Of his four beloved sons, the second, Edward, died at age four, in 1860; and the third, William, at 12, in 1862.

Throughout these years more than half a million young Americans died on battlefields during the Civil War. Lincoln's letters and diaries suggest that he felt a personal responsibility for the great slaughter, although he could see no other way to preserve the Union.

Free from the grip of the blue mass pills, he proved a calm, strong figurehead who inspired his side and led them to victory. The Civil War years are those for which Lincoln's indomitable character is famous. Lincoln the president is remembered as the soul of patience, outwardly cheering to others while remaining inwardly – eternally – the saddest of all the great men.

CALM AND COMPOSED **The statue of the president at the Lincoln Memorial, in Washington DC, immortalises him with a cool calmness and sense of solid dependability. In life, Lincoln was racked with mood swings and periods of deep despair.**

Kennedy – the sickly king of Camelot

A huge premium has always been placed on the health of a president. While Lincoln chose to confront his dependency, John F. Kennedy concealed his reliance on medication

John F. Kennedy suffered from back problems throughout his presidency. These were publicly ascribed to his war wounds: in 1943 he rescued several crewmembers when their patrol boat PT109 was sunk in the Pacific. That he could smile through the pain only added to his stature – it reminded Americans that their president was also a hero.

But Kennedy was far from healthy. He was afflicted by a range of serious illnesses that required daily medication. The extent of his ill health was kept secret from the American public. Kennedy feared that if his poor health became known before his bid for the presidency his hopes of making it to the White House would be much diminished.

Sensitive disclosures

Medical records released by the Kennedy Presidential Library in Boston revealed that Kennedy began taking corticosteroids as early as 1937, when he was 20, to relieve colitis, an inflammation of the digestive tract.

Heavy, long-term use of corticosteroids can lead to osteoporosis, a progressive bone disease, and private X-rays taken a decade later indicated that several of his vertebrae had collapsed. Among the drugs' other side effects are an increased sexual drive, a yellowing of the skin that creates a kind of permanent suntan and the growth of thick and glossy hair – all famous Kennedy characteristics. The drugs also suppress the immune system, making the user prone to other disorders.

Kennedy was later diagnosed with Addison's disease, a dysfunction of the adrenal glands, one of the symptoms of which is a progressive darkening of the skin. More steroids were prescribed. While he was carving out a career, first as a congressman and then as a senator, Kennedy always denied rumours that he suffered from Addison's disease. But this and his poor health meant he had to be secretly hospitalised nine times between 1955 and 1957.

By the time Kennedy became president in 1961, he was in constant pain, sometimes so much so that he could barely climb a flight of stairs or bend over to put on his socks. His daily medication included painkillers for his back, antispasmodics for colitis, antibiotics for urinary-tract infections and antihistamines for allergies.

SECRET PAIN John F. Kennedy's youthful and exuberant image helped him strike up a rapport with voters. They were unaware that he was on strong medication and often in chronic pain.

Keeping the legend alive

Throughout his life Kennedy sought to keep the state of his health secret. As president he projected an image of glowing vitality.

Some have argued that the revelations about Kennedy's physical state show that he misled voters – they were taking a gamble on a man who relied on medication to function normally. But it can be argued that his struggle against continual pain and the stoicism with which he bore it were evidence of his great strength of character.

DOCTORING HISTORY

Death, disease, murder and madness shape and punctuate history. Their manner and cause are often recorded, but a closer examination of images and contemporary written accounts of symptoms can lead modern medical experts to pronounce a very different diagnosis, allowing historians to get closer to the truth.

Medical examination

In 1967, an Italian surgeon visited the Rijksmuseum in Amsterdam. When he came to Rembrandt's *Bathsheba at the Well*, on loan from the Louvre, he noticed that the subject's left breast appeared swollen near the armpit, discoloured and marked with a distinctive pitting. He thought he recognised the symptoms, and a check in the history books reinforced his suspicion – Rembrandt's model, his mistress Hendrickje Stoffels, had later died after a long illness. The 20th-century doctor surmised that the 17th-century woman had been a victim of breast cancer.

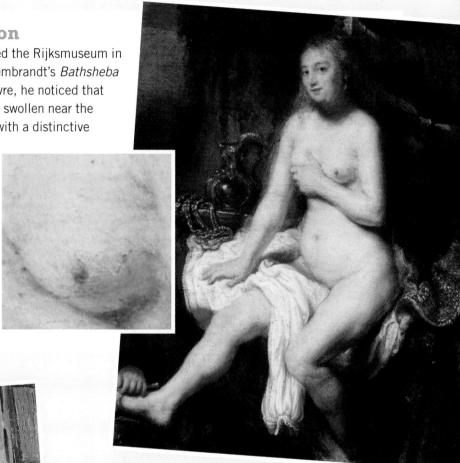

Mad with earache

Vincent van Gogh was branded insane when, in 1888, he cut off his right ear, but modern doctors who have re-examined the artist's handwritten descriptions of his condition have concluded that he was suffering from Menière's disease, a build-up of fluid in the inner ear that disturbs the sufferer's balance. The condition was not properly understood in the 1880s and almost always confused with epilepsy or madness. Driven to his life's end by earache, van Gogh spent time in an asylum before he eventually shot himself dead in 1890.

A nose for illness

In Domenico Ghirlandaio's portrait of *The Old Man and his Grandson*, painted in 1490, there is clearly something wrong with the old man's nose. But it was not until 1845 that the condition was given a name. The disease that causes a severe build-up of sebaceous (oil-producing) skin glands is now known as rhinophyma. It is similar to acne. The antibiotics that could have corrected the condition came nearly 500 years too late for the subject of this painting.

What killed the President?

The death of George Washington at the age of 67 was not suspicious, but it was certainly mysterious. He complained one day of fever, sore throat and difficulties in breathing and was dead within 24 hours. At the time his problem was diagnosed as quinsy (an abscess in the tonsils), but modern doctors who have re-examined contemporary records in the light of recent medical research think it must have been acute epiglottitis, a virus that causes the throat to swell and close.

Who protected the Protector?

Oliver Cromwell, Lord Protector of England after the execution of Charles I in 1649, died in 1658, apparently of malaria. But a study published in 1999 found that the symptoms described in contemporary accounts were not those of the mosquito-borne disease but of slow poisoning by doses of antimony, arsenic and mercury administered regularly over a period of about three months. The conclusion – widely disputed, but not incredible – was that Cromwell was murdered by Royalists anxious to bring down his Puritan Commonwealth and restore the monarchy.

SUICIDE MISSION
The kamikaze were born of pragmatism, not fanaticism

Japan's use of suicide pilots during the Second World War appeared to be an expression of its traditional warrior values of loyalty and self-sacrifice. But it was actually a last-ditch military policy aimed at getting the best value out of inexperienced pilots.

The training manual was composed of simple instructions, suitable for complete beginners. There were reminders to the pilot to 'proceed straight ahead on the runway' when taking off, and to remove the safety pin from the bomb they carried on board.

Nervous pilots were advised to urinate, as 'calm judgement' was essential. Especially when the purpose of the mission was to steer a plane laden with explosives directly into an enemy warship.

To the American seamen who witnessed Japanese kamikaze attacks during the Second World War, the notion that the pilots were not battle-hardened would have been incredible. Yet the truth is that nearly all the kamikaze were novice pilots carrying out a desperate ploy devised by a military suffering crippling losses.

By autumn 1944, it was clear that the Japanese forces were losing the war in the Pacific. At one engagement

CRIPPLING IMPACT Smoke pours out from the USS *Essex* in the aftermath of a devastating suicide attack from a kamikaze airplane in November 1944. One plane could sink a battleship in this manner.

BATTLE DRESS The tying of the *hachimaki* scarves became a sacred part of preparation for kamikaze pilots. They wore the scarves around their heads, as the samurai had done in combat to keep sweat out of their eyes.

at Saipan, pilot losses were so high that the Americans dubbed it the 'Marianas Turkey Shoot'. As Allied forces headed inexorably towards Japan, the Philippines became a crucial battleground. If the islands fell to the Allies, they would become a launching pad for strikes against the Japanese mainland.

Japan was in no position to fight a conventional battle. Handicapped by a lack of experienced pilots, it also could not spare the 100 days of training needed to give novices any level of flying proficiency. Training was limited to 25 days, which meant that the young men could just about fly, but were a long way from being competent combat pilots. As a result, they were vulnerable in dogfights with American airmen. The Japanese flying instructors likened their trainees to 'black-edged cherry blossoms' – admirable, but not expected to last long.

Vice-Admiral Takijiro Onishi was the first to propose suicide bombing missions as a tactic of war. The Japanese Admiralty persuaded themselves that they had exhausted all other alternatives. The logic of war dictated that aerial combat skills were unnecessary when a single plane loaded with explosives could inflict huge damage on the enemy.

These suicide squadrons were officially named the *Tokkotai* 'Special Attack Squadron', *Tokko* for short. They gained international renown under a different name: kamikaze. The word kamikaze means 'divine wind' and refers to an incident in Japanese history, when in 1281 a Mongol invasion fleet was wrecked by a typhoon. The Japanese High Command hoped that the young pilots who now assumed the name would provide a similarly dramatic reversal of fortune.

Samurai of the skies

Attempts to understand the kamikaze have often emphasised the influence of the Japanese samurai tradition on the pilots. These medieval warriors were bound to their masters by a strict code of obedience called *bushido*. Serving the feudal lord became the samurai's *raison d'être*: the warrior offered unwavering discipline and loyalty to the death.

The kamikaze pilots were portrayed to their country and their families as modern-day samurai, sacrificing their own lives to protect their master, the emperor. Their missions were cast in the light of the *bushido* tradition.

This noble presentation of the kamikaze struck a chord with many Japanese pilots. Some of those overlooked for suicide missions were devastated and desperately beseeched their commanders to select them. Others wrote letters in their own blood to prove their readiness to sacrifice their lives.

But no genuine parallel existed between the samurai and the kamikaze. The samurai were an elite group, most born to a noble calling, all trained for years in the warrior arts. The kamikaze, by contrast, consisted of young pilots who signed up, regardless of age or culture. Suddenly, anyone could be a samurai, so long as they were ready to die.

Taking to the air

The first kamikaze squadron was assembled by Vice-Admiral Onishi from the 201st Air Group in the Philippines. A 23-year-old lieutenant, Yukio Seki, was told by Onishi himself that he was to lead the first attack. According to one account, Seki bowed his head as he digested the news and said, 'I beg you to entrust me with this mission.' The

training manual described in poetical terms what he could expect to experience at the end:

You are two or three metres from the target. You can see clearly the muzzles of the enemy's guns. At that moment you see your mother's face... not smiling or crying – it is her usual face. You may hear a final sound like the breaking of crystal.

Considerable effort was taken to ensure that every attack counted. Pilots were told that, if they were unable to gain the correct angle of approach when attacking a warship, they were not to crash their planes in vain but to return to base. Noble sacrifices were pointless if they did not achieve the aim of halting the American advance. But about four out of five suicide planes were shot down before they reached their target.

On October 25, 1944, American warships came under attack from

ON TARGET **A kamikaze plane heads for the deck of the USS *Missouri*. In order to maximise the damage, pilots were trained to aim for certain vulnerable areas in the structure, such as the point between the bridge tower and the smoke stacks.**

WAR VETERAN Pilot Hichiro Naemura (inset, with his Zero-Sen fighter during the war) volunteered to be a kamikaze in January 1945, but never went on a mission. Almost 60 years later, he recalled envying those who had flown. 'You were able to die with rewards instead of wasting your precious life.'

suicide bombers for the first time just off the Philippine island of Samar: Seki himself was credited with the strike that sunk the escort aircraft carrier USS *St Lo*.

Once the effectiveness of the strategy was established, the Japanese High Command found new and devastating ways of applying it. Tiny aircraft called *okha* (blossoms), which were little more than piloted bombs, were attached to larger planes, flown to the battle zone and dropped onto their targets.

The kamikaze principle was applied to naval warfare too. Underneath the waves, manned torpedoes – *kaiten* (Turning of the Heavens) – were steered toward submarines and battleships. In all, some 3000 Allied servicemen died and 120 ships were sunk, at the cost of more than 7000 Japanese pilots.

The psychological impact on the Allies was profound. US personnel returning home from the Pacific were not allowed even to mention the kamikaze until the summer of 1945 – for fear of demoralising other forces. But for those who witnessed the horrific reality of a kamikaze attack the memory made a permanent scar. A seaman who served on the USS *Essex* recalled:

> *It seemed like it was coming in very slow. It was smoking but no one could shoot it down. I jumped back into the Ready Room as it hit. After the explosion I ventured back on the flight deck – and I wish I hadn't – all those people killed – most burned to death.*

The ethos of ultimate loyalty and the code of *bushido* served to mask a doctrine of military realpolitik. The suicide mission was not a traditional Japanese response: it was fighting to the death that was honourable, and only dishonour that required ritual suicide. Flying to certain death was a new variant on this ancient code. Onishi wished to give the pilots a death that would not be in vain:

> *If they are on land, they would be bombed down, and if they are in the air, they would be shot down. That's sad... too sad... To let the young men die beautifully, that's what Tokko is. To give beautiful death, that's called sympathy.*

Last letters home

Before their flights, the kamikaze pilots wrote last letters to their families. Many of them took a standardised form, which involved the rejection of nostalgic sentiment and stressed the piety of their actions. Some took on a hopeful aspect, believing that their actions would allow their names to be inscribed in the hallowed halls of Yasukuni Shrine in Tokyo, which commemorates Japan's war dead. One pilot wrote to his two young children:

Don't be envious of your friends' daddies. Your Daddy…has become a god and is always watching you.

But behind the stock phrases, the struggle to accept the enormity of their situation was still evident. Goro Nagamine recorded his feelings the night before his mission:

I would say to myself 'So are you ready now?' and there was a self that would answer 'Yes sir! I'm ready to go',

but there was still another self who never stopped yelling 'I don't want to die!'

After their letters were finished, the pilots would lay out their belongings. A piece of paper identifying the owner would be placed on top, with the phrase, 'The late', before the name. They were then ready to fly.

This 'beautiful death', Onishi realised, was also a passive death, rather than the fighting chance of survival that a wartime novice pilot – or a samurai warrior – would have.

Faced with certain death, the kamikaze pilots were not always self-assured. A top Imperial Navy pilot, Saburo Sakai, stated after the war that he did not believe all the volunteers were genuine:

…those who gave them orders and encouraged them lied. Every pilot volunteered for a kamikaze unit?

'I go! I go! I go!' – did everyone say that? That's a lie! No one wants to die. But if a pilot was ordered, we were all military men. We would go. I went too.

If pilots had doubts about the kamikaze policy, they kept them to themselves. So did their commanders. There was no open discussion of the kamikaze: the press and other media were heavily censored. No reporting of the war's casualties or defeats was allowed, and certainly not any critical assessment of military tactics.

For all the sacrifices of the kamikaze, the Japanese could not fight a nuclear war. After Hiroshima and Nagasaki were bombed, Emperor Hirohito announced Japan's surrender on August 16, 1945.

To Onishi's mind he was responsible for the failure of his pilots' honourable efforts, and had brought dishonour upon himself. He committed *hara-kiri*, disembowelling himself with his own blade.

MAN OF HONOUR In a suicide note Vice-Admiral Takijiro Onishi, the father of the kamikaze, thanked his 'brave special attackers' and hoped his death would help atone for the failure to achieve victory. He fell on his sword and died 14 hours later.

> No one wants to die. But we were all military men. We would go. I went too.
>
> SABURO SAKAI

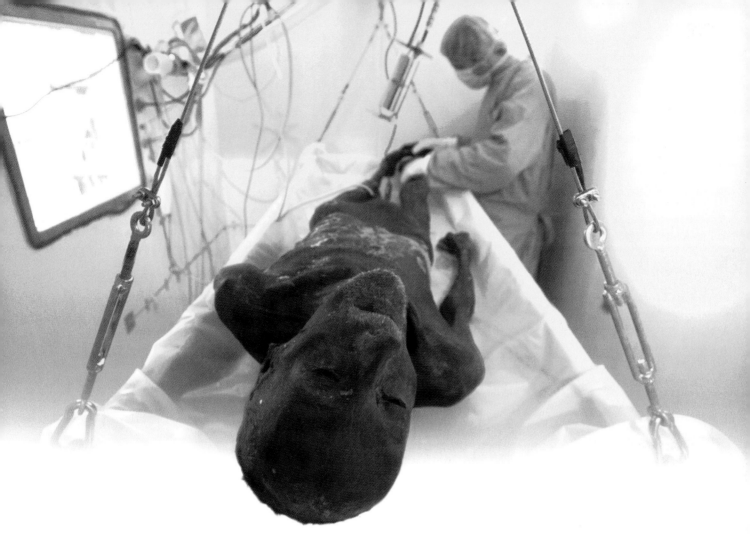

SECRETS OF THE ICE MAN
The investigation of a suspicious death more than 5000 years ago

The discovery of a Stone Age body high in the Alps was an archaeological sensation, but the mystery behind the fragile remains became a fascinating forensic puzzle. Each time a solution seemed correct, opposing evidence emerged.

As German hikers Helmut and Erika Simon set off into the mountains on the Austrian-Italian border in September 1991, the morning sun was radiating heat into a rocky hollow high above the snowline. When the couple stepped off the trail at 3191m (10,530ft), they happened to notice a body half-buried in the melting ice. Thinking that it was the corpse of an unlucky climber,

they immediately alerted the mountain rescue team.

But as the body and the belongings that surrounded it were brought down, it became clear that this person was far, far older than anyone could have possibly guessed.

The man of the mountain – whom they named Ötzi, after the Ötztal Valley in which he had been found – turned out to have lived in about 3300 BC, more than 1000 years before the construction of the Pyramids. ▶ **p.181**

EARTHLY REMAINS The Ice Man was examined on a specially refrigerated bench to limit decomposition. Scientists at Bolzano General Hospital in Italy used imaging techniques, such as X-rays and CT scanning, but it was ten years before they spotted an arrowhead buried deep in his left shoulder.

Body of evidence

The mysterious death of Ötzi was approached in much the same way as a modern murder investigation. The detectives on the case used the most up-to-date forensic techniques to examine every inch of the body. They analysed the deceased's last meal and looked for signs of a deadly struggle. Carbon dating was used to determine the date of death and DNA analysis enabled experts to pinpoint more or less exactly where he had lived.

The work of forensic pathologists has given archaeologists a clearer insight than ever before into the life of the inhabitants of Europe more than 5000 years ago.

Magic markings were a health treatment

A miniature endoscope found more than 50 incisions marking the skin. Ötzi appeared to be tattooed with coal dust, leading many to believe he could have been a shaman. But the marks were mainly on his back and legs, and would not have been readily visible.

They are now believed to have been caused by a form of acupuncture, as their locations correspond to joints affected by osteoarthritis. Some of the marks, which were made with a needle-type tool, are within 5mm (0.2in) of known acupuncture points, which could make the treatment some 2000 years older than previously thought.

Season of death

At first, scientists thought that Ötzi had died in the autumn, because the ice around his body contained the pollen of autumn-flowering plants. Perhaps he had been caught in a storm and died of exposure? But Ötzi's intestines contained cells of hop hornbeam pollen. These were so well preserved that they must have been eaten soon after the flowering of the plant. Since hop hornbeam only flowers between March and June, Ötzi must have died in the warmth of spring. This makes exposure less likely a cause of death, and violence more probable.

Age at time of death

Tests on Ötzi's bone density have fixed his age at around 46. This was elderly for his time, and it showed. He suffered from osteoarthritis – worn and stiffened cartilage – and severe whipworm, a parasite in his intestines that would have caused him intermittent wrenching pain.

Damage to the body

When Ötzi was discovered, no one knew how long he had been there. His fragile body was handled too roughly: his left hip was gouged and his wooden bow and backpack were snapped. Snow poles were used to break the ice around him, snapping off his genitals, crushing his ribs and possibly his left arm – although this may have been caused by the weight of ice. The damage created more mystery as it masked Ötzi's true injuries.

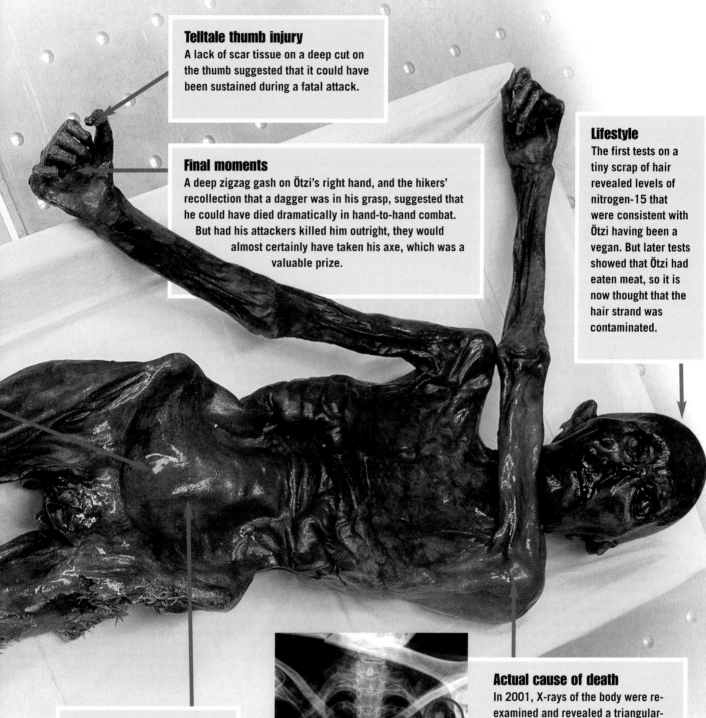

Telltale thumb injury
A lack of scar tissue on a deep cut on the thumb suggested that it could have been sustained during a fatal attack.

Final moments
A deep zigzag gash on Ötzi's right hand, and the hikers' recollection that a dagger was in his grasp, suggested that he could have died dramatically in hand-to-hand combat. But had his attackers killed him outright, they would almost certainly have taken his axe, which was a valuable prize.

Lifestyle
The first tests on a tiny scrap of hair revealed levels of nitrogen-15 that were consistent with Ötzi having been a vegan. But later tests showed that Ötzi had eaten meat, so it is now thought that the hair strand was contaminated.

Final meals
Ötzi must have been hungry when he died, since there was very little in his stomach. DNA in the cells of digested food in the colon showed that his last meals consisted of cereals together with ibex and red deer. Muscle fibres from these two meats were also found on Ötzi's skin and clothing.

Actual cause of death
In 2001, X-rays of the body were re-examined and revealed a triangular-shaped fragment, denser than human bone, in the area of Ötzi's clavicle. It turned out to be a flint arrowhead, 2cm (1in) long, that had been overlooked for a decade of detailed scientific investigation. Ötzi had been shot under his left arm, and had pulled out the shaft of the arrow. The wound would have been fatal – scientists estimate that Ötzi would have bled to death within ten hours.

The hunter's tools

At first the fact that the prehistoric body had been discovered high in the mountains led people to assume that the Ice Man must have been a shepherd. But the tools and weapons found nearby were not a herdsman's normal equipment. And the bearskin hat showed that Ötzi was probably a hunter.

Ötzi's gear made him well prepared to be self-sufficient for long periods. It is likely that he was a skilled craftsman who made modifications to his tools with his own flints. His clothing showed signs of recent repair. The new stitching was not up to the standard of the original, so it may have been his own work.

Quiver and arrows

Ötzi's deerskin quiver contained an unstrung, 1.8m (6ft) longbow made of yew wood, together with two complete arrows made from viburnum wood with flint heads and feathers, and 12 unfinished arrows. The arrows had been used and recovered – analysis highlighted bloodstains along 30cm (1ft) of the shafts, showing that Ötzi's arrows flew fast and penetrated deep into the flesh of his prey.

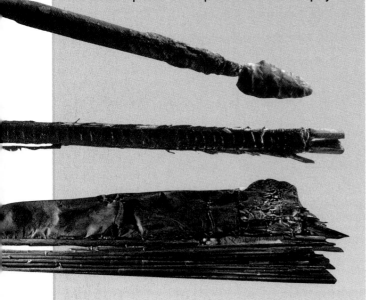

Ash-handled flint dagger

Ötzi's dagger had several different cutting edges, enabling it to be used for a variety of tasks. Also found with the dagger was its grass sheath, which would have protected Ötzi from the sharp blade. Tiny nicks on the blade fitted with incisions that had been made along the shaft of Ötzi's yew bow, suggesting that Ötzi may have used his knife to fashion the bow. Residues showed he also used it for shaping bone and antler, and scraping hides.

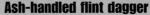

Flints

The specimens found among Ötzi's equipment were of very high quality, so he may have intended to use them for trading rather than as implements. These flints match rock found in quarries to the east of Lake Garda in Italy – further evidence that Ötzi was 'Italian' rather than 'Austrian'.

Copper axe

Estimates of the date of Ötzi's death were initially based on his axe blade. It was thought to be made of bronze, placing his death at about 2000 BC. However, this date was revised when chemical tests proved that the blade (below) was actually made of copper. It is the oldest such axe found in Europe, and high levels of copper and arsenic in Ötzi's hair show that he had smelted copper himself, or had at least been present at the foundry.

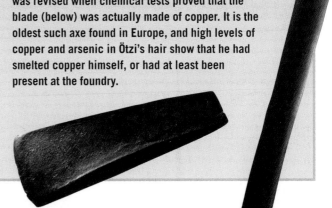

The ice tomb had preserved the man's body through several millennia. Even his eyeballs were intact. If it had not been for a freak thaw, he might have remained in his mountain grave for another thousand years or more.

The body was taken to Innsbruck, and archaeologists from all over the world converged on the Austrian city to see the mystery man.

Tests on pollen in the dead man's stomach revealed that he probably lived in a valley to the south of the Alps. But further forensic analysis was brought to an abrupt halt when Italian officials suddenly claimed that the body had been found, not in Austria, but on their own national territory. Lawyers and diplomats argued the case for years. Finally, in 1998, it was agreed that Ötzi had indeed been buried 93m (303 ft) inside the Italian border, and so his body was moved from Innsbruck to the South Tyrol Museum of Archaeology in Bolzano, Italy. At last work could begin anew.

Deadly assault

So who was Ötzi? His weapons were in a state of marked disrepair – his longbow was unstrung and he carried 12 unfinished arrows. If he was a hunter, why would he have set out so ill-equipped?

His most obvious injuries – a broken arm and ribs – initially led experts to suppose that he had been involved in a fight in his village and fled to the mountains, where, in a weakened state, he had succumbed to the cold. But further tests showed that the bones had been broken posthumously by the pressure of the ice: Ötzi had simply frozen to death. He was an old man for his time and may have been susceptible to heart attack or hypothermia.

The theory that the death was accidental had to be abandoned, however, when X-rays revealed an arrowhead lodged in his left shoulder: Ötzi had been shot through the armpit. Dried blood around the point of entry showed that it was a recent injury. The Ice Man had

Face of the Ice Man

After a cast of Ötzi's skull had been made from a 3D computer scan, scientists used plaster to simulate the soft tissue – ear lobes, nose and skin – that would have covered his skull in his lifetime. The effigy was then topped off with hair of a likely colour. The reconstruction is the closest approximation of a face-to-face encounter with Ötzi that can be achieved at this time.

died of his wounds. Someone had hunted down the hunter.

In the light of this new evidence, some people thought that Ötzi might have been the victim of a ritual killing and burial, perhaps an execution or a sacrifice. But that, too, was unlikely because there were no remains of the wooden shaft, just the tiny 2cm (1in) arrowhead. Someone – either Ötzi himself, or at least a friend rather than a foe – must have pulled the arrow out of his body. The odd angle and the awkward point of entry suggested a violent blow sustained during a running battle rather than a ceremonial death.

Ötzi's last day on Earth probably went something like this: he ate a meal in the woods, where some pollen fell into his food. He then became involved in a fight and was shot. He pulled out the arrow shaft and fled into the Alps to escape his assailant or assailants, who lost him, or left him for dead. He reached high altitude but lost so much blood that he soon died.

That Ötzi was preserved for so long is something of a miracle. Soon after his death his body was probably covered with snow, which protected it from carrion predators. The glacier that then covered him would normally have destroyed anything in its path, but his body was sheltered and secured in a rock hollow. The greatest miracle, however, is that there should have been a thaw at exactly the moment when the Simons were passing. As one commentator wrote: 'Over the past 5000 years the chance of finding the Ice Man existed for only six days'.

PATHOLOGICAL TRUTHS

Modern forensic techniques, developed for solving serious crimes, have made it possible for archaeologists and historians to make amazing discoveries by studying the bodies of long-dead people.

Dry or freezing conditions or dense, wet layers of oxygen-starved peat can preserve the soft tissue of an ancient body in a remarkably intact state. From such finds, scientists can examine flesh wounds, retrieve the contents of the stomach, test blood type and analyse fingernails and hair to build up a picture of who the dead person was and how they died. Many of the procedures are identical to those carried out on a fresh body in a police forensics lab, but to historians the discipline is known as archaeopathology.

A suspicious death

In 1984, the upper body of a man was found in a bog in north-west England at Lindow Moss. His beaten head and roped neck suggested that he was the victim of an attack, but forensic work was able to establish that Lindow Man was almost certainly executed or sacrificed rather than assaulted.

The corpse had lost its legs to modern peat cutting equipment, but swellings in the scalp tissue indicate that the head wounds – made with a bladed instrument – had been inflicted before death. Ligature marks and crushed vertebrae in the neck suggest that the leather cord around his throat had been used as a garotte by a right-handed man, tightly enough to cause death by strangulation.

The use of two separate methods is not characteristic of murder: the initial axe attack would have been sufficient to dispatch the victim. Chemical analysis of the barley flour in Lindow Man's last meal showed it had been not only baked but grains had been branded with an instrument heated directly in a fire. This led one researcher to suggest that a ritual killing had been decreed by 'drawing lots' – perhaps Lindow Man had sealed his own fate by picking the burnt cake out of a bag. Most scholars think it more likely that he was executed as punishment for a crime, as no sacrificial items have been found.

The face that fits

When an unidentified human skull is found, police sometimes hire artists to reconstruct the dead person's face by using clay or plaster to reproduce the features. This is modelled directly onto a cast of the skull at thicknesses dictated by average measurements of facial tissue at 18 key points on the human head.

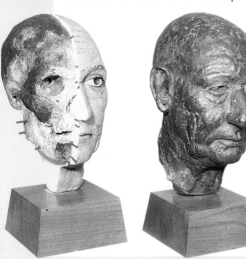

The same technique can be used to build up a likeness of a figure from history. At Bristol City Museum in 1998, specialists made a cast from the skull of a decomposed mummy. From inscriptions in the tomb, they knew they were re-creating the face of Horemkenesi, a middle-ranking priest at the temple of Karnak, from the 11th century BC. From tests on his skeleton they knew his age – about 60 – and from tomb texts they knew he also directed building works. These insights enabled the modeller to give character and expression to Horemkenesi's face.

The heart of a king?

DNA testing is the most reliable way of establishing the true identity of a victim or matching tissue samples with a suspected murderer. It can solve historical cases of questionable identity, too. The myth of the 'lost dauphin' is one of the most persistent in French history. Several impostors claimed to be Louis XVII, the son of the guillotined Marie Antoinette and Louis XVI, and the boy who died in prison at the age of 14 was often thought to have been a substitute.

The heart of the boy, preserved after the post mortem, has now been tested and its mitochondrial DNA compared with that of one of the dauphin's living maternal relatives, Queen Anna of Romania. The match proved that the child who died in the Temple jail in 1795 was the real Louis.

THE QUICK AND THE DEAD The mystery about the death of Louis XVII (effigy, far right) was solved by a genetic link with his 21st-century namesake, Louis of Bourbon (near right).

Hidden clues

● Analysis of hair belonging to Ludwig van Beethoven has revealed high concentrations of lead, which could have caused rages and even his deafness. Researchers believe the lead may have come from spa water, one of the composer's favourite tipples.

● Comparisons of people's teeth across the centuries show that although the advent of the sugar trade in the 16th century was to blame for a surge in tooth decay, the change from bread to potatoes two centuries later was just as damaging, as diets became softer and less fibrous.

● High levels of nicotine in the abdomen of the mummy of Rameses II led one scholar to propose that the pharaoh chewed tobacco. It has since been found that 19th-century archaeologists treated bug infestations in the mummy with lye and tobacco leaf.

DIGGING UP HITLER
The bizarre journey of the Nazi leader's remains after his death

Adolf Hitler died in Berlin at the end of the Second World War, but his spectre stalked Europe for decades afterwards. This is the full story of the desperate race to capture the dead Hitler's bones, and of their strange travels throughout the Cold War years.

B erlin in the spring of 1945 was a city of smoke and rubble. Soviet troops were fighting their way to its centre, street by shattered street. The war in Europe was all but over. On May 1, as the battle raged, Germans listening to radio Hamburg were warned to expect a 'grave and important announcement'. To the doleful accompaniment of Wagner, the people were informed that Adolf Hitler had fallen 'at the head of his troops' that afternoon.

Only the few Germans still in the bunker of the Reich Chancellery knew the full truth: that the Führer had shot himself the previous day, and that his body lay in the Chancellery garden. This small lie about the manner of the Führer's death soon grew into a doubt about whether he had died at all. And in the days and years that followed, an extraordinary edifice of deception – a mausoleum of lies – was built on the bones of the Nazi leader.

Hunt for a dead man

The first Soviet troops reached the Chancellery two days after Hitler's death. This was a reconnaissance party from the 3rd Shock Army. They were under orders from Soviet leader Joseph Stalin to seize Hitler or find his corpse. They immediately began searching among the rubble, and their first discovery was promising: a body with the familiar moustache and slanting fringe. But the dead man was quickly identified as a body double, who at times stood in for the Führer as a security measure.

A further search yielded two more bodies buried near the doorway to the garden. Their

LAST TESTAMENT Hitler left detailed instructions for the disposal of his body. 'My wife and I choose to die in order to escape the shame of capitulation...our bodies should be burned immediately.' These orders were followed, but not as thoroughly as he had hoped.

condition was unlike any of the other corpses found in the Chancellery, and this attracted the attention of the Soviets. A captured German soldier testified that these were the bodies of Hitler and Eva Braun, and that he had watched their cremation from an observation tower.

Red Army soldiers moved the remains to a Berlin suburb, where a military medical team carried out an autopsy. The doctor in charge of the post mortem was Faust Sherovsky; his work was personally overseen by the commander of the Soviet forces, Marshal Georgy Zhukov.

not identified Hitler's corpse. I cannot say anything definite about his fate. He may have flown out of Berlin at the last moment.'

Zhukov knew this was a lie. Perhaps it was a political move, intended to distract or wrongfoot the Western Allies; perhaps the Soviets just wanted to keep the gruesome trophy entirely to themselves. Most likely, Zhukov was giving expression to Stalin's own paranoia about Hitler. Stalin would not believe Hitler was dead until it was proven a hundred times over. He actually told the world that the Führer had escaped by

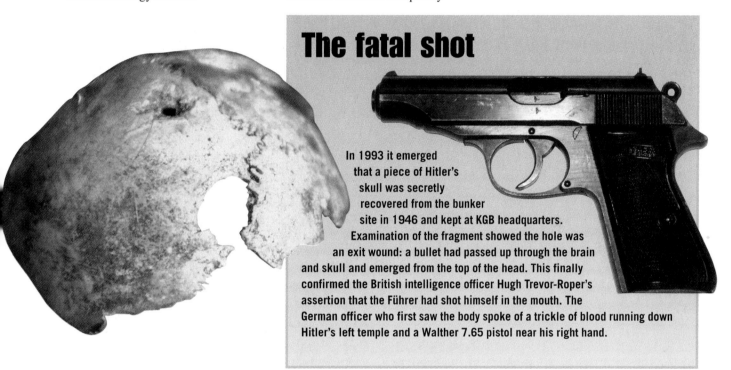

The fatal shot

In 1993 it emerged that a piece of Hitler's skull was secretly recovered from the bunker site in 1946 and kept at KGB headquarters. Examination of the fragment showed the hole was an exit wound: a bullet had passed up through the brain and skull and emerged from the top of the head. This finally confirmed the British intelligence officer Hugh Trevor-Roper's assertion that the Führer had shot himself in the mouth. The German officer who first saw the body spoke of a trickle of blood running down Hitler's left temple and a Walther 7.65 pistol near his right hand.

Soviet search teams had captured Hitler's dental records – a key piece of forensic evidence. Sherovsky matched the lower jaw of the charred corpse to the tooth X-rays, and informed Zhukov that these were indeed the remains of Adolf Hitler.

Zhukov immediately informed Stalin that Hitler's body had been recovered, and had the crucial jawbone sent to Moscow as proof. But the Soviet leadership had no intention of sharing this information with the Allies. On the contrary, Zhukov declared to Western journalists in Berlin that: 'We have

submarine from Hamburg and was hiding in Spain under the protection of the fascist leader General Franco.

But even as Zhukov announced that Hitler may have escaped, Soviet intelligence officers were moving the body out of Berlin. The remains of Hitler and Eva Braun were driven to a Russian army camp at Magdeburg, in the Soviet occupation zone, where they were secretly buried.

Meanwhile, Stalin continued to amass evidence that his enemy was dead. Soviet military intelligence scoured Berlin to find people who had been in the bunker in the last

BUNKER RUINS Private Richard Blust (right) was one of the first American soldiers to survey the fire-ravaged wreckage of Adolf Hitler's bunker. The Nazi leader had shot himself on the sofa at the rear of the picture. The conical entrance and remains of the bunker were removed (below) in 1988 to make way for a park.

Body timeline

1945 — **Hitler's suicide**
Sherovsky autopsy. Remains buried at Magdeburg.

1946 — **Re-examination of the suicide spot**
Skull fragments taken to Moscow.

1970 — **Corpse dug up from Magdeburg**
Remains incinerated and scattered in the River Elbe.

1993 — **Stored away**
Moscow announces it has skull fragments.

days. Seventy members of Hitler's staff – secretaries, bodyguards, signals officers – were rounded up and taken off to Moscow for questioning.

The interrogations were exhaustive and brutal. Heinz Linge, Hitler's personal valet, was stripped and beaten to the interrogators' repeated shouts: Hitler is alive! Hitler is alive! 'The talk was always about whether Hitler had flown out,' Linge later recalled. 'Or whether a double had been substituted in his place.'

The Soviets documented every detail recounted by Hitler's staff. Complex tables and charts plotted testimonies against each other to identify every possible inconsistency. The prisoners were even flown back to Berlin to film a re-enactment in the bunker – actors and mannequins stood in for Hitler and Braun.

A second dig

The Western powers knew nothing of this. They assumed that the Soviets had found Hitler dead, but could not be certain. With no body, sightings were reported from Argentina, Spain, Japan and even Berlin.

To put a stop to the rumours and false claims, General Dwight Eisenhower, commander of Allied forces in Europe, ordered an investigation. A British Intelligence officer, Hugh Trevor-Roper, was sent to interview any survivors from the bunker who had not been seized by the Soviets. His report, published in 1947 as *The Last Days of Hitler*, concluded that Hitler and Eva Braun had indeed committed suicide in the

bunker, and their bodies had then been cremated.

But still the Soviets would not acknowledge that the Führer was dead. In 1946 Soviet criminologists and scientists revisited the site of Hitler's suicide to gather still more evidence. Four new skull fragments were recovered from the Chancellery garden – the largest of which was punctured by a bullet hole. These pieces of bone were taken to Moscow and stored with the files in KGB headquarters. But in public the commission stated that it was 'not possible to arrive at a conclusion' about Hitler's death.

Valet's testimony

Hitler's staff and servants remained prisoners in Moscow for years after the war. The valet Linge was released in 1955. His testimony, now that he was free to speak, provided a great deal of detail about Hitler's suicide and the attempt to dispose of the body. Nearly all of it supported Hugh Trevor-Roper's account.

Linge claimed that Hitler had ordered him personally to deal with the dispersal of his and Eva Braun's bodies after their suicide, and that he was the first to see Hitler dead.

On the day of the suicide, claimed Linge, Hitler had eaten lunch with the occupants of the bunker. After the meal, he and Braun retired to their private suite. There was silence for a time, and then a single gunshot. Linge went into the room. 'There, almost upright in a sitting position on a couch, was the body of Adolf Hitler. A small hole showed on his right temple and a trickle of blood ran slowly over his cheek.' Eva Braun lay slumped to his left. The distinctive bitter-almond smell of prussic acid drifted from her body.

The two bodies were wrapped in blankets and carried up to the garden. They were doused in petrol and, with a final salute, set aflame. The intention was to consume the two bodies utterly, so that nothing remained but ash. But the funeral pyre merely rendered the bodies unrecognisable. They were hurriedly buried where they had burned before the last of Hitler's staff fled the advancing Russian troops.

The West knew no more until 1968, when a Soviet journalist named Lev Bezymensky sensationally revealed that some of Hitler's remains had been in Moscow since the war. His book included a transcript of the secret autopsy of 1945, as well as photographs of the charred bodies and of Hitler's teeth.

The Sherovsky autopsy, it turned out, had given the cause of death as 'poisoning with cyanide compounds'. But how did this fit with eyewitness accounts of a pistol shot to the head?

Bezymensky suggested that Hitler's entourage had 'tried to hide the truth in order to foster the legend that the Führer had shot himself like a man.' But Linge and other German witnesses would have had no reason to keep up the pretence during the long years of imprisonment, still less

after their release. Most likely, Sherovsky simply got it wrong: at the time of the first autopsy, the skull fragment with the bullet hole still lay buried in the Chancellery garden.

Forgotten bones

Even after Bezymensky's revelations, the whereabouts of Hitler's bones remained a secret. By 1970, the Red Army camp at Magdeburg was a Soviet military base on East German soil. It was about to be handed over to the communist German Democratic Republic when someone in Moscow recalled that Hitler's bones were still there, beneath the parade ground.

The situation was brought to the attention of Yuri Andropov, head of the KGB, who ordered that the remains be obliterated. Even though the GDR was a faithful Soviet satellite, it was unthinkable to put Hitler's bones back into German hands. The remains were exhumed at night and incinerated. The ashes were thrown in the River Elbe. Finally, reasoned Andropov, all trace of the man Hitler was gone.

But he was mistaken, because the fragments of skull and jaw remained, gathering dust in his own basement at KGB headquarters.

The small piece of skull, with its conclusive bullet-hole, was rediscovered after the collapse of the USSR. In 2000 it was put on display in Moscow, a grisly tribute to the Soviet triumph over Nazism.

True! According to some reports, Hitler and Eva Braun were not buried alone. Hitler's faithful German Shepherd dog Blondi was cremated and buried with them, having first been poisoned with cyanide.

Hitler haunted the man of steel

Why was Joseph Stalin so desperate to have Adolf Hitler's corpse? And why did he go to such lengths to hide it from the world? Perhaps the answer lies with Vladimir Lenin, founder of the Soviet state. When Lenin died in 1924, it was Stalin who arranged to have his remains embalmed and put on public display. In subsequent years Stalin encouraged the cult of Lenin: his preserved body became an object of veneration, and the mausoleum on Red Square was like a holy shrine to Bolshevism.

So Stalin understood the magical power of a leader's dead body. He was terrified that a future generation might get hold of Hitler's body and use it to breathe new life into Nazism. This fear led him to check again and again that he had the right corpse. It was the action of a paranoid and obsessive man – with the resources of a superpower at his command.

THE FLAMMABLE HINDENBURG

The airship did not explode, it burned

It has always been thought that the Hindenburg was destroyed by a hydrogen explosion. But the film footage of the disaster seemed to show effects that contradicted this explanation, setting a retired rocket scientist on a quest for the truth.

The world's largest airship was late arriving at Lakehurst, New Jersey, on the afternoon of May 6, 1937. The thunderstorms that had slowed the *Hindenburg* down were still rumbling when the landing lines were dropped to the ground in preparation for mooring. Waiting below was a posse of newsreel cameramen and reporters, a small crowd of those meeting the passengers and a ground crew of 200, responsible for slowly winching the Zeppelin to the ground. On board were 38 passengers, and a crew of 59.

The first hint that something was wrong came when someone saw a blue glow of electrical activity dancing along the airship's starboard side. One of the passengers on board later described what he saw:

With my wife I was leaning out of a window on the promenade deck... I heard a light, dull detonation from above, no louder than the sound of a beer bottle being opened. I turned my gaze toward the bow and noticed a delicate rose glow, as though the sun were about to rise. I understood immediately that the airship was aflame.

Watched by the horrified crowd on the ground and recorded on unforgettable newsreel footage, the *Hindenburg* suddenly burst into flames, hung in the air for an agonising moment, and then slowly, almost sedately, crashed down to the ground. The tragedy was vividly recorded on audio tape by radio reporter Herb Morrison: 'This is one of the worst catastrophes in the world!' he wept into his microphone. 'It's a terrific crash, ladies and gentlemen... Oh! The humanity and all the passengers!'

The mooring crew had to run for their lives. One recalled:

We started running as fast as we could and praying at the same speed. The heat, light and smoke from the explosive hydrogen gas, and the realisation that we were under the massive, sinking hulk, left the sensation of being trapped... The fiery hulk crashed just behind us with the tail section hitting the ground first... Running with my head cocked back, I heard a message from a bullhorn: 'You are all clear, turn around and give them a hand'.

Everyone who was able to help raced back to the burning wreckage to

try and rescue survivors. Amazingly, 61 of the 97 people aboard were pulled out alive.

Hydrogen theory

In the aftermath of the accident it was immediately assumed that the airship's hydrogen had somehow ignited, fulfilling the predictions of many who had warned that hydrogen was too dangerous to be used for public transport. In fact, a smaller airship, the *Graf Zeppelin*, launched in 1928, had at that time completed 144 transatlantic flights and carried more than 18,000 passengers without any mishap. But the *Hindenburg* disaster dealt a fatal blow to the airship industry nevertheless.

Investigations into the accident were conducted by the governments of the USA and Germany, and both agreed that a leak of hydrogen was responsible, perhaps caused by the whiplash of a broken tension wire. The official reports concluded that a flammable mixture of hydrogen and air had built up under the cover of the dirigible, and was probably ignited by a discharge due to the atmospheric conditions in the storm.

Curiously, none of the surviving members of the crew could recall smelling hydrogen before the accident, even though the gas had been infused with a pungent aroma of garlic to identify any leaks quickly. For years afterwards there were rumours that the investigations were compromised and that the disaster could have been caused deliberately. Hermann Goering, the Third Reich's aviation minister, certainly let it be known that he suspected sabotage. Thanks to what became known as the '*Hindenburg* syndrome', hydrogen remained deeply suspect as a source of sustainable and environmentally benign fuel.

It fell to a NASA scientist, Dr Addison Bain, to uncover the truth, more than 60 years after the disaster. Bain was manager of the hydrogen programme at the Kennedy ▶ p.192

DINING ALOFT **The *Hindenburg* was the pride of Nazi Germany and also a luxurious way to travel. Its passengers could enjoy the finest food and wine as the airship cruised at 120km/h (80mph).**

ROOM WITH A VIEW **The top deck of the airship held a lounge flanked by a windowed promenade, as well as the passenger cabins – each of which had two berths and a washbasin. The quarters occupied by the passengers and crew were located some way behind the control gondola (below).**

Countdown to catastrophe

The last minutes of the *Hindenburg* were captured on newsreel. Frame-by-frame analysis, combined with computer imaging, has made it possible to unravel the sequence of events around the fatal ignition.

-6 minutes

Descent to 55m (180ft); landing crew standing by. Rainclouds had negatively charged the airship. Charge would usually dissipate during landing, but the crew chose a high docking, meaning the charge on the ship was much greater.

-3 minutes

On the newsreel, the *Hindenburg* appeared very close to the docking tower; in fact it came no closer than 220m (700ft). Lines dropped; they were wet, allowing the internal metal frame to earth its charge at once. The skin started to heat up.

-1 minute

Ground crew realised something was wrong. Ripples in the skin reported by some witnesses who thought they were seeing gas leaking. It could have been an electrical discharge effect or stresses as the fabric heated and buckled.

First flames

The skin was not conductive. Its temperature soared as charge tried to dissipate. Components of iron oxide and cellulose acetate were highly flammable and ignited. Passengers said 'detonation' but it was spontaneous combustion.

+5 seconds

Telltale orange flames showed that the skin and not the gas inside was on fire. The flames curled around and burned downwards, not upwards as hydrogen burns. The airship stayed 'in trim' – horizontal – for a few seconds as it burned.

5s

+10 seconds

The ship was a mass of flame, still more than 30m (100ft) in the air. The fabric tore open, and witnesses heard what they thought was an explosion. In fact, the hydrogen gas burned off into the air and did not rip the frame apart.

10s

+20 seconds

Full descent took around half a minute. The hydrogen kept the ship afloat and burned off in segments as each of the 16 cells was breached. As the cells opened up a much lighter coloured hydrogen fire burned above the ship.

20s

+34 seconds

In free fall, the airship would have dropped to the ground in around 4 seconds, rather than 34. The car landed rather than crashed. Many crew and passengers managed to crawl out and run from the inferno before it reached them.

34s

Aftermath

More survivors were pulled from the car by rescuers. 36 people perished – a third of those on board. Many of the survivors suffered severe burns; some, including the captain, died later. The body search continued until midnight.

The *Hindenburg* cruises gracefully above Manhattan, New York City, on August 14, 1936, en route for the Lakehurst Naval Air Station, New Jersey, where it would meet disaster the following year. A one-way trip across the Atlantic took two days and cost $400.

Space Center, and he believed that there were good grounds to doubt the official explanation given for the *Hindenburg* disaster.

Media coverage invariably referred to the *Hindenburg* 'exploding', whereas newsreel footage clearly showed that the great airship burned quite slowly, remaining horizontal at first and taking 34 seconds after the fire started to hit the ground. Had there been a hydrogen explosion, Bain reasoned, the blast would have destroyed the airship and instantly killed everyone on board and many on the ground.

Brilliant flames

Almost all the eyewitnesses spoke of the fire burning with very bright flames; many likened it to a fireworks display. But flames from a hydrogen fire would be virtually invisible in daylight. Bain had seen enough space shuttle launches at Cape Kennedy to know that flames show only when solid fuel is burned. When hydrogen takes over, there is nothing to be seen but a rippling in the air.

The final part of the puzzle was, to Bain, the most intriguing. As the density of hydrogen is only one-fourteenth that of air, a hydrogen fire would only have burned upwards. It was quite clear that the fire on the *Hindenburg* burned downwards from the start, with flames travelling down its rippled sides like beer overflowing

a tankard. Bain embarked on a long series of tests. He acquired remnants of the airship's wreckage, including a few scraps of the outer skin, interviewed survivors and eyewitnesses, and studied newsreel footage. He also visited the airship's mooring site at Lakehurst and combed through the archives at the Zeppelin Museum at Friedrichshafen, in southern Germany. Once he had a theory, he subjected it to rigorous chemical and physical verification in the laboratory.

Crucial tests

Working with the two original samples of fabric from the *Hindenburg*, Bain analysed the outer skin. He found that it was composed of iron oxide covered with five further layers of cellulose acetate, applied to tighten the cover and protect the airframe from moisture and rot. The NASA scientist recognised the mix immediately: it was practically identical to rocket fuel. The airship was primed with one of the most combustible mixtures known to man.

The *Hindenburg* took its silvery sheen from a coating of powdered aluminium. This was a relatively recent innovation, as the older *Graf Zeppelin* had used a different paint and stiffener. Bain knew that aluminium, too, burns easily when in this form.

Bain asked the NASA Materials Science Laboratory at the Kennedy Space Center to put one of the samples through a flame propagation test. It turned out to be still extremely volatile – even after 60 years – and instantly burst into flames.

A second test showed that the airship's skin would not have conducted electricity. In Bain's opinion this would have created a build-up of static electrical charge, which could start a fire when it discharged to earth during landing.

In a third test, a sample was subjected to high-voltage electric fields similar to the atmospheric conditions existing on the night of the disaster: it, too, readily ignited and was reduced to ash in seconds.

Corroboration of Bain's tests came when a handwritten letter he had found in the Zeppelin Museum in Germany was translated. It was written by Otto Beyersdorff, an electrical engineer hired by the Zeppelin Company as an independent investigator, and was dated June 28, 1937. After carrying out a series of laboratory tests, Beyersdorff had concluded that 'the actual cause of the fire was the extremely easy flammability of the covering material brought about by discharges of an electrostatic nature'.

Denials and cover-ups

Despite this explanation, Hugo Eckener, chairman of the Zeppelin Company, continued to insist that hydrogen was to blame. But there is clear evidence that the Zeppelin Company believed Beyersdorff and knew exactly what caused the *Hindenburg* disaster. Urgent modifications were made to the *Graf Zeppelin II*, the sister ship of the *Hindenburg*, which was under construction at that time. Calcium sulfumate, a fireproofing chemical, was added to the paint, and bronze powder was substituted for the flammable aluminium dust.

It is conceivable, though unproven, that the directors of the Zeppelin Company came under pressure from the German government not to reveal the true cause of the disaster. It was unthinkable that the engineers who had developed this impressive technology were at fault. German pride was at stake and, in the Third Reich, German pride was more important than the *Hindenburg*'s fall.

EMPTY SHELL **With the dead and injured removed, only the buckled skeleton of the *Hindenburg* remained at Lakehurst. The belief that hydrogen was the cause of the disaster ended the era of the magnificent passenger airships.**

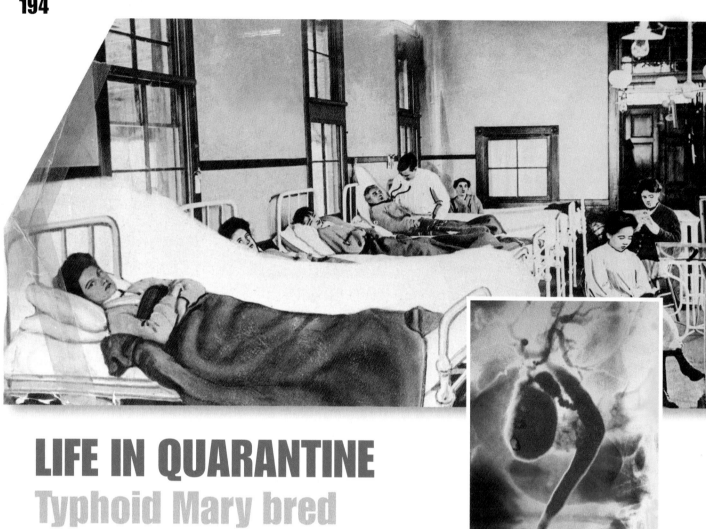

LIFE IN QUARANTINE
Typhoid Mary bred disease, but how?

America's first recorded 'healthy carrier' of typhoid, Mary Mallon, left a trail of sickness wherever she went. It is only now that we fully understand the reason for her infected condition – and how it could have been treated.

WARD OF COURT **A rare print of a news photograph shows Mary Mallon (foreground) in the Riverside Hospital, where she was detained by order of the New York Health Department. It is now known that the gall bladder (inset) – specifically gallstones (green) – can harbour typhoid bacteria in a healthy person.**

For the summer of 1906, New York banker Charles Henry Warren and his family rented a house in Oyster Bay, Long Island. They engaged a new cook, Mary Mallon. She gave them ice cream with sliced peaches – and she gave them typhoid. Six of the 11 people in the house succumbed to the disease – one of the Warren daughters later died – but Mary appeared healthy as she served up *Salmonella typhi* with the salad.

In threatening the lives of others, Mary Mallon ruined her own, gaining infamy as 'Typhoid Mary' and being forced to spend the last 23 years of her life in isolation as a threat to public health.

She might never have been caught, had it not been for the tenacity of one man: Major George Soper, a military surgeon and epidemiologist brought in by the owner of the Oyster Bay house to investigate the outbreak. By the time he was hired, in the winter of 1906, Mary had left the Warren household. At first, Soper thought that the local soft clams might have been the source of the typhoid. But his suspicions soon shifted to Mary, believing that she may have been a 'healthy' typhoid carrier – that is, one who had once had a mild case of typhoid, and was still able to spread it to others, but who was herself completely unaffected.

In March 1907, Soper tracked her down to an apartment in Manhattan, New York, where she was working as a cook. On being told that she was suspected of spreading typhoid by handling the food she served, a disbelieving Mary drove him from the house with a carving fork. The next time, Soper and a colleague lay in wait for Mary at the apartment of a friend, where she was expected: 'We wanted a small sample of urine, one of faeces and one of blood,' he related in a subsequent paper. Perhaps not surprisingly, 'Indignant and peremptory denials met our appeals.'

Taken into custody

Frustrated, Soper approached the New York Health Department, urging that Mary be confined. On March 19, officials dragged her to a detention hospital. Tests for typhoid proved positive. 'The cook was virtually a living culture tube,' Soper wrote.

Now in effect a prisoner of the authorities, Mary was transferred to Riverside Hospital on North Brother Island in the East River. Soper evidently failed to convince her of the serious risk she presented to others, as she directed her energies towards suing for her release. 'I have always been healthy. Why should I be treated like a leper?' she complained.

Soper knew that removal of the gall bladder had been an effective treatment for some carriers. Mary refused the offer of such an invasive procedure, perhaps on moral or legal grounds – but more likely because she mistrusted the man who had hounded her into a hospital prison.

The courts ruled against Mary, but in 1910, against Soper's advice, she was released, with the proviso that she would not take work as a cook and would report regularly to the authorities. For a while Mary complied, but then she moved on.

In 1915, there was an outbreak of typhoid in the Sloane Hospital for Women, New York City. Twenty-five people fell sick; two died. For three

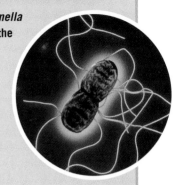

Anatomy of a typhoid carrier

Mary Mallon was a carrier of the typhoid bacilli *Salmonella typhi* (right), which attach themselves to gallstones in the gall bladder. This is the only organ that can be colonised by bacteria while the rest of the body remains healthy. The gall bladder provides an ideal condition for the bacteria to produce a glue-like substance, which they use to anchor themselves to the gallstones' rough surfaces. Research shows that if there are no gallstones present in the gall bladder, the bacteria will not multiply – so removing Mary's gall bladder would have stopped her contaminating others.

months, a 'Mrs Mary Brown' had been the hospital cook, but was unavailable for questioning. She was traced, identified as Mallon and returned to Riverside Hospital. This time, Mary remained on the little island, living alone in a small cottage in the hospital grounds until her death, aged 69, in 1938. She worked washing bottles in a laboratory and, one resident recollects, ran a sideline – baking cakes.

The humiliating nickname Typhoid Mary had long passed into the language when it came up in 2001 at a general meeting of the American Society for Microbiology. Here, finally, a scientist was able to reveal to the world why in typhoid epidemics a small proportion of those that appear unaffected will be infectious 'Typhoid Marys'.

Dr Angela Prouty of the University of Texas Health Science Center described how she had discovered that typhoid bacteria are able to cling to gallstones and multiply rapidly by secreting an adhesive film that anchors them in place.

George Soper is vindicated by the finding. Although he rarely acknowledged it, Mary's condition fascinated him as much as her willingness to risk others' lives repelled him. To him she was:

A character apart, by nature and by circumstance, strangely chosen to bear the burden of a great lesson to the world.

HEALTH WARNING Mary's case aroused mixed reactions. One newspaper illustration showed her frying skulls the size of dumplings; a kinder one portrayed her alone and dejected, with just a dog for company.

FAME
AND
REPUTATION

AGAINST ALL ODDS
Freak weather, not human error, sealed Captain Scott's fate

The British explorer Robert Scott's race to the South Pole has been seen as a heroic failure, even a self-inflicted disaster induced by bad leadership and planning. But new meteorological evidence suggests a different reason for the expedition's sorry end.

POLAR PATH A member of Scott's team poses in front of the Antarctic volcano Mount Erebus, close to the expedition's base camp on McMurdo Sound. The parallel, wave-like ridges on which he stands are known as 'sastrugi', and are formed by winds carving the hard snow.

Sunday January 21, 1912: Captain Robert Falcon Scott was leading his dispirited party home. They had lost the race to the South Pole, reaching their destination three days earlier to find a Norwegian flag billowing in the breeze. The five Englishmen faced a two-month return trek to safety, and were racing against the onset of the Antarctic winter. They were not making good time. Scott noted in his diary that the surface was horribly bad, making dragging the sledges difficult and reducing their pace. But at least they were close to the 'three degree' depot, which held the promise of food and fuel. 'Once there we ought to be safe,' Scott wrote, anticipating an improvement in conditions. Depots dotted the route home, and the temperatures would rise as the party travelled further from the Pole. Surely, he thought, it would soon get warmer.

At the South Pole itself, Scott was recording temperatures around -29°C

(-20°F). As the men walked the first hundred miles towards the Beardmore Glacier, the thermometer began to climb, but by the time they reached the Ross Ice Shelf, five weeks later, they were colder than they had been at the Pole itself.

By March 21, Scott and the two remaining members of his party, Henry 'Birdie' Bowers and Edward Wilson, were dying in the tent where their bodies would be found after the winter. There were no supplies left and the three hungry men knew that they were doomed. Of their original party, Seaman Edgar Evans had already perished, brain damaged after a fall down a crevasse, while Captain William Oates had taken his 'walk outside', leaving the shelter of the tent in the hope that – by sacrificing himself – he would secure the lives of his comrades.

It was in vain. As the three men slowly succumbed to the cold, Scott forced his frostbitten hands to write a 'Message to the Public', his explanation for the tragic end to the expedition. It was not to be recovered for another eight months, by which time the legend of Scott's courageous failure had already taken hold.

In recent years, some historians have questioned the popular perception of this heroic, particularly British, demise. The challenge to conquer the vast landmass of Antarctica was as fierce as the Soviet-American space race of the 1960s. Yet Scott was portrayed as unprepared, panicky, a poor leader of men; according to one historian, 'so consistently inept as to almost suggest the workings of a death wish.' Had he sacrificed the lives of his men in the name of competition?

It is true that some of Scott's decisions hampered the expedition's progress. He opted to take ponies, but it was their poor condition after the voyage that necessitated the fatally late start. Worse, the ponies were unable to scale the heavily crevassed Beardmore Glacier, leaving the men to haul their own supplies across 1100km (750 miles) of snow. Scott's

> We have taken a risk for the honour of our country. We knew it was a risk... we have no complaint... These rough notes and our dead bodies must tell the tale.
>
> ROBERT FALCON SCOTT

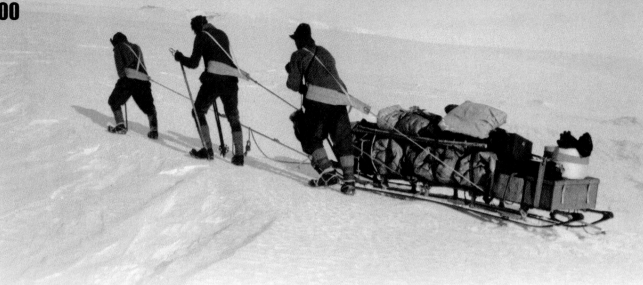

LONG HAUL **The loss of the ponies and dogs – which were eaten en route – and the breakdown of the motor sledges meant that Scott and his men had to wear harnesses and pull the heavy loads themselves.**

The fatal freeze

The polar party's low readings show how normal temperatures on the ice shelf were followed by a horrific cold that they could not have predicted.

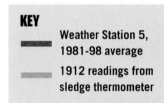

KEY

Weather Station 5, 1981-98 average

1912 readings from sledge thermometer

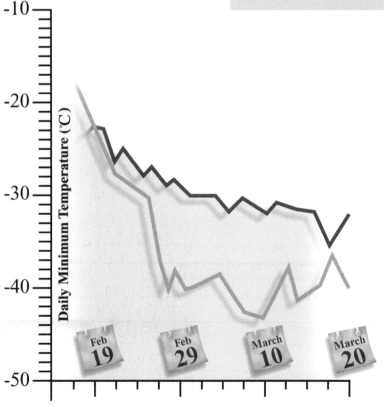

rival Roald Amundsen took only dogs. Setting off before Scott, his party reached the Pole on December 15, 1911, and travelled home through comparatively mild daily minimum temperatures of around -15°C (5°F).

Another unfortunate decision was to take along Henry Bowers on the last stretch to the Pole. The final party was supposed to comprise four men, but at the last minute Scott chose to bring one more. However, the gear and the supplies had not been tailored for five, and the extra consumption left little surplus to allow for error.

Perhaps Scott wanted to use Bowers' navigational skills, or felt that another man should share in the glory of reaching the Pole. Whatever the reason, he was signing Bowers' death warrant.

These mistakes may have cost Scott the chance to reach the Pole first, but had they been responsible for the death of his expedition team? One man who believed that other factors had been at work was the party's meteorologist, George 'Sunny Jim' Simpson. After he returned to his post at the Indian Meteorological Office in Calcutta, Simpson pored over the weather readings he had taken during his years at the South Pole. They suggested that the Antarctic temperatures of spring 1912 had been significantly colder than normal. But with no independent data to back up his theory, it went largely unheeded. It was another 70 years before an expert joined in the fight to rescue the reputation of Captain Scott. In 1986 a meteorologist with the American National Oceanic and Atmospheric Administration, Dr Susan Solomon, began studying at McMurdo Sound, the spot where Scott had set up a land base on his first trip there in 1901.

Poles apart

Scott's meteorologist George Simpson (left) sent up balloons to record air temperatures and used thermometers that had to be checked daily. By contrast the American meteorologist Dr Susan Solomon had data from six computerised weather stations printing out automatically at regular intervals. Readings were transmitted via satellite to her base station from points spaced along Scott's route. The results she obtained were a detailed confirmation of what Simpson had been struggling to prove.

From her room in the base she could see Scott's old hut across Winter Quarters Bay.

After reading papers and letters written by Simpson, Solomon looked into the temperature patterns on the Ross Ice Shelf, through which Scott's return journey led. From March 5 to 19, 1912, Scott's party recorded temperatures of as low as -40°C (-40°F). This was around 8°C (15°F) lower than the average of the minimum temperatures Solomon had recorded on the ice shelf. But could they have been mistaken? Simpson thought not: Scott had taken regular readings from two thermometers. But the dip did not show up elsewhere in the Antarctic that year.

Frozen ice and frostbite

Dr Solomon checked the records and found that in 1988 there had been just such a drop of 8 degrees on the ice shelf during late February. In every other year over 17 years of records, the drop occurred in late March. Solomon noted that 1988 was a year in which an El Niño climatic change had affected the Antarctic weather; this was the evidence of irregularity she needed. From all the data, she calculated the likelihood of the conditions Scott endured to be about one in 20.

The drop of 8 degrees did not just mean additional hardship. The actual feasibility of the journey itself was called into question. At such low temperatures, the film of water that enables skis or runners to slide will not form, making it practically impossible to pull a sledge. Scott compared the conditions to 'desert sand' and wrote in his diary:

On this surface we know we cannot equal half our old marches, and that for that effort we expend nearly double... the energy... Sledge dreadfully heavy.

At these temperatures the wind dropped – another rare climatic phenomenon. Scott's plan to return home by attaching sails to the sledges was dashed. The men were unable to cope with the physical demand of dragging the sledges themselves; they were already ravaged by frostbite. On March 18, Scott wrote: 'My right foot has gone, nearly all the toes.'

Scott made mistakes, yet the criticism levelled at him from some quarters has been as harsh as the Antarctic wind. Both Scott and Amundsen took calculated risks during their attempts to reach the Pole, but the unusually cold temperatures of 1912 compounded Scott's errors of judgment.

This did not mean there was a lack of preparation or an excess of gung-ho spirit. The British party were experienced explorers, aware of the risks they faced. Scott's final message to the public read as follows:

Our wreck is certainly due to this sudden advent of severe weather, which does not seem to have any satisfactory cause. I do not think human beings ever came through such a month as we have come through.

GREAT SCOTT Robert Falcon Scott joined his first ship, HMS *Boadicea*, at the age of just 13. Con, as he was known to his family, served as a midshipman for two years: his glittering early naval career gained him his first command of an Antarctic expedition in 1901.

GOOD CAPTAIN BLIGH
The captain of HMS Bounty was neither cruel nor tyrannical

The British sea captain William Bligh is notorious for provoking a mutiny on his ship, the Bounty. Yet this uprising was not a noble revolt against a harsh regime, as so often portrayed in films and books. In fact, Bligh was a fine sailor and one of the most lenient captains in the entire Royal Navy. The mutiny was the result of a clash of two very different personalities.

A LOYAL CREW A 1790 engraving, *The Mutineers Casting Bligh Adrift in the Launch* by Robert Dodd, depicts the moment when Captain William Bligh was thrown off his ship. He and the men with him were given only enough supplies to last five days.

On the morning of April 28, 1789, HMS *Bounty* was some 50km (30 miles) south of the Friendly Islands in the South Pacific. Captain William Bligh was awoken at bayonet point when members of the crew barged into his cabin. Bligh recalled hearing the command: 'Hold your tongue, Sir, or you are dead this instant'. His hands were bound and, still in his nightshirt, he was taken up to the deck. Fletcher Christian, the 24-year-old second-in-command, looked on, 'eyes flaming with rage', as Bligh later wrote in his evidence to the mutineers' trial.

Bligh appealed to Christian, an officer he had handpicked for the voyage: 'You have danced my children on your knee,' he said. 'It is too late,' Christian replied, 'I have been in hell for this fortnight past and cannot bear it any longer.' Bligh and 18 men loyal to him were set adrift in a small boat. As the two vessels parted company, the deposed captain recorded in his diary that he had heard a celebratory cry 'Huzza for Otaheite [Tahiti]!' from the 25 mutineers left on board the ship.

The story of the mutiny has been presented as a classic drama on the high seas: a group of impassioned young men starting a new life in an exotic paradise, breaking free from the tyranny of a sadistic and cruel captain. The first act of those 'liberated' from their obligations to Bligh and the British Navy was to throw the ship's cargo of breadfruit

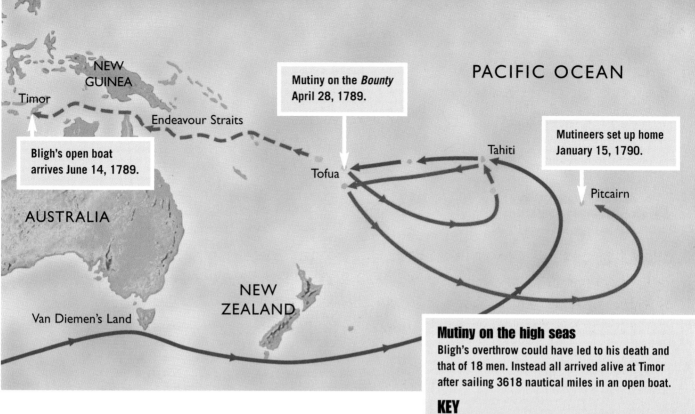

NEW GUINEA

Timor

Endeavour Straits

**Mutiny on the *Bounty*
April 28, 1789.**

PACIFIC OCEAN

Tahiti

**Mutineers set up home
January 15, 1790.**

**Bligh's open boat
arrives June 14, 1789.**

Tofua

Pitcairn

AUSTRALIA

**NEW
ZEALAND**

Van Diemen's Land

Mutiny on the high seas

Bligh's overthrow could have led to his death and
that of 18 men. Instead all arrived alive at Timor
after sailing 3618 nautical miles in an open boat.

KEY

→ The *Bounty*'s route before the mutiny

➤ The mutineers' escape

--- Bligh's voyage to safety

plants overboard. Fletcher Christian was then elected leader and some of the sails were torn up to make identical canvas uniforms that signified equal status for all. With that, the men turned the ship around and headed back to Tahiti.

The *Bounty* had just spent six months on the island and many had fallen under its spell. Bligh and his men had been sent to the South Pacific to collect cuttings of the breadfruit tree, whose fruit was to be used as food for Caribbean slaves. The long shore leave in Tahiti had been necessary to allow the breadfruit seedlings to grow into plants strong enough to survive a long voyage. The time the crew spent on 'the finest island in the world', with its friendly people and their relaxed lifestyle, captivated them. Many had Tahitian lovers, some had themselves tattooed: plenty began seriously to consider settling there. With the captain removed, it seemed that they would now get their chance.

Maritime miracle

Set adrift and left to the mercy of the sea, Bligh first headed for Tofua, where he and his men narrowly escaped death at the hands of hostile islanders. He then set course for the nearest European settlement, on Timor, an island in the Dutch East

Indies, some 6400km (4000 miles) away. It was a terrible voyage in the 7m (23ft) open boat. Living off only a few loaves of bread, raw fish and the occasional sea bird, the men constantly had to bail water as the sea broke over them. Although violent rainstorms provided drinking water, they induced 'cold and shiverings scarcely to be conceived.'

Bligh navigated the Endeavour Straits and its treacherous reefs without the aid of a map. It was one of the greatest feats of navigation – and survival – in history. Seven weeks after the mutiny, on June 14, 1789, the boat arrived at Kupang, Timor.

On his return to England, Bligh was praised and the mutiny condemned, but there was some puzzlement as to the motives of its leader, Fletcher Christian, an officer with respectable connections. Bligh blamed the temptations of Tahitian life – the offers of great possessions by its chiefs and the promiscuity of its women. He was exonerated for the loss of his ship and given a second breadfruit voyage.

Another ship, meanwhile, set sail to find the mutineers. Fourteen of them were found easily enough – on Tahiti

BITTER HARVEST The object of the *Bounty*'s mission was to collect breadfruit trees, as it was hoped that they would provide a cheap food source for Caribbean slaves. In fact, the slaves loathed the breadfruit and refused to eat it.

The mutineers on Pitcairn

During shore leave, many mutineers had established relationships with Tahitian women. None was more besotted than Fletcher Christian, whose lover Maimiti was said to be older than him and very striking in appearance. Many – including Bligh – suggested that the allure of these women was the prime reason for the mutiny. According to surviving mutineers, Christian and Maimiti were married on Tahiti.

American sealing boats landing on Pitcairn Island in 1808 were startled to find English-speaking inhabitants. The islanders said that they were children of the *Bounty* mutineers and had one survivor among them, John Adams, to tell the story.

Bloody feud

After a dispute in Tahiti, the mutineers had split into two groups – one group stayed and they were later captured and brought to trial. The others sailed east with some Tahitian women and men in search of an uninhabited island. On discovering Pitcairn Island, they burnt the ship to avoid detection, built houses and farmed land. But life became difficult when one mutineer laid claim to a woman who was spoken for. The Tahitian men who objected were flogged by the sailors; they then broke away from the settlement and began a series of ambush killings. Ten were murdered in the feud, including Fletcher Christian.

Maimiti and several of her children (including her son named Thursday, above) survived the feud and remained devoted to Christian's memory. In 1841, George Gardner, a British navigator visiting the island, described Maimiti as 'surprisingly active, her age being estimated between 80 and 90.' Her looks had not survived, as she was 'the most perfect picture of an old hag I ever saw'.

seems to have abounded with men above the common herd of illiterates', wrote one observer, impressed by the impromptu cross-examination of Boatswain James Morrison.

For others, like James Heywood, family influence was on hand to help them to escape the noose. In all, only three men were hanged. One of them was aged just 17, and he had been asleep when the *Bounty* was taken.

Under the strict rules for evidence, no one could record the events that had actually caused the mutiny. This only encouraged the rumours surrounding the case. The public was hungry for details of Bligh's 'tyranny' and avidly consumed the contents of a pamphlet published after the trial by Fletcher Christian's brother Edward.

Christian himself was still at large, by now married to a Tahitian and living on the remote Pitcairn Island in the Pacific Ocean. But he had his brother – a professor of law at Cambridge – back in England to defend him.

Edward Christian set up a kind of parallel 'trial', parading several witnesses to the events on the *Bounty* before a panel of 'respectable gentlemen'. This unofficial panel concluded that Bligh had exceeded the accepted limits of command.

Violent temper

Bligh had no such champion. He was a simple self-educated Cornishman who had entered the Navy as a seaman at 16. He lacked the refined manners of some officers, but worse than that was his line in insults.

Bligh's temper was instrumental in creating a rift between him and his first mate. In the three weeks following the *Bounty*'s departure from Tahiti, Fletcher Christian became the object of a series of Bligh's violent tirades.

Christian was a sensitive man, apparently unable to cope with Bligh's temper. If he felt himself 'in hell', it was the result of accumulated criticisms and disparagement. One witness reported to Edward Christian that: 'Whatever fault was found, Mr

– but it was discovered that the rest, including Fletcher Christian, had disappeared with the *Bounty*. Those who were caught were manacled naked for two months below decks and, when the ship struck reefs, four of them drowned in their chains.

Having survived shipwreck and starvation, the rest of the captured mutineers had to plead for their lives at a court martial on HMS *Duke* in Portsmouth harbour. Only two had legal representation; the others had to manage by their own wits. 'The ship

 False! Captain Bligh was not actually a captain when he took the Bounty to Tahiti. Promised a captaincy after the voyage, the 33-year-old Bligh was only a lieutenant.

Christian was sure to bear the brunt of the captain's anger'.

During an ill-judged raid on the island of Aitutaki, part of the Cook Group, Christian's foraging party had a narrow escape when they were attacked by natives. He received a barrage of abuse from his captain upon his return to the ship: 'God damn your blood, why did you not fire?' Bligh seemed to have forgotten that he had ordered his men not to use their weapons, for fear of provoking further conflict.

Bligh continued to single out his first mate for criticism. The night before the mutiny, he was heard to call Christian 'a cowardly rascal' and then a 'lying thief' for taking coconuts not apportioned to him.

Polite society seemed disposed to believe one of its own, and Bligh's reputation became tarnished, paving the way for the modern depiction of Fletcher Christian as a heroic young idealist, standing up to a violent and despotic commanding officer.

But some evidence had been overlooked. The ship's log actually proved that, despite the lash of his tongue, Bligh was the most lenient captain in the Navy. The record shows the captain's average of floggings per seaman to be lower than on any other British ship in the Pacific in the 18th century. After one such punishment, four months into the *Bounty*'s journey, Bligh wrote that 'until this afternoon I had hoped I could have performed the voyage without punishment to anyone'. During the *Bounty*'s long stay in Tahiti, he was lenient with two deserters, ordering them lashed when he was within his rights to have them hanged.

Cleaning and dancing

Throughout the voyage of the *Bounty*, Bligh's actions were those of a reforming humanitarian rather than the brutal tyrant of popular legend. He introduced a three-watch system that had seamen on duty four hours in 12 instead of four in eight, and he had vegetables included in the men's diet.

Ironically, it was precisely these attempts to institute a rational, humane regime that turned the crew

FILM VILLAIN Charles Laughton played the role of Captain Bligh in the 1935 film *Mutiny on the Bounty*. Bligh was portrayed as a cruel and abusive captain. In one scene he flogged a dead man, and in another ordered the keelhauling of a sailor who had requested a sip of water.

against Bligh. They resented having to eat sauerkraut and malt extract. His paternal efforts to ensure that their clothes were dry and hammocks clean bordered on the obsessive: 'Seamen will seldom attend to themselves,' he once wrote, 'they must be watched like children'.

Even Bligh's introduction of the 'cheerful exercise' of compulsory dancing in the evenings led to one flogging and caused such discontent that the men invented their own dances to mock the captain. And Bligh's ban on the sadistic practice of dunking crewmen over the side when 'Crossing the Line' of the Equator brought even more outrage. Bligh had interfered with a time-honoured ritual of baptism in the ocean. The men did not care that the captain thought it 'brutal and inhuman'.

Supporters of the mutineers also made much of Bligh's mean-spirited use of the ship's provisions, but it was a role forced upon him by the Admiralty, who had decreed that any shortfall in stock would come from the captain's own pocket.

Fletcher Christian's explanation for the mutiny will never be known: he and the other sailors fell out with the Tahitians they had sought to befriend, and were murdered in a series of violent ambushes on Pitcairn Island.

A captain vindicated

By contrast, Bligh's career after the *Bounty* was marked by success. In 1797, he commanded HMS *Director* at the battle of Camperdown and, as captain of HMS *Glatton* in 1801, took part in the Battle of Copenhagen, after which he was commended for his bravery by Admiral Horatio Nelson. Also in 1801, Bligh was elected a Fellow of the Royal Society – a prestigious scientific academy – for his distinguished services to navigation and natural history.

Perhaps more important is the character reference provided by the 18 crewmen of the *Bounty* who chose to stay in a rowing boat with their captain rather than return to the paradise of Tahiti. More would have travelled with him, but the boat was overloaded and some had to clamber back onto the *Bounty* with the mutineers. A seaman from the boat recalled: 'I felt the unbridled licence of his power of speech, yet never without soon receiving something like a plaster to heal the wound.'

> **More would have been set adrift with Bligh, but the boat became overloaded and they had to climb back onto the *Bounty*.**

LIVING LEGACY **A tinted photograph of the descendants of John Adams, the sole *Bounty* survivor on Pitcairn, was taken by a Captain Cator at the end of the 19th century. January 23 is celebrated as 'Bounty Day' and commemorates the day in 1790 when the mutineers burned their ship and settled on the island.**

HURRICANE FORCE
Statistics reveal the Battle of Britain's unsung hero

In 1940, a battle raged in the skies above southern England that would change the course of the Second World War. The decisive factor was widely believed to be the fast and manoeuvrable Spitfire, but in fact it was the durable Hurricane that saved the day.

AT CLOSE QUARTERS As an RAF Spitfire overtakes a slower Heinkel HE III bomber, a brave German airman in the Heinkel snatches a photograph through the nose of his plane. The Spit was fast and deft in flight, but its contribution to the British victory may have been overemphasised by its dashing tactical superiority.

The series of aerial combats fought over southern England in the summer of 1940 – collectively known as the Battle of Britain – was of crucial strategic importance in the Second World War. If the Battle of Britain had been won by the Germans – that is, if the Nazi leader Adolf Hitler had gained air supremacy over the English Channel and landed his troops on the beaches of Kent and Sussex – then it is not just the history of the United Kingdom that would have been different. With Britain beaten, German troops,

armour and aircraft concentrated in the west would have been redeployed against the Russians on the Eastern Front in 1941. This could have tipped the balance of the entire war in the Germans' favour.

The British prime minister Winston Churchill's tribute to the RAF pilots – 'Never in the field of human conflict was so much owed by so many to so few' – captured both the scale of their achievement and the mood of the nation. It also played its part in the creation of the myth of the Spitfire – a myth that took hold even before victory had been secured, and lodged in the mind of every civilian in the south of England who turned to look skyward in the long summer of 1940.

What they might have seen was a droning pack of German bombers – Dorniers, Junkers, Heinkels – and their escort of fighter aircraft, Messerschmitt Me 109Es and 110s, diving and scattering at the sudden, ferocious onslaught unleashed upon them from above. Spitfires!

Magic in a name

The Supermarine Spitfire, armed with eight Browning .303 machine guns, was one of the most celebrated aircraft of the war. Sleekly beautiful, manoeuvrable and fast, the plane was the airborne equivalent of the wire-wheeled MGs favoured by some of its fast-living young pilots. It was glamour with wings.

Luftwaffe crews dreaded it. When the German air ace Adolf Galland was asked by his Commander-in-Chief Hermann Goering what he needed to turn the tide of battle, he replied: 'A squadron of Spitfires'. The aeroplane was lauded by newspapers and film-makers as England's saviour.

This was true, but only in the same way as a dedicated team player contributes to a shared victory. From a distance, the black specks in the sky, harrying the enemy, all looked alike – agile, single-seat fighters with enclosed cockpits, RAF roundels and racketing machine guns. Observers on the ground could be forgiven their assumption, but in fact most of these planes were not Spitfires but Hurricanes. To insist on the Hurricane receiving its due, however,

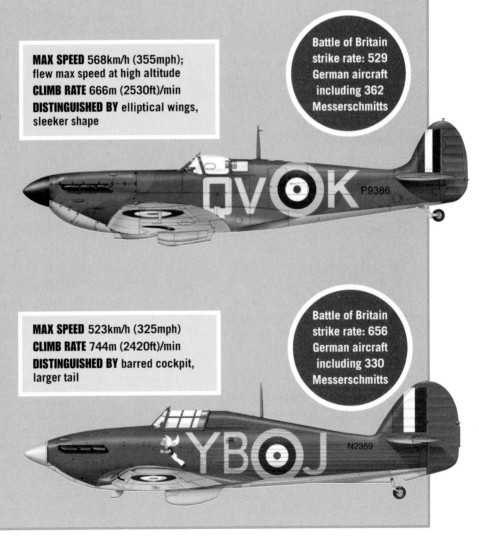

Spitfire Mk I

● First plane flew in May 1938, but the Mk I proved slow to construct.

● 1583 Mk Is were built. The Mk II appeared in July 1940, only just in time for a few hundred to take part in the Battle of Britain.

● Comprised 31 per cent of the RAF fighters in the Battle of Britain.

● Highly effective at altitudes of more than 4600m (15,000ft), where most Battle of Britain dogfights took place.

MAX SPEED 568km/h (355mph); flew max speed at high altitude
CLIMB RATE 666m (2530ft)/min
DISTINGUISHED BY elliptical wings, sleeker shape

Battle of Britain strike rate: 529 German aircraft including 362 Messerschmitts

Hurricane Mk I

● Went into production in 1936 at the Hawker works and other factories by tender.

● By September 1939, 497 had been built, by early 1940, a total of 3774.

● Comprised 55 per cent of the RAF fighters in the Battle of Britain.

● Although slower, easier than the Spitfire to land, and simpler to maintain and repair.

MAX SPEED 523km/h (325mph)
CLIMB RATE 744m (2420ft)/min
DISTINGUISHED BY barred cockpit, larger tail

Battle of Britain strike rate: 656 German aircraft including 330 Messerschmitts

is not to deny that the Spitfire was the superior aircraft. As one pilot wrote:

Flying the Spitfire was like driving a sports car. It was faster than the old Hurricane, much more delicate. You couldn't roll it very fast, but you could make it go up and down much easier… It wouldn't do anything wrong. The Hurricane would drop a wing if you stalled it coming in, but a Spitfire would come wafting down… And so fast! If you shut the throttle on a Hurricane you'd come to a grinding halt. In a Spitfire you just go whistling on.

It was not until early 1941 that the production of Spitfires caught up with that of Hurricanes. In August 1940, Spitfires accounted for only 31 per cent of the operational fighter force. Some researchers claim that, owing to time spent on repairs, during August and September there were about twice as many Hurricanes as Spitfires in the air. But the Spitfire made its mark. At the end of the Battle of Britain, on October 31, 1940, the Spitfire had shot down 529 enemy aircraft; the Hurricane, 656.

German disadvantages

Analysis of German strategy shows that the Battle of Britain was swung in the Allies' favour by German miscalculation at command level rather than by any significant advantage owed to the Allies' flying skill or the quality of their aircraft. The Luftwaffe had the disadvantage of fighting over enemy territory far from home, when its pilots were already tired. If British pilots ran low on fuel or ammunition they could easily land to pick up more and quickly be back in the air again.

The Germans had no option but to run for home, severely limiting their capacity for engagement. And as the fighters had a significantly shorter range than that of the bombers, the latter frequently had to fly on without escort protection.

It was worse for the Luftwaffe, too, when they were hit. When RAF flyers bailed out or crash-landed, they were often picked up from the sea by Coastal Command. On land, they could walk or take the train back to their airfields. In total, throughout the battle, 1220 British planes were

FACTORY FLAW With advanced stressed-skin construction and a complex moulded shape, the Spitfire (above) was not easy to build. By contrast, Hurricanes, with their tubular metal structure, could be run rapidly off the production line.

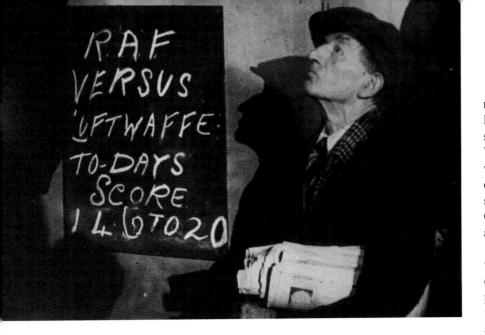

DOGFIGHT SCORES For civilians looking up, aerial combats between the Royal Air Force and the German Luftwaffe often had the feel of a game. Scores were sometimes chalked up on blackboards, though the deadly seriousness of the battles was never in doubt.

destroyed at a cost of 443 pilots' lives – a survival rate of 60 per cent.

German crews that were forced to land fell into enemy hands and were lost for the duration of the war. Many Luftwaffe planes were bombers rather than single-seat fighters, so their human losses were much heavier.

The RAF built more planes and had better ground crews to repair damage quickly. Britain also had a Ground Controlled Interception System, based on radar, which gave vital early warning of the enemy's approach. The Germans lacked any such system, and so were easily ambushed.

Goering's mistakes

Many of the decisions that were made by Hermann Goering made these disadvantages even more acute. He underestimated the importance of the radar stations and called off the Luftwaffe's attacks on them. The station at Ventnor on the Isle of Wight, just off England's south coast, would have been an easy target, but it operated unimpeded throughout summer 1940 and supplied Fighter Command with accurate information about the Germans' likely missions.

Goering was also deaf to his pilots' views on flight formation. On his orders, the Messerschmitt fighters played a purely defensive role. They flew in close escort to the bombers and were denied the freedom to go hunting for Hurricanes and Spitfires.

Major Adolf Galland was a brilliant fighter pilot who was given command of the Luftwaffe's Fighter Wing 26 in August 1940. He was later made General of the Luftwaffe, but his leadership came too late for the Germans fighting the Battle of Britain. Galland had clear opinions on Goering's abilities as a tactician, and wrote after the war:

The theme of fighter protection was chewed over again and again. Goering clearly represented the point of view of the bombers and demanded close and rigid protection. The bomber, he said, was more important than record bag [kill] figures.

I tried to point out that the Me 109 was superior in the attack and not so suitable for purely

More about 'the few'

If the Hurricane had not been so easy to fly, British losses would probably have been far greater, because 70 per cent of RAF Battle of Britain pilots were new recruits who had never previously flown in action. After the war, 'the few' were often portrayed as upper-class, public school types. But in fact, of the 3500 Fighter Command pilots, only 200 had been educated at such schools. The majority came from humbler backgrounds and 20 per cent of them were from overseas, notably New Zealand, Canada and the USA. There were also Czechs and Poles, some of whom had to suffer the consequences of being mistaken for Germans when they were shot down in rural England.

defensive purposes as the Spitfire, which, although a little slower, was much more manoeuvrable. He rejected my objection.

But Galland was right. Although the Hurricane outnumbered the Spitfire and outscored it in total kills during the Battle of Britain, against Me 109s it was the Spitfire – with 282 kills against the Hurricane's 222 – that had the higher strike rate.

The two aircraft worked in partnership. While the Spitfires distracted the German fighters, the Hurricanes flying at a lower altitude could concentrate on shooting down the bombers. In an inspired strategy, outfits of Spitfires were sent purposely to draw off the German fighter contingents. The Hurricanes would then step in to shoot down the bombers left temporarily unprotected.

By mid-September, Hitler made what many analysts have identified as his fatal mistake – abandoning the invasion plan and switching the emphasis to night-time raids on London and other cities, thus bringing an end to the Battle of Britain and giving Fighter Command time to recover its strength. It was not long before the Spitfire truly did become the RAF's premier fighter – a machine that appealed as much to the aesthetic sense of the men who flew it as to their instinct for adventure.

'The Spit didn't look as if it was meant to be a fighting machine', said one pilot. 'It looked as if it would be beautiful to fly – which it was.'

SCRAMBLE! Squadrons of Hurricane pilots based at an airfield in southern England race for their planes. Their aim was to intercept German aircraft at the earliest possible moment as they flew across the Channel.

MALIGNED MADONNA
Lucrezia Borgia's bad reputation stems from her family's dark deeds

Lucrezia Borgia is known to history as a murderess, a husband killer and a monster of sexual depravity. But there is no evidence that she ever poisoned anyone; in fact, she appears to have been a helpless victim whose reputation was poisoned by the enemies of her family.

HIS FATHER'S SON **Cesare Borgia was made a cardinal by his father at the age of 17; later he gained infamy as a ruthless general. His government of the Romagna region in northern Italy inspired Niccolò Machiavelli's treatise on leadership, *The Prince*.**

The Catholic Church in the Middle Ages was the most powerful political organisation in the world. The Vatican, the pope's seat of power in Rome, levied taxes, sold 'indulgences' – pardons for sins – and ran lucrative industries throughout Europe. The pope commanded vast personal wealth and had to be a consummate politician. Rodrigo Borgia, father of Lucrezia, was just such a man.

The Borgia family had arrived in Italy from Spain and bought and bargained their way into the Vatican during the 15th century. In 1492 Cardinal Rodrigo was elected Pope Alexander VI and became the archetype of the Renaissance popes: lustful, scheming and brutal in his dealings with his enemies.

Lucrezia Borgia was 12 years old when her father became pope – old enough to be a useful pawn in Rodrigo's dynastic scheming. She had already been betrothed twice before her first marriage, at the age of 13. Her husband was Giovanni Sforza, a prominent member of a powerful Milanese family.

If the extravagance of the wedding was any indication, the prospect of forming such an alliance delighted Rodrigo. The young couple were married in the Vatican in 1494. Guilia Farnese, Rodrigo's latest and youngest mistress, led the bride's attendants – a procession of 500 women. But not every onlooker was impressed: the ceremony caused a scandal in Rome, where outspoken churchmen were vocal in their criticism of papal excesses.

Incest and impotence
But the Sforza family did not prove powerful enough to satisfy the ambition of Lucrezia's father. When they failed to deliver their promised alliances, Rodrigo decided to annul his daughter's marriage. The only legitimate reason for this was non-consummation, and Rodrigo accordingly requested a declaration of impotency from Giovanni Sforza. The Sforza family, unwilling to quarrel with the pope, forced Giovanni into signing a confession of non-consummation before an audience of doctors and theologians.

The confession was almost certainly untrue: by now Lucrezia was 17 and Sforza, already a father by a previous marriage, had no reason to abstain from sex with his wife. To complete the proceedings, Lucrezia was examined and declared a virgin.

After the episode was over, Giovanni Sforza, angered by his humiliation at the whim of his father-in-law, told Duke Ludovico of Milan that Rodrigo's motives for arranging the annulment amounted to more than

POETIC POSE **Lucrezia Borgia became Duchess of Ferrara in 1502, presiding over her court of poets and artists as a muse. Almost certainly she inspired the enigmatic *Portrait of a Woman* by Bartolomeo Veneto.**

FAMILY PORTRAIT The pre-Raphaelite artist Dante Gabriel Rossetti was intrigued by the destructive power of women's sexuality. In *Lucrezia Borgia's Family*, painted in the 1850s, Rodrigo and Cesare fawn over a wanton, reclining Lucrezia. The allusion to incest is clear.

fatherly concern. In starting this rumour he laid the foundations for the slanderous charges of incest that would later dog his former wife.

Lucrezia was now married off to Alfonso, Duke of Bisceglie, whose Neapolitan family Rodrigo considered to be a useful ally. But within two years the pope had forged an alliance with Louis XII of France, who was an enemy of the Naples principalities. Lucrezia's marriage had again been rendered unadvantageous by political circumstance.

According to the detailed diary of the Papal Master of Ceremonies, Johannes Burchard, in 1500 Lucrezia's brother Cesare ordered his men to attack Alfonso in St Peter's Square. The duke survived the ambush only to be finished off in the Vatican apartments where Lucrezia was attempting to treat him. Burchard

observed drily: 'Since Don Alfonso refused to die of his wounds, he was strangled in his bed.'

By all accounts Lucrezia was devastated. Archdeacon Gian Lucido Cattanei wrote: 'The pope is out of humour because his own daughter is in despair.' Lucrezia fled to her castle in the principality of Nepi to recover. Her letters to her servant Giordano were full of melancholy and signed 'the unhappy Princess of Salerno'.

Vicious accusations

But in the rival courts of Venice and Naples, Lucrezia's evident sorrow could not make up for the damage caused by her family's machinations. She took the blame for events brought about by her father's scheming and her brother's violence. The Venetian chronicler Girolamo Priuli called her the greatest whore in all Rome, while the satirist Sannazaro was no more subtle. In this epigram he compares her with the legendary prostitute Thais and accuses her of incest with her father:

Here in her grave lies Lucrezia in name, but Thais in truth: daughter, bride and daughter-in-law of Alexander.

In the centuries after her death, it would be these accusations of sexual insatiability that inspired the dramatisations of Lucrezia's life. The myth of the incestuous poisoner was born, but the truth was that the deaths and intrigues that occurred in the Vatican were arranged by other members of her family.

Cesare and Rodrigo were certainly notorious for poisoning their enemies. Chroniclers described both men ordering their cooks to add poison to wine and food served to the guests they wished to eliminate.

Cesare's violent temper was notorious. He was even suspected of murdering his own brother Juan simply to displace his father's favourite from prime position. Juan Borgia disappeared after a family meal and was later found floating in the Tiber, a fate that would befall many of Cesare's enemies.

Another victim was a court official named Perotto. On March 2, 1498, the Bolognan informant Cristofero Poggio wrote that: 'Perotto, the first chamberlain of our Lord... I now understand to be in prison for having made His Holiness's daughter, Madonna Lucrezia, pregnant.' As this pregnancy was fully visible at the time that Lucrezia was being pronounced 'intacta' by the Vatican, Perotto was an embarrassment: after being chased through the streets he

was caught by Cesare, murdered then thrown into the Tiber. Informants reported that Lucrezia gave birth later that month: a baby boy certainly appeared in the Borgia household around this time, but was not seen publicly until he was around the age of three. This child – known as the 'Infans Romanus' – was rumoured to be the product of a union between Lucrezia and her father.

Married again

In the face of public mistrust and opprobrium Lucrezia's next marriage proved difficult to arrange. Her reputation had been tainted by the widespread rumours of infidelity and incest. Cesare favoured a union with Alfonso d'Este, the Duke of Ferrara,

RUTHLESS KILLER When Rodrigo Borgia became Pope Alexander VI (right) he resorted to violent repression to maintain power. The preacher Savonarola (top right) was simultaneously hanged and burned on Rodrigo's orders in the Piazza della Signoria in Florence for accusing the pope of corruption.

as this state bordered his own, but the duke and his family were apparently wary of the Borgias.

Lucrezia took the bold step of presenting herself personally to the duke's ambassador Johannes Lucas. It was his report on Lucrezia's character and looks that apparently laid the Este family's fears to rest. The ambassador would have been ill-advised to mislead his employer, and so his description does carry some weight:

She is a most intelligent and lovely, and also exceedingly gracious lady... Moreover, she is a devout and God-fearing Christian... In short, her character is such that it is impossible to suspect anything 'sinister' of her; but on the contrary, we look only for the best.

A subsequent meeting must have verified Lucas's words, but it is probable that an offer to repeal the Duke of Ferrara's papal tax and a large dowry were even more persuasive. Lucrezia married Alfonso in 1502, and moved to Ferrara, where she lived out her days as a wife and mother, and the patron of poetry and fine art.

Niccolò Cagnolo, a courtier from the retinue of the French ambassador, described Lucrezia at the time of her third wedding, aged 21:

She is of middle height and graceful of form; her face is rather long, as is her nose; her hair is golden, her eyes grey, her mouth rather large, the teeth brilliantly white, her bosom smooth and white and admirably proportioned.

Her whole being exudes good humour and gaiety.

Now distanced from the poisonous family intrigues in Rome, Lucrezia

STEALING BEAUTY **A lock of Lucrezia Borgia's hair is kept in a tiny glass case in the Ambrosian Library, Milan. After the English poet Byron had seen it, he admitted in a letter that he had stolen a strand, 'blonder than blond' as a keepsake.**

settled gracefully into the calmer routine of Ferrara.

Lucrezia had seven children with Alfonso, and when her firstborn son Rodrigo died, she went into mourning and lived in a convent for several months. Though her powerful family had, more than anyone else, been the authors of her suffering, she was distraught at the deaths of her father and her brother. After Cesare died in battle, on March 11 1507, she locked herself in a convent and prayed for two days.

In 1519 Lucrezia herself died from complications following childbirth. She was 39 years old. At her death a cousin of Federico Gonzaga – the Renaissance art collector, whose mother presided over a rival court during Lucrezia's time at Ferrara – wrote of:

One... universally beloved not only for the habitual piety of her life, but for her unbounded charity and kindness of heart.

Dubious legacy

But Lucrezia would not be remembered in such glowing terms: her reputation for licentiousness far outlived her, since the backdrop of power struggles and sexual intrigue to the Borgias' rule proved irresistible to artists and writers, and several literary works of the 19th century used the moral dissolution of Lucrezia as their central theme. In his play *Lucrezia Borgia*, the French playwright Victor Hugo depicted a woman trapped in the darkness of her past deeds, 'a golden ducat, stamped with the effigy of Satan.'

During the play Lucrezia makes advances to her illegitimate son. She then revenges herself upon his scornful friends by poisoning their drinks. Her character is summed up by Don Apostolo, who calls her 'an adultress... one who drugs the wine cup at the feast'.

Hugo's compatriot Alexander Dumas describes Lucrezia in his work *Les Crimes Célèbres*, as being 'wanton in imagination, godless by nature, ambitious and designing'. He

Lucrezia's love letters

In her later years, Lucrezia Borgia became an important patron of the arts: the poets Pietro Bembo and Ludovico Ariosto, the painter Titian and the musician Bartolomeo Tromboncino frequented her court.

The letters written by Bembo to Lucrezia are classic examples of the literature of courtly love. The poet often spoke of a love denied: 'With my heart I kiss your Ladyship's hand, since I cannot with my lips.' For her part, Lucrezia wrote to 'Messer Pietro mio' and in her first letter (above) signed a delicate pseudonym: 'This henceforth shall be my name, f.f.' The letters reveal a playful side to Lucrezia, rather than proof of an affair between the two.

Bembo dedicated his book *Gli Asolani* – a dialogue on love – to Lucrezia. Bowing to political pressure, he removed the dedication from later editions.

also gave credence to the rumours of incest: she is both 'a daughter and a mistress' to Rodrigo, and she sleeps with Cesare. Despite the varied crimes of her father and brother, it was Lucrezia who earned most of Dumas' moral censure against this 'diabolical trio'.

Lucrezia's reputation also suffered from the fact that some 19th-century commentators refer to 'the Borgias' as a clan rather than specifying any individual members. For instance, Guillaume Apollinaire describes the poison La Cantarella as 'that which the Borgias utilised in conjunction with arsenic'.

There is not a single instance of a writer of Lucrezia's time implicating her in poisoning or murder, although there are many who make such accusations against her brother and father. But in death as in life, Lucrezia Borgia remains overshadowed by the malevolent plotting of the men she loved most: her family.

ELEVATED TO SAINTHOOD Lucrezia Borgia's father commissioned the artist Pinturicchio to paint frescoes throughout six rooms in the Vatican apartments in Rome. The richly gilded St Catherine, completed around 1496, is thought to be based on the 16-year-old Lucrezia.

SOPHISTICATED PHILISTINES
The brutes of the Bible were music lovers and gastronomes

The Old Testament recounts tales of the Philistines who made war with the Israelites. Now their name doubles for anyone ill-mannered and uncultured, but recent archaeological finds reveal a different side to the barbarian settlers.

Twelve centuries before the birth of Christ, when tribal boundaries and allegiances were as shifting as the sands, waves of migrants swept on to the shores of the Levant. The Egyptians called them the 'Sea Peoples', and among them were the Philistines, who conquered the Canaanites and established themselves on the eastern shores of the Mediterranean.

They settled along a lush coastal strip from Gaza to Tell Qasile, near modern-day Tel Aviv, on the trade route from Egypt to Syria. There, in a territory they named 'Philistia', they built a league of five fortified cities – Ashdod, Ekron, Ashkelon, Gath and Gaza. These were each governed by lords, who made joint decisions on important matters and formed a cohesive social, economic and military unit.

Warring neighbours

The struggle between the Israelites and Philistines was born of territorial conflict. The Bible related how the Lord told Moses:

When ye are passed over Jordan into the land of Canaan, then ye shall drive out all of the inhabitants of the land from before you... Those which ye let remain of them shall be pricks in your eyes and thorns in your sides, and shall vex you in the land wherein ye dwell. [Numbers 33: 50-53; 55]

The Israelites believed that the Philistines were encroaching on land that had long ago been vouchsafed to them by God, and Biblical accounts of the struggles between the two tribes go some way to explaining the Philistines' reputation for aggression. The Bible also recounts how the Philistines stole the Ark of the

LADY WITH A LYRE **A clay figurine dating from the 8th century BC shows that the Philistines enjoyed music. Other small figurines were found, many of them hollow and used for making offerings of wine to the gods at temples or shrines.**

Covenant, the sacred symbol created by Moses of God's presence among the Hebrew people.

Over the centuries, between territorial skirmishing, there were long, productive periods of peace within Philistia, which the Bible does not mention. Nor does the Bible describe the Philistines' sophisticated way of life. In modern usage the term 'philistine' has come to be a byword for all that is brutish and bloodthirsty, but in reality the Philistines were a cultured people.

In recent years, systematic excavation of the Philistine cities, particularly Ashkelon and Ekron, has revealed that they were master builders and skilled artisans. They built well-planned, walled cities with palaces and temples, and sturdy dwellings with street drainage.

Loom weights attest to a weaving industry; vats, presses and amphorae to a thriving trade in wine and olive oil. Delicate pieces of silver jewellery suggest that the Philistines did have an aesthetic sense. A terracotta statuette of a woman playing a lyre shows that music was appreciated.

Clear evidence has been unearthed that the Philistines had also mastered the art of smelting iron and copper. The narrative in the Bible suggests that they also kept control of the means of production. Strict laws prevented the Israelites from owning any iron weapons forged in Philistia, and even decreed that agricultural implements such as sickles and

EARLY CAPTURE In the mortuary temple of Rameses III, a frieze celebrating Egypt's victories over the newly arrived 'Sea Peoples' shows several Philistines taken prisoner during the 12th century BC.

German slander

The explanation for the modern meaning of the term 'philistine' lies in events much more recent than those recounted in the Bible.

In the German town of Jena in the late 17th century, a confrontation between the townspeople and the students from the local university resulted in the death of a student. During a memorial for him the minister preached a sermon and quoted the line 'The Philistines be upon thee, Samson'. German students adopted the word to mean an untutored person, and the name stuck.

IRON GRIP According to the Bible, the Philistines monopolised the production of iron weaponry and tools. This was probably because their technology was more advanced than the Israelites'. An iron dagger found at Ekron, one of the five cities of Philistia, shows that they could forge strong and durable blades.

ploughshares could only be repaired by Philistine metalsmiths. The work would be done – at a price – and the ruling was greatly resented:

Now there was no smith to be found through the land of Israel; for the Philistines said, Lest the Hebrews makes swords or spears.
[1 Samuel, 13:19]

The victory of David over Goliath with a sling and stone, then, was more than the triumph of a slight boy over a monster. The story was a powerful allegory for the victory of a disadvantaged but godly people over pagan braggarts.

The victory turned out to be a fleeting one. For David and his kinsmen, the lack of iron weapons would lead to their their subsequent defeat and death in battle.

[For] it came about on the day of battle, that there was neither sword nor spear found in the hand of any of the people. *[I Samuel 13: 22]*

David's searing lament for the Israelites' defeat has done much to burn into the imagination the idea of the barbarian who kills the thing that is beautiful:

The beauty of Israel is slain upon the high places: how are the mighty fallen! Tell it not in Gath, publish it not in the streets of Ashkelon; lest the daughters of the Philistines rejoice. *[2 Samuel 1: 19-20]*

The Philistines have long since vanished into history, leaving only a name, 'Palestine'. The last record of them as a distinct society is in the 7th century BC, when the Babylonian king Nebuchadnezzar invaded Philistia and took many hostages.

The uncircumcised Philistines ate pork and worshipped 'false gods', yet they were clearly not the vulgarians that their name now implies. The archaeological evidence of their food and cloth industries, their artwork and pottery, and their literacy and numeracy shows them to have been – on the contrary – a cultured people for their time.

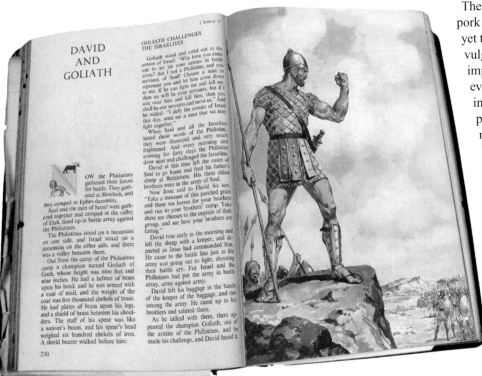

THE BIBLE'S BADDIES The image of the Philistines as aggressors is epitomised by Goliath, champion of the Philistine army. He challenged the Israelites to find him an opponent, while his compatriots jeered at them.

A cultured people

The finds that reveal most about the Philistines are examples of their pottery. Pieces dated to the 12th and 11th centuries BC hint at the Philistines' Aegean origins, and subsequent developments of the Mycenean style show the way that they assimilated the techniques of other settlements around the coast.

The Philistines were a literate and numerate people. Impressions left in clay by stamp seals have been found at Ashdod, while bronze and stone scales unearthed at Ashkelon show the importance of trade and commerce.

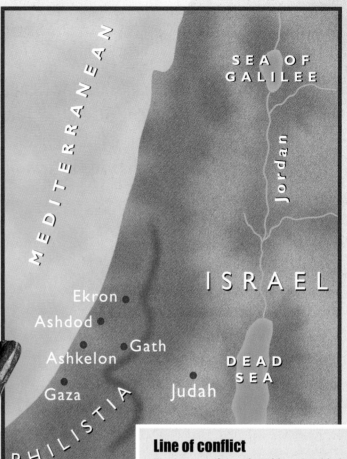

MEDITERRANEAN

SEA OF GALILEE

Jordan

ISRAEL

Ekron

Ashdod

Ashkelon

Gath

Gaza

PHILISTIA

Judah

DEAD SEA

Line of conflict

The 'pentapolis' or five cities of Philistia were Ekron, Ashdod, Ashkelon, Gaza and Gath. The Israelites, centred around Judah, resisted further advances east.

Approximate line of territorial conflict *c.*1200 BC to 600 BC.

Large cauldrons called kraters were used to mix wine and water after the Greek fashion. This suggests that eating and drinking were social occasions.

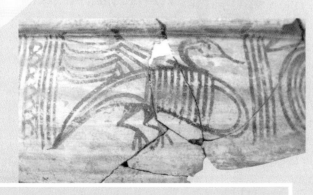

Philistine pottery was decorated with motifs of birds and fishes in the Mycenean style. The manner of clay work, firing and paint preparation are widely taken as proof that the Philistines were originally from the Aegean.

The earliest Philistine pottery was black and white. Later pots had more colour as the 'Sea Peoples' learned about the different pigments used by the Canaanites.

BASED ON A TRUE STORY

History has provided Hollywood with a wealth of juicy stories. But how faithful to the facts have the big screen versions been? Sometimes movie-makers get the details wrong by mistake, but more often they change the facts deliberately. Either way, it is not always easy to separate truth from fiction.

There are two ways to give a film historical authenticity. The first is to get the incidental details right – the costumes, locations and weapons. Big-budget Hollywood productions can afford to research well. With digital imagery, battles can be fought with a cast of thousands or the ruins of antiquity can be rebuilt in their original splendour.

The second way is to stick to the facts of the story, but that may not suit the dramatic requirements of the film-makers. If the hero needs a love interest, he'll get one. If one general in the war needs to be the 'bad guy', that is how he'll be portrayed, even if he wasn't. Scriptwriters go to work on a 'treatment', and history gets a makeover.

Killer fact

The writers of *Wyatt Earp* (1994), starring Kevin Costner (centre), took several liberties with the facts. In the film, the US lawman's brothers Morgan and Virgil are shot dead on the same evening. In fact, they were killed more than three months apart.

Out of time

In the 1966 Hollywood film *One Million Years BC*, Raquel Welch dodges fierce dinosaurs. The last dinosaur became extinct 65 million years before the first modern human appeared on Earth.

Misleading sub plot

U-571 (2000) recounts the bravery of a US Navy team on a daring mission in World War II. Led by Lt Andrew Tyler (Matthew McConaughey), they risk their lives to board an enemy submarine (U-571), capture a German Enigma code machine and change the course of the war. But the film should have been called 'U-110' and the hero should have been Sub-Lieutenant David Balme of the Royal Navy. During filming, outraged Britons complained to US President Bill Clinton, who reminded them that the film was, after all, only a work of fiction.

Go west, young man

Krakatoa, East of Java (1969) was unfortunately named. The volcano that erupted catastrophically in 1883 is in fact 50 km (30 miles) west of the Indonesian island. No one realised until release date.

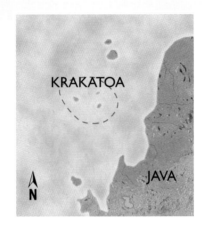

KRAKATOA

JAVA

N

Navel gazing

Belly dancers never used to wear jewels in their navels. Back in the 1920s, when harem films were all the rage, it was illegal to show a woman's bare navel on screen. But Hollywood producers found a way round the problem by 'dressing' the navel with a jewel. The image has become so well-known that real belly dancers now often wear jewels to make themselves look more 'authentic'.

BELLY FULL Anita Ekberg observes the dress code as Salma in the 1957 film *Zarak*.

Artistic licence

● At the end of Stanley Kubrick's *Spartacus* (1960), the hero, played by Kirk Douglas, is crucified. The historical hero was killed in battle against the Roman legions.

● *Independence Day* (1996) shows the US flag still standing on the surface of the Moon, where it had been placed by Neil Armstrong and Buzz Aldrin. In fact, it was blown over as soon as the two astronauts blasted off in Apollo 11 in 1969.

● In *Braveheart*, the 1995 historical epic starring Mel Gibson, when William Wallace first leads his men against the English the year shown on screen is 'AD 1280'. But the Scots patriot first came to prominence in 1297 – although his exact date of birth is uncertain, in 1280 he could have been no more than eight years old.

● *Bridge On The River Kwai* (1957) was based on the story of the Burma railway but filmed in Thailand. As a result of the film's popularity the Thai authorities later renamed the stretch of the Mae Klong River where the film set was built. 'The Kwai' is now a big tourist attraction.

TAKING THE STAND
New evidence on an old battleground

The legend of Custer's Last Stand grew from speculation based on the position of the fallen bodies of the Seventh Cavalry troopers. Now the battle site has yielded up fired bullets and spent cartridge cases which tell a very different tale.

Custer's Last Stand is part of the mythology of the Wild West. The defeated yet defiant figure of General George Armstrong Custer at the battle of the Little Bighorn, surrounded by the bodies of his dead comrades, besieged on all sides by enemies yet still firing his gun, is an image that is portrayed in poetry, plays, books and films and is the inspiration for countless paintings.

The site of the battle in Montana is a major tourist attraction. Every year thousands of pilgrims visit the exact spot where the general made his last stand and took his place in history as a symbol of American fighting spirit.

The newspaper records of what happened at Little Bighorn on that hot summer day in 1876 were not based on white eye-witness accounts – the American Indians wiped out every last man, scalping and mutilating the bodies. There were plenty of Lakota, Sioux and Cheyenne who had been at Little Bighorn and were willing, later, to talk about what they had seen, but their testimony was ignored, perhaps because it was so damning. They spoke of Custer's men running away 'like a buffalo stampede' and shooting 'like drunken men, into the ground, into the air'. One warrior named Wooden Leg claimed that the soldiers had turned their guns on themselves.

Trail of bullets

It took a prairie fire in 1983 to uncover the first of some uncomfortable truths. Before the fire, the scenic battlefield was a protected monument to the memory of the Seventh Cavalry and a no-go area for archaeologists. But with the scrub and bushes burned to the ground, permission to excavate was now granted to Dr Richard Fox and his team from the University of South Dakota.

The site's protected status had kept it free of unauthorised trophy hunters: it was rich in relics. Fox's team spent several years unearthing

PIN-UP POSE Pictures of George Armstrong Custer in his famous buckskin jacket gave the impression to the public that America was protected by tough outdoor heroes.

human remains, artefacts and, most importantly, cartridges, cartridge cases and firearm parts. These were used to determine the positions of combatants and the role of individual weapons in the battle. They have described what they have found as 'chaos in a desperate situation'. The locations of fired bullets and the cartridges that discharged them show that many soldiers were running and shooting over their shoulders ('vectoring'), rather than standing still to shoot.

No time to shoot

A soldier who is vectoring leaves his cartridge cases in a trail rather than in a pile at one location; bullets fired from his gun, identified by the scratches of the firing pin, show the direction of the shots. Perhaps most tellingly, Fox's team found not a single bullet or case from a Colt revolver that had been fired from the last stand position.

Discredited statements from Sioux and Cheyenne who fought at Little Bighorn claimed Custer's men hardly had time to switch from rifles to revolvers to confront their attackers in the final moments, and were all dead within 'the time it takes a hungry man to eat his dinner'.

Fox's overall conclusion is that the evidence he has found supports the Native American testimonies, and that these should now be re-evaluated.

It was the discovery of gold in the Black Hills of Dakota in 1870 that set in motion a chain of events leading to Little Bighorn. Prospectors and settlers flooded into the area, ignoring the fact that the Black Hills were sacred territory which had been guaranteed to the Lakota Indians. In the autumn of 1875, realising they would have to fight for their

DOUBLE VISION The 'guns-blazing' painting, above, is not supported by archaeological evidence. The Sioux drawing, top, shows soldiers dying in a disorganised killing field, and is the more accurate picture.

▶ **p.228**

The firearms evidence

Richard Fox and his team found artefacts belonging to 81 of the weapons in Custer's command at the last stand. The most famous of these was the Colt revolver, with its distinctive metal backstrap (right). Altogether, the soldiers carried 250 weapons at the last stand, so Fox realised he had found signs of about a third of these. He therefore calculated that the 124 non-Army firearms artefacts recovered must represent around 400 guns in use by the braves. This was the first time that an evidence-based figure had been suggested for the number of guns used against Custer.

Fox also estimated that about half of the Native Americans' weapons were repeating Winchester-type rifles that could fire 16 bullets before each reloading. The cavalry, on the other hand, were mostly armed with single-shot Springfield .45s, which the Army had issued in preference to repeating rifles. This was intended to save on ammunition and encourage more accurate sniper shooting. But at close quarters, the Native Americans, firing successively, had the advantage.

Clues to Custer's endgame

Archaeologists working at the Little Bighorn site used metal detectors to locate spent cartridge cases and bullets. Nearly every one of these could be matched to an individual weapon by the signature firing pin marks.

The cartridge case pinpoints the place where a gun was fired, while a corresponding bullet shows where it was aimed. For the first time, hard evidence could be used to see where Custer's men had grouped to defend themselves, and – more importantly – the key attacking positions of the warriors who surrounded them on four sides.

 The marble markers that dot the battlefield do not correspond exactly to the soldiers killed – numbering around 225. The men represented companies C, E, F, I and L of the Seventh Cavalry. Archaeologists have excavated the markers to try to verify how many fell at each position.

1 Custer does not appear to have entered the Indian encampment; he moved straight up into the hilly territory. This may have been because there were too many warriors armed and mounted.

2 Custer deployed Lt Calhoun and company L on the eastern ridge, but they came under heavy fire. Hunkpapa Sioux warriors were streaming out of the Indian village, packing at least 78 guns, mostly repeating rifles. At least 30 soldiers were killed here, others moved back along the ridge.

3 Captain Keogh and Company I were deployed to either support Lt Calhoun or cover his retreat. They too were overrun by Sioux warriors: the remains suggest up to 80 men fell here.

4 Companies E and F dismounted along the southern ridge and formed a skirmish line. But as they faced Crazy Horse and the Cheyenne to the west, a contingent of Oglala Sioux came up Deep Ravine while the Hunkpapa Sioux fired into the line from behind. About 65 died here, some are lost in the ravine.

5 Custer had deployed all his companies except C. Indians took up four positions, each one better sheltered than Custer's. There was no regrouping. Escape was impossible and the remaining men – about 50 of them – bunched as they were shot down.

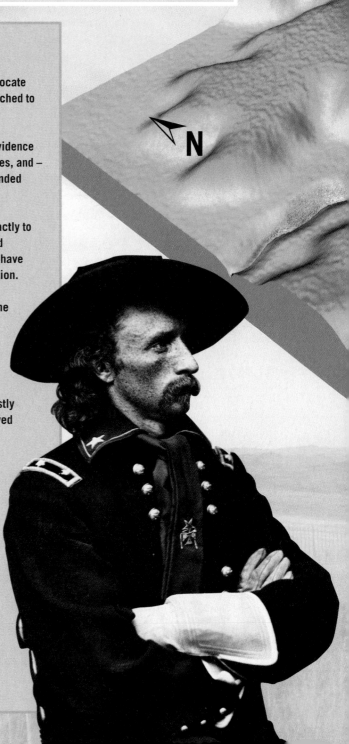

Bullets and cartridge cases
Of 1453 bullets found, only 41 were Colt revolver bullets (near right). About a third of these had not been fired but were still undischarged in their cartridges (far right). Another third were impacted on the ground along the ridges, probably fired down into dead or dying enemies, by soldiers or by warriors who took the Colts as trophies.

HUNKPAPA SIOUX

Little Bighorn River

Sitting Bull's Village

OGLALA SIOUX

Last Stand Hill

Deep Ravine

CHEYENNE

Warrior wisdom
Sitting Bull did not tell his warriors how to fight or participate in the battle, but he foretold their victory, describing the soldiers 'falling like grasshoppers'.

The Native American accounts of the last stand tell how the converging of small tribal groups from different starting points amounted to a tactical triumph. The rapid movements and well-protected positions are mapped by spent cartridge cases and impacted army bullets fired at them. From seven distinct positions they overwhelmed the Seventh, pinning them in criss-crossing lines of fire.

land, Lakota, Sioux and Cheyenne warriors gathered in Montana under the great war chief Sitting Bull. The US Government raised a force of 2500 men to crush them.

The Army's assumption was that the tribes would repeat their earlier tactic of avoiding direct clashes and instead play a run-and-hide game around the plains. The plan was to track them, surprise them, and overwhelm them quickly with superior numbers and firepower.

Pushing west across the Great Plains, Custer's Seventh Cavalry moved ahead of the infantry, covering 70 miles in three days. The unit was made up of 586 troopers, 31 officers, 33 Indian scouts, and a mule train carrying supplies and ammunition. Custer's orders were to wait for the infantry column led by General John Gibbon before engaging in any action against Sitting Bull. But, on the evening of June 24, while camped at Mud Creek, his scouts returned to report they had located 'hostiles' in a valley to the west. Custer ordered his men back into their saddles and they set off in pursuit, riding until well past midnight.

Custer's folly

At 9 o'clock on the morning of June 25, Custer's Crow scouts told him they had observed 'more Indians than the white men had bullets'.

Custer was worried not so much by the reported size of the force, as by the possibility that they might scatter. He did not know that he was about to launch an attack on the largest concentration of American Indian tribes in history, or that his quarry was in possession of between 600 and 700 firearms, a figure estimated by the archaeologists based on the recovered remains. About 400 of these guns would be used against Custer at the last stand battle.

Custer split the Seventh into three battalions. One, under Captain Frederick Benteen, was assigned to scour the southern bluffs and cut off the most likely escape route, while a second, under Major Marcus Reno, was to cross the Little Bighorn and attack from the east. Custer, with 225 men, moved along the opposite bank.

Reno was soon in trouble. He said later that he had expected the villagers to flee in the face of his charge, but they mounted an effective counter-attack. He ordered his men into a defensive 'skirmish line' but the battalion was forced to retreat into a wood, where it was joined by Benteen's group. The two commands survived the night with the loss of about a third of their number. Crucially, no word was sent to Custer.

Four miles upstream, Custer led his men towards the Indian encampment. It is possible that he planned to repeat the success of a brutal 'sweeping' operation he had carried out in 1868 on the Washita river, riding through a teepee village and gunning down anyone within range. The action had grabbed headlines and made him a national hero, but it had also made the Seventh hated by the Sioux.

FIELD OF THE FALLEN The Custer dead were buried where they had died; troop details returned to the battlefield in later years to reinter exposed remains. In 1881 the remains were dug up and placed in a mass grave, with wooden posts marking the places where they fell.

Conduct unbecoming an officer

Details of the death of the renowned General Custer and all his five companies reached the East Coast on, of all days, July 4, when the nation was celebrating the centennial of its independence.

In the patriotic wave of anger and grief that followed, no one questioned how it was that different Indian tribes had suddenly acquired the tactical skills of a trained army. Instead, while army generals condemned Custer's rashness, the public wanted the blame for the 'massacre' pinned elsewhere. Bowing to popular opinion, the Army hauled Major Marcus Reno before a court martial and accused him of withholding support from Custer. Although he was officially cleared of this charge, he never lived down his branding as a coward.

Custer must have realised that the village was a clustering of several camps, as he sent to Benteen a young private with the written instruction, 'Big village, come quick, bring packs'. In the packs were extra rounds of ammunition that mounted troops did not carry.

The last stand

Custer had expected to meet a rout of panic-stricken warriors driven from the village by Reno's attack. His last words were recalled by Sergeant Kanipe, sent to hurry along the packs: 'Hold your horses, boys, there's plenty down there for all of us!' But there was no charge. Wooden Leg describes the men strung out on the ridge, unsure of where to aim:

The soldiers could not see our warriors, [who] had left their ponies and were crawling in the gullies through the sagebrush.

The tracing of the firearms now shows how every deployment was met with a new line of attack. The movements were swift; the last stand was no more than the final, desperate position of men with nowhere else to go. Kanipe, whose errand saved his life, identified the dead two days later. A letter he wrote in 1908 makes clear that another part of the legend – that Custer barricaded himself and his men behind horses – is false:

There was not hardly any horses around where he was lying... There is no such thing as to corral... or make a fortification out of horses.

The defeat still brought money, morale and new recruits to the demoralised US Army – young men eager to 'avenge Custer'.

The American Indians' greatest military victory led to their greatest defeat. After the death of Custer, they were ruthlessly driven back into reservations. The Black Hills would never again be their homeland.

DEADLIER THAN BATTLE
Poor hygiene made Florence Nightingale's wards lethal

The 'Lady with the Lamp' raised morale in Scutari, but her improvements at the hospital led, with tragic irony, to the deaths of many patients. Nightingale regretted the errors of the Crimea for the rest of her life.

Florence Nightingale arrived to take charge of the Barrack Hospital at Scutari on the outskirts of Constantinople on September 4, 1854. It was the height of the Crimean War – ten days after the battle of Balaclava and one day before the battle of Inkerman. Nightingale was 34 years old and possessed of a steely determination. Before her lay four miles of beds, closely packed on wooden floors so rotten that they could not be properly cleaned. The walls were thick with grime. Through the wards wafted the stink of blocked drains and cesspools. Nightingale's efforts in this hellhole became legend and helped to make nursing an acceptable profession for well-to-do young women.

Nightingale had travelled to the war zone in the wake of 28,000 British troops. Russian armies had annexed a corner of the Ottoman Empire, and the troops were sent to block further Russian expansion. By the time Nightingale arrived in the Turkish city of Scutari, British forces had taken the fight onto Russian soil. The war was proving

HIDDEN DANGER The artist William Simpson travelled to Scutari and made sketches of the wards from life. Although Nightingale is shown in clean and calm surroundings, blocked drains and sewage made the hospital a haven for disease.

costly and bloody; sick and wounded soldiers were being transported by the shipload from the Crimean peninsula across the Black Sea to the hospital at Scutari. The journey took a fortnight. Some of the wounded had lost limbs, some were delirious. But the hospital brought them no relief.

The situation there belied the assurance given to Nightingale in London by the head of the Army Medical Board that 'nothing was needed'. The hospital had only canvas bedding. There were shortages of stretchers, splints, bandages and bedding. There was no fresh clothing for those whose coats or trousers had been shot away with their limbs; no adequate kitchen to prepare their food. There was no proper laundry, no hot water; nothing for the patients to wash or eat with. Even for world-weary surgeons and soldiers whose nerves had been hardened by war, the scenes of mutilation and death were shocking.

Forward into battle

All this Nightingale believed she would change. Using money she had raised herself, and donations sent by readers of *The Times,* she reorganised and accelerated the flow of medical supplies. She acquired fresh clothing, soap, towels and cutlery. Aided by her team of 38 nurses she re-equipped the hospital laundry and the kitchen, and ensured that men for the first time had clean linen and regular, nourishing meals.

She achieved this in spite of the conservatism, complacency and chauvinism of male doctors and the inertia of the political establishment. Through sheer strength of will, Nightingale did indeed perform miracles. Guided by the glow of her famous lamp, she brought comfort

not only to the sick and dying, but also to the bereaved families of the dead, to whom she would write long, detailed letters. Under her influence, mutilated men found new hope, mastered their fears and surrendered to the agonies of amputation.

Winter of death

But it is not enough to bring mere comfort to the sick, or to ease the pain of death. Comfort is not the same as cure, and it is here that the case turns against her. For all her efforts, and the efforts of her nurses, the men simply went on dying. In the winter of 1854-5, the mortality rate at Scutari was double the death rates in the smaller regimental hospitals at the Russian front.

In that winter, 5000 men – half of Nightingale's patients – died in her care. That was about 50 a day. Worse still, many died not from wounds or fevers contracted en route to Scutari, but from virulent diseases caught on the wards. They were victims not of war, but of poor hygiene.

The tragedy was that the cleaner and more efficient the Barrack Hospital became under Nightingale's command, the more soldiers were brought in for treatment. But the germs harboured in the sewage in the frequently blocked drains continued to spread death among the ever-growing numbers of patients. The truth was that, for all Nightingale's impressive discipline, passion and hard work, she was – in matters of medicine and hygiene – an amateur.

Florence Nightingale had learned nursing through private study. She came from a wealthy family and was expected by her parents to tread the conventional pathway of society balls and marriage to a man of property. In

SISTER OF MERCY It has been said that grateful soldiers kissed Florence Nightingale's shadow as she passed through the wards with her lamp (opposite). But she knew that she had made fatal errors in Scutari. Her long devotion to nursing was a kind of atonement for this failure.

232

The legacy of Nightingale's data

Florence Nightingale never forgot the huge losses of soldiers to typhoid, cholera and dysentery at Scutari. In 1858 she showed the great toll taken by 'preventable or mitigable' diseases: the revelation shocked the public.

One of her diagrams (below right) shows deaths from April 1854 to March 1855. Improvements made to sanitation in April 1855 lowered the death rate dramatically (below left).

Nightingale was critical of those who considered infection inevitable and, in works such as *Notes on Nursing* (right), she campaigned for better germ prevention through good hygiene.

NOTES ON NURSING:

WHAT IT IS, AND WHAT IT IS NOT.

BY

FLORENCE NIGHTINGALE.

LONDON:
HARRISON, 59, PALL MALL,
BOOKSELLER TO THE QUEEN.

DIAGRAM OF THE CAUSES OF MORTALITY
IN THE ARMY IN THE EAST.

2. APRIL 1855 TO MARCH 1856.

1. APRIL 1854 TO MARCH 1855.

The red shading showed the number of deaths from wounds – about one in ten.

Black areas showed deaths from causes such as dysentery and other bowel diseases.

The biggest blue areas represented deaths from contagious diseases, such as cholera and typhoid.

Deaths peaked in January 1855: out of 3168 soldiers, 3085 died of disease, but only 83 of their wounds.

her childhood she showed a different inclination – mending broken dolls and fitting splints to injured pets. Nightingale was 25 when her mother decisively blocked her intention to become a nurse at Salisbury Hospital, but the parental opposition was born of more than snobbery. Nursing in the mid 19th century was not a career for any woman of virtue, let alone the daughter of a gentleman. Nurses in those days were better known for drunkenness and immorality than for the dispensing of medicine or the dressing of wounds.

But still Nightingale persisted. Finally, at the age of 34, without any kind of training, she was engaged as superintendent of a nursing home in Harley Street, London. Within a year the Crimean War broke out and she was able to use her friendship with a Cabinet minister, the Secretary-at-War, Sir Sidney Herbert, to get herself appointed to Scutari. Two years later, she returned to England a national celebrity and trail-blazing heroine, who had proved that female nurses could contribute significantly to army welfare.

Within a year of this apparent vindication of her intentions and abilities, Nightingale was a changed woman, in poor health and confined to her home for days and weeks at a time. The cause of her illness is unclear. In the Crimea she had been unstoppable, although as a younger woman she had often taken to her bed. Nightingale was never in good health again, though the most important phase of her life was only just beginning.

Ignoring her doctors' advice that a prolonged rest was crucial to her recovery, Nightingale asked William Farr, a government statistician, to show her how to analyse data. She set to work on the meticulous records she had kept of the mortalities at Scutari.

By 1857, having collated figures from other field hospitals to use for comparison, Nightingale had worked out that her hospital had not merely dealt with existing sickness, but, as she wrote to Sir John MacNeill, leader of the Supplies Commission, disease had been 'generated within the building itself'. Mortality in the Barrack Hospital from dysentery and other bowel conditions had been 25 per cent higher on her wards than in front-line hospitals.

The realisation that the conditions at Scutari had been taking the lives of those it was supposed to be saving may have been the shock that propelled her into a long illness.

War on germs

It is for the achievements of the second chapter of her life that Florence Nightingale deserves to be celebrated. Far from attempting to conceal the awful truth of Scutari, she wanted to publish a full account. Only government intervention kept the details from the public. A more general report on the causes of mortality in the army was published, for which Nightingale was elected to the Royal Statistical Society.

Now that she had a clearly defined mission, she channelled all her efforts into fighting for it. When the French chemist Louis Pasteur proposed the notion that microbes were responsible for disease, Nightingale positioned herself in the vanguard of the antiseptic movement.

'Sanitation!' became her war cry. Despite the furious opposition of the War Office, she successfully fought for a Royal Commission on the health of the army; the commission's eventual report relied heavily upon her work. She was the driving force behind the Sanitary Commission, which introduced better hospital practices and saved the lives of many British soldiers fighting colonial wars in India.

In 1859, Nightingale's *Notes on Nursing* proposed methods that are still used in hospitals throughout the world today. Among these practices is the 'Nightingale ward', in which one nurse cares for her own room of patients from a central work station and store. Although still in poor health, Nightingale campaigned for improvements in hospital hygiene and nurses' training. In the late 1870s she wrote: 'Always have chlorinated soda for the nurses to wash their hands, especially after handling a suspicious case.' Even in old age she was receptive to new ideas, such as steam sterilisation of instruments and the use of new swabs to dress wounds.

In the 1890s, Nightingale attacked medical science for turning germ theory into an excuse to ignore poor hygiene. Her outbursts were interpreted by the English biographer and critic Lytton Strachey (in his book *Eminent Victorians*) to mean that Nightingale did not believe in germs. She actually wrote that:

God forbid that the Bucks Sanitary Conference should come to the conclusion that typhoid fever, diphtheria &c &c are the direct consequences of Bacillus F and Bacillus D instead of bad drainage, cess pools and foul water.

Nightingale could easily accept that 'germs' infected the body, but it was how the body could be better safeguarded that interested her. She was well aware that prevention involved hard work, which public authorities preferred to shirk. Nightingale was not able to avoid the issue so easily: Scutari, with its tubs of fetid waste, collapsed drains and swirling sewage, was forever lodged in her memory.

True! Florence Nightingale kept a pet owl, which died on the day she was to travel to the Crimea. She delayed her departure in order to have it embalmed. In Scutari, soldiers gave her another owl.

CENTRE STAGE After her Crimean experiences Florence Nightingale devoted her life to medicine, founding a training school for nurses at St Thomas' Hospital in 1860, where she was photographed with staff in the final year of her life. She died, aged 90, three years after being awarded the Order of Merit.

ARTISTS' IMPRESSIONS

Portraits are complex historical documents. They are never the whole truth because they represent the subjective opinions, prejudices and hidden agendas of the artist – and often those of the sitter, too.

No matter how realistic they may look, portraits can never be taken at face value. A historian must consider the painter, his opinion of the subject, who paid him to do it, and when he worked – some of the portraits on which we base our view of historical figures were painted long after the subjects' deaths, by artists who never met them. Some paintings flatter to deceive; others are informed by malice: the artist dislikes the subject, and the feeling shows in the work. And some pictures contain secret messages that may be missed by the untrained eye.

Misleading advertising

When Henry VIII was looking for a new wife after the death of Jane Seymour, he heard favourable reports of Anne of Cleves. His chief minister, Thomas Cromwell, was keen that Henry should marry her to forge stronger links between England and Protestant allies in Germany, but before the king committed himself to a fourth marriage, he wanted to know what she looked like. He commissioned Hans Holbein the Younger to go to Europe and paint her portrait. Pleased with the result, Henry summoned Anne to England. But when he met her face to face, he thought she was excessively plain, and dubbed her 'the Flanders mare'.

The union was doomed from the start – Anne was Queen of England for only four months in 1540. Anne lived a long life as a divorcée, but Cromwell was executed as a traitor.

Whose dress?

Portraits can teach historians much about period fashions but *Mrs Bowers* teaches us to be cautious. In this portrait, the American artist John Singleton Copley depicts her in a draped satin gown. We might assume that this is what affluent Boston women of the 1770s were wearing, but we would be wrong: keen to emulate English fashions, which Americans thought the height of fine style, Copley copied the gown, the rose, the pose and even the dog from a portrait of Lady Caroline Russell by the English artist Sir Joshua Reynolds. At this time American society dresses were much higher necked, often of lace-trimmed calico.

A true likeness?

This is the public face of John Milton, author of *Paradise Lost* and *Paradise Regained*. The poet commissioned the engraving himself for the frontispiece of the 1645 collected edition of his poems.

What many readers of the work may not know is that when Milton saw the result he was appalled. He demanded that the engraver, William Marshall, put beneath it an

inscription in Greek. Marshall knew no Greek, so unless someone translated it for him he would have been unaware that the text made him the butt of a rather cruel joke, in which Milton invites onlookers to 'laugh at a rotten image by a good-for-nothing artist'.

Persuasive guesswork

In Titian's portrait of Francis I, an artist at the height of his powers shows a mighty monarch at the height of his. The painting captures a splendid image of pride and vitality. But the Venetian master never set eyes on the French king – he based his work on earlier likenesses by Parisian court painters. It turns out to be a picture of what Titian thought the king should look like, not how he was. The work is the end result of a game of artistic Chinese whispers.

Auspicious imagery

At first glance, Jan van Eyck's *The Arnolfini Wedding* (1434) may appear to be no more than its title suggests. The portrait is filled with details that appear to be incidental clutter, but are in fact loaded with symbolism. The bedpost at the back of the room is carved with a likeness of St Margaret, patron saint of women in childbirth. The oranges beneath the window stand for fertility; the dog for marital fidelity. The cast-off clogs show that the floor is sacred ground. Despite her appearance, the bride is not about to give birth – wedding dresses of the period were cut to suggest pregnancy. The mirror on the back wall reflects not only the couple in the painting but also the artist and a third man, perhaps a marriage witness. There is more to this work than meets the modern eye.

A NEW SHAPE FOR THE DODO
The most absurd bird in history was neither fat nor slow

Our idea of the dodo is unfairly based on unflattering paintings of unrepresentative individuals. Scientific reconstruction has shown that in its natural environment the dodo was lively and athletic.

The sad story of the dodo is well known. It was too flabby and too indolent to fly and it did not even have the sense to run away when it was attacked. So when Dutch sailors landed on Mauritius at the end of the 16th century, all they saw was an easy meal: within a lifetime every last dodo on the island had been clubbed and roasted. All that remained of the bird was a collection of bones, a few paintings and a proverbial expression: something that is as dead as a dodo is very dead indeed.

But 400 years after the first dodo waddled into oblivion, scientists are looking again at the world's least attractive bird. Its appearance, its habitat and the circumstances of its demise have all been reassessed. Because it might be that the creature that is the very symbol of extinction was not so useless after all. Perhaps the dodo was, on the contrary, a perfectly wrought product of its island environment.

From an evolutionary point of view, the dodo's large size and flightlessness can be seen as typical adaptations to a life without predators. Being big allowed a more efficient use of energy and meant the birds could withstand food shortages caused by hurricanes and droughts. With no enemies to flee from, flight

UGLY DUCKLING The dodo appears large and awkward in contrast to the naturalistic portrayal of the other bird species. The Dutch painter Roelandt Savery spent ten years in Prague recording the specimens kept by Rudolf II in his palace menagerie, but the emperor never owned a live dodo.

became an unnecessary use of energy. At some point during millions of years of isolation on its Indian Ocean island, the dodo evolved into a giant with tiny wings.

The dodos' paradise was shattered by the arrival of human sailors in the 16th century. Having never needed to defend themselves from any other creature, they stood their ground rather than fleeing – though dodos could be aggressive: some sailors reported receiving a nasty peck. But the idea that sailors ate the dodos to extinction is wrong. In fact those who did try roasting the dodos were unimpressed by their meat, which was leathery, so they took a step that was to prove fatal for the species. They released goats and pigs onto the islands so that other voyagers could be certain of a meal in future. Pests such as rats set up home too. These foreign animals preyed on the eggs and nestlings of the dodo. By the 1660s the creature had disappeared from the island.

DNA evidence
The reputation of the dodo went into a headlong posthumous decline. Lewis Carroll heaped scorn on the bird in *Alice's Adventures in Wonderland,* in 1865. But new evidence has shown that the dodo was not as fat or as useless as has been portrayed. The genetic identity of the dodo has been determined by testing DNA extracted from a skull, and it turns out that the dodo is not some outlandish ostrich, but is in fact a

giant pigeon.

Armed with this classification, Andrew Kitchener, curator of birds and mammals at the National Museum of Scotland, used a technique of tissue and muscle reconstruction to try to establish how the dodo looked in its native habitat. He studied the earliest descriptions made by Dutch sailors who saw live birds in the 1590s. Apart from complaining about their tough meat and dangerous bite, their accounts do

> The dodo today is the ultimate symbol of extinction: something that is as dead as a dodo is very dead indeed.

LAZY BONES? The dodo's reconstructed skeleton showed it was of an athletic build. Tests of the load-bearing ability of the bones confirmed this more upright stance.

They make no claims that the birds were abnormally shaped, saying only that they were the largest birds on the island.

One account was of particular interest. In 1662 a shipwrecked sailor, Volquard Iversen, described the behaviour of dodos on a small island off the south-east coast of Mauritius:

Among other birds were those which men in the Indies called 'doddaersen' ('round bottoms'); they were larger than geese but not able to fly. Instead of wings they had small flaps; but they could run very fast.

Iversen's account was wholly inconsistent with the size and shape of the bird depicted in the oil paintings of the dodo by the Dutch artist Roelandt Savery. Kitchener grew suspicious: all the paintings of live dodos seem to have been of captive birds belonging to European collectors. Live dodos were certainly transported back to Europe to take pride of place in the menageries of aristocrats and rich collectors.

As the public interest in new and exotic flora and fauna grew, accounts of expeditions were published as exciting and often exaggerated travelogues. These were written more for commercial gain than scientific accuracy, and illustrations for them did not include careful studies of the dodo observed in a natural setting.

Instead, illustrations were often based on rough sketches of dodos kept as pets on Mauritius or on specimens brought back to Europe. Kitchener wondered if these dodos could have been overfed. Tame birds would be given scraps; on board ships they could have been fed biscuits or cornmeal rather than their natural diet. Kitchener used a dodo skeleton

to calculate the bird's natural weight. Although no full skeletons of any captive dodos have been kept, there are plenty of bones: a 19th-century naturalist brought a huge haul of them back from Mauritius; they are now stored in the Natural History Museum in London and Cambridge University's Zoology Museum.

Kitchener measured hundreds of these bones so he could reconstruct a one-fifth scale model of the skeleton. To this he added plasticine muscles based on the anatomical rules of other birds' skeletons.

The reconstructed dodo was found to be consistent with the earliest descriptions of the bird given by the first sailors to see it on Mauritius. The model's weight was calculated by measuring its volume and testing the tissue of other birds for density. The weight range given by this method was between 12.5kg (28lb) and 16.1kg (35lb) – nothing like the 50lb (23kg) claimed by one account written in the mid 17th century. Rather than weighing three times as much as the average Christmas turkey, the dodo was a substantial – but not a gigantic – bird, strong enough to carry its bulk comfortably.

Naturally pacy

A Dutch ornithologist, W. C. Oudemans, suggested that the dodo fattened up when food was abundant and slimmed down during the dry season. But Kitchener found that the bones he had tested were able to discredit this as a sufficient explanation for a 50lb bird.

Knowing that the dodo belonged to the pigeon family meant he could calculate how the lengths of the leg bones varied with body weight in the smallest to the largest pigeons.

By extrapolating from these relationships, the dodo's weight was

DODO IN WONDERLAND The image of the dodo as an ungainly giant was reinforced by this illustration, by John Tenniel, for Lewis Carroll's popular children's fantasy *Alice in Wonderland*. Carroll himself is said to have been inspired by a stuffed dodo at the Oxford University Museum of Natural History.

Reconstructed in its true form
This model shows the dodo as it really was –
slim, upright and muscular. The plumage has
been matched in colour to the Savery paintings,
although the type of feather is less downy and
more streamlined, like a pigeon's.

Tests on DNA extracted from a
surviving dodo skull have proven
that the giant bird was a member
of the pigeon family. Its closest
living relative is the Nicobar
pigeon, *Caloenas nicobarica*, of
South-east Asia.

The dodo dwarfs its more
distant relative, the common
(feral) pigeon, which is about
32cm (13in) in length compared
with the dodo's 100cm (40in).

fixed between 10.6kg (23lb) and
17.5kg (38lb), helping to confirm the
weight given by the model.

The dodo now looked as though it
might well have been able to run, just
as the shipwrecked Iversen had
described. To confirm this
observation, Kitchener cut three of
the principal leg bones in half and
measured the thickness of the bone
walls. Two of the bones matched the
strength of known sprinters such as
the guineafowl and the ostrich. The

third bone – the femur – was weaker,
but functioned better when held
vertically. So the model was adapted
to show this revised gait – less of a
waddle and more of a stride.

The dodo has now shown itself to
have been a naturally pacy bird with a
large but streamlined body. It had a
tendency to overeat and this small
fault turned it into an ornithological
laughing stock. The injustice is
enough to make the sharp, athletic
dodo of history turn in its grave.

INVENTION AND DISCOVERY

DRIVEN BY IDEAS
Ancient engineers had the scientific knowledge to build a steam engine

The concept of steam-driven machines is usually associated with the giant engines of the Industrial Revolution. But nearly 2000 years before the age of steam, an Alexandrian inventor designed a working steam engine. He was one of many ancient thinkers who understood the basic principles of modern engineering.

HERO'S WELCOME In the history of inventions, Hero of Alexandria occupies a prime place among the ancients, having invented some 80 ingenious devices. His rotating wind ball – which was driven by jets of steam created by a fire-heated cauldron (below left) – must have astonished his contemporaries.

A visit to Alexandria in the 1st century AD was a trip to the pulsating technological heart of the ancient world. There, in the shadow of Pharos, the wondrous lighthouse, were buildings dedicated to the increase of human knowledge. A main street 30m (100ft) wide and 5km (3 miles) long brought scholars to a famous library that contained about half a million books written on papyrus; or to the Museion, a centre for study, where scholars sat among artists, poets and craftsmen and worked to further the growth of debate and discovery.

The city had been founded by Alexander the Great in 331 BC. Over succeeding centuries, Alexandria became a centre for science, philosophy and engineering. It was also home to some of the greatest geniuses the world has ever produced.

It was in Alexandria that invention was truly invented. The Egyptians had achieved mighty memorials to their

Hero's steam engine

Hero is usually said to be Alexandria's greatest inventor. His writings show that he was fascinated by air and water pressure, siphons, pulleys, counterweights and concealed reservoirs. His most striking invention was a 'wind ball'. It converted energy into mechanical motion and so can be defined as an engine – the first ever to be powered by steam. It was never used for any practical purpose, but its underlying principles are central to modern engineering.

1 Water heated in the sealed cauldron starts to boil and turn to steam.

2 A pipe, probably copper, feeds the steam from the cauldron into the metal ball.

3 The steam inside the ball builds up.

4 Jets of steam are forced out through the two L-shaped, copper tubes on opposite sides of the ball: the ball starts to spin.

5 A pivot helps support the ball at the other side, allowing it to spin freely. As the heat builds up, the ball spins faster and faster.

pharaohs; the Babylonians had invented the calendar and much of mathematics, but the word 'idea' was a Greek one.

Alexandria was the seat of the Ptolemaic dynasty, the Macedonian rulers of Egypt. The city united Persian, Egyptian, Babylonian and Greek ideas, and applied science was as important as philosophy to the Greeks. The pulley, the windlass (winch) and the crank get their first mention in *Mechanica*, a book from the school of Aristotle.

The pursuit of knowledge

The Greeks are best known for their achievements in the arts and philosophy. For practical results, it is wrongly believed, you have to wait until the Roman Empire. But in fact the Greeks built lighthouses, canals, tunnels, steam engines, pumps, presses, astronomical calculators,

clocks and automata. In a society based upon the labour of slaves, the Greeks did not need to apply all they knew in a practical fashion.

They had plenty of manpower to call on if they needed to lift or shift raw materials or erect buildings. Besides, their inspiration was the pursuit of pure knowledge, rather than economic gain. And this explains why harnessing the energy they created – a vital part of the Industrial Revolution, for trains, barges and ultimately the motor car – was of little consequence to the ancient engineers.

Nonetheless, it was an Alexandrian, working on small-scale engineering projects nearly 2000 years ago, who first understood the potential of steam power. Hero, widely recognised as Alexandria's greatest engineer, lived in the 1st century AD. Though heir to a rich Greek tradition, he may

BALL PLAY In one of Hero's inventions steam produced by a cauldron of water runs up a tube to a cup-like opening, where the force of the upward jet keeps a tiny metal sphere suspended in mid air.

Open Sesame!

Hero's showmanship was evident in his temple doors that opened and closed by expansion and contraction of air.

1 A fire lit on the altar heats the air in the altar cavity below.

2 The heated air expands down a tube and into a globe, which is half filled with water.

3 The hot, expanding air forces water up through a bent pipe and into a suspended bucket.

4 As the bucket fills with water, it falls steadily, pulling on the ropes wound around two poles.

5 These are the pivots of the temple doors. As the ropes tighten, the doors open.

6 A counterweight pulls on a second pair of ropes. When the altar fire is put out and the heated air contracts, water is drawn back and poles swivel back to their starting point, closing the temple doors.

MODEL DEVICE In 1988, a team at Reading University, England, made a 'wind ball' to Hero's design. It was timed at 1500 rotations a minute, but was hopelessly inefficient in its use of fuel.

well have been of Egyptian origin. Hero was a showman, who fascinated his fellow citizens with scientific wizardry: we know this because he was often asked to supply mechanical 'diversions', much in the tradition of the Victorian era.

But the showman made a clear distinction between mechanical devices that 'supply the most necessary wants of life' and those that 'produce astonishment and wonder'. He devoted equal energy to both.

The 'wind ball'

One of Hero's most striking inventions was the first engine to be powered by steam. Sometimes called a 'wind ball', it comprised a hollow sphere with two bent tubes attached to it. When steam was fed through a pipe into the ball from a cauldron of boiling water, jets of compressed steam drove the ball round and round like a Catherine wheel. Though it was driven by steam, the engineering principle is identical to jet propulsion – 2000 years before it was used to power aeroplanes.

But could this device have been put to use? Its weakness was the joint between the revolving sphere and the steam pipe, which had to be both loose enough to let the ball spin, and tight enough to prevent the escape of too much steam. Modern engineers who reconstructed a working model found the machine was inefficient.

Energy lost through escaping steam and friction at the clumsy pivot joint meant that a scaled-up machine, built to the best standards of the day, would have required vast amounts of energy to heat the water and turn the ball.

Going one better than Hero

The earliest steam engines of the 18th century improved on Hero's invention by employing pistons. Beam engines designed by Thomas Newcomen provided power for pumps; they were later refined by James Watt, who made the separate condensing engine in 1770, and George Stephenson.

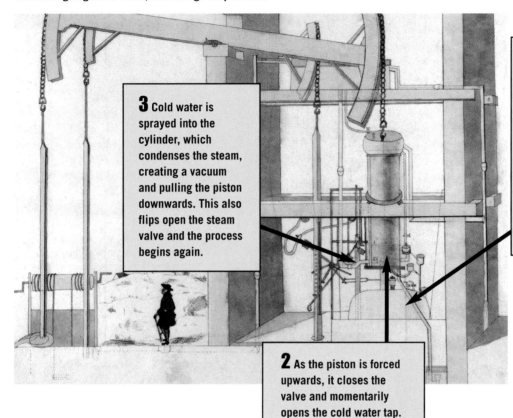

3 Cold water is sprayed into the cylinder, which condenses the steam, creating a vacuum and pulling the piston downwards. This also flips open the steam valve and the process begins again.

1 Water in the boiler is heated to a high temperature, forcing steam through a valve into the piston chamber and raising the piston. The beam is released and its weight pulls it down on the other side, driving the pump action.

2 As the piston is forced upwards, it closes the valve and momentarily opens the cold water tap.

Hero's *Treatise on Pneumatics* shows he was familiar with pistons, which had been used for siphoning water and even for simple pumps. One of his inventions uses a wind vane to drive a piston pump which pushes air through organ pipes to play them. It is the first documented use of wind to drive machinery.

It seems never to have occurred to Hero that a better engine could be made by forcing steam into a cylinder to drive just such a piston. Not until the 18th century was the piston employed to harness steam power. Greek metalworking techniques were in any case unable to produce pistons of sufficient precision.

Hero's automatic temple doors had no practical purpose; his coin-fed slot machine, designed to deliver water for ritual washing on entering a temple, offered amusement rather than actual assistance. A coin put in the slot fell on a pan balanced at the end of a pivoted beam. The other end of the beam was attached to a valve, which opened momentarily as the coin hit the pan, delivering a splash of water to rinse face and hands.

But perhaps Alexandrian society was most impressed by Hero's magic drinking horns, which could be filled with water and wine, and pour both at the same time from different spouts.

Hero's mechanical ingenuity should not be disparaged just because it was not applied. To Hero, it was the technique that was important, not its application, and the invention itself that mattered, rather than its inventor. Although he acknowledges a debt to other, earlier scientists in his *Treatise,* he does not name them.

COINING IT Hero invented a slot machine that, for the price of a five-drachma bronze coin, dispensed water for devotees to ritually cleanse themselves.

NEW NOSES AND MENDED EARS

The secrets of plastic surgery were known for thousands of years

With no anaesthesia except opium, and using pieces of straw for nostrils, Indian medicine men were carrying out nose jobs in ancient times. The demand came mostly from men mutilated by war or punishment.

Walking down the dusty streets of 18th-century Mysore, India, a British officer was startled by a local merchant with a scarred forehead and misshapen nose. Intrigued, he asked about the man's appearance, and learned that he had been found guilty of adultery and had had his nose cut off as punishment. A *vaidya* – a Hindu holy man – had fashioned him a replacement using the man's own skin. This chance meeting introduced the notion of plastic surgery to America and Europe.

Reconstructive surgery had been practised in India for more than 2000 years, but it was a medical feat unknown in the West. When an account of a grafting operation was published in the *Gentleman's Magazine* of London in October 1794, it attracted much interest.

It has long been accepted that

CASE STUDY Plastic surgery of the nose was first carried out in the West by surgeons in the 19th century. J. Mason Warren's 1840 academic paper on the operation (illustrated by a satisfied patient, left) was a landmark.

ancient civilisations possessed the ability to carry out basic surgical operations. An ancient Egyptian manuscript known as the 'Edwin Smith Papyrus' dating from about 3000 BC contains advice on how to treat fractured noses and jaws, and directions on stitching and cauterising (sealing wounds by burning). Skeletons excavated from a craftsmen's village near the Valley of the Kings show that when these labourers sustained fractures their bones could be reset and splinted. But medical historians are still surprised by the discovery that plastic surgery involving extensive reconstruction was carried out centuries before the invention of anaesthesia.

Ancient Hindu surgery

The term 'plastic surgery' has nothing to do with artificial substances – it derives from the Greek word *plastikos*, meaning 'able to be moulded or formed'. It is concerned with modifying deformations that have been caused by disease or injury, and the basic principles behind it had been discovered in ancient India.

One of the eight branches of Ayurveda, the Indian system of medicine, is shastrakarma, the practice of surgical techniques. Practitioners of Ayurveda rejected magical remedies and sought the link between the disease and the cure. The world's first medical school was founded around 1500 BC in the city of Taxila, in modern Pakistan.

The Hindu author Sushruta compiled an encyclopedia of medical treatments in about 600 BC. It contained detailed anatomical information and descriptions of 300 surgical procedures, among them the first descriptions of rhinoplasty and octoplasty: plastic surgery of the nose and the ear.

Injuries to noses were a common occurrence in ancient India. Noses were considered a symbol of pride and dignity, and as such presented a tempting target in combat. The justice system also prescribed amputation of the nose for crimes such as adultery; consequently the demand for nasal reconstruction was widespread. Sushruta described how a new nose could be created by attaching skin from the cheek to the nasal remnants:

A careful physician having taken a plant leaf of the size of the nose of that person, and having cut the

adjoining cheek according to that measurement, and having scarified [scraped] the nose tip should attach it to that nose tip and quickly join it with perfect sutures… When the healing is complete and the parts united, remove the excess skin.

Even the nasal passages could be reconstructed using short lengths of hollow sticks. Honey and oil were applied, and oil-soaked cotton was used to dress the repaired nose. This complex operation would eventually become known in the West as the 'Indian Method'.

There was also a demand for facial reconstruction from adults and children whose heavy ear jewellery had split and infected their earlobes. Sushruta's discourse implies that this was a common problem, easily remedied by taking skin from the cheek and suturing it into the torn lobe. He describes performing this operation even on tiny infants.

The methods passed from India to the classical civilisations of Greece and Rome. In his book *De Medecina*, the Roman writer Aulus Cornelius

INDIAN PIONEER The 6th-century BC surgeon Sushruta (shown above in a painting by R.A. Thom) was notable for his ground-breaking writings on plastic surgery. He was also the first to record how to operate on cataracts.

HOW TO MAKE A NEW NOSE An article in the *Gentleman's Magazine* in 1794 revealed to Western medicine what had long been known in the East: delicate surgery with the patient's own skin could miraculously reverse severe mutilation.

HARD GRAFT A self-grafting nose operation was performed in the 16th century by the Italian surgeon Gaspare Tagliacozzi. The detailed lithographs of the procedure, which takes skin from the underside of the arm and grafts it to the nose, are copies from Tagliacozzi's textbook, showing how to implant the skin (1), and how to imobilise the patient to allow the graft to 'take' (2).

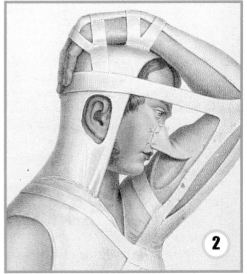

Celsus described almost identical procedures to Sushruta's for repairing mutilated noses, lips and ears. The most famous recipient of this treatment was Justinian II, the Byzantine emperor. In AD 695 he was deposed and his nose amputated, in the hope that the stigma of this disfigurement would prevent him from regaining power. Justinian went into exile, but by AD 705 was emperor again. He had reportedly been operated on and had a new nose, which earned him the nickname Rhinometus – 'Cut Nose'.

But surgery was viewed as ungodly in medieval Europe, and in 1163 Pope Innocent III and the Council of Tours passed a resolution stating that 'Surgery is to be abandoned by the schools of medicine and by all decent physicians'. Clerics were forbidden to practise bloodletting; it was left to barbers and butchers to carry out surgical procedures.

When Gaspare Tagliacozzi, a professor at the University of Bologna, published a work of surgical techniques in 1594, the church excommunicated him. On his death, they even ensured that his remains were buried in unconsecrated ground, by digging them up and removing them from a churchyard.

RECUPERATION As soon as the skin attached to the nose, the graft was likely to be successful. In time the excess skin could be cut away from the arm, which then healed as though from a superficial injury.

Tagliacozzi's methods continued to be mocked in the decades following his death. His pioneering grafting of skin directly from the arm to the face was criticised by some Renaissance writers. The French satirist Voltaire wrote a poem lampooning Tagliacozzi, in which he performed an operation that stretched a patient's skin from his buttock to his nose.

Western response

It was not until the 18th century that plastic surgery gained real acceptance in Western Europe. Some surgeons carrying out amputations on ships or in field hospitals were aware that skin could re-attach itself to flesh. Before the amputation, skin could be trimmed from the leg or arm to fold back over the stump. But many still preferred the traditional method of cauterising open wounds or amputated limbs with hot oil.

Then the *Gentleman's Magazine* article of 1794 introduced the West to the Indian reconstructive techniques. Two British doctors, Thomas Cruso and James Findlay, documented the procedure. They watched as an Indian cart-driver named Kawasajee – whose nose had been cut off as a penalty for treason – had his nose rebuilt, and concluded that the operation was likely to succeed in most cases.

The artificial nose is secured and looks nearly as well as the natural nose, nor is the scar on the forehead very observable after a length of time.

The account inspired an Englishman named Joseph Carpue to perform two similar operations. He reportedly took only 15 minutes to complete each reconstruction.

But after this first step towards assimilating Indian medical techniques, the British then made a complete about-turn. By 1835 they had closed down all the schools of Ayurvedic medicine, replacing them with Western medical colleges. That the methods did not disappear completely was thanks to a handful of determined private practitioners who offered Ayurvedic treatment from their own homes.

Finally, in 1914, Europe was thrown into circumstances that forced hospitals to train their surgeons in the techniques of plastic surgery and to develop new techniques as quickly as possible. Trench warfare was inflicting terrible injuries with shrapnel and shells, and surgeons were suddenly confronted with thousands of young men in dire need of facial or bodily reconstruction. The wounded from the Western Front were coming home.

It was not until the 18th century that plastic surgery gained real acceptance in Western Europe.

How doctors dulled the pain

Ancient doctors were almost as skilled with anaesthesia as they were with the scalpel. Ways to alleviate pain during surgery were known to ancient Egyptian physicians, who combined water and vinegar over Memphite stone to produce carbon dioxide. This gas had an analgesic effect not very different from modern anaesthetic practice.

In the 2nd century AD the Roman physician Galen advised using a potion, 'theriac', which contained more than 100 ingredients. Theriac was still taken in the 19th century, its success perhaps due to the fact that it contained opium.

In the 4th century AD Hilary, Bishop of Poitiers, was exiled to the Orient, where he too encountered opium. He compiled a medical textbook which advised: 'If anyone is to have a limb mutilated, burnt or sawn, he may drink a half ounce with wine, and whilst he sleeps the member may be cut off without any pain or sense.' Later use of a 'sleeping sponge' showed that inhalation of opium had been recognised as valuable for prolonging the stupor.

Drugs and alcohol

Alcohol was the most popular anaesthetic when in 1800 the English chemist Humphry Davy inhaled the gas nitrous oxide, and discovered that it not only dulled pain but induced a mild euphoria. He suggested its use in minor surgical procedures, claiming it did not produce the hangover brought on by alcohol. His proposal was ignored, although nitrous oxide became popular at society parties. As 'gas and air' it is used for pain relief in hospitals today.

WHO DISCOVERED AMERICA?
The New World has been known by explorers for 1500 years

The belief that Christopher Columbus discovered America is a fallacy. He was following in well-trodden footsteps. Centuries before his birth, pioneers had travelled across the Pacific and Atlantic Oceans.

Children in classrooms across the world are taught that the Genoese sailor Christopher Columbus discovered America, that 'In fourteen hundred and ninety two, Columbus sailed the ocean blue'. The rhyme may be true, but many of the other aspects of Columbus's journey have been mythologised. He did not set sail to prove that the Earth was round – he was hoping to find a lucrative trade route through to Asia. He didn't even land in the modern United States; his ship came ashore on the island of San Salvador in the Bahamas.

In any case, the notion of 'discovering' the American continent is itself a dubious one. Archaeological evidence tells us that North America has been inhabited for nearly 20,000 years. Columbus's voyage represents little more than the first step towards the colonisation of the continent by European settlers.

The earliest civilisations that would have had ships capable of reaching America were the Egyptians or even the Phoenicians. Although claims that they did reach the continent have been made, the evidence is scant. A more convincing case has been made for the Romans, although nothing has been written about such a voyage.

The Roman Empire stretched from Hadrian's Wall on the England-Scotland border to the deserts of Syria, encompassing almost the entire known world. Their galleys were certainly capable of the journey across the Atlantic; some were as large as 18th-century battleships. Low in the bow and rounded at the stern like trawlers, they were designed for the calmer waters of Mare Nostrum (our sea) – the Mediterranean.

Mysterious find

There are no Roman settlements or archaeological remains, but physical evidence does exist in the form of a tiny terracotta head of a bearded

ROMAN TRACES A tiny terracotta head found in the Toluca valley, Mexico could indicate that Roman galleys reached America, or that Roman shipwrecks washed up on her shores. Soil dating suggests that the Toluca head was already buried long before the Spanish came to Central America.

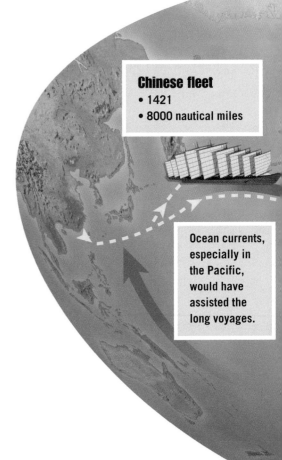

Chinese fleet
- 1421
- 8000 nautical miles

Ocean currents, especially in the Pacific, would have assisted the long voyages.

man. It was found in the Toluca Valley, 40 miles west of Mexico City. Just 5cm (2in) tall, the head is unlike any other pre-Columbian artefact and has been a source of controversy since it was unearthed in 1933.

Scientists at the Max Planck Institute for Nuclear Physics in Heidelberg recently used an advanced method to determine the age of the head. High-energy electrons that had accumulated in the sample were made to release their energy as light. The amount of light released gave a measure of the time elapsed since the clay was fired. The head was dated to AD 200, and is thought by many to match the style of objects being made in Rome at around that time.

The mystery of the Toluca head is how it could have travelled from Rome to Mexico. The original archaeological records suggest that it had been buried around 1510, a little before European colonists might have

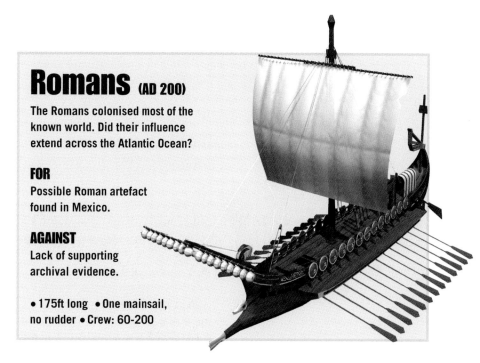

Romans (AD 200)

The Romans colonised most of the known world. Did their influence extend across the Atlantic Ocean?

FOR
Possible Roman artefact found in Mexico.

AGAINST
Lack of supporting archival evidence.

- 175ft long • One mainsail, no rudder • Crew: 60-200

brought it to America. Could such a tiny object have been washed up in a shipwreck, retrieved from a beach and brought inland as far as Mexico? Most scholars agree that for a

REDRAWING THE MAP The tantalising clues to America's earliest discoverers suggest routes of exploration dating back to more than a thousand years before Columbus.

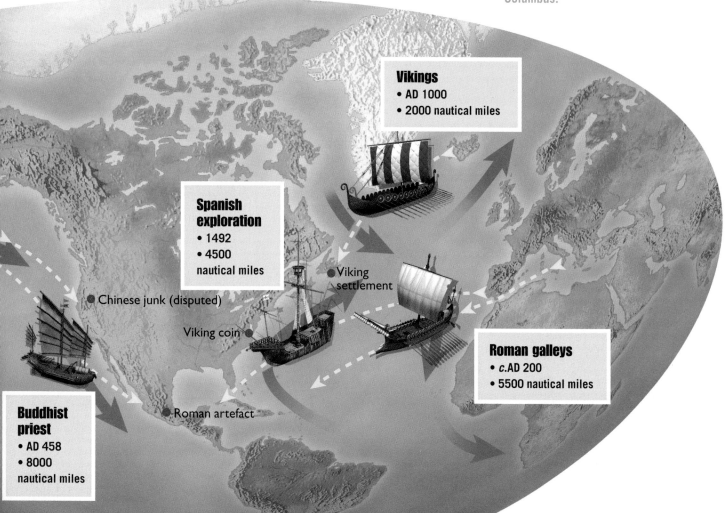

Vikings
- AD 1000
- 2000 nautical miles

Spanish exploration
- 1492
- 4500 nautical miles

Viking settlement

Chinese junk (disputed)

Viking coin

Roman galleys
- c.AD 200
- 5500 nautical miles

Roman artefact

Buddhist priest
- AD 458
- 8000 nautical miles

civilisation that usually left a clear footprint anywhere it ventured, the archaeological evidence for Romans discovering America is slight.

The Viking connection

The evidence that Viking traders reached the American continent is, by contrast, almost incontrovertible, and backs up claims made in the Norse sagas – literary works from the Middle Ages that record the deeds of Scandinavian heroes. According to *The Greenlanders' Saga*, the first discovery was an accident. A trader called Bjarni Herjulfsson set sail from Norway for his home in Iceland in AD 986. But when he got there he heard that his father Herjulf had left to join the newly established settlement in Greenland, and he impulsively followed him. In fog and strong north winds he became lost at sea and finished up within sight of a land covered with forest and low hills.

Bjarni never set foot ashore, but the story he brought home inspired others, including Leif Ericsson, who bought Bjarni's boat and set sail with 35 crewmen in 1000. Leif apparently landed in several places before returning home; if the account is true these would have been on the Canadian mainland.

Archaeological evidence now shows that this tale is very close to the truth. In the 1960s Norwegian

archaeologists uncovered an entire Norse settlement on the north coast of Newfoundland. At L'Anse aux Meadows they found a place that seemed to match the descriptions given by Bjarni and Leif. There were seven buildings in three complexes, enough for a small settlement of some 100 people. The style of the buildings is typical of Icelandic houses of about 1000, and carbon dates point to the same period. There are no such remains on the mainland, but three butternuts found in the settlement must have come from much farther south in America itself.

A thousand miles south, in Maine, a single Norse coin found at the mouth of Penobscot Bay is evidence that Norse settlers did make contact with indigenous people, who would have lived on the mainland. The so-called Maine Penny was found in 1957 by amateur archaeologists amid a mass of Native American stone tools and pottery. The coin has been identified as a Norwegian penny minted by King Olaf Kyrre between 1067 and 1092.

Fragmentary as these traces are, they have convinced many scholars that the Vikings did reach the American mainland. But they do not seem to have had a long-term impact. No trace of their influence remains among the indigenous peoples.

Eastern explorers

A recent, controversial theory has proposed that another great seafaring civilisation may have reached America before Columbus. In 1421, the Chinese emperor Zhu Di ordered a huge fleet to sail from Nanking to return a party of visiting rulers and envoys to their homes. The fleet was then to 'proceed all the way to the end of the Earth to collect tribute from the barbarians beyond the seas… to attract all under heaven to be civilised in Confucian harmony'. Admiral Zheng He was placed in charge, commanding ships of a size and power that would not be seen again for centuries, fitted with bulkheads and numerous

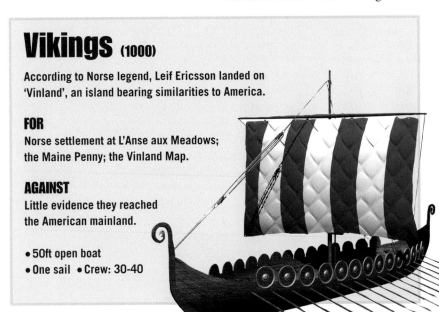

Vikings (1000)

According to Norse legend, Leif Ericsson landed on 'Vinland', an island bearing similarities to America.

FOR
Norse settlement at L'Anse aux Meadows; the Maine Penny; the Vinland Map.

AGAINST
Little evidence they reached the American mainland.

- 50ft open boat
- One sail • Crew: 30-40

Mapping out the past

In 1958 a map dealer put up for sale an ancient parchment map showing Europe, North Africa, Greenland and the Canadian island of Newfoundland. It was immediately bought for $1 million by the philanthropist Paul A. Mellon, who donated it to Yale University, where scholars declared it genuine – a true Norse map, drawn between 1420 and 1440. Some historians believe that this map – known as the Vinland Map – proves that the Vikings reached America. The creative journey the map itself has taken is far from clear.

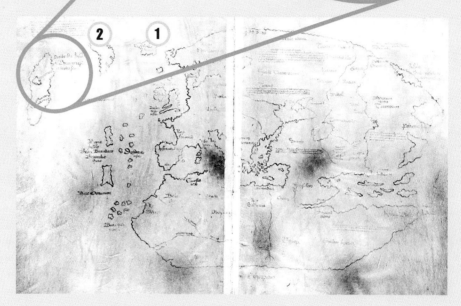

PUSHING BACK THE FRONTIER
The map includes Iceland (1), then Greenland (2 – shown as an island). They would be reached before Vinland Island, which is clearly labelled, by ships sailing west. But some scholars think that, although the map is genuine, Vinland and these islands were later additions.

'Vinland Island' is clearly labelled at the top left hand corner of the map. Lower down, an inscription relates how 'the companions Bjarni and Leif Ericsson, sailing south through the ice, discovered a new land, which was very rich and even had vines; they called it Vinland Island'.

The cartographer credited with drawing the map, Claudius Clavius, was a Dane who had copied the information from an earlier Viking map. But the map's provenance was highly dubious, with no recorded history from before 1958, when it was discovered. Critics have claimed that the Norse settlers of Greenland had no cartographic knowledge, relying instead on an oral tradition.

In 1972, scientific analysis of the ink used in the map seemed finally to have proved it a fake. This showed the presence of anastase, a form of titanium dioxide pigment, which had not been synthesised before 1923. Anastase leaves traces of yellow, and one theory was that anastase had been added by a forger to simulate the ageing of iron gall ink. So the map had to be a clever forgery. But other scientists contested the finding, finally proving that the amount of anastase present could be accounted for by accidental contamination.

Radiocarbon dating of the parchment itself, published in 2002, showed that it was made in 1434, give or take 11 years – exactly the period when the Yale scholars believe the map was drawn. They had previously decided that the language used and the form of writing matched records written at the Council of Basle, convened by the Church between 1431 and 1449.

Too incredible to be fake

It is of course possible that the map is a fake, but drawn on genuine medieval parchment. If so, it is an extraordinary fluke that the forger found parchment of exactly the right age to support the Yale theory. 'If it is a forgery, then the forger was surely one of the most skilful criminals ever to pursue that line of work,' concludes a member of the team that dated the parchment.

Chinese fleet (1421)

Imperial archives record that a huge treasure fleet of 317 ships sailed from China in the early 15th century. It is not widely accepted that they got beyond Africa, but one historian argues that they reached American shores.

FOR
Disputed junk in Sacramento River.
Traces of Chinese claimed in Californian language.

AGAINST
Evidence scant.

• Treasure ships up to 800 x 180ft • Crew: 1000+

cabins. The navigators who sailed in them had magnetic compasses and maps, and followed well-charted routes. Just how far Zheng He's fleet travelled was never recorded. By the time it returned two years later the policy of exploration had changed, and China had entered a period of isolation that lasted 600 years. Zhu Di had been replaced by his son, who slammed the door to the world, and left the great fleets to rot.

Could a boat from Zheng He's fleet have reached the west coast of the New World? A medieval Chinese junk at the bottom of the Sacramento River, nearly a hundred miles inland, would be compelling evidence, if experts could agree it existed. Core samples taken from wood fragments recovered from the location have been carbon dated to 1410. Fragments of wood were also sent to China, where they were analysed by the Chinese Academy of Forestry. The samples were identified as having come from the Keteleria conifer, which is native to south-east China, but not North America.

But there is debate surrounding the validity of this evidence. Many doubt there is actually a junk in the river, as no actual part of it has been brought to the surface. The wood fragments are minuscule.

Supporters of the junk propose the theory that the ship ran aground in the

Sacramento River, forcing the Chinese crew to settle in America. The remains of a walled stone village 70 miles from the site bear some hallmarks of Chinese construction. Other tantalising clues have been found. In 1874 a United States government report contained a claim from a linguistic expert, Stephen Powers, that traces of the Chinese language could be found among the tribes of California. Powers argued that the Chinese had intermixed with Native Americans, only to fall prey to the diseases that the Europeans settlers brought with them in the 15th century. Officials at the time were unimpressed with this theory and suppressed his findings, but they could represent a crucial piece of the jigsaw.

Intrepid missionary
Chinese records show that the treasure fleet of 1421 already knew about the great landmass across the Pacific Ocean. The earliest claim for discovering America can be found in Volume 231 of the eminent 13th-century historian Ma Tuan-Lin's *Great Chinese Encyclopedia*. In AD 458 a Buddhist priest, Hoei-Shin ('Universal Compassion'), left China to spread the word of his faith. He sailed across the vast 'Great Eastern Sea', returning 40 years later with incredible tales of a land he called 'Fusang'. The detailed account of his journey has allowed some experts to speculate that Fusang was actually America.

The priest spoke of the arid landscape that he had found, and how it was dominated by the fusang tree, after which the land was named. He described its edible shoots and how 'Its fruit resembles the pear, but is red; the bark is spun into cloth for dresses, and woven into brocade'. The fusang bears a striking resemblance to the *Agave americana* (maguey plant), which is widely found in Mexico to this day. This supposition is backed up by Hoei-Shin's assertion that the local area was devoid of any source of iron: Central America is one of few parts of

BORN LEADER Admiral Zheng He was a seasoned explorer. After a voyage to East Africa in 1405, the admiral had presented the emperor with a giraffe, which many at the time believed to be a mythological beast.

the world where this is the case.

According to the *Great Chinese Encyclopedia*, the inhabitants of Fusang were known as the Ichi. It was written in the archives that the Ichi had 'no mailed soldiers; for they do not carry on war'. This echoes Mexican historical accounts of the Itza tribe, an apparently peace-loving people whose architectural and artistic achievements were greatly to influence the Mayan civilisation.

Modern nautical studies suggest that Hoei-Shin's story could be genuine. The account of his journey states that he travelled 20,000 *li* across the Pacific Ocean. This distance was roughly equivalent to 8000 nautical miles, and placed Fusang somewhere along the coastline of Central America. The prevailing currents provided a natural guide, as they flow up and around the east Asian coast to Alaska, and back down the coast of America to Mexico.

On his return home, in AD 499, civil war prevented Hoei-Shin from gaining an audience at the imperial court for three years. In AD 502 he finally met the emperor Wu Ti who, impressed by his story, ordered that Hoei-Shin's testimony be included in the Imperial archives of the Liang dynasty. The legend of Hoei-Shin's journey passed into popular culture, inspiring later Chinese explorers – perhaps even Admiral Zheng He – with tales of the distant and mysterious land of Fusang.

It is impossible to say with any certainty whether the Chinese records are accurate. Stories may have been exaggerated, or mistold. Even if Hoei-Shin did set foot on American soil, there might have been others before him. Archaeological sites in North America may reveal new clues, traces of pioneers from other nations.

But there is enough evidence to treat the claims we have heard seriously. The story of the discovery of the American continent is richer and more complex than the classroom would have children believe.

> *Chinese explorers would be inspired by tales of the distant and mysterious land of Fusang.*

Buddhist priest (AD 458)

Archives tell how, in the 5th century AD, a monk called Hoei-Shin left China. He returned 40 years later with tales of a land called 'Fusang': was this place America?

FOR
Certain features of 'Fusang' unique to Central America. Distance of journey given in Imperial records correct.

AGAINST
No archaeological evidence.

- **70ft junk** • **Multi-masted, ruddered**
- **Crew: unknown**

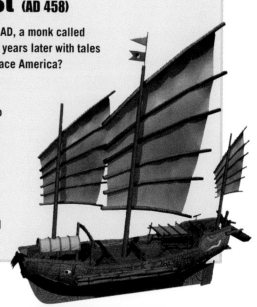

MONOPOLY ON IDEAS
To Park Lane and Broadway via Poverty Place and Easy Street

For nearly 70 years players have enjoyed the risky financial speculations of the Monopoly board. But the original version of the property-buying game was intended to satirise capitalism – not celebrate it.

One evening in 1930, so the story accompanying the rules in the board game Monopoly tells us, an unemployed boiler salesman by the name of Charles Darrow sketched out some Atlantic City street names at his kitchen table, when 'a new game began to take form in his mind'. Encouraged by his prototype's popularity among friends, Darrow began selling handmade sets. His initial approach to the games company Parker Brothers was rebuffed – it cited '52 fundamental errors', including that the game took too long to play, the rules were too complicated and there was no clear goal for the winner.

But Darrow was undeterred, and with the aid of a printer friend, he sold 5000 sets to a local F.A.O. Schwarz department store. Impressive sales swayed Parker Brothers and, within six months of striking a deal, they were producing 20,000 Monopoly games a week. Darrow was on his way to becoming the world's first millionaire board game designer.

The history of Monopoly's invention features the same spirit of single-minded speculation and initiative that the game itself rewards. But there is another side to the story. During a bitter and protracted trademark lawsuit some years after Darrow's death, it emerged that a very similar board game had been played by Quakers living on the east coast of America for more than 30 years

before Darrow 'invented' it. Although it comprised a board covered with properties, the Quaker game had quite the opposite object, and taught the evils of speculation and profiteering rather than rewarding their success. According to one acquaintance Darrow played this game, and even borrowed a set of its rules.

Quaker protest
An economics professor, Ralph Anspach, uncovered this story during a battle against the games company Parker-General Mills, over the rights to his game 'Anti-Monopoly', in which the aim was to break up large companies. After appearing on television in 1974, Anspach received a call from an elderly woman.

'I think Parker Brothers has a lot of nerve suing you for getting a free ride on their game,' she told him. She then spoke of a college friend whose family used to play a Quaker version of a property board game long before Monopoly appeared. Ralph Anspach traced several such folk games going back to Elizabeth Magie of Maryland, who patented her 'Landlord's Game' in 1904.

Magie was a committed 'single-taxer', supporter of a single federal tax designed to discourage property speculation. The Landlord's Game board was square, with property blocks arranged around the edges. There were banks, a poorhouse, railroads, utilities, a jail, and 'Mother Earth' at one of the corners. Around the board, the players might stop at

Poverty Place or Easy Street. The game grew popular in the economics faculties of east coast universities, where students added a new rule by which rents increased when little cardboard houses were set on properties. In this form, it became known as Auction Monopoly, then Monopoly. The Landlord's Game was patented by Magie again in 1924.

Few people actually bought Magie's home-produced game, which she distributed herself. Instead they sketched out their own boards using local street names for added amusement, and copied out the rules from one another. Ralph Anspach eventually found out how Charles Darrow came across it.

An advertisement placed in the *Christian Science Monitor* delivered the breakthrough. Charles Todd of Philadelphia recalled the day in 1932 he ran into a childhood friend, Esther Jones, now married to Darrow, and invited her and her husband Charles over for dinner. After the meal they played Magie's game. 'It was entirely new to them,' Todd said. 'They had never seen anything like it before and showed a great deal of interest… we could see Darrow really loved the game.' They played together another five or six times; at the last Charles asked for a set of written rules. 'He said this was such a great game he wanted to get it right.' The Todds never spoke to the Darrows again.

Roaring success

Much of the appeal of Darrow's Monopoly was in his distinctive modern designs, the quirky tone of the Chance and Community Chest cards and the unusual play tokens. The flat-iron, hat, shoe and so on were said to have been appropriated from Esther Darrow's charm bracelet. The new game was the parlour craze of 1934 and its sensational earnings revived Parker Brothers' fortunes.

Parker Brothers' chairman Robert Barton wrote to Darrow, 'We have been doing very well with Monopoly and we want to do everything that we can to protect its reputation and

position.' He invited Darrow to sign an affidavit that the game was entirely his own creation.

Elizabeth Magie never contested Parker Brothers' issue of Monopoly. Instead, she entered into negotiations with them. Her only concern was to popularise the idea of a single taxation policy and prove that an unfair financial advantage was enjoyed by property speculators. Parker Brothers secured the rights to her patent for $500, without royalties, but with the promise that the Landlord's Game would go into production and reach the public in its original form. They kept to the letter of this agreement, although sales amounted only to a few hundred.

In the accompanying notes, Magie outlined how the object of the game was to illustrate 'how the landlord has an advantage over other enterprises'. In Monopoly – the biggest-selling board game in the world – to capitalise on this advantage is, of course, the whole point.

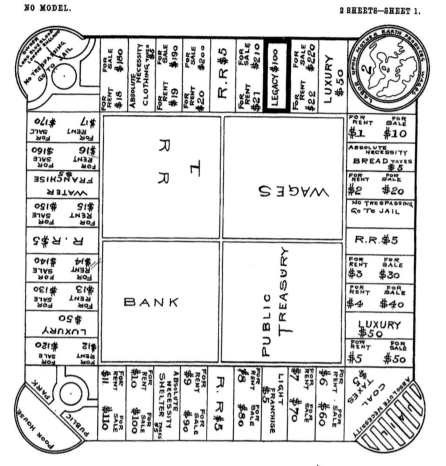

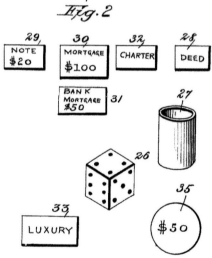

RAGS TO RICHES The patent for the 'Landlord's Game' was awarded to Elizabeth 'Lizzie' Magie in 1904. The original board layout included the jail, public park, water and electrical franchises, with simple cards for deeds and banknotes.

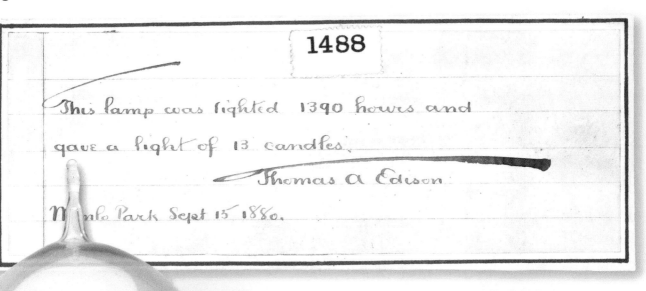

1488

This lamp was lighted 1390 hours and gave a light of 13 candles.

Thomas A Edison

Menlo Park Sept 15 1880.

LET THERE BE LIGHT
Thomas Edison did not invent the light bulb

The invention of the light bulb came as a result of a series of scientific breakthroughs. But shady commercial practices meant that the inventor truly responsible lost his rightful place in history.

At the end of the Civil War in 1865, the reunited states of America entered a new era of commerce and entrepreneurship. Businessmen made their fortunes supplying the vast marketplace of the Midwest with the latest domestic appliances and tools. Lighting was one area in which huge technological strides were made. And with the development of electricity as a reliable power source, a race began in the late 1870s to patent an efficient form of electrical lighting. At the forefront of this contest were two American inventors, Thomas Alva Edison and Hiram Maxim.

Edison was already famous for his invention of the phonograph and various telegraph instruments. But he was at least as much a businessman as he was an inventor. Edison approached investors directly rather than submit himself to the industrialists and their specifications. His experience of developing prototypes of other inventions had made him familiar with the loopholes in patent laws. As a result Edison's usual practice was to patent every advance made by his research team, however small.

SECOND PLACE Edison signed a certificate of performance for his light bulb in September 1880. But the bulb in his 'standard lamp' was suitable only for demonstration, and lagged a year behind Hiram Maxim's own model.

Hiram Maxim, on the other hand, was an archetypal inventor – ploughing away, busily working on ideas, but not giving a thought to their commercial potential until after the final 'eureka' moment.

In his mid 20s he had invented the first sprinkler system in Boston, only to fail to impress investors of its worth. In 1878 he was hired by Hans Schuyler of the US Electric Lighting Company in New York. As a further incentive, over and beyond his wages of $10 a day, Maxim was due a quarter share in anything he produced for the company. Aware of the inventor's work on gas machine lighting in Massachusetts, Schuyler placed him in charge of operations to produce electric light. Within a year Maxim had installed the first electrical 'arc' lighting system in the Equitable Insurance Company building in New York.

Out of the arc

Arc lights worked by building up charge on a carbon rod until an 'arc' of electricity crossed to a second rod. With sustained charge build-up, the arc sparked continuously, producing light. Arc lights wasted a great deal of energy and could be dangerous. It became a question of who would be first to find a way to channel current through a filament and sustain it without burn-out.

Edison witnessed demonstrations of an early version of an unstable arc

light in 1877, and in an interview with the *New York Tribune* in 1878, announced his intentions to design an incandescent lamp. When asked about the financial rewards of being the first man to make such a product, he replied: 'I don't so much care for fortune as I do for getting ahead of the other fellow.' He revealed that his platinum wire filament kept melting, and said, 'I want to find something better.' To help him in this quest, he founded his own fully staffed laboratory, complete with skilled glass blowers.

For all his rhetoric Edison had a lot of ground to make up. By 1878 Hiram Maxim had built a working light bulb using a filament made of

---

Early bulb burn-outs

Most light bulbs work by a process known as 'incandescent filament lighting'. An electric current is passed through a filament – a very thin piece of material. The electical resistance of the material causes it to heat up and incandesce – glow brightly.

Although the principle was well known in the 1870s, a major problem remained unsolved. The material for the filament had to be made of either carbon or platinum, as they alone were able to withstand the great heat. The high cost of platinum prohibited its use, while carbon filaments were too uneven in thickness, allowing the thinner parts to burn out.

Hiram Maxim solved this problem by putting petroleum into the sealed bulb. As it heated up, the petroleum gave off a carbon vapour, which deposited carbon onto the thinnest (and therefore hottest) parts of the filament. The filament was self-repairing in its weakened parts, a process known as 'flashing'. The bulb gave out a more constant and durable light.

IDEAS MEN Thomas Edison (far left) patented more than 1000 inventions, and was known as the 'Wizard of Menlo Park'. Hiram Maxim (left) was an inveterate inventor who applied for his first patent – a hair-curling iron – at the age of 26.

Leading light

Hiram Maxim was the first to crack the light bulb's innate problem of burn-out, but it was Edison who came up with the best idea to protect the filament from burning. He used suction to remove oxygen from the bulb, creating a vacuum inside it.

Once they were commercially produced, Edison's bulbs would glow for longer than 40 hours. With his name clearly displayed on every one, the light bulb became the invention with which Edison would be forever associated.

carbon inside a bulb filled with petrol vapour. The bulb stayed lit and did not burn out. Maxim applied for a patent on October 4 'on the principle of preserving and building up carbons in an incandescent lamp'. If his application had been successful he would now be recognised as the official inventor of the light bulb. But he was to run into a quagmire of bureaucracy, bitter lawsuits and deliberate obstruction.

The interfering 'Mr D'

Maxim's patent was being processed when a former employee, sacked from the company for drunkenness, stepped forward to deny the claim. The man, who Maxim discreetly referred to as 'Mr D' (in fact, William Edward Sawyer) had also worked for Hans Schuyler at the Electrical Lighting Company: he had been a member of Maxim's team. After seeing a demonstration of the new, longer-lasting filament, Mr D

challenged Maxim's patent, bringing his father and brother forward as witnesses to testify that he had invented the heat-induced carbonising of the filament years before Maxim had. Mr D's claim was upheld, and he was granted the patent.

There was an extra injustice in the claim. Mr D had actually slowed Maxim's progress by making alarmist comments about the petrol vapour used in the bulb cavity. He persuaded Schuyler that the bulb would be too dangerous to sell, and work on the project had been delayed as a result.

Just as Maxim seemed to have been beaten, help arrived from an unlikely quarter. Edison, probably realising that the carbon filament was the only practical material suitable for the bulb's filament, challenged the award of the patent to Mr D. The subsequent proceedings revealed that Maxim was the real inventor and revoked the patent awarded to Mr D.

Then came the sting – one that Edison could not have planned even if he had wished to. American law at the time stated that, as the patent granted to Mr D had been fraudulently obtained, it could not subsequently be granted to any other individual and became the common property of the United States. Mr D had lost Maxim a patent he valued at 'at least a million dollars a year'.

Maxim also found himself losing out to Edison in the propaganda war. Edison piqued public curiosity with optimistic statements of progress and

True! On October 21, 1931, several days after the death of Thomas Edison, electric lights across the United States were dimmed in tribute to the inventor.

daring demonstrations. In 1878, he announced cryptically that 'I have just solved the problem of the subdivision of the electric light indefinitely'. This statement meant nothing scientifically, and belied the fact that he still had lots of problems with his platinum filament, which had to be switched off at frequent intervals to prevent it overheating.

Maxim dismissed Edison as a publicity seeker, noting bitterly in 1879 that 'every time I put up a light a crowd would gather, everyone asking "Is it Edison's?" ' Yet Maxim had produced the first saleable light bulb, and Edison had still to make a lamp that worked.

War of the lamps

The rivalry between the two men intensified when Edison finally produced his own lamp. Though the two lamps were very similar, Edison's gift for self-promotion again gave him the upper hand. At the Congress of Electricians in Paris in 1881, Edison and Maxim both set up displays of their lamps. Edison's designs dominated the headlines, in part because his own Parisian staff had written many of the press reports.

Edison flourished in the world of commerce, too. His company bought up almost all the stocks of a rare chemical that was essential for making the filament lamps, which almost scuppered the rival Electric Lighting Company.

With his usual business acumen, Edison acquired patents in several European countries with prospects for his invention. He even arranged for a farmer on the Japanese island of Kyushu to cultivate a particular type of bamboo exclusively for the Edison Swan Electric Company. When carbonised, it made an ideal filament,

and was used in the Edison standard lamp until 1894.

Maxim had abandoned his attempts to sell his light bulb by 1883. But the loss of the light bulb did not dim his innovative mind. At the Parisian Congress of Electricians, a friend told him that instead of appliances Maxim should 'invent a killing machine that will let these Europeans cut each other's throats more easily'.

Maxim was inspired. For two years he worked on the world's first automatic gun. He took a Winchester repeating rifle and reconfigured it with a reloading action. The power from the recoil slotted the next cartridge into position. By 1883, Maxim had a working prototype of a gun that fired bullets at the touch of a lever. 'They all went off in about half a second,' he wrote. 'I was delighted.'

The Maxim machine gun was able to shoot 500 rounds in a minute and was far lighter and more portable than the manually operated Gatling machine guns. By 1890, the British, German and Russian armies had all adopted the devastating new weapon.

By the time of his death, Hiram Maxim had learned more about the role commerce played in finding and developing original ideas. He had amassed 122 American and 149 British patents, from a mousetrap that reset itself to automatic weaponry. But for Edison's business nous, he would have had the one that got away.

> Every time I put up a light a crowd would gather, everyone asking, 'Is it Edison's?'
>
> HIRAM MAXIM

MASS DESTRUCTION The Maxim machine gun was first used in battle by British colonial forces during the Matabele War, in southern Africa, in 1893. In one engagement, 50 soldiers with just four Maxim guns were able to kill 5000 warriors.

PATRONS AND PATENTS

Necessity is the mother of invention, but its paternity is sometimes a matter of dispute. The names associated with particular well-known inventions are not always those that most deserve the credit.

Many inventors have learned to their cost that, in the competitive world of commerce, there is no premium on talent and originality. Often the key to getting a breakthrough noticed is to get the innovation patented in your name and have the backing to manufacture it. In America, early patent law was powerless to prevent individuals making improvements to someone else's invention and taking out a new patent.

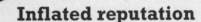

Inflated reputation

The first British patent for a pneumatic tyre was granted to Robert William Thomson in 1845, 40 years before the first car hit the streets. But he was too far ahead of his time. The tyres were too awkward to use on bikes, so it was not until motor transport became widespread that there was a demand for his invention. In the end, the man to profit was not Thomson but John Boyd Dunlop (left), who in 1888 patented a refinement of Thomson's tyre, an air-filled inner tube tucked inside a durable rubber outer casing.

Hoovering up the profits

Few people talk about vacuum cleaning a room – they talk about Hoovering it. But William H. Hoover was not the inventor of the vacuum cleaner; rather he was a man who saw the potential of a portable electric cleaning device and turned it into a world-famous company. In 1869, Ives McGaffey patented a 'sweeping machine' that picked up dirt from rugs. Hubert Cecil Booth took out a British patent on a similar device in 1901. Then in 1907 James Murray Spangler, a cleaner in a department store in Ohio, rigged up an old sewing machine fan motor to a soapbox stapled to a broom handle and attached a pillowcase at the rear to collect dust. Hoover, a leather merchant, was so impressed that he bought the patent, retained Spangler as his superintendent, and marketed the machine through US retail outlets. He renamed the Electric Suction Sweeper Company after himself in 1922.

Picture credits

The man recognised as the inventor of photography is Louis Daguerre, in 1839. Yet a French-born scientist living in Brazil, Louis Florence, was using a working camera six years earlier. He also worked out how to fix the images, a process which had Daguerre stumped for several years.

Florence called his pictures 'photographs', but they were never seen in Europe, and so missed out on the publicity that attracted a ready market. There, the first photographic images unveiled were the other Louis' 'daguerreotypes'.

WINNING ON EXPOSURE Louis Daguerre's camera was not the first, but it was enthusiastically received by the French public and immediately attracted commercial backing.

Who made the call?

Today it is generally thought that the telephone was invented by Alexander Graham Bell – but was it? Bell made his breakthrough in 1875 and acquired a US patent on March 7, 1876. Three days later he transmitted the first message ever sent by telephone.

But an Italian American, Antonio Meucci, began work on transmitting speech by electricity as early as 1857. He filed a 'notice to patent' his invention in 1871, but could not raise $250 for the patent itself. Although he was at least four years ahead of Bell in development, Meucci had little success with backers; one even lost his prototype model. Bell, by contrast, was an established inventor with commercial backing already in place.

There was a long legal dispute between Bell's company and the rival Globe Telephone Company, which sponsored Meucci. Although the courts ruled in favour of Bell, the judgment conceded that Meucci had been the first to 'convey speech mechanically by means of a wire telephone'.

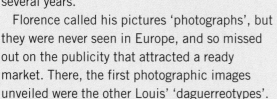

Spotting an opportunity

No one knows for sure who built the first telescope, but of the leading candidates it is the Italian scientist Galileo Galilei who usually gets the credit. However, most historians accept that the device was invented by Hans Lippershey (below right), a spectacle-maker from Middelburg in Holland. He applied for a patent in Holland in 1608 but it was denied, as the product was too easily assembled to count as an invention. When news reached Italy that this man was on his way to Venice to sell telescopes to the doge, Galileo quickly built his own, thus getting in first to secure the money, the place in history and a distinguished career in astronomical observation and research.

BIRTH OF THE BLAST FURNACE
Smelting plants could produce up to a tonne of iron a day – 500 years ago

Pre-industrial Europe was a tough farming culture, where the land was worked with crude tools. But although there was no machinery, the technology was very advanced. In the 1500s, blast furnaces smelted iron of a quality to match the factory iron produced in the 19th century.

TELLING DETAILS Evidence of the spread of iron-smelting plants through Europe appears in a work painted by the Flemish artist Lucas van Valckenborch in 1585. The key constituents of an early blast furnace are present in the detail of the 400-year-old painting: the water wheel, the bellows and the tanks to catch the molten iron.

M onasteries in the Middle Ages were wealthy institutions. Set in countryside or woodland, they were abundantly supplied by surrounding farms, orchards, beehives and hop-presses. Peasants cured pork and made bread, ale and honey, while the monks laboured over manuscripts or knelt at prayer. But in the silence of the cloisters the monks would have heard the thumping of forge hammers, shaping thick bars of wrought iron. A little farther away the furnace would have belched flame, as a workforce engaged in the hazardous business of producing iron on an industrial scale.

Medieval monks are not thought to have been at the cutting edge of heavy industry. But in fact they were technological pioneers. After the fall of the Roman Empire the Church had enjoyed a near monopoly of education for centuries. In the great new universities of Europe, almost all teachers and their students were clerics of one sort or another. Cistercian monks were a driving force in devising

new metallurgical methods, and spreading it throughout the Continent. As early as 1323, French monks were using water-driven bellows to raise furnace temperatures to about 1500˚C (2700˚F) – hot enough to liquefy iron ore, while the first blast furnace is thought to have been built 65 years later.

We imagine that when the Industrial Revolution began in Britain it was kick-started by a few key inventions, chief among these being the blast furnace. Now this view is changing because of archaeological evidence about the quality of iron produced much earlier. Blast furnaces seem to have been in operation for several hundred years before Thomas Telford or Isambard Kingdom Brunel, and iron was produced on a greater scale than previously thought.

For centuries, people had been smelting iron in Britain by traditional methods. The arms and armour of the medieval knight were made of iron. The 12th and 13th-century castles and manor houses; the abbeys, cathedrals, churches and chapels required ever greater quantities of iron. Every building site had a forge to make chains and claws for lifting stone blocks, and clamps for strengthening walls. 'Iron is more useful to man than gold,' a Franciscan remarked in 1260.

The evidence for the trailblazing skills of the monks comes not from their years of industrial success, but from the time of their downfall. When the Cistercians of Rievaulx in North Yorkshire were expelled from their abbey during Henry VIII's destruction of the monasteries,

The wheel powered the bellows, boosting the temperature of the fire as high as 1500°C.

Water was forced through a narrow channel (leat) to drive the water wheel.

Molten iron from the smelting chamber was 99 per cent pure and suitable for casting.

The smelting chamber was fuelled by wood hewn from the surrounding forests.

Iron smelting at Rievaulx

In the summer of 2002, archaeologists at Bradford University built a clay bloomery shaft furnace and smelted iron from local ore. The leftover lumps of slag had a high content of iron, indicating a poor-quality extraction.

The 500-year-old remains of the slag dug up at Laskill, near Rievaulx, contained a much lower proportion of iron. To achieve this, the temperature must have been far higher than in the clay bloomery. The team concluded that the furnace in use in the 16th century at Laskill must have been more advanced than the one they had built, and was probably an early blast furnace.

Efficient smelting produces dry, porous-looking waste slag

Inefficient smelting leaves rivulets of iron visible in the slag

TECHNICAL SERVICE Cistercian monks relied on lay brothers (recognisable by their beards and fringes) to mine the iron ore and operate the furnaces. These carvings are on the abbey church in Aubazine, south-west France.

the king was anxious to profit from their many treasures: he ordered detailed inventories to be made of the contents of all abbeys. The Rievaulx inventory still survives today, and contains an entry referring to 'the Iron Smythes sett & beyng on the westsyd of the Abbott'.

Two items on the abbey inventory intrigued Gerry McDonnell, an archaeo-metallurgist at the University of Bradford. Mention was made of a 'bloomsmithy' at Laskill, about 6km (4 miles) from the abbey, and a 'hammersmithy' at Rievaulx itself. McDonnell decided to investigate the two sites.

A geophysical survey of the landscape at Laskill and Rievaulx picked up variations in the magnetic field caused by the buried remains of iron and slag, the rock and metal waste left behind after smelting.

The monks had smelted iron since they first arrived at Rievaulx in 1132, and evidence of traditional smelting was also found in the abbey grounds. Analysis of the slag showed these furnaces were the highly wasteful old-fashioned clay bloomery type. Workers would have spent hours reheating and hammering the impure iron (known as bloom) to clean it.

But the Laskill slag was different: it had a low iron content, proving that the monks must have found a much more efficient way to extract the iron from the ore.

McDonnell's excavation uncovered the new method. Buried beneath the ancient slag and soil was a large structure below the ground – quite unlike the circular stack furnaces. There were also signs of a stream, and indications that alongside the stream the labourers had dug out a 'leat', a trench through which water is channelled to power a water wheel.

From wood to iron

The land around Rievaulx would have been able to provide all the resources necessary for a well-functioning blast furnace. There were plentiful supplies of iron ore in the hills close by. Beech, oak and alder for charcoal grew locally. The monks also had a strong workforce of lay brothers who mined the ore and chopped the wood. Running water was used to power the bellows and the forge hammer. Thanks to traditions and technology developed over many centuries, the monks were in a position to take full advantage of these natural resources.

They needed a large and constant supply of high-grade metal. Iron was used to make horseshoes and nails, as well as tools for stonemasons, carpenters, foresters and woodcarvers. The monks needed shears to clip the wool from 14,000 sheep. They were also in business, supplying cast iron and steel on a large scale.

In strictly technical terms, what McDonnell found may have been a 'high bloomery', dating from around 1538, which marks the transition

between the traditional bloomery and the blast furnace. A true blast furnace is known to have been built at Rievaulx in about 1570. This charcoal blast furnace achieved very high temperatures and could produce over a tonne of metal a day.

By this time the Earl of Rutland had taken over the abbey and its lands. The monks had left to escape Henry VIII's persecution – probably moving to the Continent.

Now that England was officially Protestant, the lay brothers – local men who had been attached to the abbey – would have reverted to being labourers. The earl would probably have utilised their know-how to help to run the blast furnace. So the iron industry continued to flourish after the monks who had established it had gone.

This giant furnace operated until the mid 17th century, when evidence of ironmaking at Rievaulx comes to a halt. The furnace had become a victim of its own success. It produced great quantities of iron, but its appetite for charcoal was prodigious – ten tonnes of wood were needed to

make a tonne of charcoal, and the supply had simply run out. Coal was an economical alternative to charcoal, but around Rievaulx there was none available. In any case, the high carbon content of coal tended to contaminate the iron.

Production of iron took off again in England – though not at Rievaulx – when in 1709 Abraham Darby introduced the use of coke rather than coal. It was to transform Britain into the largest, most successful producer of iron and steel in Europe. By then the contribution of the monks was faded and forgotten, like their ruined abbeys, which are still scattered across the English landscape.

LOST SKILLS By the late 17th century the woods around Rievaulx were stripped of the timber used for charcoal. The blast furnace in the abbey's grounds became uncommercial and the iron production plant fell into ruin.

BREAKING THE WAVES
Uncovering the ancient heritage – and religious origins – of surfing

Some surfers believe that their pastime harks back only as far as the 1960s. Yet surfing is an ancient skill: the Hawaiian Islanders have been riding the waves for at least 1500 years.

To its legions of devotees across the globe, surfing is not so much a sport as a way of life. But the enthusiasts who scour coastlines around the world in search of the perfect wave would perhaps be surprised to learn that the origins of surfing go back centuries.

The Polynesians who came to Hawaii from Tahiti in the 4th century AD possessed an array of ocean skills. They were deft canoeists, and they had also developed the art of catching waves while riding on belly boards, which they called *paipo*.

The islanders found that they could cross the coral reefs around the shore much more quickly on a flat plank of wood than in outriggers or double-hulled canoes. More than that, in the giant curling Hawaiian breakers, they could angle their boards and ride at speed across the face of a wave. In time they learned to build longer boards on which they could ride while standing upright.

But for these ancient people surfing was more than a practical skill; it had spiritual significance too. The Hawaiian word for surfing – *he'henalu* – also meant something akin to 'meditation' or 'communion'.

FIRST SURFERS The earliest images of surfing are sketches made in Hawaii. Although there are records of Tahitians playing in the surf on belly boards, it was in Hawaii that surfers first stood upright.

In search of the Big One

Surfing's renaissance in the 20th century was largely due to the Hawaiian swimmer Duke Kahanamoku. Kahanamoku was the Olympic 100m freestyle champion, eventually defeated at the 1924 Paris Olympics by Johnny Weissmuller (left, with robed Duke). 'It took Tarzan to beat me', Kahanamoku would joke. Kahanamoku used his fame to promote surfing across the world. Even after he retired he would talk of how 'the Big One' still awaited him in the Hawaiian surf.

The Big One came to Kahanamoku in the summer of 1932. Offshore earth tremors combined with a stiff offshore wind to form 'The Bluebirds', a rare swell of 9m (30ft) waves between gaping troughs 'the depth of elevator shafts'.

Duke recalled one wave in particular: 'It seemed very personal and special – the kind that I had seen in my mind's eye in a night of tangled dreaming. There was just this one wave and myself – no more. I got to my feet when the pitch, slant and speed seemed right. Left foot forwards, knees slightly bent, I rode the board down that precipitous slope like a man tobogganing down a glacier'.

Duke Kahanamoku clung on for more than a mile, before the wave finally expired in waist-high water before a crowd of stunned onlookers.

And in Hawaiian mythology, gods were known to surf celestial waves.

Surfboards became status symbols: the rich and powerful rode the waves on hollowed-out boards up to 6m (20ft) long that were practically boats, crafted from the light, buoyant wood of the *wili wili* tree. The poor made do with smaller, more modest craft carved out of breadfruit or banana palm wood.

Carnival time

For most of the year Hawaiian society was regulated by *kapu* – a strict hierarchical code that set the chiefs apart from the ordinary people. Surfing was controlled by this law: certain reefs and beaches were reserved for the use of high-ranking dignitaries only. But every year *kapu* was suspended for a period of feasting and games. This holiday season lasted from October to January, and culminated in the Makahiki festival, which marked the return of the god Lono, who came every year to renew the earth.

It was at the height of this celebration that the English explorer Captain James Cook anchored at Kealakekua Bay in January 1778. His first sighting of Hawaii featured a thousand canoes and ten thousand jubilant islanders performing ancient rituals in the surf. Cook's imposing ship awed the Hawaiians, who thought he was none other than Lono himself – though Cook had no idea of the impact of his arrival, or the reason for the joyful welcome.

The islanders surfed with such 'boldness and address' as 'scarcely to be credited', Cook wrote. They would wait until the surf reached 'its utmost heights', swim in groups of 20 or 30 past two sets of breaking waves, and place themselves 'on the summit of the largest surge, by which they are driven along with amazing rapidity toward the shore'.

They then had to jump clear of the board before it crashed, with no margin for error. One of Cook's lieutenants wrote: 'On first seeing this very dangerous diversion I did not conceive it possible but that some of them must be dashed to mummy against the sharp rocks, but just before they reach the shore, they quit their plank, and dive under till the Surf is broke'. He also noted that those who got closest to the rocks before jumping were 'much prais'd'.

The decline of surfing as a religious ritual in Hawaii can be dated from the arrival of European explorers. Within 20 years of Cook's visit, whalers and sandalwood traders had brought agricultural settlers and Christian missionaries to the islands. Their arrival spelt the end of *kapu*.

The missionaries discouraged surfing, which they regarded as a sinful waste of time. One minister wrote disapprovingly of how, when the surf was up, 'the thatch houses of a whole village stood empty, daily tasks such as farming, fishing, and tapa-making were left undone while an entire community – men, women and children – enjoyed themselves.'

Immoral pleasure

The surf was also the scene of courtship rituals, and many settlers regarded such immorality as an even greater danger than the rocks. American Congregationalist Hiram Bingham complained:

The evils resulting from these sports and amusements have in part to be named. Some lost their lives thereby, some were severely wounded, maimed or crippled, but the greatest evil of all resulted from constant intermingling without any restraint of persons of both sexes and of all ages at all times of the day and at all hours of the night.

Not all Westerners welcomed the restrictions on surfing. In 1892, Nathaniel Emerson wrote: 'We cannot but mourn its decline, it too has felt the touch of civilisation, and today it is hard to find a surfboard outside of our museums and private collections.'

Yet despite the missionaries' zeal, surfing survived. In 1905, a group of teenagers at Waikiki beach formed

Hui Nalu, 'The Club of the Waves'. This was more than just a club for amateur sportsmen. It was part of a wider assertion of Hawaiian identity following the island's annexation by the United States. It was, in a sense, a kind of rediscovery of *he'henalu,* the spiritual and cultural roots of surfing. International interest in surfing grew, and surf schools and equipment suppliers sprang up across the USA, then Australia. For those seeking the thrill of a power greater than themselves, to surf is still to be borne in the arms of nature – or of the gods.

SURFING GOES WEST Little more than 100 years after Europeans and Americans had tried to discourage surfing in Hawaii, they had taken to the waves themselves. Since the 1950s surfboards have been made of synthetic materials – polystyrene foam and glass fibre – but they are otherwise little different from the *he'henalu* of 1500 years ago.

GENETIC HISTORY

Every human being carries their own unique history in their DNA – in a genetic code that scientists are increasingly able to understand. Now that methods have been developed to extract DNA from ancient remains, scientists have begun to compile a whole new library of historical source material.

DNA (deoxyribonucleic acid) is a gigantic molecule that holds the encoded genetic information specific to every individual. It comes in two types – nuclear DNA (so called because it is found within the nucleus of each cell in our bodies) and mitochondrial DNA (hundreds of copies of which can be found outside the nucleus in every cell). Because nuclear DNA degrades quickly after death, scientists and historians base their studies on mitochondrial DNA (mtDNA). This type of DNA, which is passed on through the female line, relatively unaffected by sex and selection, mutates at a rapid but steady rate. By comparing the mtDNA of ancient remains with other ancient or modern mtDNA, it is possible to identify the ancestral population to which the subject belonged and the time at which they lived.

Examining the evidence

The likelihood of recovering mitochondrial DNA from a fresh biological sample is greater than for nuclear DNA because there are hundreds or even thousands of mtDNA molecules in each cell compared to just two nuclear molecules. Even so, until the mid-1980s it was possible to extract a useful amount of mtDNA from only the most well-preserved remains. This meant that DNA analysis was restricted to samples of a few thousand years old at best.

All this changed when a method was devised for replicating genes called 'PCR' (polymerase chain reaction). Using PCR, a researcher can 'amplify' even the smallest amount of mtDNA into a workable amount for analysis. This allowed samples to be taken from much older remains. The strands of DNA created by PCR are then separated according to size by an automated sequencing machine that uses a laser to 'read' the sequence of the genetic code. The various fragments of DNA are pieced together according to the established sequence until a strand is created which is long enough to support successful analysis.

In 1997, a 379-pair sequence (from a possible total of around 16,000) of mtDNA was taken from Neanderthal bones. Comparison with modern human DNA showed that there was no direct ancestral link between the two species.

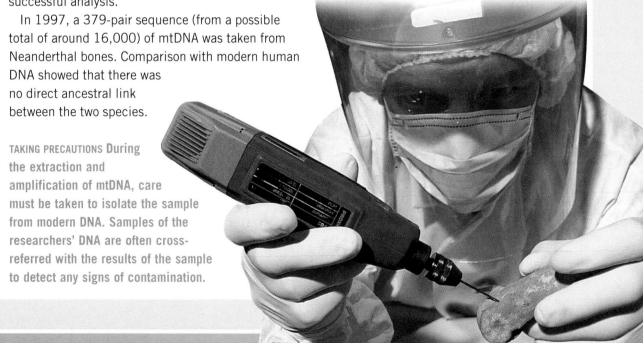

TAKING PRECAUTIONS During the extraction and amplification of mtDNA, care must be taken to isolate the sample from modern DNA. Samples of the researchers' DNA are often cross-referred with the results of the sample to detect any signs of contamination.

The molecular timepiece

The only way in which mitochondrial DNA changes over time is through mutations – molecular changes – caused by tiny random radioactive events. This allows scientists to calculate the date of a sample of mtDNA from the number of mutations that have taken place.

This method has established to many geneticists' satisfaction that our ancestral population arose 200,000 years ago, as this is the age of the oldest mtDNA molecules still found in people today. Critics of the theory say that a mitochondrial lineage might only survive for a finite length of time. At some point, statistically dependent upon the size of the population and its rate of growth, the women carrying a particular mtDNA will fail to pass it on when they bear no children or only sons. These experts believe that the data shows only that maternal lineages reach back 200,000 years, and propose that other, older ancestors could also have contributed to our gene pool.

In 2001, mtDNA was extracted from Mungo Man, a human dated to 41,000 years old, whose remains were found near Lake Mungo in Australia. His DNA matches poorly to that of modern humans, suggesting that he could have been part of a population that died out before the present day, and whose genetic heritage did not survive.

NO RELATION
When Mungo Man was found, he was first thought to be the forefather of modern Australian aborigines. DNA profiling has disproved this theory.

People watching

The mutations in mitochondrial DNA can reveal more than age. If a mutation is present in the mtDNA of some women in one population, but entirely absent in another, then these populations must have separated before the mutation occurred. If the mutation is evenly spread in two separate populations, then they must have been part of a single population when the mutation took place.

The diversity of genetic sequences within a population is a reflection of its original size: larger populations give rise to more diversity; smaller ones contain more similarity. Such observations can establish the ancient locations of today's ethnic groups, as well as how groups have moved and interrelated.

One study may explain the rapid rise in farming in Europe around 9000 years ago. DNA analysis of several population samples suggests that at about this time a small influx of people moved into Europe from the Middle East, where farming was already widespread.

Related in the sagas

Historians have long known that Vikings from Norway raided the Orkney Islands in the far north of Scotland in the 9th century AD, and that the islands later adopted Norse culture. Some believed that, like the Romans, the Vikings formed a small elite and allowed the most amenable Orkney families to wield limited power to keep control. But a study of the nuclear DNA of 71 adult men from the islands proves otherwise. The Vikings interbred so successfully with local women that the Y chromosomes from Orkney men today are a much better match with those of modern Norwegians than with their own Celtic neighbours.

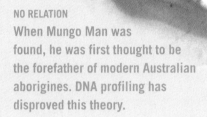

FAMILY HEIRLOOM The marauding Vikings in the Orkney Islands left treasures such as the Pitney brooch (above), coins, echoes of their language and a permanent genetic legacy.

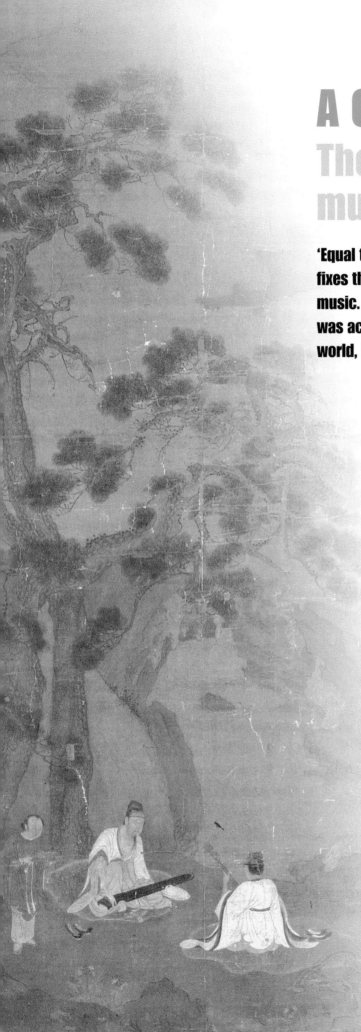

A CHANGE OF TUNE
The answer to a musical conundrum

'Equal temperament', the system that defines and fixes the notes of the scale, is a core idea in Western music. Long thought to be a European innovation, it was actually discovered on the other side of the world, in a land that had no need for it.

Anyone who has ever plucked a guitar or tootled on a recorder can tell you that there are 12 notes in the musical scale, each a semitone higher than the last. Every piece of music, from the simplest melody to the most complex symphony, is constructed with these 12 notes – just as every piece of writing is made up of the 26 letters of the alphabet.

In one sense the notes we hear are ordained by nature, or rather by the laws of physics. A high C sounds like the same note as a low C because there is a fixed ratio between their sound-wave frequencies. There is also a fixed ratio, a very significant one, between the first and fifth note in the scale. On the doh-ray-me-fah-soh-la-te-doh scale in any key, the note called soh (the fifth) resonates with a frequency that is precisely two-thirds that of doh (the first).

The troublesome fifth

It follows that if you skip up the scale from one fifth to the next – C to G, G to D, D to A, and so on – then after 12 steps and seven octaves you will land back at the note where you started: on C. That is what should happen, but it doesn't. If you judge the fifths perfectly, with the ratio between them set at precisely two-thirds, then your top C will be way out, and you will hear it as tooth-grindingly out-of-tune. It is a problem that has dogged Western music for centuries because the notes of the scale are not like the letters of the alphabet. They are more like the days in a calendar, which do not fit exactly into a lunar month, or like the months, which do not fit into the 365-day solar year. Calendars have leap years to take up the slack, but the musical scale has no such neat solution. The misfit between the seven octaves

MAKING MUSIC **In a garden landscape, two Chinese scholars play the qin (a zither) and the ehru (a stringed instrument). A Chinese mathematician calculated the formula on which every tune and jingle played in the West is founded.**

and the 12 perfect fifths has been known to musicians for centuries, and the difficult gap it produces is called the 'Pythagorean comma'. The age-old problem for players and tuners of musical instruments has been how to get round the comma.

In the early Middle Ages instruments could only play in one key, harmonies were simple or non-existent, and melodies rarely moved from one key to another. This allowed the Pythagorean comma to be hidden in a part of the scale where the tune never ventured. If there is no B in your song it does not matter if the B sounds out of tune, and you can tune the other notes to the perfect, rational intervals.

But this solution could not last. By the 17th century, composers were writing music that ranged widely across the scale, exploring new harmonies and moving unexpectedly into different keys. This advance was accompanied by the appearance of instruments such as harpsichords and organs that could produce all the notes in the scale.

These early keyboard instruments left the Pythagorean comma with no hiding-place. Players now needed to find a means of disposing of the comma so that a chord or a melody could be played in any key. And they needed to be able to do it without re-tuning or 'tempering' the instrument every time the key changed.

European musicians were aware of a number of solutions to the problem. The composer Johann Sebastian Bach was a pioneer in the search for a temperament to suit all tonalities: his collection *The Well-Tempered Clavier*, completed in 1738, contains a piece written in every key to show that it could be done. But Bach never explained exactly what temperament he used, as he always tuned his instrument himself, by ear.

Other temperaments had been described mathematically, but no-one had formulated the simplest solution to the dilemma, the tuning method we call equal temperament. This system simply shares the comma evenly between the 12 notes of the scale, or rather shaves a minute fraction off each note, making all of them slightly, almost imperceptibly flat. Some players and instrument makers could achieve this using their musical intuition, as Bach did. But there still had to be a mathematical formula, so that instruments could be made with their various holes, strings and frets at the right size and in the right position.

Extraordinarily, the solution had already been found, 150 years earlier, by a mathematician living in solitude in Ming dynasty China.

Mathematical harmony

Chu Tsai-yü, the man who discovered equal temperament, was born in 1536. He was a prince, a member of the Ming dynasty. In 1550 his father Chu Hou-huan was imprisoned for criticising the emperor and, in protest at his father's treatment, the 14-year-old Chu Tsai-yü moved into a mud hut in the grounds of his family's

KEY NOTES As soon as J.S. Bach published *The Well-Tempered Clavier*, with a piece in every key, keyboard players wanted their instruments to have 'equal temperament', so that they could play without constant re-tuning. Bach tuned his clavier this way by ear, but the less gifted needed an authoritative solution.

BOOK MAN Matteo Ricci (above, left) was an Italian Jesuit priest who spent 30 years studying in China, even adopting the empire's dress and manners. He may have been the first European to hear the solution to the equal temperament problem.

estate. He spent the next 19 years in the hut, until his father was released.

During his long years of protest, Chu Tsai-yü immersed himself in mathematics. He set himself the task of correcting the inaccuracies in the Ming calendar, which had gone so far awry that it had become impossible to predict eclipses accurately.

From there it was a short step to the study of music. The Chinese believed in a strong link between astronomy, time and music. Both the year and the octave were divided into 12, and each semitone was named after a month of the year. Chu Tsai-yü would certainly have been aware of the Pythagorean comma (though he would not have called it that) and must have seen that this was a problem not unlike the one caused by the inaccuracies in the calendar that he had just rectified.

After long experimentation with pitch-pipes Chu Tsai-yü realised that the key to equal temperament was not the division of lengths between the pipes, but the ratios of their different sizes. He calculated the exact formula required to produce evenly spaced notes and so yield a scale in which all the semitones fitted exactly into the space of an octave. Here was the formula that had eluded every Western mathematician and music theorist.

Chu Tsai-yü published his findings in 1584 in a work entitled *A New Account of the Science of the Pitch-pipes*. He understood its great significance, but it was an academic irrelevance in China, which uses a five-tone scale in its music.

Chu Tsai-yü could not have known that the formula was to become vital to Western music. Although he never published his theory outside China, there are tantalising clues that lead from the Chinese province of Kuangtung (Canton) to the Belgian city of Bruges, bringing the theory to Europe. Here, Chu Tsai-yü's work was to influence the course of Western musical history.

Temperament trail

China in the Middle Ages was not a closed society. There were many thriving communities of foreigners in the country, including a group of Jesuit missionaries with a house of learning in the southern port of Macao, where they taught spoken and written Cantonese. The foremost European scholar in China was a Jesuit priest named Matteo Ricci. He spent most of his life there and even used a Chinese name, Li Matou.

Ricci is known to have read Chu Tsai-yü's thoughts on the calendar. It is more than likely that he also studied the new work on the pitch-pipes. Moreover, Ricci is known to have been in Nanking in 1595, while Chu Tsai-yü was presenting his ideas on tonal scale to the emperor. It may well be that the two distinguished scholars met. Perhaps Chu Tsai-yü even gave a copy of the work to his strange foreign admirer. Certainly Ricci is likely to have been the first European to see the solution to the riddle of equal temperament.

So could Ricci be the first link in a chain that leads back to the musicians of Western Europe? The Jesuits' house of learning was based in the province of Kuangtung, which at that time was the centre of trade between East and West. There were huge fairs twice a year, where goods and ideas were exchanged.

Perhaps Ricci passed news of Chu Tsai-yü's breakthrough in a letter to his brethren, sent with a merchant. Maybe he just spoke of it, and the knowledge somehow filtered to the west along with the panniers of silk and fine porcelain. Either way, the first person known to have the proof in Europe was a man with strong Chinese connections.

Wind wagoner

In 1620 a respected Belgian mathematician named Simon Stevin died in Bruges. He had been responsible for introducing the concept of decimal fractions into mathematical theory. He was also famous for inventing a new form of transport. In 1600 he rigged up a sail to a large cart and took 26 passengers on an exhilarating 80km (50-mile) journey from Scheveningen to Petten, travelling at an average speed of 25 miles an hour. He called his exciting new invention a 'Chinese sailing carriage'. In China itself, where such vehicles had been used for many centuries, they were known as 'wind wagons'.

Stevin had long been interested in Oriental science. The wind carriages were one spectacular result of this. A more understated Chinese idea was found among his papers after his death: it was Chu Tsai-yü's formula for equal temperament.

It is not known whether Stevin shared the formula with anyone, but the date is uncanny. It was precisely at this time that the temperament problem was becoming acute, and somehow the formula had become widely known in Europe by the end of the century.

Yet while equal temperament worked mathematically, many musicians deplored the effect on the ear of squeezing the fifths into the straitjacket of the octave. The 17th-century Italian composer Giovanni Battista Doni was one such critic, carping that 'good singers did not want to sing with such instruments'. It was, after all, a compromise – a fudge – in which every note was played slightly flat, albeit by a precisely calculated amount.

Not until the era of Beethoven was equal temperament adopted by every musician, making all Western music, in effect, slightly out of tune. It is a testament to the triumph of equal temperament that, 200 years later, we cannot hear it at all.

IN HARMONY By 1620, the Belgian mathematician Simon Stevin knew of the formula to establish equal temperament. The fact that his unpublished notes contained no calculations suggested that this was a formula that had been given to him by another person.

CLAIM TO A CONTINENT
Captain Cook knew he was not the first to reach Australia

Ancient charts suggest that – despite its isolated geographical position – sailors were mapping the Australian landmass hundreds of years before Captain Cook discovered it.

LAYING CLAIM In a 1902 painting celebrating the first steps on the sand of Botany Bay, the British naval commander James Cook is shown restraining his men from attacking the Aboriginal people. He had been instructed to 'make presents of Trifles' to gain their consent to take possession of the land for Britain.

April 1770 marked two years since the British ship *Endeavour* had left Plymouth in southern England. Having sailed all the way round South Africa's Cape Horn, it now ploughed through the choppy waters of the South Pacific. The crew had witnessed Venus moving across the sun, in accordance with the instructions for their voyage, and taken measurements from a number of locations. But as the crew navigated towards a known island,

Van Diemen's Land (now Tasmania), they were blown off course by a storm and the ship pitched up in a secluded bay on a distant landmass to the north-west. The *Endeavour*'s captain, James Cook, went down in history as the man who first discovered and charted the continent of Australia.

But in truth there was more to this discovery than the mere vagaries of the weather. Unbeknown to his crew, Cook was in possession of additional secret 'Instructions'. It is now widely accepted that the observations of Venus were a smokescreen for Cook's real orders, which were to 'set up proper marks and inscriptions as [the continent's] first discoverers and possessors'. The orders issued to Cook by the Admiralty contained the following words: that there was 'reason to imagine that a continent or land of great extent' was to be found south of New Guinea.

The reason for such a supposition was well founded: Dutch explorers for the East India Company had already charted the land and claimed it. Cook followed his orders to the letter, charting almost the full length of the eastern coast of Australia,

which he christened 'New South Wales'. He went ashore at regular intervals to stake the required marks and inscriptions, but sailed past the entrance to Sydney Harbour, which would remain undiscovered for another 17 years, until a small fleet of British ships packed with convicts dropped anchor in its calm waters.

The unknown land

Many of the Pacific islands of Oceania were familiar to European sailors by the time of Cook's voyage. Ships from Portugal, Spain and the Netherlands crisscrossed the

Traces of a continent

In 2002 a naval historian, Gavin Menzies, proposed that the first European explorers based their charts of Australia on maps already in existence. He believes that these maps, since lost, came from the Chinese, as the only nation with the capacity for such voyages was China. In the British Library Menzies discovered a map by the cartographer Jean Rotz, who worked for the English king Henry VIII. The map, drawn in 1542, depicts a continent called 'Greater Java'.

Menzies claims that he can redraw the outline of Greater Java allowing for navigational errors made at the time, such as the underestimation of some distances. The finished

result is, he claims, much closer to Australia's actual outline. The land that appears to join Australia to Tasmania and beyond was in fact pack ice, which extended much further north in the 15th century.

There are startling similarities on the Rotz map itself (below). The northern tip of Greater Java resembles Cape York (circled) on the northernmost tip of Australia, while the Auckland Islands and Campbell Island (circled) also match almost perfectly. The landmarks of Port Stephens, Broken Bay and Botany Bay are also claimed as close matches by Menzies.

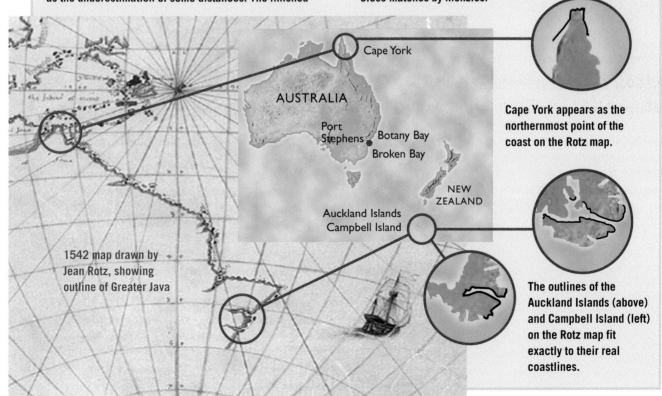

1542 map drawn by Jean Rotz, showing outline of Greater Java

Cape York

AUSTRALIA

Port Stephens — Botany Bay
Broken Bay

NEW ZEALAND

Auckland Islands
Campbell Island

Cape York appears as the northernmost point of the coast on the Rotz map.

The outlines of the Auckland Islands (above) and Campbell Island (left) on the Rotz map fit exactly to their real coastlines.

Southern Ocean during the 16th and 17th centuries, using the Spanish-ruled Philippines and the Dutch colonies in the East Indies as bases.

The islands of Java and New Guinea were mapped during this period, and it was commonly thought that they formed part of a huge continent that stretched across the base of the world, from south of the

FROM THE EAST A 15th-century French painting shows explorers in the Indian Ocean using an astronomical instrument for navigation and even encountering a kangaroo-like creature on foreign shores. It was probably copied from an older Chinese watercolour, suggesting that the Chinese knew of Australia long before Captain Cook.

East Indies to the tip of South America. This landmass was called *Terra Incognito* (unknown land) or *Terra Australis* (southern land).

The first European ship to chart the territory was the Dutch vessel *Duyfken* (Little Dove) in 1605. The *Duyfken* was part of a fleet of ships carrying out exploration for the United East Indies Company. The captain, Willem Jansz, took the ship through the Torres Straits and, unwittingly, along the northern coast of Australia. Though the crew were unaware of their discovery, and may never have actually gone ashore, the cartographic evidence of their presence is undeniable. A chart of the Pacific made for the East India Company in 1622 – and copied from manuscripts made on the *Duyfken* – shows 'Nova Guinea' (New Guinea)

with recognisably Australian landmarks such as Pennyfather River and Albatross Bay.

The *Eendracht* (Concord) sailed for Java from the East Indies in 1616 along a new route: south-east for 1000 miles after rounding the Cape of Good Hope, and then turn north. The captain, Dirk Hartog, thought that the 'Roaring Forties', strong westerly winds in the Southern Ocean, would improve journey times. But Hartog's ship overshot, coming up against the western coast of Australia.

The crew went ashore and explored several uninhabited islands (one of which is now known as Dirk Hartog Island), although not the mainland. They left a commemorative pewter plate erected on a pole, etched with a description of the *Eendracht*'s voyage. The plate was found there 80 years later and is now displayed in the Rijksmuseum in Amsterdam.

Eastern pioneers

Jansz's map, if it was indeed drawn by him, is only part of a story that began centuries earlier, according to a British maritime researcher, Gavin Menzies. He believes that it was only with charts drawn by Chinese explorers – and copied by European cartographers – that Dutch, Portuguese and British expeditions were able to cross the Pacific and Atlantic Oceans, and reach the New World and Australia.

Unlike the Europeans, the Chinese did not announce themselves as the first discoverers of Australia. But it could be that their ancestors had been aware of Australia as long ago as the 6th century AD. The official history of the Sui Dynasty (AD 589-618) recorded the presence of a landmass some 100 days' sailing south of China.

It describes a creature known as Shan Lai Jing, which possessed the head of a deer, hopped, and had a second head in the middle of its body. This was no mythical creature, but surely the earliest record of a bounding kangaroo, carrying a young joey in its pouch.

Fruits of labour

The arches of the Sydney Opera House are assumed to have been inspired by sails. In fact they were modelled on a far less romantic object.

Its gracefully overlapping nine shells make the Sydney Opera House one of the world's most recognised buildings. But most of the 2 million tourists who visit it each year are unaware of the inspiration behind this modern architectural wonder – and its controversial past.

The idea of building a new concert hall was first proposed in the 1950s by the conductor of the Sydney Symphony Orchestra, Eugene Goossens. A site was found at a disused tram depot on Bennelong Point and in 1956 a competition was announced to design the building.

The winner was a Dane, Jørn Utzon. His revolutionary design – with its huge shells radiating out from the centre – stood out from the more conventional square and circular buildings that other architects suggested. But although the Opera House was built on the waterfront, Utzon was not attempting to represent the sails of a ship. He was actually inspired by a piece of fruit: the segments of an orange, with the individual shells all being cut from a single sphere.

Construction started in 1959, but it soon became clear that the initial estimate of a four-year project was wildly optimistic. Behind the scenes there were political wrangles over the number of performance spaces in the interior. In 1966 Utzon walked out on the project, frustrated by the interference of the New South Wales government. Building work was further delayed by the discovery that the columns could not support the roof – they had to be demolished and replaced.

The Opera House was finally finished in 1973. It had taken 14 years and run 90 million Australian dollars over budget. For all the acclaim heaped on the completed building, there were still some dissenting voices. The great American architect Frank Lloyd Wright remarked acidly that, 'The circus tent is not architecture'.

FACT
AND
FABLE

NOAH'S FLOOD
The facts behind the Biblical legend

'And the waters prevailed exceedingly upon the Earth,' says the Bible. 'And all the high hills that were under the whole heaven were covered.' Modern archaeology has confirmed the Genesis story: we now know exactly where, when and how the Biblical deluge occurred.

According to Genesis, God in his rage against mankind sent a great flood that took 150 days to abate. Every creature on Earth drowned except Noah, his family and the animals – 'two of every sort' – that he took with him aboard his homemade lifeboat.

The suggestion that one man and his sons could have built a vessel capable of holding a breeding population for the entire living world is now hard to take literally. Similarly, the assertion that Noah at the time was 600 years old, and that he lived for another 350 years, tends to place the story squarely in the category of Biblical myth and metaphor.

Yet this need not mean that the story of Noah is entirely without foundation in fact. More than 200 legends of great floods have been recorded throughout the world, including the Epic of Gilgamesh, a Sumerian king whose story was inscribed on clay tablets in around 2000 BC. In this legend the king is warned by a god to build a great boat to protect 'all the living things of the Earth'. There then ensues a great flood that frightens even the gods.

But why are there so many ancient stories about a catastrophic flood? The likeliest explanation is that they arose from real events which, over the centuries, were inflated and obscured by story-tellers. Local floods became great inundations that drowned the entire world. Natural disasters became the vengeance of the gods. Looked at in this way, Noah's Flood suddenly seems much easier to accept. Indeed, scientists now believe they know the exact date and location of the occurence. And, they confirm, it was a flood so great that any man who saw it might have thought that it covered the entire earth from one end to the other.

The Bible speaks

And every living substance was destroyed which was upon the face of the ground, both man, and cattle, and the creeping things, and the fowl of the heaven; and they were destroyed from the earth: and Noah only remained alive, and they that were with him in the ark.

The evidence for this passage from the Book of Genesis does not come from the place where archaeologists have traditionally sought it, on the slopes of Mount Ararat, but deep beneath the waters of the Black Sea. To find the beginning of the story we have to go back 12,000 years to the last few millennia of the Ice Age. As the earth warmed and the glaciers gradually dripped towards extinction, so freshwater lakes began to gather. One of these filled a small part of the area now covered by the Black Sea. It grew slowly over the centuries and became, in effect, a large ▶ **p.286**

The fossil evidence
Shells taken from the bottom of the Black Sea proved that there had been a sudden change from fresh to salt water some 7500 years ago. The transitional layer between the fresh and saltwater sediments was so thin – less than a millimetre – that the switch must have been almost instantaneous.

The site of the flood

Until 7000 years ago the Black Sea was a freshwater lake, fed by melt water from the dwindling glaciers of the Ice Age. It was a natural oasis in the arid world, and there is evidence of human settlement on its shores. The people who lived here would have had no idea why the waters rose so quickly and with such catastrophic consequences. As their homes disappeared below the sea, it would have seemed to them that the whole world was being drowned.

BULGARIA

1 Looming disaster
As the Ice Age came to an end, the waters of the Mediterranean rose. They overflowed into the Sea of Marmara, where an irresistible pressure built up behind the narrow neck of land that separated Marmara from the lake in the Black Sea basin.

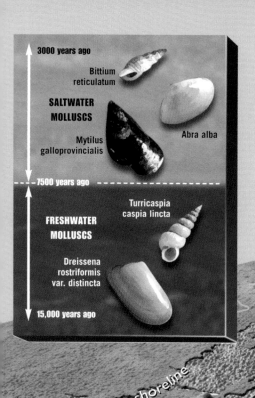

3000 years ago

Bittium
reticulatum

**SALTWATER
MOLLUSCS**

Mytilus
galloprovincialis

Abra alba

7500 years ago

Turricaspia
caspia lincta

**FRESHWATER
MOLLUSCS**

Dreissena
rostriformis
var. distincta

15,000 years ago

The search for the ark

Until recently, the quest to find evidence for the great flood centred on Mount Ararat in Turkey, which is named in the Bible as the final resting place of Noah's ark. Much was made of a boat-shaped outcrop of rock, first spotted in 1948, but it turned out to be a natural geological feature. The truth is that the flood happened far from Ararat. And if anyone escaped in boats, there is no evidence for it in the archaeology. But this does not make the Noah story untrue: it merely places his tale in the realm of the unknowable.

RUSSIA

GEORGIA

Modern shoreline

Ancient shoreline

BLACK SEA

Area of flood

BOSPORUS POINT OF BREACH

SEA of MARMARA

TURKEY

AEGEAN

2 Wall of water

The sea broke through the natural dam of the Bosporus with the force of 200 Niagaras. In less than a year 150,000km² (60,000 sq miles) of land had been covered. The freshwater lake became a salt sea, and settled at a level 150m (500ft) higher than before.

3 Escaping the flood

The spectacular dramatisations of the Biblical flood by Victorian painters were not far from the reality. The waters would have risen by about 15cm (6in) a day. An event of this magnitude would have created a folk memory that grew over time into myths such as the story of Noah and his ark.

oasis around which settlements were built. These villages lay about 152m (500ft) lower than the level of the Mediterranean.

As the ice went on melting, so sea levels across the world continued to rise. What then occurred, some 7500 years ago, was so sudden, cataclysmic and terrifying that only one explanation would have seemed credible: the gods were in a rage, and the mortals below were condemned to suffer the consequences.

The dam breaks

To understand what actually happened, you need only look at a modern map of the Mediterranean. The northern spur, between Greece and Turkey, is what we now know as the Aegean Sea. In the north-east of this, taking a bite out of western Turkey, is a narrow inlet called the Sea of Marmara. Seven-and-a-half millennia ago, this was the very engine of catastrophe.

Between Marmara and the low-lying ground that contained the freshwater lake lay a narrow ridge of land. Higher and higher on this ridge crept the swelling waters of the Mediterranean. Heavier and heavier became the pressure on the fragile neck of land.

With all the weight of the Mediterranean behind it, the Sea of Marmara, like a liquid stiletto, became a highly concentrated, irresistible force. Something had to give, and it did. In what perhaps

began as a trickle but rapidly grew to a torrent that may have had no equal in the whole of geological time, the sea broke through the barrier and roared into the land on the other side.

Imagine Niagara Falls and multiply it by 200. That is the estimated force of the influx that created the Black Sea. Every day 42km^3 (10 cu miles) of seawater would have poured through the gap now overlooked by the city of Istanbul. The inundation probably changed the weather patterns of the whole region; with the resulting evaporation causing torrential rain, the like of which would not have been seen before.

Settlements around the rim, in modern-day Turkey, Bulgaria, Moldova, Ukraine, Russia and Georgia, disappeared beneath the waves. The low flat nature of the land bordering the Black Sea meant that the onrushing flood would have quickly scoured away all the surface soil, sediment and loose rock.

Villagers caught up in the floods fled to the mountains, but they would have had to move at least a kilometre a day in order to escape the encroaching waters. Some of them – not knowing when, if ever, the waters would stop rising – may have built rafts or boats. Legend insists that Noah came to rest on Mount Ararat, near the Armenian border in north-east Turkey, but if we are to look for a literal truth this is no more believable than the floating zoo itself, and is probably the result of mistranslation or garbling of earlier accounts. If a family was washed up anywhere in a boat, then a low hill somewhere far to the west is much more likely.

Drowned shore

The true story of Noah's flood was revealed recently by two marine biologists from Columbia University in the USA, William Ryan and Walter Pitman. In 1993, in an area just off the Black Sea's northern shoreline, they put their Great Flood theory to the test with an examination of sediments and mollusc shells taken from the bottom. The freshwater

EARLIER DATE In Greek and Aramaic versions of the Old Testament the Flood takes place around 3100 BC, more than 800 years prior to the date suggested by the Hebrew text from which later Latin and English translations derive.

The Epic of Gilgamesh

The Sumerian flood myth known as the Epic of Gilgamesh probably derives from an earlier story which survives on a large clay fragment known as the Nippur tablet (right) as well as recorded Mesopotamian literature. It certainly dates from earlier than 1650 BC and tells of when the god Enlil decided to wipe out the people on Earth. A kindly god, Enki, warns Atrahasis, the king, of the coming flood and the royal family build a reed boat coated with bitumen which they fill with animals and birds. Many scholars believe that certain details from the Mesopotamian legend could have found their way into the Biblical epic, although it is clearly not the same story.

In 1923 a British archaeologist, Leonard Woolley, excavating the Mesopotamian city of Ur, had his workmen dig through 2.44m (8ft) of 'virgin' soil, to find flint implements and pottery fragments beneath. He was filled with excitement, and described his wife looking at the huge layer of empty clay sediment: 'She turned away remarking casually, "Well, of course it's the flood".'

Archaeologists today prefer to take the find as a part of the evidence for extensive localised flooding of the rivers Tigris and Euphrates. At 4000 BC Woolley's find does not correspond in date either to the king referred to in the Sumerian epics or the timeline of the Bible.

shells were all older than the earliest marine ones, suggesting that there had been a change from freshwater to saltwater some 7500 years ago.

Closer to the coastline, core samples from the sea bed produced sun-bleached shells, plant roots and a layer of mud – powerful evidence of a land surface that had once been flooded. Radiocarbon dating showed that these mollusc shells had all started to decay at the same time: the creatures within them could have all died in a single catastrophic incident.

Ryan and Pitman's hypothesis was cogent and persuasive, but if the water level in the Black Sea had indeed risen as far and as fast as they suggested, then relics of the old lake shoreline should still be there somewhere very deep beneath the sea's surface. If evidence for it could be found, the flood theory would be cemented into hard historical fact.

In 1999 an expedition led by the ocean explorer Robert Ballard duly put flesh on the bones. Using sonar and a remote-controlled underwater camera, Ballard's team found an ancient shoreline exactly where Ryan and Pitman had predicted – 167m (550ft) down, 32km (20 miles) off the Turkish coast. There were beaches,

headlands, sand-bars and yet more mollusc shells showing exactly the same age-profile and freshwater to saltwater transformation that Ryan and Pitman had identified in 1993. The flood was real.

The Noah myth

The evidence, then, conclusively points to the reality of a great flood. But was it truly Noah's Flood? Although the question ultimately remains unanswerable, there are good reasons to suspect that the creation of the Black Sea was at least the source of the legend. It was in the right part of the world, and on a scale sufficient to explain the apocalyptic visions of its later chroniclers.

It would be little surprise if the story had grown in the telling. For 3000 years before the invention of writing it would have been handed down as oral history from parent to child, gathering on the way 100 generations' worth of dramatic embellishment. By the time it was written down, fact and legend had become so enmeshed that, until Ryan, Pitman and Ballard's investigations, it was impossible to know how much real history lay drowned beneath the myth.

PLAIN AND POKER-FACED
Cleopatra's supposed beauty went unnoticed during her lifetime

That Cleopatra was beautiful has been accepted without question. Yet no contemporary source mentions her beauty, and a later writer describes her looks as 'not incomparable'. Studies of coins and statues are now revealing the face of the woman no man could resist.

Her erotic entanglements shaped the classical world. She was the consort of the powerful Roman general, Julius Caesar. Unbowed by his assassination she took one of his successors, Mark Antony, as her lover, and together they fought to the death against the might of Rome. The story of Cleopatra's life – and suicide – has inspired countless works of art and literature. In films she has been played by the most beautiful women of recent times: Claudette Colbert; Vivien Leigh; Elizabeth Taylor. Yet the evidence of contemporary portraits and sculptures suggests that the romantic notion of her enchanting beauty is completely inaccurate.

Jewel of the Nile

Almost every portrayal of the queen seems to be idealised, symbolic, purposely caricatured, or else it turns out not to be Cleopatra after all. But a reappraisal of the images that do survive provides some tantalising glimpses. They are all the evidence available to historians, as there are no contemporary descriptions of her physical appearance. The most credible source we have is the Greek essayist Plutarch, who knew the grandson of one of her courtiers and wrote a century after her death that:

As far as they say, her beauty was not in and for itself incomparable... but her conversation had an irresistible charm; and from the one side, her appearance, together with the seduction of her speech, from the other, her character,

TWO-FACED Silver and bronze coins minted in Alexandria give Cleopatra a hooked nose and prominent chin. But on coins the nose and eyes were often accentuated to confer an air of authority and strong will.

which pervaded her actions in an inexplicable way… was utterly spellbinding. The sound of her voice was sweet.

It can be said with some certainty that Cleopatra would not have conformed to modern notions of beauty. Their mummies show that most of the Ptolemy women were around 1.5m (5ft) in height. Slim they were not. Coins and busts of Cleopatra show accumulated fat deposits around her neck, described as the 'Venus rings' on a statue. The rolls may have signified wealth and fine living, but several experts believe this feature is more than mere symbolism. If they are right, the queen's neck was decidedly thick-set. Other details shown on some of the statues are a generously proportioned nose and larger than average ears.

Queen of diplomacy

Cleopatra was born into the Ptolemaic dynasty in 69 BC. The Ptolemies were puppet monarchs, dependent on the Roman senate for their position. But what they lacked in power they made up for in pomp and ceremony: Cleopatra was highly educated and by all accounts had an

extraordinary regal presence by a very early age.

A talent for diplomacy was crucial to her survival. Inheriting the throne at 17, she was trapped between a populace disenchanted with the Ptolemies and the scheming advisers who filled her court at Alexandria. Across the Mediterranean, Roman power cast a long and threatening shadow over Egypt.

When Julius Caesar entered Alexandria in 48 BC, Cleopatra was in exile, following her brother taking sole possession of the throne of Egypt. To outwit him, or perhaps in fear of her life, she had herself carried across defensive lines and presented to Caesar wrapped up in a linen sack.

Recording the event, Plutarch does not say that the emperor was stunned by her physical appearance; rather, he was 'immediately taken [by] the coquettish impression it made'.

The description of Caesar's amusement does not fuel the romantic claim that he had fallen

False! Cleopatra could not have been bitten by an asp, as the species does not live in Egypt. The Egyptian cobra depicted on her headdress kills painlessly and quickly and is the more likely culprit.

Seductive siren...

Descriptions of Cleopatra as a sultry temptress appeared in Rome in the decades after her death, when her name was used to sell cosmetics and beauty advice. In medieval times she was accused of having seduced Mark Antony with potions and magic. Shakespeare restored some queenly dignity to her image by relying on the accounts of the writers Plutarch and Suetonius, but the notion has persisted that her beauty, as portrayed by Elizabeth Taylor (right), literally bewitched men.

Rolling out a carpet at the feet of Julius Caesar is, to modern sensibilities, a bold introduction with erotic overtones. At the time, Cleopatra feared for her life and probably made an appeal to Caesar because he was her only chance of protection. There is no evidence as to which one seduced the other.

The facts are these: she was 20, in an unconsummated marriage to her much younger brother; he was 52 with a wife, mistresses and a string of sexual partners.

so deeply in love with the alluring
20-year-old that he could refuse her
nothing. He certainly took her as a
lover and brought her to live in
Rome, but his reasons for supporting
her claim to the throne were probably
self-serving. According to the author
Suetonius, he decided Cleopatra
would be easier for him to control
than a newly appointed governor.

Caesar was not a man to fall under
the spell of any one woman. Roman
writers such as Suetonius agree that
he was lecherous throughout his life
and was the lover of many senators'
wives and even other foreign queens,
such as Eunoe the Mauretanian.
Suetonius adds that Cleopatra's
'impudence charmed him', but in the
two years between 46 and 44 BC
Caesar failed to establish her status in
Rome as a queen, or even as a
mistress. To conservative citizens the
Egyptian queen appeared little more
than an exotic courtesan.

But Cleopatra gave Caesar what his
wife had not: a son, Caesarion.
According to Suetonius, Caesar
spoke to one of the tribunes about a
law that would allow him to marry
'what wives he wished, and as many
as he wished, for the purpose of
begetting children'. If Caesar had
succeeded in marrying Cleopatra,
some historians have suggested that
she could have become Empress of
Rome, and her son could have
inherited Caesar's dictatorship.

But such a bill was never proposed
to the senate, and Caesar was
murdered by conspirators in 44
BC. His will – rewritten only a
few months previously – was
a bitter disappointment for
Cleopatra. It named Caesar's
great nephew Octavian as the
inheritor of his estate and

family name. Caesar could not break the law that prohibited foreigners from inheriting the property or titles of Roman citizens. Octavian became Caesar's heir and Cleopatra and Caesarion fled back to Alexandria.

Beguiling Antony

Within three years Cleopatra was romantically entangled with another powerful Roman: the politician and soldier Mark Antony. She is widely believed to have seduced him purely to further her own power, having picked him out as the most likely to emerge as Rome's next leader. Biased historians writing in the age of Augustus usually describe her as the dominant partner, claiming that the besotted Antony lived only to serve

her: 'Whatever Cleopatra ordered was done, regardless of laws, human or divine,' mocked the Alexandrian historian Appian in his *Civil Wars*.

The relationship between Antony and Cleopatra began in 41 BC, when the queen was 29. She was summoned by Mark Antony to Tarsus (in modern southern Turkey) to explain Egypt's poor support for his army at the battle of Philippi. There the conspirators against Julius Caesar had been defeated by the armies of Antony and Octavian.

Choosing to interpret the order as an invitation, she arrived in high style. Plutarch described the scene:

She came sailing up the Cydnus in a barge with gilded stern and outspread sails of purple, while oars of silver beat time to the music of flutes, fifes and harps. She lay all along under a canopy of cloth of gold, dressed as Venus.

It was a show calculated to beguile Mark Antony, and it appears that he willingly succumbed to it. The pair became lovers and Cleopatra was soon pregnant again.

Antony's visit to Egypt became a year-long stay. He attended the games and shows and immersed himself in the society of Alexandria. Cleopatra's political position was immeasurably strengthened by his presence at her side; she would have worked her hardest to keep the soon-to-be father within her domain. But early in 40 BC

RING OF TRUTH **A gold finger ring from 50-30 BC shows Cleopatra wearing Egyptian regalia. Her prominent nose and chin are shown in a more life-like manner than in other Egyptian carvings. This may make the portrait better evidence of how the queen looked in life.**

Regal icon...

Cleopatra's Egyptian attire was intricate and ornate. Her handmaidens defined her eyes with kohl and stained her nails, palms and feet with henna. Plant extracts reddened her lips. Her hair was not dressed, but her wig and crown were secured in place. The effect would have been pure costume drama.

Egyptian statues of Cleopatra are distinguished from those of earlier queens by the triple uraeus – the three cobra heads on the crown. Such statues do not convey a genuine likeness of the queen, as they conform to a conventional representation of the Ptolemaic royal family. The shortened neck and large ears may denote some recognisable characteristics of Cleopatra herself.

Demure lady...

A bust held in the British Museum was originally identified as Cleopatra on the strength of its similarities to other portraits of her on coins, but the lack of a royal diadem (the headband with a single jewel) has changed expert opinion.

The head is now believed to represent a woman who modelled herself on Cleopatra. During the queen's time in Rome (46-44 BC) her notoriety made her an instant celebrity, and her Macedonian style of hair-braiding would have been copied by many Roman women. It is even possible that this woman was one of Cleopatra's own attendants.

Plain Jane...

It is thought that a bust from the Depsuig Collection is a genuine image of Cleopatra. The hairstyle and diadem are characteristic of other images of the queen.

In particular, there is an encouraging match to a bust identified as Cleopatra in 1933, known as the Vatican Head. This bust is missing the nose preserved in the Depsuig head, which has a downturned end and slightly flared nostrils. The precision of the features suggests these details have been purposely included. The outlines are softer and more delicate than in other works, but this may be due to the bust having been treated in recent times with abrasive chemicals.

Antony did return to Rome and made peace with Octavian. Presumably to the consternation of the abandoned Cleopatra, who had just given birth to his twins – Alexander Helios and Cleopatra Selene – Antony wed Octavia, the widowed sister of his comrade in power, Octavian.

Appian offers an explanation for the turn of events. At first, Antony had 'lost his head' to Cleopatra, 'like a young man'. Now he wintered in Athens with Octavia just as he had in Alexandria with Cleopatra:

He dined in the Greek manner and... attended festivals in Octavia's company, in which he took great delight. With her, too, he was very much in love, because he was easily attracted by women.

Reunited lovers

But Antony's marriage was not to last. Four years after deserting her, he returned to Cleopatra. Was this, finally, the evidence of her famed sexual allure? The available evidence suggests not. Now well into her thirties, the queen is shown on busts and coin portraits from this time as a lonely ruler: she wears a severe hairstyle and a stern profile.

Most striking to modern eyes of the attributes associated with the queen's appearance is the long, 'hooked' nose. But Mark Antony was a Greek, and no doubt would have been accustomed to what is a common trait among many eastern Mediterranean women.

Love alone might not have been sufficient to bring him back – it will never be proven. But his relationship with Octavian, long tainted by rivalry, was deteriorating, and it is possible he had decided on political grounds to split from Octavia and her brother and build a new power base in Egypt. Cleopatra's fleet was the strongest in the Mediterranean, so some historians suspect a solely political motive for his return.

But we do know that Antony also chose to recognise and honour his Alexandrian family; there are references to a celebration – the Donations – and a marriage in 34 BC. Soon Cleopatra became pregnant with the couple's third child.

In Rome, supporters of Octavian poured scorn on the union. Orators presented the Donations as a riotous carve-up, in which Antony bestowed dominions of the Roman Empire on his children and newlywed wife. Cleopatra's drunken and crazed ambition was blamed for Antony's lapse into emasculated subordination. When the inevitable clash came, Octavian had already won the propaganda war in Rome.

War on Cleopatra

In 32 BC Antony divorced Octavia. Octavian's response – a declaration of war – was swift. But despite the alliance between Cleopatra and Antony, Octavian declared war on Cleopatra alone. For as long as Mark Antony remained popular in Rome, Octavian took care that the blame for his defection was laid on the Egyptian queen, implying witchcraft and sexual depravity.

Mark Antony was forced to abandon a large portion of his army and was swiftly defeated by Octavian. Both he and Cleopatra killed themselves. Octavian restyled himself as the Emperor Augustus and ruled

for 43 years. His victory paved the way for the creation of the Cleopatra myth. Antony was presented as a feckless opportunist unable to measure up to the demands of power; Cleopatra was the debauched but irresistible temptress who had stolen him from his duty. This image of Cleopatra became romanticised over the centuries until she was a fabled beauty, while her true face was obscured – visible only on damaged statues and tarnished coins.

...or Macedonian matron

A possible representation of Cleopatra has been uncovered on the Greek island of Delos. Susan Walker, Deputy Keeper in the Department of Greek and Roman Antiquities at the British Museum, has argued that the hairstyle and hooked nose correspond to other portraits of Cleopatra. The bust is also noticeable for the rolls of fat – known as Venus rings – on the neck. Coins minted at Ascalon portray an 18-year-old Cleopatra with similar physical characteristics, suggesting that the Delos image could well be of the Egyptian queen.

THE REAL PIED PIPER
The old fairy tale has a sinister background

The rat charmer who lured away the children is more than a character in a bedtime story – a stranger did visit the town of Hameln in 13th-century Germany and, when he left, he took the children with him.

Children everywhere know the story. The people of Hamelin were desperate. Their homes were alive with rats and nothing could shift them. Then a stranger appeared who offered to rid the town of the rats – for a fee. The people eagerly agreed, so the man in the strange suit took out a pipe and began to play. Entranced, the rats followed the musician to the river, where they fell into the water and drowned. The town rejoiced, but the mayor refused to pay the stranger as agreed. So the angry piper played once more, and this time he led the children away. They were never seen again.

The Pied Piper of Hamelin is one of the darker European folk tales. Its themes of ingratitude and terrible vengeance are troubling to say the least: there is no 'happy ever after' in this bedtime story.

But the tale is more than mere fiction. Something deeply traumatic did happen in the German town of Hameln – there are documents that speak of it. We may even be able to pinpoint the day on which it occurred.

The date is long remembered from an inscription on a stained-glass window, now lost, in a Hameln church. The window was said to bear the image of a piper, with the words

In the year 1284, on the day of John and Paul, it was the 26th of June, came a colourful Piper to Hameln and led 130 children away.

The first written reference to the piper can be found in Hameln's book of statutes. In 1351 it began to date all proclamations according to the 'years after our children left'.

Another reference is found in the Lüneburg Manuscript of 1450 which speaks of a young man who 'began to whistle through the whole town on a silver flute of wondrous shape'.

Who was the piper?

In fact medieval pipers did not always play the flute: many had whistles or bagpipes. Players were sometimes employed in the late Middle Ages to lead civic celebrations (it is not by chance that the stranger in the story is hired by the mayor). The depiction of the Hameln piper at the head of an unruly parade of rats may be a folk memory of that role.

As for the piper's colourful dress, this is not just an embellishment to the tale. Multi-coloured – or 'pied' – clothes were a symbol of low status, and were worn by other 'entertainers' such as court fools and executioners.

For pipers were often troublemakers in the Middle Ages. Despised for their work-shy, itinerant ways, some were even barred from taking communion. They were dangerous too. There was a uprising in Würzburg in 1476 that was said to have been led by a figure called the Piper of Niklashausen.

Rats do not figure in the story until the 16th century. Europe was gripped by plague, and it would not have been difficult to make a connection

between the piper who brought trouble and the vermin that brought illness. At any rate, in the first complete version of the legend, printed in 1556, the piper is described as a rat-catcher. It was the Brothers Grimm, with their taste for the macabre, who linked the expulsion of the rats to the fate of the children.

Missing children

But what happened to the children of Hameln? Some writers believe the story is about an epidemic – rat-borne plague. The children may have been taken out of the town for quarantine reasons.

Others think they may have joined the 'Children's Crusade' of 1212. Thousands of children set off for the Holy Land, but many were sold into slavery or died on the way. But this theory does not explain why the story is set so firmly in Hameln.

A tantalising new theory has been proposed by the historian Juergen Udolph. He believes that many of the townspeople were persuaded to leave Hameln and settle near Brandenburg. Udolph found there were families in Brandenburg with the same dynastic names as in Hameln. In 13th century Germany urban people were known as the 'children of the town', so perhaps the story is a parable of the uprooting of an entire community, not just the children.

But there remains that troublesome date, June 26, 1284, when 130 children were apparently lost. Was it some terrible accident or crime, too painful to recall except in sideways references? There is nothing more in the historical record that throws light on that day, but the people of Hameln remembered it for generations afterwards – and they laid the blame on the piper.

FANCIFUL TUNE The piper was recast as a harlequin by the fairy tale illustrator Arthur Rackham. This was probably not what Robert Browning had intended by the verse: 'His queer long coat from heel to head was half of yellow and half of red.'

ENDURING IMAGE The Pied Piper (der Rattenfänger) is a central figure in Hameln today. The dark elements to his tale are overlaid with a spirit of fun and merriment: even restaurants (above) bear his name.

True! The German town of Brandenburg has a legend that is strangely similar to the Pied Piper story. It tells of a man with a hurdy-gurdy whose beautiful music lured the children of the town away.

A SAINT PRESERVED
Faith in holy relics is sensationally vindicated by science

Although first viewed with scepticism, the venerated remains in an ornate coffin in Italy have had each and every doubt systematically eliminated by DNA tests and dating. There is every reason to believe that the skeleton in the coffin is that of St Luke.

He was an old man, short and stocky. Perhaps he had lost something in stature, for his bones were thinning and he had arthritis of the spine. He would have breathed with difficulty; the curvature of his ribs suggested emphysema. Since 1177, his remains had lain in an ornate lead coffin in the Basilica of Santa Giustina in Padua, Italy. They were venerated, but as time passed, almost forgotten. He either was, or was not, St Luke the Evangelist.

For many of the faithful, the relics of saints are unquestionably authentic and a source of sanctity. For out-and-out sceptics, they are no more than human debris of doubtful provenance. Yet believer and sceptic alike felt a frisson of excitement when in 2001 scientists concluded that, in all probability, the relics kept in the Santa Giustina basilica were his remains. They were indeed the bones of Luke, the patron saint of physicians and artists, whom the Italian poet Dante called *scriba mansuetudinis Christi* – scribe of Christ's gentleness. For the faithful it was confirmation of their belief; for everyone else, a great detective story.

Who was St Luke?

What do we know of the historical Luke? He came from the city of Antioch, now Hatay in southern Turkey. He was a doctor. He was erudite. His legacy to the world was the third Gospel of the New Testament – far more detailed than the others – and the Acts of the Apostles. These are in fact a single work, a seamless narrative addressed to someone called Theophilus, whom many commentators have concluded was a high-ranking Roman government official. There are ancient clues about the identity of this historian of the first days of the Christian religion. A prefacing note to the Gospel, written in the second half of the 2nd century, states

SCRIBE OF CHRIST Luke is described in an early preface to his Gospel as 'Syrian'. Icons of the saint, like this one from the Chilandar monastery in Greece, often show him holding a book or a quill.

that the author was 'Luke, a Syrian from Antioch', while Irenaeus, the Bishop of Lyons, writing in around AD 170, made mention of 'Luke, a companion of Paul [who] recorded in a book, the Gospel'.

Luke was a friend and travelling companion of Paul of Tarsus, who called him 'the beloved physician' (Colossians 4:14) and his 'fellow labourer' (Philemon v 24).

Luke's gospel followed the order of Mark's, but it is fleshed out lyrically and extensively with oral testimony, which commentators believe Luke collected himself. The Acts of the Apostles continue the story with the Ascension, the Pentecost and an account of the Christian church, up to Paul's final imprisonment by the Romans. This was the time when Luke alone stood by him and Paul wrote bleakly:

> *Demas hath forsaken me and is departed unto Thessalonica; Crescens to Galatia, Titus unto Dalmatia. Only Luke is with me. (2 Timothy 4:10-11).*

Prized relics

In the years after Paul's martyrdom, Luke travelled widely continuing his missionary work. Most sources say he died at the age of 84 in about AD 150. St Hippolytus claims he was crucified at Elaea in the Peloponnese. Modern Greeks hold that he was hanged from an olive tree. Martyrologists such as Bede say only that he suffered for his faith and died at a great age in what is now Turkey.

Whatever the truth about his biography, it was generally written that Luke was buried at Thebes in

Greece. Indeed, in 1992, the Greek Orthodox Church laid claim to the bones, insisting that they be returned to Greece. So how could Luke's bones have finished up in Padua?

In AD 330, the hilltop Church of the Holy Apostles was erected in Constantinople for the vainglorious Roman Emperor Constantine. Within the church, Constantine ordered a cross-shaped tomb for himself to be built, and commissioned 12 further caskets alongside it to receive the relics of the Apostles.

According to the testimony of the 4th-century theologian and writer St Jerome, in AD 356 the emperor successfully brought the remains of the Apostle Andrew from Achaia in Greece and the missionary Timothy from the Turkish city of Ephesus, along with Luke from Thebes. Luke's bones were then transferred to Padua, probably for safekeeping during the reign of the pagan emperor Julian the Apostate, or in the anti-religious iconoclast period of the 8th century.

FINAL RESTING PLACE The ornate lead sarcophagus in the Benedictine Basilica of Santa Giustina in Padua, northern Italy, holds the skeleton thought to be St Luke's. Church records show that the bones have been there for at least 900 years.

HOLY REMAINS The skeleton said to be St Luke – topped by a plaster cast to replace the skull – lies exposed after tests to assess its authenticity. The missing skull was proved to be the one held, and still venerated, at the Cathedral of St Vitus in Prague.

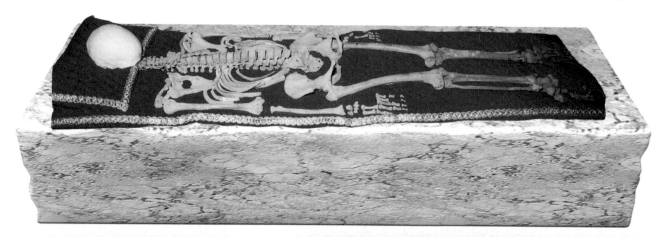

Tooth extraction

Radiocarbon dating indicated that the two teeth found in the Santa Giustina coffin belonged to someone who had died between AD 72 and AD 416. St Luke's year of death is estimated to be AD150. The teeth were ideal subjects for analysis; their DNA was relatively easy to extract. Both teeth were also found to fit into a socket on the jawbone of a skull said to be St Luke's, brought from St Vitus Cathedral in Prague, in the Czech Republic.

To complicate matters further, there were two skulls that were said to be St Luke's. The 16th-century ecclesiastical historian Cardinal Baronius records that the head of Luke was brought by St Gregory from Constantinople to Rome, to the church of his monastery of St Andrew. But other historical documents state that, in 1354, the king of Bohemia, Charles IV, took Luke's skull from Padua to the Cathedral of St Vitus in Prague, then the capital of the Bohemian Empire.

Calling in experts

With the historical record supporting – but by no means proving – the authenticity of Luke's remains, the Bishop of Padua, Antonio Mattiazzo, called on secular experts to help the investigation. An international team of scientists was brought together to test the Padua coffin's contents.

The sarcophagus had last been open to the public in 1562, the bones having lain revered and unseen for over 400 years. In 1998, the seals were cut and the tomb reopened. A skeleton of a man was revealed. He was about 1.6m (5ft 4in) tall and aged between 70 and 85 when he died. As expected, the skull was missing.

The Deacon of Prague Cathedral crossed Europe to bring the skull from St Vitus to northern Italy. It was examined to see if it was compatible with the atlas – the topmost vertebra – of the Santa Giustina skeleton.

The skull fitted as a key fits a lock. Tellingly, it was dolichocephalic – elongated towards the back – a skull shape typical of the population of Antioch in Luke's day. Moreover,

teeth from the Padua coffin fitted perfectly into the Prague skull.

The two teeth were also given to Dr Guido Barbujani, a population geneticist (and life-long atheist) from the University of Ferrara. He compared DNA extracted from one of the teeth with modern samples taken from Syrian and Greek populations.

If the body was somebody other than Luke, it would more likely be a Greek corpse than a Syrian one. If authentic, it had to be Syrian. Barbujani found that the DNA was three times more likely to have come from a Syrian than a Greek.

Traces of pollen taken from the bones of the skeleton's pelvis were also tested and found to be of Mediterranean origin, which was consistent with St Luke's death and burial having taken place in Greece.

Everything now pointed to this being the great evangelist himself. It was good enough for Bishop Mattiazzo, who, in October 2000, took from Luke's skeleton the rib closest to the heart and personally delivered it to Thebes – the saint's original burial site. The bone was placed ceremonially in an empty tomb – a marble sepulchre into which the 1.9m (6ft) lead coffin would have fitted exactly.

'Our data tell us the body is absolutely compatible with a Syrian origin,' declared Barbujani. Behind his cautious words, however, there was a hint of jubilation. His scientific training prevented him from making a definite assertion. But maybe he was sending a coded message: the date he chose to make his announcement was October 18, the feast day of St Luke.

PRIZE COLLECTION **Emperor Constantine (below) placed Luke's relics in the Basilica of the Twelve Apostles. In later years the Basilica would house the relics of one of the great fathers of the Church, St John Chrysostom.**

THE ORIGINAL CASTAWAY
The true identity of the man who inspired Robinson Crusoe

A marooned Scottish sailor was always thought to be the inspiration for Defoe's best-seller. But another man's survival story, written 20 years earlier, has been revealed as the real model for Robinson Crusoe.

To be a man marooned on an island, facing the hell of isolation, is one of the most enduring literary images of the human predicament. Daniel Defoe's *Robinson Crusoe*, published in 1719, was an instant best-seller and has been reprinted in English over a thousand times. Part of the book's appeal lies in its convincing attention to detail, to the minutiae of survival. Yet the clarity with which Crusoe is portrayed owes little to the man thought to be his real-life inspiration.

Alexander Selkirk was a famous maroon during the lifetime of Crusoe's author, Daniel Defoe. His four-year, solitary ordeal on Más á Tierra, one of the volcanic islands in the Juan Fernández group, 600km (370 miles) off the coast of Chile, had been widely publicised in the English press. When Daniel Defoe published *Robinson Crusoe*, its success owed much to Selkirk's celebrity. A second edition was run off after just two weeks and two sequels followed.

Mundane lifestyle

But Selkirk's mundane experiences in the Pacific bore little resemblance to Crusoe's adventures in the tropical Caribbean. In an article in *The Englishman* in 1713 the essayist Richard Steele described as vividly as he could Selkirk's tamed cats, fishing trips, goatskin clothes and his hide-and-seek with Spanish ships; but the story of his years on Más á Tierra lacked the dramatic impact of Robinson Crusoe's experiences with pirates, cannibals and coral reefs.

In fact, very little of Selkirk's experience bears any resemblance to the events of Defoe's novel. Unlike the resourceful and energetic Crusoe, Selkirk never fully explored his island, although it was an easy 100km² (40 sq miles). He was not shipwrecked like

GOATSKIN GARMENTS Illustrations for *Robinson Crusoe* **drew on accounts of Alexander Selkirk's well-publicised appearance at the time of his rescue. But the facts of his adventure do not figure in the novel.**

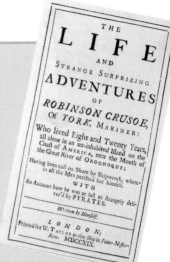

Crusoe versus Pitman: the texts compared

The titles are not the only similarity between *A Relation of the Great Sufferings and Strange Adventures of Henry Pitman* and *The Life And Strange Surprizing Adventures of Robinson Crusoe.* In fact, there are far too many features in common for it to be simply a coincidence: Defoe must have used Pitman's book as a source.

Survival packs
Pitman and Crusoe took similar equipment with them when they escaped.

Among other things, Pitman packed 'a hatchet, a hammer, saw and nails... and candles'

Crusoe's survival pack included 'a great lump of beeswax to make candles' and 'a hatchet, a saw and a hammer'.

Turtles
These creatures formed a large part of the diet of both Crusoe and Pitman. Turtles are unable to right themselves when caught and turned over and would have provided a ready supply of food.

Both men tried to construct pots to cook the turtles in, but Pitman enthused in particular about eating 'turtle roasted by the fire on wooden spits'.

The June 17 entry in Crusoe's diary records a memorable meal. '*June 17. I spent in cooking the turtle... her Flesh was to me at that Time the most savoury and pleasant that ever I had tasted in my Life.*'

Stormy weather
Both characters were thrown into the water during storms and forced to cling to the rocks for safety.

During his journey to Saltatudos, Pitman encountered waves the size of 'mountains and vales' and was 'violently driven... by the fury of the wind and the sea.'

Defoe's description of a storm in *Robinson Crusoe* is remarkably similar to an analogous passage in the Pitman book. '*... a raging Wave, Mountain-like, came rowling a-stern of us... it took us with such a Fury, that it overset the Boat at once.*'

Cannibals
The prospect of encountering hostile natives – maybe cannibals – held back both men from landing on islands that may have offered them safe shelter.

Pitman refused to land on Margarita, an island off the Venezuelan coast, fearing that fires on the beach had been lit by 'savage cannibals'. This was something of a misjudgment. The island's populace had been Roman Catholic for over 200 years.

'*... we were rather in Danger of being devoured by Savages than ever returning to our own Country.*' Crusoe's fears of being eaten by Moors led him to avoid landing on islands 'out of the... Way of all humane Conference'.

Manservants
Both castaways had the help and company of a manservant, but they were aquired by very different means.

Henry Pitman bought a native servant from privateers for 30 pieces of eight. He described how 'his servant would shoot a small fish at a great distance' with his bow and arrow, a weapon that Crusoe's Man Friday could also use 'very dextrously'.

Crusoe rescued his servant from an execution by 'savages' – a better story than Pitman's purchase – and gained a companion with an ethos of 'servitude and submission'. '*... he lays His Head flat upon the Ground... to let me know, how he would serve me as long as he liv'd... I made him know his name should be Friday.*'

Crusoe; he had gone ashore after an argument with his captain, and then been abandoned. He did the bare minimum to survive: his goatskin clothes were untanned and smelly, he constructed no furniture, made no medicines. A shack provided barely adequate shelter; his 'pet' goats were purposely lamed so they could be more easily caught.

By contrast, the fictional Crusoe is a diligent and ingenious shipwrecked mariner, who makes pots, sews, brews and bakes. He keeps himself clean with soap he makes from vegetable fat and tends his wounds with his own poultices. This was no Alexander Selkirk, but the detail of the descriptions suggests it was not entirely the product of a landlubber's imagination either.

True inspiration

So who was the real Robinson Crusoe, and how did Daniel Defoe learn of him? The answer lies in a failed rebellion in 1685 by the Duke of Monmouth against James II, challenging his claim to the throne. The attending surgeon on his force was Henry Pitman. The rebellion was crushed and most of the rebels were killed; about 300 men were captured and stood trial under Judge Jeffreys. Despite pleas that his presence was one of a medical observer only, Pitman was sentenced to ten years' hard labour in the West Indies.

After 15 months of brutal captivity, he escaped in a boat with seven other men, finally washing up on the Caribbean island of Saltatudos. There they encountered shipwrecked privateers, their boat was set on fire and they had to live in isolation for safety. But at no point was Pitman alone. After just three months his surgical skills won him a passage on a passing pirate ship (Defoe's Crusoe was marooned for 28 years). Pitman returned to England in disguise to find that his family had gained him a pardon. He wrote of his experiences in *A Relation of the Great Sufferings and Strange Adventures of Henry Pitman,* published in 1689.

Evidence suggests that though these events occurred 30 years before the similarly titled *The Life And Strange Surprizing Adventures of Robinson Crusoe* was written, Defoe knew of Pitman's book. The two works show startling similarities in portions of the text. Now it has also been argued that the two authors knew each other well. Defoe, like Pitman, had taken part in the Monmouth rebellion. He stood trial and was pardoned.

Tim Severin, a British writer and explorer, has found that after Pitman returned to England, the two men frequented the same neighbourhood. Pitman signed his book 'from my lodgings at the sign of the Ship in St Paul's Churchyard, London'. At the same time as Pitman, now a pharmacist, was putting the finishing touches to his work, Defoe was working as a hosier and would have traded with cloth merchants just around the corner in Paternoster Row.

It is not difficult to imagine that these two literary men, veterans of the same campaign, might have visited the same bookshops and taverns in this small corner of London, or even been acquaintances. Maybe they swapped stories; maybe Pitman's anecdotes gave Defoe material for a fictional narrative.

One more connection takes this beyond speculation. Pitman's book was published by his landlord, a bookseller named John Taylor. In 1711 Taylor's son William moved the family business to Paternoster Row, where he became the publisher of *Robinson Crusoe.* Even if Henry Pitman had died by this time, it is almost inconceivable that William Taylor would not ever have remarked to Daniel Defoe: 'I know a book you might be interested to read...'

FALL FROM GRACE A woodcut showed the rescued Alexander Selkirk's weathered appearance. He made little money from his fame. A violent, heavy-drinking man, he returned to sea and died of fever in Africa, at the age of 45.

RAISING THE DEAD Daniel Defoe saw the name 'Robinson Crusoe' on a tombstone when he was hiding in a graveyard after the failure of the Monmouth uprising. He wrote the novel in under six months, and a sequel in four. He died 12 years later, a rich man.

THE HERO THAT NEVER WAS
Why the character of King Arthur was created

The legend of the heroic King Arthur and his Knights of the Round Table is woven into the early history of England. Yet Arthur was the fictional creation of an imaginative writer, who was desperate to create a national hero.

A visitor to the ancient abbey of Glastonbury in the year 1191 might have seen a crowd gathering round a deep pit being dug between two high-standing crosses in the cemetery. Excitedly, they tried to peer around a set of curtains put up to shield the excavation. Sixteen feet down the monks found an oak coffin, and within it the bones of a man and a woman. An eager monk jumped in and held aloft a plaited coil of golden hair, its sheen still as bright as on the day it was buried, only to see it crumble to fine powder in his hand. In the grave under a stone slab was a lead cross, inscribed in Latin with the words: 'Here lies the famous King Arthur, buried on the Isle of Avalon, with Guinevere his second wife'. The monks had discovered the remains of England's greatest hero, lying side by side with his greatest love.

Or had they? No modern scholars would credit it. This was a convenient time for such a momentous discovery. The abbey urgently needed to attract visitors, after a fire in 1184 left it seeking public donations for rebuilding work. King Arthur was a name at the forefront of the popular consciousness. Only a year earlier the king of England, Richard the Lionheart, had left on crusade to Jerusalem, taking with him a sword reputed to be Excalibur itself. Nowadays it is assumed that the excavation was stage-managed by Abbot Henry, a kinsman of King Richard. But whether it was a fraud or a genuine discovery, the fact is that the finding of the bones became one of the most talked-of events of the year. It tells us a great deal about the popular faith invested in one of the greatest literary creations of all time: *The History of the Kings of Britain* written by Geoffrey of Monmouth.

An over-imaginative Welsh patriot

Geoffrey was a Welshman who, frustrated by the absence of a good history of his people, took a few disjointed Welsh legends and turned them into a coherent and majestic narrative covering almost 2000 years and the reigns of 99 Celtic kings. He called his work a history, and claimed that all he had done was translate into Latin 'a certain very ancient book written in the British language'.

This was a well-known trick used by authors who wanted to give the

BUILDING ON A THEME A 14th-century French manuscript, *Romance de Roi Artus* (*Romance of King Arthur*), brought new elements to the Welsh telling of Arthur's battle-driven story. A French author added romance to the tale and introduced the quest for the Holy Grail.

appearance of authenticity to their own words, although historians still argue over whether by 'British' Geoffrey meant Welsh or Breton (the Celtic tongue of north-west France). In fact the *History* was a skilful mix of things his readers already knew – Julius Caesar's British campaign, for example – and things they did not. The 'historical' King Arthur was almost entirely the product of Geoffrey's own imagination.

We will never know if there was any factual basis for the existence of Arthur. None of the early genealogies of Welsh royal and noble families claimed an Arthur among their ancestors – at any rate not until long after the first Tudor king of England, Henry VII, named his own first-born son Arthur in 1486.

Some say the name links him to Arcturus, the bright star in the constellation of the Great Bear, and hold that he was a Celtic hero, the leader of a band of warriors who cleared the land of the giants. Others argue that the name derived from the Roman name Artorius, and that there must have been a real Arthur, a Romanised Briton.

A 9th-century Welsh writer, Nennius, portrayed Arthur as a war leader uniting the Britons against the invading Saxons, who were forcing people from their homes into the poorer uplands of western Britain: Wales, Cornwall and Cumberland. Exiled Britons were encouraged by the telling of Arthur's legend to dream of the day when he would return. The day of his death was said to have

FULL CIRCLE **A wooden round table in Winchester Great Hall is 5.4m (18ft) in diameter, and has places to seat 25 around it. Tree-ring dating of the wood, and the carpentry used in the construction, suggest that it was made in the 13th century during the reign of Edward I, a great admirer of the legendary Arthur. The painted monarch is the Tudor king Henry VIII, whose elder brother was named after Arthur.**

seen a terrible fire in the sky, marking the end of an age of glory.

The fire has been assumed to be an embellishment of Arthur's myth, but it may have been the start of it. Such a 'fire' may actually have happened: a British scientist believes he can show that a huge comet bombardment occurred in AD 540; its effects included slow growth rings on trees during this year. By the time of Geoffrey's boyhood, the memory had entwined itself with Arthur's story: his heroic deeds were familiar to all.

This Arthur was the figure of Celtic legend whom Geoffrey transformed into the central figure of his book. In Geoffrey's hands Arthur was still the Welsh champion who fought against invading Saxons, but also became much more. He was conqueror of Scotland, Iceland, Ireland, Norway, Denmark and Gaul, victor over the Romans in battles, his achievements equal to those of empire-builders such as Alexander the Great and Charlemagne. It was Geoffrey who made Arthur from a warrior into a king, and introduced the figure of the sorcerer Merlin. Arthur's court was presented as a hub of international chivalry and high fashion.

But from the moment of its appearance there were those who doubted the veracity of Geoffrey's history. 'How could it be,' asked the 12th-century English historian William of Newburgh, 'that a king called Arthur defeated the Romans and conquered half of Europe when not a single author who actually lived in those times so much as mentions his name?' Nonetheless, Geoffrey's book became an instant best-seller, translated into many languages.

In the 1170s and 80s the writer Chrétien of Troyes, a founding father of French literature, produced Arthurian romances that completed the cast of characters recognisable today: the lovers Lancelot and Guinevere, Gawain, and Perceval. This was the epic story that the Glastonbury monks hoped would draw hordes of eager donors.

England's hero

Overlooking Arthur's Welsh origins, English kings were quick to associate themselves with their country's new mythical leader. In 1278 Edward I came to Glastonbury, inspected Arthur's tomb, and had it moved to the place of honour before the high altar. Edward had a keen interest in all things Arthurian and the huge round table that can still be seen at Winchester Great Hall in England was probably made specially for him. Later on, in the 14th century, Edward III drew upon ideas of the round table when he founded the Order of the Garter – a chivalric order comprised of his most loyal knights.

The great 15th-century romance, the *Morte d'Arthur*, written by Sir Thomas Malory and printed by William Caxton, England's first

LEGENDARY LEADER Heroic depictions of Arthur, such as this 1903 painting by the artist Charles Butler, suggest a kingly ideal.

publisher of printed books, bolstered the belief that the table at Winchester was actually Arthur's. The preface to the book stated that the table was proof of Arthur's existence. And Winchester, the Saxon capital of Wessex in the south of England, was the place where Arthur founded his court of Camelot.

Also Merlin let make by his subtlety that Balin's sword was put in a marble stone standing upright as great as a mill stone, and the stone hoved always above the water and did many years, and so by adventure it swamm down the stream to the City of Camelot, that is in English Winchester.

The book ensured that the cult of Arthur survived. Writers such as Alfred, Lord Tennyson and Mark Twain, and illustrators including Aubrey Beardsley, found inspiration

CLASSIC SCENE **The Art Nouveau artist Aubrey Beardsley made woodcuts to illustrate the *Morte d'Arthur* in 1893. One showed how Arthur's sword Excalibur was returned to the hand of the Lady of the Lake.**

in the stories, re-interpreting them in a more poetic vein.

There will always be those who will seek the historical Arthur, whether at 'Dark Age' sites such as Tintagel and South Cadbury (rather than Caerleon in South Wales, where Geoffrey set Arthur's court) or at the supposed burial place of Glastonbury, the legendary 'Isle of Avalon'. But Arthur transcended history long ago. As G.K. Chesterton observed in his 1930 poem *The Grave of Arthur*, the heroic leader is a paradox: a British king who may never have lived, but whose legend will never die.

The making of other national heroes

Many nations have legendary figureheads who have helped to shape their identity; usually these are real leaders whose deeds have been exaggerated in ballads or folk tales. But if history cannot provide such a figure, the imagination will.

German seeks grail

A legend with close similarities to Arthur's created Germany's hero Parsifal, celebrated in the 12th century by the poet Wolfram von Eschenbach. Parsifal may be the same mythical character as Arthur's Sir Perceval: both knights were dedicated to a search for the Holy Grail.

French toast

In France, the nation honours the 8th-century king Charlemagne, whose armies Christianised pagan Europe. By the year 800, when Charlemagne was crowned Holy Roman Emperor, his vast realm included most of Europe. By the 15th century, poets' versions of Charlemagne's story rivalled Arthur's.

Spanish rhymers

Spain's El Cid was a real person – Rodrigo Diaz, Count of Bivar. His heroic exploits against Moorish invaders in the 11th century were mythologised

when reinvented as a poem more than a hundred years later. Even so, the Moors were sufficiently impressed by their enemy to give Diaz his nickname – El Cid translates as 'The Chief'.

The Swiss won't Tell

Legend has it that Switzerland's national hero William Tell refused to bow down before the hat of the Austrian governor Gessler. As a punishment, he had to shoot an apple off the top of his young son's head with a crossbow. Tell's brave defiance inspired his countrymen to rebel against the Austrians, creating the forerunner of the modern Swiss state in 1308. But the apple story was just a myth, imported from Persia, and Tell may never have existed.

The Aussie anti-hero

In some nations, even bad guys can become heroes. Many Australians revere Ned Kelly, a horse dealer and rustler who was apparently persecuted by the police. Having rescued his sister Kate from assault by a policeman, Ned and his brother Dan were accused of murder, went on the run and became genuine criminals, robbing banks and wearing the home-made armour for which they became famous. Ned was hanged in 1880.

HOW LEGENDS ARE BORN

Many of the best-known stories from history simply aren't true. Or at least they didn't happen in the way described. Some chroniclers used to invent stories to illustrate the character of one of their protagonists; some recorded folklore as if it were established fact; others simply made mistakes.

Bloody myths

The legend of Dracula is often thought to have originated with a 15th-century east European prince. His father was known as Dracul (Dragon) and so Prince Vlad became famous as Dracula (Little Dragon). A warlord who was made king of Walachia (part of Hungary) at the age of 17, Vlad fought for power in Turkey, Transylvania and Moldavia. His absurdly cruel punishments earned him the nickname in later years of Vlad the Impaler, which echoed the mode of death that would destroy the legendary Count Dracula.

But the name was all that Vlad bequeathed to Bram Stoker for his 1897 horror classic, *Dracula*. All the other elements of the story came from eastern European superstitions about the dead and how to ward away the devil found in vampire stories by earlier writers. Stoker came across the name Dracula in a history book – which mistranslated it as 'Wallachian for devil' – and substituted it for his character's original name, Count Wampyr.

Try, try and try again

The story of Robert the Bruce, alone and despairing in a cave, but inspired to make one last attempt to defeat the English by the persistence of a spider trying to climb the cave wall, is one of Scottish history's best known legends. But a legend is all it is.

The version now told first appeared in *Tales of a Grandfather*, written by Sir Walter Scott in 1828, 500 years after Bruce fought for Scottish independence. A history of the Douglas family from 200 years earlier may be more truthful. In this account, Bruce's ally Sir James Douglas encourages him to put behind him 12 failed attempts to drive out the English with these words: 'I spied a spider clymbing by his webb to the height of an trie and at 12 several times I perceived his web broke. But the 13 tyme he clambe up the trie.' Scott, it seems, took the spider and transported it for dramatic effect into his hero's hideaway.

The real golden fleece

The legend of Jason and the Argonauts is traceable to the 8th century BC, when it is referred to, though not told, in Homer's epics. Heracles, Orpheus and Theseus – wholly mythical heroes – join Jason's crew, but the route described in later versions may be based on actual voyages made by Greek explorers of the 5th century BC, who sailed between the two rocks, the Symplegades, that mark the entry to the Black Sea at the Bosporus.

Jason's destination, Colchis, was home to the Svans, to whom the ram was a sacred symbol and was often described as golden. Historians suggest that news of this culture influenced the development of Jason's legend. Even more intriguingly, sheep's wool was used until recent times in this part of Georgia to sieve gold dust from mountain streams. Jason, if he had existed, might have been able to find a fleece at Colchis that glittered with real gold.

NEW ARGONAUTS The British maritime explorer Tim Severin found a plausible route for Jason's voyage in the *Argo*, a modern reconstruction based on Greek vessels of the Bronze Age.

Missing nose

In one of history's most wanton acts of vandalism, Napoleon's troops supposedly used the Great Sphinx of Giza for target practice during their 1798 Egypt campaign, blasting off the famous effigy's nose. But a drawing made in 1755 by a Danish architect, Frederick Norden, shows that the damage had already been done before Napoleon arrived. In fact a 15th-century Muslim historian, Muhammad al-Husayni Taqi al-Din al-Maqrizi, recounts that a religious leader ordered the sphinx to be disfigured to punish the Egyptians for indulging in cult practices in front of the monument.

A British traveller may be to blame for the mistake. He drew the sphinx – nose intact – in 1737, but his inclusion of other details that would have been lost to erosion by the time of his visit shows that he was using artistic licence for the sake of a pleasing picture.

Stories without substance

◉ Nero did not fiddle while Rome burned. According to Tacitus, the emperor sang about the destruction of Troy, likening 'present misfortunes to the calamities of antiquity'. But any musical accompaniment would have been played on a lyre.

◉ 'I can't tell a lie, Pa; I did cut it with my hatchet.' George Washington's admission to chopping down a cherry tree helped to cement his image as the embodiment of republican virtue. But a political propagandist, Mason Locke Weems, first wrote about the episode long after Washington's death, claiming it to be a story told to him by an 'aged lady'.

◉ Until around 8000 years ago a species of mammoth smaller than an Indian elephant lived on Sicily and the Greek islands. Skulls found on the islands have a socket-like opening in the centre for the trunk: this looks very much like a giant eye. Such skulls would often have been dug up by Greek farmers, and almost certainly gave rise to the myth of the giant, one-eyed Cyclops that terrorises the hero of Homer's *Odyssey*.

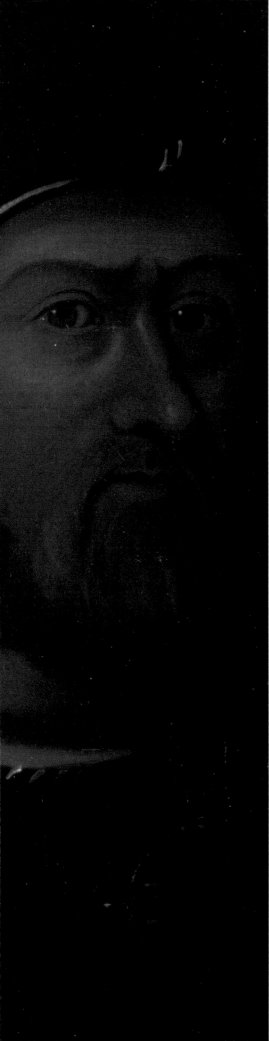

THE REAL BRAVEHEART
Scotland's freedom fighter is more myth than history

In Scotland, William Wallace is revered as a national hero and a martyr to the patriotic cause. But all the sources for his life are fanciful or biased; the true Wallace was very different from the cherished legend.

W illiam Wallace is universally acknowledged as the founding father of Scottish nationalism. He is celebrated in his homeland as a kind of medieval guerilla, a kilted Guevara who led his people in the struggle against English tyranny. Today, there are more than 80 places in Scotland that proudly claim an association with him, as well as dozens of statues and monuments to his memory throughout the country. And the plaque that marks the site of his brutal execution, outside St Bartholemew's hospital at Smithfield in London, is always adorned with fresh flowers.

But what kind of man was William Wallace? How is it that, 700 years after his death, he still inspires an almost religious devotion? And, in the end, what do we know for certain about the man that the chronicles call 'malleus Anglicorum', the hammer of the English?

In search of The Wallace

These are the facts of Wallace's life. He was born between 1260 and 1278 – no one knows where, though the town of Elderslie in Renfrewshire claims that honour. He was one of the leaders of the resistance in the years when Edward I – the English king known as 'Longshanks' – sought sovereignty over the Scots.

After a stunning victory over the English at Stirling Bridge in 1297, Wallace became sole Guardian of Scotland. This was the high-point of his military and political career. In the absence of the Scottish king John Balliol, who was under house arrest in Edward's court, he became the ruler of Scotland. But ten months later Wallace's army was crushed at the battle of Falkirk. After this defeat, William Wallace disappeared from view; it is probable that he fled to Europe. Seven years later, back in Scotland, he was betrayed by his own side to the English. Though he was not by now a figure of great political importance, the vindictive Longshanks had him put on trial and executed for treason.

A colourful legend has accrued to these bare biographical bones. Wallace's deeds have been grossly

FIGMENT OF IMAGINATION Paintings of William Wallace are all based on an engraving made more than 300 years after his death. Artists usually showed him as bearded, which is credible, and dressed in plate armour, which is not.

exaggerated by admirers and detractors alike, and the truth of the man has been distorted beyond recognition.

The main friendly source is a long epic poem called *The Wallace*. It was written a full 170 years after Wallace's death by a Scots bard known as Blind Harry. The text is full of factual errors and entirely imaginary episodes. All kinds of swashbuckling adventures are ascribed to the young Wallace, who is portrayed in superhero terms:

> *Nine quarters large was he in length... third part his length in shoulders broad was he. Right seemly, strong, and handsome for to see... His brows were hard, his arms were great and round... eyes clear and piercing, like to diamonds bright...*

A fighting Adonis, in other words: nine quarters is about 2.1m (6ft 9in). Early in his account Harry has this Celtic Goliath evading capture by dressing as a woman and sitting quietly at a spinning wheel while English soldiers search the house around him. Blind Harry also

provides a tale of love, loss and vengeance as Wallace's newlywed sweetheart is captured and murdered by the English. Intriguingly, given the Robin Hood-like overtones of his exploits, Wallace's lover is called Marian. In fact it is unlikely that he ever married.

Historians, Scottish ones in particular, have always clung to Blind Harry because he is the sole source for the events of Wallace's life up to 1296. Much is made of Harry's claim to have made use of an earlier account written by John Blair, Wallace's friend and chaplain. But this first-hand biography is lost, if indeed it existed in the first place. Were there a more trustworthy source, then it would be easier for people to see *The Wallace* for what it is, an engaging and romantic piece of epic fiction.

The first contemporary reference to Wallace occurs in the Lanercost Chronicle, a pro-English source which describes Wallace as 'a certain bloody man... a chief of brigands in Scotland...[in] revolt against the King.' But this hostile sketch is as

ACTION HERO The film *Braveheart* is based on a semi-fictional account, and contains many historical inaccuracies. It claims that Wallace, a minor noble, was an oppressed peasant, and – most ludicrously – that he seduced the future Queen of England while awaiting execution in London.

False! Robert the Bruce is hailed as a Scottish hero, but he was actually a French-speaking Norman knight. He held lands in England and France as well as Scotland, and even fought for England against Wallace. After Wallace's death he won independence for Scotland.

LONGSHANKS Edward I subjugated Wales to the English crown, and spent much of his life trying to do the same to Scotland. On his deathbed he decreed that his bones be boiled from his body and carried into battle against the Scots.

wide of the mark as Harry's glowing portrait. Wallace was not a brigand in the sense of a common robber, and he was not by any stretch of the imagination a victim of oppression. He grew up in a time when Scotland was at peace with its powerful southern neighbour. His family was a well-connected but minor branch of the Scottish nobility. In another age, suggests one biographer, Wallace would have been a country gentleman.

Wallace's privileged background informed his political agenda. The idea that he was some kind of freedom fighter is totally misplaced. He never said that he was fighting for the rights of the common Scottish people; his stated aim was the restoration of the deposed Scottish king, John Balliol.

Puppet and warrior
This was itself a strange political goal for a champion of Scottish independence. John Balliol's election to the Scottish throne was engineered by Edward I, and he was permitted to rule only as a puppet of the English. Edward delighted in treating him as a lackey, but in 1296 John rebelled against Edward's routine humiliation of him. There was a short and vicious war, after which the defeated King John was forced to undergo a ceremony in which Edward tore off John's royal insignia and imprisoned him in London. Wallace's goal was to bring this weak and discredited leader back to Scotland. It was for this that he fomented a national uprising which – for 300 days or so – made him the head of the Scottish nation.

We do not know what William Wallace was doing during King John's war with England. If Blind Harry is to be believed, he had a string of adventures in which he was provoked beyond measure by heavy-handed English bullies; he triumphed against overwhelming odds; and he made one daring escape after another.

The probable truth is that he was leader of a band of irregular troops in the south of Scotland. In the many local uprisings against the English, Wallace was gaining experience as a fighter and a commander. But even his military prowess is questionable. His reputation as a general rests on the battle of Stirling Bridge, where the English cavalry were lured across the narrow bridge and slaughtered before they could regroup.

Wallace's co-commander on that day was Andrew Moray, an

SWORD IN STONE A monument raised in 1814 in Melrose was the first of countless statues of Wallace erected throughout Scotland, affirming the noble and romantic notion of the country's national hero.

Kilts and tartan: a manufactured tradition

William Wallace is often depicted, as in the film *Braveheart*, wearing something resembling a kilt with a distinctively Scottish tartan pattern. It is commonly held that the kilt is the ancient dress of the Scots people, and that clan tartans have developed over the centuries as the distinctive badge of clan loyalty.

But the historian Hugh Trevor Roper has shown that the kilt and the tartan are modern inventions. The kilt was designed and first worn by an 18th-century English industrialist named Thomas Rawlinson, who intended it as a convenient form of dress for his Scottish labourers. He adapted it from the more traditional belted cloak, but never meant it to become a national costume. This idea arose only in the 19th century, when this highly fanciful form of Scottish peasant dress was reclaimed by genteel, romantically minded Scots patriots.

Tartans were worn in Scotland from the 16th century: the design was imported from Flanders. But the idea that that certain patterns have historic connections with particular families came from two brothers named Allen who claimed to have an ancient book entitled *The Garde-Robe of Scotland*. They published a book, *The Costume of the Clans*, which was supposedly based on the precious manuscript. By the time the brothers were exposed as frauds (they claimed to be descended from Bonnie Prince Charlie), their work had been plagiarised by others. It was enthusiastically adopted by the Scottish textile industry, eager to cash in on the tartan boom with novel garments and accessories (left).

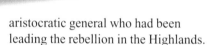

aristocratic general who had been leading the rebellion in the Highlands.

Wallace, contrary to what many historians have said of him, was not a practitioner of guerrilla warfare: he preferred the set-piece pitched battle. It is entirely plausible that the tactics that won the day for the Scots at Stirling Bridge were Moray's, not Wallace's, for when Wallace tried to repeat the trick on his own at Falkirk, the result was the disastrous defeat that ended his rule. In years as a military commander he never won another battle, or wrested a castle from the control of the English.

But none of this matters. Wallace's significance lies not in what he did, but in what he represents. Even in his own lifetime he embodied the idea of Scotland as a separate country with its own history and identity – and this is why Edward went to such lengths to capture and kill him. He hoped that by destroying the man Wallace he could annihilate the idea of Scottish nationhood.

But Edward failed. Blind Harry used the fantastical tales that accrued to Wallace to create a parable for the birth of a national consciousness. Some peoples never produce heroes who can serve that purpose: the English, for example, have to make do with the entirely fictional figures of King Arthur and Robin Hood. William Wallace lived a life that was heroic enough and true enough to be turned into myth. That is his legacy, and Scotland's good fortune.

STIRLING BRIDGE The Wallace Monument at Abbey Craig commemorates the Battle of Stirling Bridge. This victory was the high point of Wallace's career and made him sole ruler of Scotland for nine months.

INDEX

Page numbers in **bold** indicate main entries; those in *italics* indicate illustrations/captions only.

ACKNOWLEDGMENTS

Artworks: **10/11b** & **12/13b** Tony Morris/Linda Rogers Associates 2003
All others Planet Three Publishing Network

Photographs in *The Truth about History* came from the following sources, indicated by the abbreviations given below.

AKG London (AKG)
The Ancient Egypt Picture Library (AEPL)
The Bridgeman Art Library (BAL)
The British Library (BL)
British Museum (BM)
Corbis (C)
Corbis Bettmann (CB)
Corbis Sygma (CS)
Getty Images (GI)
Heritage Image Partnership (HIP)
Imperial War Museum London (IWM)

The Kobal Collection (Kobal)
Mary Evans Picture Library (MEPL)
The Natural History Museum London (NHM)
National Geographic Image Collection (NGIC)
Rex Features (Rex)
Robert Hunt Library (RHL)
The Ronald Grant Archive (RGA)
Science and Society Picture Library (SSPL)
Science Photo Library (SPL)
TRH Pictures (TRH)

The position of an image on the page is signified by **t** top, **c** centre, **b** bottom, **l** left, **r** right, **bg** background.

10tl MEPL **12** Katz/Gamma/Mark Deville **14bg** SPL/John Reader **14br** Image no. 4744 American Museum of Natural History Library/J Beckett & D Finnin **15** Katz/Gamma **16** NHM **17** AKG **18** NHM **20** C/P Johnson **21** SPL/John Reader **22b** HIP/Museum of London **22-23** AKG **23t** SPL/John Reader **24** MEPL **25tl** CB **tc&tr** MEPL **b** AKG **26** Image no.4937American Museum of Natural History Library/D Finnin & C Chesek **27** Vito Cannella **28** C/W Morgan **30tl&tr** CS/J Langevin **c** C/M Beebe **31tl** C/M Sedam **tr** C/N Fobes **cl** C/E Stolzenberg **cr** CS/G Tim **bl** CB **br** Hutchison Picture Library **32cl** C/Sakamoto Photo Research Laboratory **b** Popperfoto/Reuters **33tr** C/J Sugar **c** SPL/James King Holmes **32-33** French Ministry of Culture, Rhone, Alps Jean Clottes **34/35** C/G Jecan **36tr** C/M Bridges **38-39** GI **40** & **41b** C/L de Selva **41t** MEPL **42** C/Stapleton Coll. **43** AEPL/Bob Partridge **44br** Ashmolean Museum, Oxford **bl** AEPL/Bob Partridge **45tr** AKG **cl&cr** AEPL/Bob Partridge **46** C **47t&cr** John & Deborah Darnell/Theban Desert Road Survey **b** C/R Watts **48tr** NASA/JPL **bl** C/K Westermann **49cl** Saqqara Geophysical Survey Project **br** NASA/JPL **50** C/K Schafer **51** BM **52tl&tr** C/W Kaehler **b** C/G Berto Vanni **54/55** NGIC/REZA **55** C **56** & **57bl** Victor H Mair **57br** After Albert von Le Coq, Chotscho, Berlin 1913 **58** C/J Newbury **59** MEPL **60** CS/M Rick **61** Produced by The Rochester Institute of Technology, John Hopkins University and the Xerox Corporation. Copyright resides with the owner of the Archimedes Palimpsest **62** BAL/Museo della Civiltà Romana **64bl** SPL/Martin Dohrn **cr** SPL/London School of Hygiene & Tropical Medicine **65** Noelle Soren **66** Wiltshire Archaeological & Natural History Society Library **67t** BAL/V&A Museum **b** C/Archivo Iconografico **68c** GI **69** Alexander Keiller Museum, Avebury Marlborough Wiltshire **70-71** C/R Wood **70b** BM **7 1b** Photoservice Electa, Milan **72t** BAL/Phoenix Art Museum **73** Kobal/Dreamworks/Universal/Buitendijk Jaap **76** AKG/Erich Lessing **77, 78, 79, 80** AKG **81** GI **82 l** MEPL **r** Shakespeare's Birthplace Trust **83 l** C/R Jack **r** BAL/Petworth House, W Sussex **84** MEPL **85t** BAL/Musee de la Ville de Paris, Musee Carnavalet/Archives Charmet **86** AKG **87t** AKG **b** North Carolina Collection, Univ. of North Carolina Library at Chapel Hill **88, 89, 90tl** BAL **90tr** BAL/Kunsthistorisches Museum **91** BM **92** C/B **93tl** HIP/BL **c** C/A de Luca **94** AKG **95cr** C/W Kaehler **95** Anne Frank House Museum **97** GI **98** Courtesy of Massachusetts Historical Society **99t** Courtesy of Peabody Essex Museum **b** Courtesy of the Trustees of the Boston Public Library/Rare Books Dept. **100** Courtesy of the Massachusetts Historical Society **101b** MEPL **t** Charles Upham Map/Salem Witch Trials Documentary Archive **102** Courtesy of the Massachusetts Historical Society **103, 104, 105** MEPL **107** AKG/Eric Lessing **108tl&tr** BAL/Egyptian National Museum **109** Gina Mosti **110, 111t** AKG **b** AKG/Eric Lessing **112cl** SPL/Philippe Psaila **tr** C/J Blair **bc** Franck Goddio/Hilti Foundation/Christophe Gerigk **113tr** SPL/Alexis Rosenfeld **bl** C/R White **116** MEPL **117, 118, 119, 120** AKG **121c** C **r** CB **122tl** MEPL **tr** Topham **123tr** The National Archives **c** NGIC/Patrick O'Sullivan **s** MEPL **126** IWM **127** National Archives **128bl** BAL/ILN **tr** BAL/with special authorisation of the City of Bayeux **129tl** C/R Ressmeyer **cr** C/Y Arthus-Bertrand **130** Scala, Florence **131** Private source **132, 133** Scala, Florence **134t, cr, b** Scala, Florence **cl** BAL/Santa Cecilia in Trastevere **135** Scala, Florence **136** AKG/BL **136-137c** BAL/Dept. of the Environment **138** AKG/BL **140** GI **141** BAL/Museum of the Revolution **142t** GI **b** C **144** RHL **145** Novosti **146** BAL/Archives Charmet **147** BAL/Biblotheque de Lyon **148** BAL/Bibliotheque Nationale **150** SSPL **151t** AKG **c** Private Collection **152c** GI **153t** Courtesy of the Bletchley Park Trust **154** The National Archives **155** AKG **159t** GI **b** Rex **160br** TRH **162t** The National Archives **b** GI **163** C/S Raymer **165** SPL/D A Peel **166** C **167, 168t** BAL **b** GI **169** Topham

170t C/F G Meyer **b** BAL/Courtauld Inst. Gallery **171tr** GI **cl** The Art Archive/Musee du Louvre **br** Museum of London **172** TRH **173t** TRH/US Navy **174** GI **175** Popper/Reuters/Peter Macdiarmid **176** TRH **177** CS/G Gianni **178-179c** Photo Archives South Tyrol Museum of Archaeology **179b** Photo Archives South Tyrol Museum of Archaeology/Regional Hospital of Bolzano **180-181** NGIC/Kenneth Garrett **182** HIP/BM **183t** Bristol Museums & Art Gallery **b** CS/H Julien **184** GI **185cl** C/G Antoine **cr** TRH **186, 187** GI **188** Topham **189** C **190-191bg** Topham **192** GI **193** C **194t** CB **cr** SPL/Dept. of Clinical Radiology, Salisbury District Hospital **195t** SPL/eye of science **b** MEPL **198-199** Popper/Herbert Ponting **200** CB/H Ponting **201t** Popper/E W Nelson **b** GI **202** BAL/National Library of Australia **203b** BAL/Michael Graham Stewart **204** MEPL **205t** Popper/HO/Reuters **b** CB **206** MEPL **207** GI **208** R J Caruana 2003 **209** RHL **210t** IWM **211t** IWM **210-211b** GI **212, 213** AKG **214** BAL/Victoria & Albert Museum **215t** BAL/Museo de San Marco dell'Angelico **b** BAL/Musee de Beaux Arts /Lauros/Giraudon **216** copyright Biblioteca Ambrosiana – Auth. No.03/0156 **217t** copyright Biblioteca Ambrosiana – Auth No.03/0267 **b** Scala, Florence **218** courtesy Israel Antiquities Authority **219** AKG **220t** C/D Rubinger **220b** Fratelli Fabbri **221tl&br** AKG/Eric Lessing **bl** Aren Maier **222b** Kobal/Warner Bros. Ben Glass **222t, 223** RGA **224** MEPL **225t** Courtesy of the Southwest Museum, Los Angeles CT.1-D no. 1026G.I **225c** C, **226t** & **227t** Archaeological Perspectives on the Battle of Little Big Horn by D Scott, R Fox, M Connor and D Harman 1989, University of Oklahoma Press Reprinted by Permission **226b** AKG **226-227bg** C/B May **227b** C/D Barry **228-229b** CB **229t** Peter Newark's American Pictures **230t** C/Stapleton Coll **b, 231** CB **232** Courtesy of the Florence Nightingale Museum Trust, London **233** GI **234t** BAL/Louvre,Paris **b** The Metropolitan Museum of Art-Rogers Fund 1915 C15.128 photograph copyright 1998 **235tr** BAL/Louvre,Paris **tl** C **br** Art Archive/National Gallery, London.Eileen Tweedy **236** AKG/Erich Lessing **237** Oxford University Museum of Natural History **b** BAL **239** National Museums of Scotland **242** AKG **244b, 245t** SSPL **245b** MEPL **246** Boston Medical Journal **247t** AKG/Bibliotheque Nationale **b** Wellcome Library, London **248t** AKG **b** CB **250** Romeo H Hristov **252** Maine State Museum **253** Image courtesy of Yale University Press **255** Zheng He Research Institute, Nanjing, China **257** US Patent & Trademark Office **258** SSPL **259bl** CB **br** GI **260** Doug Brackett, Edisonian.com **261, 262cl** CB **t** C/R Raymond **b** Advertising Archives **263t** Art Archive/Musee Francais de la photographie Bievres/Dagli Orti **b** C **264** AKG/Erich Lessing **266t** Dan Scheid **b** AKG/Jean-Francois Amelot **267t** Popper/Reuters Jocken Eckel **b** C/Patrick Ward **bg** C/B Ross **268/269** Bishop Museum, Hawaii **270** CB **271** Advertising Archives **272** SPL/Volker Steger **273t** Three Traditional Tribal Groups **b** HIP/BM **274** BAL/Christies Images **275** BAL/Roger-Viollet **276** C/Archivo Iconografico **277** CB **278** BAL/National Gallery of Victoria, Melbourne **279** British Library **280** BAL/Bibliotheque Nationale **281** C/L Clarke **285tl, c, bc** NGIC **tr** C/A Woolfitt **cr** AKG **286b** AKG **287** BAL/BM **288l, br** copyright Huntarian Museum, Glasgow Univ. **bc** BM **289** RGA **290** BAL/Temple of Hathor **291** copyright The St. Hermitage Museum, St Petersburg **291t** V&A **292t** BM **b** Staatliches Museen zu Berlin – Preu.ishcher Kulturbesitz, Antikensammlung/ Johannes Laurentis/bpk 2003 **293** Delos Archaeological Museum **294-295** BAL/Chris Beetles Ltd **295** C/D Bartruff **296** BAL **297** Archivio Abbazia Santa Giustina **298t** National Academy of Science, USA Oct.16 2001, 10.1073/pnas 211540498 **b** MEPL **299** BAL/Roger-Viollet **300t** British Library **b** CB **301t** MEPL **b** BAL/K Walsh **302** MEPL **303** Fortean **304** BAL **305** MEPL **306** GI **307cl** C/K Fleming **b** MEPL **308** BAL/Smith Art Gallery & Museum **309** RGA **310t** MEPL **b** Scottish Viewpoint **311t** MEPL **b** BAL/Ken Welsh

Edited, designed and produced by
Planet Three Publishing Network
Northburgh House, 10 Northburgh Street, London EC1V OAT

PLANET THREE
PUBLISHING

FOR READER'S DIGEST
Editors Jonathan Bastable, Alison Candlin
Art Editor Louise Turpin

FOR PLANET THREE
Project Editor Liz Hitchcock
Assistant Editor Tom Beckerlegge
Features Editor Henry Russell
Sub Editors Mike Brown, Gaia Vince, Peter Hogan
Art Directors Michael Yeowell, Paul Southcombe
Art Editor Nancy Dunkerley
Designers Terry Sambridge, Yuen Ching Lam
Illustrators Paul Southcombe, Peter Cerpnjak, Paul Jackson
Picture Editor Kate Pink
Picture Researchers Tara McCormack,
Moira McIlroy, Liz Heasman

FOR READER'S DIGEST
GENERAL BOOKS
Editor Cortina Butler
Executive Editor Julian Browne
Art Director Nick Clark
Managing Editor Alastair Holmes
Picture Resource Manager Martin Smith
Style Editor Ron Pankhurst
Pre-press Account Manager Penny Grose
Book Production Manager Fiona McIntosh

RESEARCHERS
Alexander Capon, James Ewing, Julian Fenner, Jeremy Pilch, Zoe Taylor, Vicky Wayman

WRITERS
Russell Miller, Richard Girling, Rose Shepherd, Jonathan Bastable, Professor John Gillingham, Dr Paul Pettitt,
Tom Beckerlegge, Habie Schwarz, Henry Russell, Nigel Hawkes, Dr Andrew Kitchener, David Glen

AUTHENTICATION
Professor Jeremy Black, Dr Paul Pettitt, Professor John Gillingham, Dr Rod Thornton, Dr Simon Rofe, Claire Imber MS

Proofreader Barry Gage
Indexer Laura Hicks

Permission to reproduce lines from 'What Say the Reeds at Runnymede?', by Rudyard Kipling, kindly granted by A.P. Watt Ltd, on behalf
of The National Trust for Places of Historical Interest or Natural Beauty.

THE TRUTH ABOUT HISTORY

was published by The Reader's Digest Association Limited, London.
First edition Copyright © 2003 The Reader's Digest Association Limited, 11 Westferry Circus, Canary Wharf, London E14 4HE
www.readersdigest.co.uk

We are committed to both the quality of our products and the service we provide to our customers. We value your comments,
so please feel free to contact us on 08705 113366, or via our web site at www.readersdigest.co.uk

If you have any comments or suggestions about the content of our books you can contact us at gbeditorial@readersdigest.co.uk

Origination Colour Systems Ltd

Printing and binding Maury / Brun, Malesherbes, France

Concept code UK1427/G
Book code 400-094-01
ISBN 0 276 42751 3
Oracle code 250007464H.00.24